BORN IN BONDAGE

BORN IN BONDAGE

Growing Up Enslaved in the Antebellum South

MARIE JENKINS SCHWARTZ

Harvard University Press
Cambridge, Massachusetts
London, England

Third printing, 2001

Library of Congress Cataloging-in-Publication Data
Schwartz, Marie Jenkins, 1946–
Born in bondage : growing up enslaved in the antebellum South / Marie Jenkins Schwartz.
p.   cm.
Includes bibliographical references (p.) and index.
ISBN 0-674-00162-1 (cloth)
ISBN 0-674-00720-4 (pbk.)
1. Child slaves—Southern States—Social conditions—19th century.
2. Slavery—Southern States—History—19th century.
3. Southern States—Social conditions—19th century.
4. Afro-American children—Southern States—Social conditions—19th century.   I. Title.
E443.S39   2000
306.3′62′0830975—dc21
99-087747

For my family

CONTENTS

ILLUSTRATIONS

Sunday Morning at the Great House, by Alice R. H. Smith, ca. 1930–1947. Watercolor on paper (37.09.02). Gibbes Museum of Art/Carolina Art Association.

The Stack Yard, by Alice R. H. Smith, ca. 1930–1947. Watercolor on paper (37.09.20). Gibbes Museum of Art/Carolina Art Association.

Plantation Scene, ca. 1840s. Woodcut. Library of Congress, Prints and Photographs Division, LC-USZ62-31015.

Anna and Matile, attributed to Alice R. H. Smith, ca. 1900–1920. Photograph (A86.15.02.02.48). Gibbes Museum of Art/Carolina Art Association.

Doll sewn by a slave child, undated. Historic Stagville, Division of Archives and History, North Carolina Department of Cultural Resources.

Southern Cornfield, 1861, by T. W. Wood. Oil on canvas. T. W. Wood Art Gallery, Montpelier, Vermont.

Advertising for purchase of slaves, 1835. Broadside. Library of Congress, Prints and Photographs Division, LC-USZ62-62799.

"Human Flesh at Auction," by Vanigen-Snyder, in *The Suppressed Book about Slavery,* 1864. Woodcut. Library of Congress, Prints and Photographs Division, LC-USZ62-30797.

Virginian Luxuries, ca. 1815. Artist unknown. Colonial Williamsburg Foundation, accession no. 1993.100.1.

Lynchburg Negro Dance, 1853, by Lewis Miller. Watercolor. Abby Aldrich Rockefeller Folk Art Center, Williamsburg, Virginia, accession no. 1978.301.1p.17B.

Marriage of a Colored Soldier at Vicksburg by Chaplain Warner of Freedmans Bureau, ca. 1866–1871, by Alfred R. Waud. Pencil. The Historic New Orleans Collection, accession no. 1965.71.

Former slaves Laura Clark (1937) and Ben Horry (ca. 1938), United States Works Progress Administration. Photographs. Library of Congress, Manuscripts Division.

EDITORIAL NOTE

Quotations have been reproduced verbatim from sources—including any unusual spellings—without employing the notation *"sic."* Readers should be aware that people who interviewed former slaves, often decades after the end of slavery, frequently and deliberately inserted misspellings into slave narratives such as those published under the editorship of George P. Rawick as *The American Slave: A Composite Autobiography.* Consequently, the presence of unusual spelling in quotations attributed to many former slaves and to a limited number of former owners should not be taken to reflect the inability of slaves or slaveholders to spell by modern standards.

Throughout this book I refer to children in second references by their first names, in contrast to adults, who are referred to in second references by surnames. Exceptions occur only when the practice would create confusion, as in the case of spouses using the same surname, or when surnames do not appear in the sources. Thus when I refer to adult slaves in second references by first names only, I do not mean to imply that the slaves had no surnames.

BORN IN BONDAGE

INTRODUCTION

"Lord, I done been threw somepin'," marveled Caroline Hunter of Virginia, as she related her experiences under slavery to an agent of the United States government collecting memories from former slaves in 1937. Though seventy-two years had passed since the Civil War had brought about the end of slavery, tears filled Hunter's eyes as she recalled a childhood of hardships endured. "During slavery it seemed lak yo' chillun b'long to ev'ybody but you," she lamented.[1] Mothers and fathers alike found their roles circumscribed by owners who considered it their right—even their duty—to oversee a slave child's upbringing.

Slaveholders interjected themselves between parent and child by interfering in all aspects of family life. Owners disciplined children, forcibly separated them from families, and dictated the type of work they should perform, according to Hunter. "Many a day my ole mama has stood by an' watched massa beat her chillun 'till dey bled an' she couldn' open her mouf," she recalled. Her father had been driven from his family by the owner's lash. A free man, he had left the area to join the army rather than endure beatings imposed by his wife's owner. Hunter's brothers fared no better. All three were badly battered, then sold following their recovery. The abuse Hunter bore included the trauma of watching her mother strapped "to a bench or box an' beat . . . wid a wooden paddle while she was naked." Before she reached maturity, Hunter "was put out in de fiel's to wuk all day" at exacting tasks. She dreamed of escape and learned to interpret everyday sights and sounds as signs of trouble to come: a turtledove's whistle was thought to warn of an impending beating. Hunter knew her childhood experiences would shock her interlocutor from the government's Works Progress Administration, who had no firsthand knowledge of slavery. "It's hard to believe dat dese things did happen, but dey did," she attested.

Once freed, some former slaves recalled a point in time—"a traumatic moment" in the words of the historian Willie Lee Rose—when they became subject to their owners' discipline and realized they belonged to someone other than their parents. For Jacob Stroyer, this moment of perception occurred while he was learning to ride his owner's racing horses. The instructor's reliance on corporal punishment as a training tactic prompted the would-be jockey to seek help from his parents. To the boy's astonishment, neither could protect him from the capriciousness of his teacher. Indeed, his father merely advised Jacob to "be a good boy." The moment stood apart in Stroyer's memory, and he later recorded the incident and his reaction in writing. Many other former slaves did the same, although none so vividly perhaps as Stroyer.[2]

One can sympathize with young Jacob, who had stepped beyond a circle of family and friends to confront the slaveholder's power to punish at will— exercised in this case through the riding instructor. But in truth Jacob fared better than many slave children, who endured slavery as a series of traumatic moments from birth. Caroline Hunter recalled no happy time before she realized the fact of her enslavement. Neither did Ishrael Massie, who throughout childhood witnessed and endured firsthand many horrors, including the forced parting of families and punishments so harsh they left men unable to stand—or worse. Members of Massie's own family were sold to different planters, and he once saw a man burned alive. Yet Massie and Hunter were fortunate in one sense: both escaped an untimely death—the ultimate horror of a childhood in slavery. Many of the boys and girls born in bondage never grew to adulthood, because infant and child mortality rates among slaves in the antebellum South were high. This demographic fact alone confirms Massie's judgment that antebellum slavery days were "terrible, terrible times."[3]

By law, slaveholders determined the conditions under which bonded children grew to adulthood. Slave parents as a result of their servitude forfeited the right to shape their sons' and daughters' lives. Slaveowners considered themselves the rightful heads of plantation households, responsible for directing the lives of all members whether black or white. But the owners were unwilling to carry out the work of child rearing themselves and left these tasks to the slaves, content to fulfill the role of supervisor. And neither masters nor mistresses could be everywhere at once, which placed slaves in charge of children to a greater or lesser degree depending in part on the individual owner's level of interest.

If slaveholders were willing to leave some child-rearing tasks in the hands of parents, slaves gladly accepted the responsibility. Indeed, they resented any usurpation of parental rights by slaveholders, and they advanced their rights in ways that were subtle but determined. The willingness of slaves to protest conditions of servitude that deprived them of parenting roles influenced owners to allow women and men time for their families. Owners relied on slaves to cooperate at the work site and worried that they might rebel against working in the conventional manner if provoked. Slaveholders held the power to force slaves to work through the use (or the threat) of harsh punishment, but in fact slaves did not always react to brutality by working harder at assigned tasks. Resentful slaves sometimes became truants, slowed the pace of work, or performed tasks poorly. Their actions could result in financial disaster for plantation owners, especially if they affected planting or harvesting of crops intended for market. If miserable and desperate enough, slaves might strike back for perceived wrongs by destroying property or inflicting harm on members of the owning class. Consequently, slaveowners hesitated to roil relations in the slave quarter by refusing parents of young children—particularly mothers, who were thought more suited to the task of child rearing than fathers—time for their youngsters.

Allowing parents to attend to slave children, even at the expense of the marketable crop, held additional advantages for owners, who could increase their wealth and ensure the perpetuation of the southern slave system through the reproduction of the labor force. Well-nurtured children were more likely to survive to adulthood and become working hands than neglected ones. But the decision whether to allocate the work of slaves—particularly that of women—to crop or child posed a dilemma. On the one hand, owners wanted as many slaves as possible working in the field or at other productive labor. On the other, they wanted to see their wealth increase as slave populations expanded. One strategy promised immediate profits; the other assured long-term gain. Many owners held conflicting opinions about the best course of action, and slaves seized on such indecision to gain opportunities to care for their children according to their own notions of proper parenting.

Slaves struggled to secure time for their families with varying degrees of success. They were seldom able to overcome the constraints imposed by enslavement; the long hours consumed by their owners' work left them little opportunity for nurturing children and completing household tasks. That many slaves failed to achieve independence in family matters or even to keep their families together should not obscure the successes they experienced, however. Even the enslaved parents of Caroline Hunter and Ishrael Massie managed to create some form of family life for their children, even if it was truncated and fraught with tension. Through their attempts to shape childhood according to their own ideals, slaves created a world of their own making and refuted the slaveholder's belief that the babies slave women bore in bondage belonged to no one but the owners.

The expansion of the nation in its early years and a congressional prohibition effective in 1808 against participation in the international slave trade persuaded slaveholders to pay increased attention to nurturing slave children. By the 1820s, cotton planting had become profitable in a wide stretch of the South previously unavailable for settlement. Planters and would-be planters moved westward in large numbers to grow the fiber for sale in Europe and New England, where the textile industry was burgeoning. This extension of the Cotton Kingdom called for new laborers. Following the ban on slave importation, some smuggling of slaves occurred, but never in numbers sufficient to meet labor needs. The only practical way to increase the pool of slave laborers was through the birth of children. Without children born in bondage, the South could not continue as a slave society.

Well before Congress voted to end the international slave trade, slave women had been giving birth to enough children to increase the slave population. As early as 1720, the number of children born began exceeding the number of slaves who died in the Chesapeake (colonial Virginia and Maryland); by the 1750s, the same could be said for coastal South Carolina.[4] Indeed, the demography of slavery made possible the ending of the international slave trade as of 1808 without major protest from the slave states because the population trend helped to ease the minds of slaveholders about the future profitability of southern agriculture and the continuation of slavery through subsequent generations.

The same developments that reassured slaveholders heightened anxiety among slaves, who feared the dissolution of family ties. The planters' inability to import "salt-water" slaves, coupled with a demand for more laborers in the cotton-producing South, threatened slave families, whose members could be bought and sold from one area of the country to another. By relocating slaves from areas where their labor was not needed to regions where the economy was booming, planters could make plantation slavery more efficient—but at the price of human misery. The matter was of grave consequence for slaves. Slave parents loved their children and despaired at their loss. Moreover, the family served as an important locus of resistance to the dehumanization that slavery entailed. The presence of sons and daughters on the plantation or farm affirmed the slaves' humanity, and caring for children offered welcome respite from the harsh realities of slave life. Creating and nurturing families ensured the continuation of a people who shared a sense of identity grounded in a common past and in the everyday experience of enslavement. When they joined together to raise children, slaves brought profit to their owners, who watched their slaveholdings multiply, but they also benefited themselves by creating a cultural space apart from that inhabited by the owning class. Through families, children learned to judge bondage, and the men and women who enslaved them, in terms other than those employed to justify the institution. By wielding superior power, slaveholders might force slaves to accommodate their desire for services, but they could not compel slaves to accept slavery as a morally and ethically legitimate institution. As long as slaves maintained parental prerogatives, they held an effective means of countering their owners' attempts to impose upon slave children their ideas of a proper social order. When owners bought, sold, or relocated slaves, they scattered slaves and broke kinship ties, threatening the source of the slave's power to resist psychological domination. Slaves responded by developing strategies to avoid family separations or—when that proved impossible—to postpone them or at least to ensure that their children developed caring relationships and received the material goods necessary for survival in their parents' absence.

The significance of children was shown by their numbers in the antebellum years, defined in this study as the period from 1820 to 1860. More than two-fifths of antebellum slaves were younger than age fifteen; one-third were younger than age ten. The large numbers of slave children living within the South's borders contrasted with trends in other parts of the Americas. In Latin American and Caribbean slave societies, slave deaths generally exceeded births, and planters continued to enslave and import Africans to sustain their slave systems until late in the development of the plantation regime. In contrast, the slave population in the United States was largely native-born. Only in America did large numbers of slaves learn from birth to endure the conditions of oppression associated with chattel bondage. By 1860, the United States had achieved the dubious distinction of becoming the largest slaveholding nation in the world, with more than four million slaves.[5]

The phenomenal growth of an indigenous slave population in the United States appears to have resulted from many factors, some beyond human control. A greater proportion of women in the population helped ensure a large number of births, and a relatively healthy climate and the absence of tropical disease helped children survive. Work regimens associated with crops grown in the United States appear to have been less demanding than those for crops cultivated in other parts of the Americas. In addition, more limited opportunities for slaves to achieve freedom in the United States, the closing of the international slave trade, and the ability of southern planters to sell "home-grown" slaves for profit played a role. Nevertheless, masters and mistresses preferred to interpret the numbers as evidence that United States slaveholders treated slaves better than owners elsewhere. At a time when abolitionists in the North portrayed slaveholders as cruel and despotic, slaveholders convinced themselves that they were the benefactors of slaves, caretakers who assumed the burden of providing for an inferior people. Aware of abolitionism's growing appeal throughout the Atlantic world, antebellum southern slaveowners were eager to demonstrate that the form of slavery they imposed on people of African descent benefited the enslaved as well as the enslaver. They bragged of their own slaves' supposed contentedness and argued that bondage in the United States was more humane, less cruel, than it was on the sugar, coffee, and cocoa plantations of Latin America and the Caribbean, where bonded children did not thrive. Indeed, they believed that southern slaves were better fed, clothed, and housed than many free laborers in the North.[6]

Slave parents were determined that their children would endure and a people persist. When southern planters boasted that they treated their slaves better than any other working people, free or slave, slaves demanded that they live up to the claim. To ensure their children's survival, slaves enlisted the sympathies of those they feared, calling upon owners to act on the

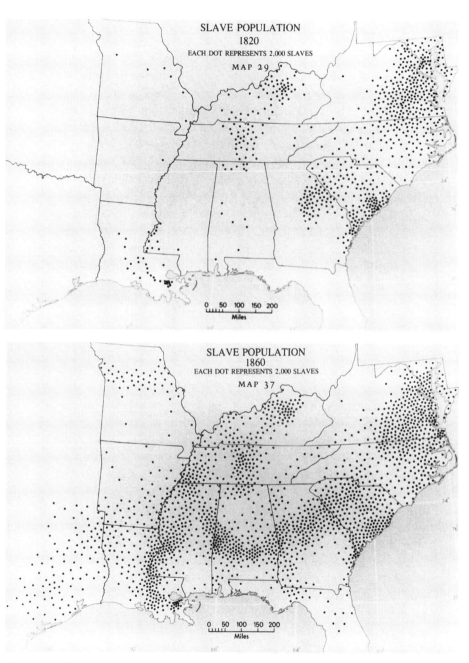

Slave population in 1820 and 1860. Reprinted by permission of Louisiana State University Press from *Atlas of Antebellum Southern Agriculture* by Sam Bowers Hilliard. Copyright © 1984 by Louisiana State University Press.

human impulse to care for children too young to survive on their own. Slaveowners responded to parents' appeals, but not consistently and certainly not always in the way parents hoped. Consequently, slaves employed time-honored patterns of resistance to change plantation practices that put children at risk. They feigned illness or incompetence, worked slowly or not at all, and undertook other actions designed to pressure owners into making provisions for children that ensured their health and safety.

This book tells the story of slave children and the efforts of parents and owners to raise them. The children occupied an unusual position in that two sets of adults valued them, laying claim to their economic worth and attaching an emotional significance to their presence. Slaveholders hoped to establish plantation policies that fostered children's survival without interfering with agricultural routines. They took steps to ensure that boys and girls learned how to work as well as how to play subservient parts in the paternalistic drama that passed for southern race relations. They also acted to secure children's faithfulness to slaveowning families. Of course, the owners' personal relationships with slave children were tempered by their concern for crops, but their attention to securing the emotional attachment of the youths cannot be discounted. Owners disciplined children and insisted that they learn to labor, but they also courted their fidelity and affection.

Although slave parents encouraged slaveholders to behave benevolently, even paternalistically, toward their children, their commitment to paternalism was incomplete. There existed a real danger that in recognizing their owners' responsibilities toward their sons and daughters, they would surrender their own. Consequently, they vied with slaveholders to retain authority over child rearing, even as they pleaded for their masters and mistresses to provide for the children's well-being. Negotiations were ongoing because the needs and abilities of children changed as they grew older. The bargaining was not between equals. The owners' overwhelming power and willingness to use force gave them the ability to shape childhood experiences through fiat, direct intervention, and subtle pressures. Slaveholders by law and custom could separate families at will by selling parents or children if they wished; they could beat into submission slaves who protested their orders. Owners also could grant parents time away from field and other duties to care for their families, or they could keep mothers or fathers so long in the field that they had little time to spend with their children. In addition, owners could provide children special treats and favors that parents could not replicate.

Slaves countered this power through subtle influences, prolonged negotiations, and direct confrontation. For slaves, more was at stake than simply winning the children's affection, although this too was a matter of considerable importance. Slave children contributed to the welfare of their families and communities through work, as did most other nineteenth-century children, and slave parents hoped to keep slaveholders from appropriating this work for their own benefit. Parents also hoped to keep children from tattling, since slaves relied on one another to remain silent about what went on in the slave living quarters or at least to be discreet in their everyday encounters with whites.

As they grew, children found themselves torn between the demands of owners and those of parents. Theirs was a world in which the lines of authority were murky. They needed to please owners; a wrong deed, word, or look could bring harsh consequences. But they also needed to please parents and other slaves upon whom they depended for survival. Children under these circumstances could find themselves in a precarious position, needing to understand and to separate the requirements of owners and parents. Mattie Gilmore's experience illustrates the slave child's dilemma. Her mistress, who suspected theft of household goods by other slaves, held the young Alabama girl responsible for watching any slaves who entered the owner's home (or "big house," as it was sometimes called) and reporting any acts of theft that she witnessed. Mattie understood the consequence of not following her mistress's order: a whipping by the mistress. Unfortunately for Mattie, her stepmother expected the child to remain silent if she saw slaves appropriating the property of her owners. When Mattie conformed to her mistress's order and tattled, the stepmother whipped the child herself. Lewis Jenkins as a young boy confronted a situation even more ambiguous than Mattie's. When he was seven or eight, his owning family appointed him to the position of "watchman," which entailed spying among the slaves. The cook put an end to his sleuthing by threatening violence should he report her activities. Jenkins later maintained that he could "see nothin', tell nothin'" after receiving the warning. The boy, whose situation was complicated by his mixed race, lived an unusual and especially perilous existence.[7] The stories of Mattie Gilmore and Lewis Jenkins—and those of Carolyn Hunter, Ishrael Massie, Jacob Stroyer, and other children—reveal much about how people experienced enslavement.

ONLY since the civil rights era have historians focused on the everyday experiences of the enslaved. During the first half of the twentieth century, studies of slavery in antebellum America tended to ignore the slave's humanity and to focus on how slaves were treated and whether slavery was profitable. The ideas of U. B. Phillips (*American Negro Slavery*, 1918) dominated thinking about slavery and slave life into the 1950s. Phillips saw southern slaves as a racially inferior people who benefited from being part of a patriarchal system and whose labor was neither profitable nor efficient. As the civil rights movement gained ground in the 1950s and 1960s, historians began to explore the nation's past in an effort to explain the origins of contemporary racial problems and the persistence of poverty among African Americans. Enslavement seemed a possible explanation for both, and scholars soon discovered flaws in Phillips's analysis. Slaves had been victims, not beneficiaries, of a labor system that profited owners but not workers. This idea influenced the thinking behind proposed changes in public policy intended to eradicate modern social ills, especially poverty. As Assistant Secretary of Labor in the Lyndon B. Johnson administration, Daniel Patrick Moynihan issued a report (*The Negro Family*, 1965) that purported to explain the plight of the nation's poor black families, alleging that African American families were entangled in a cultural pathology born of past enslavement.[8]

Among scholars, the debate shifted to consider how enslavement had affected the men and women who experienced it. Stanley M. Elkins (*Slavery*, 1959) believed that half of all plantation slaves were infantile "Sambos," a caricature with which southern slaveholders would have felt comfortable. His influential work painted adult slaves as childlike, docile, dependent, and irresponsible—the psychological victims of repression. The slave personality had succumbed to the oppression of chattel bondage, he concluded. Other historians soon called into question his characterization of slaves, but out of Elkins's work, the slave emerged as a historical actor. According to scholars such as John W. Blassingame (*The Slave Community*, 1972), Eugene D. Genovese (*Roll, Jordan, Roll*, 1974), George P. Rawick *(From Sundown to Sunup*, 1972), and Herbert G. Gutman *(The Black Family in Slavery and Freedom*, 1976), slaves were not merely objects of benevolence or victims of oppression but helped to shape life in the South. Local studies, such as Charles Joyner's investigation of slave life along the Waccamaw River in South Carolina (*Down by the Riverside*, 1984), confirmed the participation of slaves in the creation of southern culture.[9]

Although a new generation of scholars agreed that slaves had been actors on the southern stage, they disputed the nature of power and the ability of slaves to resist the cultural domination that enslavement implied. For some the hegemony of slaveholders crippled the slave's ability to resist the institution's dehumanizing tendencies. Generally, these scholars began with an examination of the slaveholder's world and extrapolated from that the conditions under which bonded people lived. By uncovering the treatment slaves received at the hands of their oppressors, they sought to understand the slave experience. Critics of this school saw slave culture as transcending the hegemonic power of the slaveholder and furnishing slaves with inspiration to resist their owners' views of the southern social order. To appreciate the situation of slaves, they began by studying what happened in the slaves' living quarters. Their interest lay not so much in learning how slaves were treated but in exploring how slaves shaped their own lives despite the manner in which they were treated.

Perceived weaknesses and strengths of the slave family have figured in the debate about the ability of slaves to counter their owners' interpretation of southern society. Kenneth M. Stampp (*The Peculiar Institution,* 1956), who defined slaves in terms of their victimization, was unable to see how the slave family might function to prevent its members from succumbing to the cultural supremacy of the owning class. He saw slaves living "in a kind of cultural chaos" where parents exerted little influence in the raising of their children. Fathers in particular lacked authority; their only important family function "was that of siring offspring." Two decades later, Herbert G. Gutman—in a work that represented a major turning point in the historiography of slavery—refuted Stampp's contention that slaves had no meaningful family relationships. Most slave children lived in households headed by two parents, Gutman argued. The majority of slave marriages endured, and when death or the slave trade intervened to disrupt marriages, other slaves assumed kinship roles in place of parents. Family connections—both biological and "fictive"—served as conduits for cultural continuity between generations. Young slaves learned about marriage, family, and the limits of the owner's power in the slave cabin, not in the owner's house. Extensive family networks among slaves formed the social basis for African-American communities and fostered the development and spread of an African-American culture with rules of conduct differing from those of owners. This cultural space offered slaves a vantage point from which they could critique the conditions of their lives.[10]

Around the same time that Gutman was developing his ideas about power and culture, Eugene D. Genovese was formulating an alternate view of slavery that characterized the relationship between slaveholders and slaves in familial terms. Genovese argued that the two had bonded in an association "so complex and ambivalent that neither could express the simplest human feelings without reference to the other." Slaveholders spoke of slaves as members of their families and ran their plantations as if they were patriarchal households. They offered paternalistic protection and direction to slaves and assumed the burdens of providing slaves with adequate food, clothing, and shelter; of keeping families intact unless economic need or the slave's disobedience forced their separation; and of disciplining slaves only when necessary to ensure order and a level of production profitable to the planter. In return, slaves owed their masters and mistresses their labor. Slaves accepted their owners' paternalism out of necessity, but they interpreted it differently from owners. Whereas slaveholders conferred mutual duties, slaves claimed reciprocal rights. Rather than bestowing upon slaves the material goods necessary for survival, family security, and kindly treatment, planters owed slaves this as their due. By asserting their rights under paternalism, slaves extracted some advantages from the system, but only by accommodating themselves to it and signaling their "acceptance of an imposed white dominion."[11]

Children were among the prime beneficiaries of the slaveholder's paternalistic impulses, according to Genovese. Owners petted and pampered their young charges. "Occasionally masters and mistresses mistreated the slave children," he acknowledged, "but generally they doted on them as if they were playthings or pets." Children were excused from field work, except during cotton picking season when they might be expected to help. Even then, "they often enjoyed themselves." The same children worked "willingly" around the family cabin to ease the lives of overworked parents. Yet their work burdens were light, compared with those of poor children of the industrializing nations or even the children of southern yeomen. In contrast, "slave children had a childhood." Indeed, their experiences in childhood helped slaves adjust to paternalism. As they grew, children "absorbed the rules and culture of the dominant society."[12]

Genovese's and Gutman's work led to new research by scholars who defended or refuted the concept of paternalism or explored the structure and functioning of the slave household. Generally, historians only indirectly or occasionally addressed the issue of how children fared under the conditions of slavery.

James Oakes (*The Ruling Race,* 1982) was more interested in refuting Genovese's doctrine of paternalism than in examining children's experiences, but his work, which concentrated on slaveholders, acknowledged the high proportion of youths in the slave population. In 1850 the average master was forty-three years old, but the majority of slaves were younger than age eighteen; Oakes noted that "demographically . . . the most common master-slave relationship was between a middle-aged white man and a black child." Slaveholders used the language associated with paternalism, he admitted, but merely because large numbers of slave children were present in southern society and because the owners' racist view characterized slaves as childlike. Materialism motivated planters more than did paternalism, he maintained. Slaveholders were entrepreneurs and slaves akin to employees. When slaves failed to carry out their work in a manner satisfactory to their owners, they were in effect striking, and slaveholders sought the good will of their slaves to avoid work slowdowns and other tried-and-true forms of worker resistance. The culture of the slave quarter held little interest for Oakes.[13]

Another approach to understanding the nature of slavery focused on women in bondage and often took issue with Herbert Gutman's depiction of slave households. Families helped slaves survive, as Gutman suggested, but the family was matriarchal or matrifocal, according to these scholars. Slave households were often truncated, especially in the upper South where the small size of slaveholdings made it difficult for women to find marriage partners living on the same estate. Husbands often lived apart from wives and children, but even when men were present in the household, slavery deprived them of their traditional role of supporting their families. A "community of women" took charge of child rearing. For Gutman, two-parent households represented the ideal to which slaves aspired; to the degree that slaves achieved that ideal, they also achieved the means to raise children according to criteria acceptable to the slaves. Yet Deborah Gray White (*Ar'n't I a Woman?*, 1985), Brenda E. Stevenson (*Life in Black and White*, 1996), and other historians addressing the experiences of women have shown that households headed by women could and did function effectively to raise children in the absence of a resident man.[14]

Although the majority of scholars have focused on adults in slavery, Thomas L. Webber (*Deep Like the Rivers*, 1978) and Wilma King (*Stolen Childhood*, 1995) have sought to understand the lives of slave children. Webber dissented from Genovese's view that the solicitous attitude of slaveholders created opportunities for slaves to experience childhood. He agreed that slave children were insulated from slavery's worst features, but he attributed this to their isolation from members of the owning class. Slave families nurtured and provided for their children, who, he maintained, spent the great majority of their time with other slaves before beginning to work in their owners' fields—generally between the ages of eight and fourteen. More recently, King has argued that children were not shielded from the terrors of slave life. Early and relentless encounters with brutality robbed children of childhood in a manner similar to that experienced by children in times of war. "To be sure, enslaved nineteenth-century children and youth did not live continuously amid the actual bombardment of war," King wrote in the introduction to her work, "but their experiences with separations, terror, misery, and despair reduced them to children without childhoods."[15]

My book has benefited from engaging with these earlier debates about the nature of slavery, the slave family, and slave childhood. One purpose of this study has been to understand how children—and a people—endured the conditions associated with chattel bondage. Because children do not fend for themselves, particularly at young ages, this book focuses on the adults responsible for children, as well as on the children themselves and their interactions with one another. Another aim has been to view paternalism from the slave quarter, to determine how parents cultivated or resisted paternalistic influences as they raised their children to adulthood. Finally, I have sought to understand the slave child's stages of development and the nature of a childhood in bondage. Slave children did experience childhood, if one defines the concept as a distinct stage of life separate from that of adulthood. But a childhood in bondage was peculiar, bounded by the constraints of slavery and shaped by slaveholders and slaves—both adults and children—as they went about their everyday activities.

For slaves, as for other children, important milestones marked developmental categories. Weaning signaled the end of infancy. Early childhood concluded when the children grew old enough to obey and to serve. By the age of five or six, children were initiated into the world of work through education and training intended to enhance a slave's economic worth. During this stage of development, harsh punishments were introduced to prevent children from performing duties poorly. Another significant event was the assumption of adult work responsibilities, usually between the ages of ten and twelve. The mid-teen years of slaves were shaped by their vulnerability to sale and, in the case of girls, sexual exploitation. Courtship, marriage, and the start of parenting signaled separate stages of life, although they were usually collapsed into a brief period—as short as one or two years—between the mid to late teens or early twenties. These stages, different as they are from those associated with modern childhood, serve as reminders that notions of child development have differed over time, and from place to place, and from one social group to another, despite an apparent grounding in biological processes.

One challenge in writing about slave children has been to identify the chronology of their maturation. Neither slaveholders nor slaves placed importance on keeping complete or accurate written accounts of slaves' ages. They could have done so, but slaves made few efforts to recall or record the exact ages of their children. Although most slaves lacked the means of recording births in writing, they had other methods of noting important events. Betty Farrow of Virginia, an exception to the rule that slaves did not know their exact birth dates, learned of her age from her mother, who could neither read nor write but had the date of her daughter's birth etched in her memory. In addition to preserving dates in memory, slaves could use "notching sticks"—long sticks carved with knives—to keep track of dates. Their intricate inscriptions marked months, years, and holidays, but not birthdays. Generally, slaves considered birthdays of little importance, although following emancipation some regretted not knowing their ages.[16]

Owners exhibited more concern about slaves' birth dates than did slaves. Slaveholders wanted to know the ages of any slaves they bought, and they often were required by law to maintain records of their slaves' ages, for slaves were taxable property and the rates varied by age. Those wishing to purchase insurance against the possible loss of valuable slave property needed to maintain records of slave births, because rates were based on a slave's age and occupation. Many owners recorded birth dates in their account books. When they purchased slaves of unknown ages, owners estimated the year of birth, using a variety of methods. Some examined teeth: children's ages could be calculated by the number of teeth in the mouth, adults' by the condition and absence of permanent teeth. Another method of separating older from youthful slaves involved pinching the skin on the back of the hand. "If the person is very far advanced in life, when the skin is pricked up, the pucker will stand so many seconds on the back of the hand," one observer noted.[17] Slaveholders dutifully recorded these estimated ages, rendering surviving slave lists of doubtful accuracy. Not only were methods of estimating ages imprecise, but slaveholders also had incentives to misrepresent their slaves' ages. They might avoid taxes or more easily sell a slave by recording adult slaves as being younger than they were.

Although no birthday celebrations occurred in the slave cabin or quarter and lists of birth dates recorded by owners remain of dubious accuracy, archival and other sources reveal a vocabulary used by slaves and owners to depict the various stages of child development. Assorted terms, generally gender-specific for older children but gender-neutral for infants and toddlers, described the various stages associated with childhood and youth. "In her lap" referred to infants who were not yet crawling, "creepin' days" to children old enough to crawl but not walk. "Little tot" described a child so young he or she could barely remember later the events or people in that time of life. A "little pig-tailed" girl or a "shirt-tail" boy was older, the age of each reflected in her hairstyle and his clothing. The terms "big missy" and "half grown" man referred to adolescent girls and boys.[18] If these age categories are imprecise by modern standards, they nevertheless were noted by adults who concerned themselves with slave children's welfare. They serve to organize the following chapters, which examine the experiences of children who bore slavery's burden.

In writing this book I have consulted both slaveholder records and documents created by and for former slaves to recreate the experiences of children and their parents. Important documents about slavery from the perspective of slaves include oral history projects. The most notable and ambitious of these is the Federal Writers' Project of the Works Progress Administration (WPA). Under the auspices of this New Deal program, more than 2,000 former slaves were interviewed between 1936 and 1938 about their lives in bondage. By the 1930s, many years had passed since the Civil War brought about the end of slavery, and most of the project's informants had been infants or young children when they were enslaved. Because so much time had elapsed before these former slaves recorded their experiences, some historians have questioned the worth of the documents. Yet it is important to include them in a study of slave children precisely because the majority of informants experienced bondage as children. I have taken care to compare the interviews of former slaves with other sources, including interviews with former slaveholders completed decades following slavery's collapse. In 1912–1913, the Southern Renaissance writer and educator H. C. Nixon, perhaps best known as a contributor to *I'll Take My Stand, by Twelve Southerners,* distributed a questionnaire on Alabama slavery to former slaveholders and members of their families. The survey addressed topics similar to those covered in the WPA interviews, including slave housing, clothing, food, work, courtship, marriage, family relationships, religion, child-care arrangements, and leisure activities. The respondents' assessments of slavery and slave life reflected the racial prejudices of the time, but details on the material conditions of slave life and the day-to-day experiences of slaves generally do not differ in substance from those found in other sources, including the interviews collected by the WPA.[19]

The South in which the former slaves lived was not monolithic. Regional variations existed, and in this book I draw primarily on interviews and other types of records—including documents created by slaveholders—from three distinct regions. The main purpose of studying contrasting geographic regions in the antebellum era is to determine whether a uniform African-American culture traveled with the slaves as southern society expanded westward. Significant variations in child-rearing practices in the different regions would indicate that slaves had not formed a common identity, based either in a shared past or in the everyday experience of enslavement. On the other hand, continuities in child-care practices would offer evidence that African Americans had forged a common culture, especially if they differed from those of owners.

The three regions of concentration—central Virginia, central Alabama, and the area consisting of coastal South Carolina and Georgia—grew different crops for market, which affected the economic prospects of slaveholders. Central Virginia is part of the piedmont, a rolling plateau that within the state's borders extends from the fall line running through Richmond west to the Blue Ridge Mountains. Central Alabama is located within the southern black belt and consists of a stretch of prairie and woodland twenty to twenty-five miles in width that girds the state. The coastal region, or low country, in South Carolina and Georgia forms part of a narrow belt that stretches along the eastern seaboard from North Carolina to Florida. Slaveholders in central Virginia, whose mixed agricultural economy produced tobacco, wheat, other cereal crops, and livestock for market, succeeded financially but to a lesser extent than did slaveholders in the other two regions of study. Rice in coastal South Carolina and Georgia and cotton in central Alabama proved more lucrative than did the agricultural products of Virginia, with the result that planters in these areas were among the South's wealthiest slaveholders. Sizeable slaveholdings were typical in the two regions, in contrast to the Virginia piedmont where small farms predominated.

Virginians—including piedmont planters—partially compensated for a lagging agricultural economy by selling slaves to the rapidly expanding states of the lower South and West, including Alabama; and some planters, many of whom caught "cotton fever," left the state hoping to improve their financial situations with a change of location.[20] At times, planters along the South Carolina and Georgia coasts also caught "cotton fever," but the ma-

jority stayed put. They participated in the interregional trade by purchasing
some slaves in the upper South and selling other slaves to the expanding
cotton region in the West, although the preponderance of the trade in slaves
along the rice coast occurred through local exchanges.[21]

Alabama's black belt achieved a phenomenal growth as slavery expanded
westward. The area attained statehood in 1819. After that, immigrants—free
and unfree—flocked to the area rapidly and in large numbers. For the first
two decades, Alabama remained something of a frontier country, importing
slaves as necessary to meet a growing need for labor created by newly arriving planters. By the 1840s, Alabama slave society had matured, and slaveholders had begun to export, rather than to import, slaves. Sons and
daughters of Alabama cotton planters ventured farther west into new states
such as Arkansas and Texas, which began to attract the "excess" slave and
free populations of the older regions of settlement. Despite sending slaves
to the West, the slave population of central Alabama increased from 10,000
in 1820 to more than 210,000 by 1860.[22] In comparison, central Virginia's
slave population grew from 200,000 to 250,000 in the same four decades,
while the slave population in the South Carolina and Georgia coastal area
increased from under 130,000 to 160,000.[23]

Although the patterns of settlement, the size of slaveholdings, and the
crops grown varied in the three regions, these differences are easily over-
stated. Cotton grew in the low country, along with rice, and planters with
large and small slaveholdings could be found in each of the three regions of
study. More important, children born in bondage made up a substantial
portion of the population in all three areas. In 1860, 45 and 46 percent of
slaves were under the age of fifteen in the Alabama black belt and in the
Virginia piedmont, respectively; children age fourteen or younger constituted 38 percent of the slave population in coastal South Carolina and
Georgia.[24]

Each time a child was born in bondage, the process of enslavement began anew, as owners attempted to teach these children how to be a slave
and parents struggled to give them a sense of self and belonging which denied the owner complete control over their lives. The following pages
counter the commonly held vision of the paternalistic slaveholder who de-
termines the life and welfare of his passive chattel. They recreate the experiences of a bound but resilient people as they learned to negotiate between
acts of submission and selfhood, between the worlds of commodity and
community, as they grew to adulthood.

1

❋

BIRTH OF A SLAVE

SLAVE WOMEN tended to give birth before a "crowded bedside." Midwives, mothers, women friends, and other family members were present—including at times the expectant father. Emma Coker relied on her mother to help with the birth of her son, despite the presence of a physician, and she apparently witnessed the birth of her sister's many children. Even young siblings could be drawn into the drama. Phillip Evans, former slave of South Carolina, recalled long afterward the time when he ran for the midwife when his mother "got in de pains." His memory of his brother Richard's birth—to the hour and the minute—remained vivid into old age.[1] Slaves in attendance were there to assist the mother, rejoice in the occasion, and ensure their ideas of proper procedures were followed.

The onlookers included owners, who claimed a right to direct the unfolding events. When the slave woman Sally gave birth early one Sunday morning in August 1845, her Alabama master missed church to oversee the birth. The seventeen-hour labor of a slave named Celia also kept her South Carolina owner at home. The attendance of John Brown's mistress at his birth was expected, as this was her custom with all slave children born on the estate.[2] Whatever pleasure the owners took in attending slave births reflected the monetary and emotional value slaveholders placed on the births of slave children, their desire to see the southern social order perpetuated, and their sense of entitlement to meddle in the private lives of slaves.

Slaves and slaveholders alike welcomed the news of pregnancy and celebrated its successful conclusion. As they gathered around the mother, they admired the newborn and marked the importance of the event by giving gifts. Slaves offered simple gifts such as home-grown food, assistance with infant care or other work, and respect for the role of mother. Masters and mistresses gave material goods—a new dress for the mother, perhaps—and time off from the field or other chores to care for the infant. The most generous might grant the mother permanent freedom from the field, although this was rare and restricted to women who had already given birth to a requisite number of children. "When the family increases to ten children living, I require no other labour from the mother than to attend to her children," a Georgia planter explained to readers of the *Southern Agriculturalist*. At times the offer was for a woman to care for all the plantation's slave children—hers included—instead of returning to field work. Either way, the mothers who met the criteria for avoiding field work tended to be older and less able to carry out hard physical labor than those with fewer children.[3]

Although slaveholders and slaves joined together to celebrate a slave child's birth, they each had different reasons. Owners applauded the mother's fecundity, her contribution to a growing labor force, and her role in helping to perpetuate slave society, as well as what they thought of as their own enlightened management, which supposedly made family life possible for slaves. For their part, slaves honored the woman who ensured the continuation of a family and a people. Their different interests in slave infants shaped the beliefs of each about how pregnancy and childbirth should proceed. Whose ideas prevailed depended on a variety of factors, some of which the slaveholder controlled and some of which fell within the domain of the slaves. Even though owners had the advantage of superior resources, slaves found ways to make many decisions about pregnancy and childbirth.

The slaveholder's response to childbirth reflected in large part a financial calculation. Owners wanted to cultivate and harvest a cash crop: a combination of tobacco, grains, and livestock in central Virginia and the rest of the upper South; rice and cotton in the coastal regions of South Carolina and Georgia; and cotton throughout Alabama's black belt and most of the lower South. They also wanted to raise hardy slave babies and preserve the health of new mothers. Slaveowners understood the link between taxing work and miscarriage, or "abortion" as the failure of pregnancy was termed. Pushing women too hard in the field put not only the pregnancy at risk, but also the health of the expectant mother. Time and again owners found themselves torn between the desire to accommodate pregnant women and infants by releasing expectant mothers from field work and the conflicting wish to use all resources at hand—including the labor of all adults—to produce the largest possible crop. Each strategy held economic advantage, which posed a dilemma for the slaveholder. Even a planter with large numbers of slaves could place a crop in jeopardy by excusing women from field work. No planter wanted to sacrifice a crop, but excusing pregnant women from rigorous field work served to protect an owner's future crops and other economic interests as much as sending the women to work in the field.

Keeping too many slaves out of the field could spell disaster for the owner, but also for any overseer whom the owner hired to manage agricultural routines. Overseers usually worked only on the largest plantations. Their reputations—and often their pay—depended on getting the crop in and out of the ground efficiently. Those who did not expect to remain at a job long had little incentive to place the planter's long-term interests above short-term profits. They viewed pregnancy and childbirth as impediments to getting a job done and kept their employers informed about the number of pending and recent births among the hands to ensure that an owner knew the overseer did not bear the responsibility for any delay in planting or harvesting. In 1844 the overseer A. R. Bagshaw, hired by Charles Manigault to manage his rice plantation along the Savannah River, complained of slave pregnancies. "The worst is Pregnant women," Bagshaw wrote. "There is now five which weakens the force very much."[4] Overseers who wanted to remain long in a planter's employ had to worry more about the long-term consequences of pushing pregnant women and new mothers in the field for fear that their employers would complain of low birth rates among slaves or days of work lost because of miscarriage.

The majority of overseers, many of whom hoped to quit overseeing and establish their own farms someday, appear to have been driven by the fear that they might not get the crop planted or harvested in a timely manner. They drove the women to complete laborious jobs and took the risk that owners would blame them for any unfavorable outcome. Stancil Barwick was clearly on the defensive when he informed his employer about the circumstances surrounding two miscarriages on the cotton plantation he managed in central Georgia. Neither he nor Treaty realized she was pregnant, he insisted, and she had not been working in the field when the miscarriage occurred. Rather, "she was at the house all the time, I never made her do any work at all." Louisine miscarried "in the field it is true but she was workt as she please." She was about five months along. When she complained of sickness, "I told her to go home. She started an on the way she miscarried."[5] Barwick offered this explanation because some of the slave men had complained to the master about the overseer's treatment of the women. By bringing the situation to their owner's attention, the men intended to protect childbearing women by reminding the owner of his obligation to ensure their welfare.

Slaves found it difficult to persuade planters, as well as overseers, to release pregnant women from arduous chores. No planter could assume a happy outcome from pregnancy. A high infant mortality rate among slaves, combined with miscarriages and stillbirths, meant that some proportion of pregnancies would not end with the birth of a living child. Only a foolish owner forfeited a woman's labor or assumed any extra expense associated with pregnancy before the pregnancy seemed likely to be carried to term; consequently, slaveholders withheld special accommodations for pregnant women until late in the gestation period. Even then, owners with good intentions might be dissuaded from excusing women from field work if market prices for staple crops soared, tempting them to push slaves toward greater levels of productivity in order to gain short-term profits. Rice planters along the Atlantic coast of South Carolina and Georgia proved particularly vulnerable to the lure of large profits, and they taxed the physical endurance of mother and child to such an extent that slaves growing rice experienced higher rates of mortality than those producing tobacco and cotton in other regions of the South, even though the death toll among rice workers never reached the catastrophic levels associated with the production of sugar in other parts of the Americas.[6]

Slaves employed more than one strategy to persuade owners to lighten the work of pregnant women by assigning them shorter, less demanding tasks. They appealed to their owners' sense of benevolence and economy by reminding them of their human responsibility to care for slave mothers and the promise of increased financial assets. Generally, they concentrated their efforts to win accommodations for women during the last month or months of pregnancy when the likelihood increased that the pregnancy would result in the birth of a healthy infant. In the last stages of pregnancy, slave women constantly complained to their masters, overseers, and mistresses of fatigue and other ailments. "A gang of pregnant women" took their complaints of being overworked to owner Pierce Butler shortly after his arrival at his Butler Island, Georgia, plantation in 1839 following a lengthy stay in the North. When Pierce proved unsympathetic, the slave women petitioned his wife, Fanny Kemble Butler, to influence her husband on their behalf. Fanny, English in origin and new to the ways of slavery, zealously took up the cause. At first Pierce proved patient, but he eventually ordered his wife to cease her efforts at reforming plantation practices. Even a planter such as Butler, who prided himself on being a "good" master, resisted granting concessions during pregnancy.[7]

When their pleas to masters for leniency went unheeded, enslaved women frequently took their complaints to mistresses, who they thought understood better than masters and overseers the special needs of childbearing women. Slaveholding women were considered less concerned with financial than private matters, and so might be enlisted in the struggle to obtain better working conditions for pregnant and new mothers. The strategy posed a risk: women who sought relief in this manner could incur the wrath of an overseer or master, who might retaliate. On one of Butler's plantations, a slave woman told Fanny that overwork accounted for her poor health, only to receive a flogging from the overseer for her effort to improve her situation. Pierce would eventually try to prohibit such reprisals, but in this instance he simply warned his wife that she might be too sympathetic.[8] The persistence of slave women in taking complaints to the mistress despite such rebuffs suggests that they either found relief at times or had reached a point of desperation.

Treating female health problems frequently fell under the purview of the mistress, and this served as an added incentive for pregnant slaves to tell her tales of woe related to pregnancy. On plantations without mistresses, slave women could enlist the sympathy of the overseer's wife, if one resided on the plantation; but not all overseers' wives proved interested, and not all overseers had wives. Charles Manigault did his best to avoid married overseers, believing that their wives only created problems on the plantation. A fear, probably unfounded, that overseers' wives would meddle in plantation policies affecting slave women may have figured in his thinking. Fanny Kemble Butler's efforts to improve the situation of slave women on her husband's estate were short-lived, for she and Pierce stayed less than four months in the South. Although Pierce employed a married overseer,

Fanny expressed little faith in his wife's ability or inclination to carry out the reforms she had begun.[9]

The need of pregnant women for relief from arduous work was not feigned. Slave women suffered frequently from gynecological problems, a situation that Fanny Kemble Butler documented in her diary. "A great many of the women are victims to falling of the womb," she wrote. Auger, the mother of five children, surprised Fanny by complaining of menstrual flooding and intolerable backaches. Fanny had thought on first seeing the "stooping, halting hag" that she was past menopause. "Constant child-bearing, and the life of labor, exposure, and privation which they lead, ages these poor creatures prematurely," she noted. Owners recognized gynecological problems by excusing women from the field. One physician reported that a slave woman might miss up to eight days of work during her menstrual cycle. Planter John Fitzgerald of Virginia accepted his slave Mobrina's absence for "a day or two . . . from too great a flow of Her menses."[10]

Knowing the special hardships pregnant women underwent, relatives and friends pleaded with owners not to require heavy work from them or inflict severe punishments upon them. Husbands, fathers, brothers, mothers, sisters, and other slaves joined their voices in a chorus of requests for such accommodations from the owner. Every owner understood only too well that many enslaved men and women stood ready to back their pleas for better treatment with actions that threatened financial ruin. If a mother or her baby were injured by the mother's being pushed too hard, men might run away or break tools; women might burn the barn or poison the owner's son. Pregnant women risked harm to themselves and their unborn children by suffering the punishments inflicted upon recalcitrant slaves, and they could not easily take to the woods to avoid them. Therefore, others stepped in, running away or refusing to work until they elicited promises from owners to spare pregnant women from harsh treatment. Through such actions, husbands, fathers, mothers, brothers, and others invested family relationships with meaning grounded in the everyday experience of enslavement. "Husbands allays went to de woods when dey know de wives was due fo' a whippin'," reported one former slave. The strategy whereby other slaves threatened retaliation for harm to a pregnant woman was never foolproof, however. Virginia slave Charlie Jones stood by helplessly as the overseer whipped his pregnant wife, "not darin' to look at her or even say a word." In this case, the whipping had been unexpected and the husband had too little advance notice to arrange a getaway.[11]

The protection of extended family and friends was crucial since pregnant women did not live always with the expectant father. Sale or death separated some spouses; other couples lived on separate slaveholdings, particularly in the upper South where the small size of many slaveholdings prevented men and women from finding suitable partners on the home estate. Young women who entered into sexual liaisons with men on other plantations and farms and who were carrying their first child often lived with their parents rather than in a separate cabin, which allowed the parents to assume the role of protector. Mothers with several children might live in separate cabins with just their children if their spouse resided on another estate, but they too might have relatives and friends who looked out for their interests. A spouse, parent, uncle, or other relative did not always need to go so far as to run away or to damage property to influence the behavior of an owner. An owner might have had to cope previously with a slave's disappearance under similar circumstances or have heard of a neighbor whose barn had gone up in flames. Generally, the presence of caring relatives and friends capable of taking action was enough to worry owners about possible reprisals for subjecting a pregnant woman to especially abusive treatment.

Owners held themselves accountable for the treatment of their bondsmen and women, although their behavior fell far short of what slaves considered compassionate. They agreed collectively to abide by somewhat nebulous standards, some of which were codified into law while others had been agreed upon more informally. These called for slaves to have adequate food, clothing, shelter, and rest, which kept them alive and (not incidentally) working in their owners' fields. Judging by their own criteria, many slaveholders failed to measure up to the standards associated with the "good" master or mistress, but most owners believed in the concept at least as a worthy goal. A "good" slaveholder cared about pregnant women and their infants and considered their welfare in assigning tasks and allocating resources. The presence of slave children in the back yards of plantation houses throughout the South served, in the owners' minds, as a badge of honor, attesting to the kindliness of the southern slaveholder and the superiority of the South's slaveholding regime, which made it possible for slaves to enjoy the benefits of family life.

Fostering the maternal care of infants enabled owners to view themselves as humane and enlightened managers, or even parent figures, rather than as cruel overlords and despotic exploiters, as they were portrayed in the abolitionist tracts that circulated increasingly in the North. Slaveholders placed importance on the personal relationships that developed between owners and slaves, in part because they believed that cordial behavior between individual owners and their slaves proved the legitimacy of the institution of slavery.[12] Consequently, even the most heartless of slaveowners did not always adopt the most financially expedient rules for pregnant slaves. They more readily showed consideration for a favorite slave or one with whom they interacted frequently than for slaves seldom seen, but many established policies they considered lenient toward all or most of their slaves. Such policies helped them deny—even to themselves—that they exploited slaves for their own gain. As the voices of abolitionists grew louder in opposition to slavery during the antebellum years, slaveowners pointed with pride to their benevolent rule as proof that the southern slave system benefited everyone, black and white alike.

Weighing both financial and ideological concerns, and worried about the consequence to property and persons of not doing so, most owners concluded that they should excuse pregnant women from the most onerous farm chores during the last month or months of pregnancy when the signs of impending birth were clearly visible. Planters who engaged in the practice urged others to excuse pregnant women from arduous chores to prevent harm to mother *and* child. Ideally, no pregnant woman would engage in "lifting, pulling fodder, or hard work." One set of instructions for overseers advised them "to preserve the health of the negroes" by relieving pregnant women of "any but the lightest labor for several months before and after confinement."[13]

Not all planters followed the same practice, because they interpreted such advice according to their individual understanding of pregnancy, economy, and race. Some customarily kept pregnant women out of the field and had them perform lighter tasks; others did so only if they had alternate work that required attention. Still others agreed in principle that pregnant women should be excused from difficult labor, but they did not consider hoeing or even picking cotton arduous enough for black women to warrant such action, even as an expected delivery date drew near. On one of Pierce Butler's Georgia plantations, pregnant women burned stubble in the field one day, work that was evidently considered less difficult than the normal task; but on another occasion a slave named Leah, despite her advanced stage of pregnancy, performed "task work in the fields" until she grew "quite helpless from exhaustion." Former slave Annie Jones of Virginia chopped tobacco shoots with a hoe even though she "was big wid chile an' gittin' near her time," and other pregnant women routinely performed the same work as other slaves. The slave Betty worked in the Alabama cotton fields during the spring months of 1845 almost to the day she bore her child, which may explain why her baby died within the week. In the fall of 1844, Charity's owner did not excuse her from cotton picking until the day of her baby's birth. A resident of coastal South Carolina later recalled that the slave women she knew could not put down the hoe until labor pains began, no matter how poorly they felt. The weight of the hoes ranged from six to nine or twelve pounds each. When not working with a hoe, this informant said, expectant women performed other arduous chores, such as wading into a river to fill baskets or tubs with mud to enrich the soil. The women had no choice in the matter. They "hab to do it to de very hou'" of their labor. Many, if not most, owners believed that pregnant women of African descent could withstand such work without harm to themselves or their babies, even though they recognized the correlation between heavy work loads and unsuccessful pregnancies.[14]

Their desire to increase their human property and to appear humane made owners reluctant to deny pregnant slaves relief from difficult work assignments for fear they would miscarry or produce a sickly or stillborn baby. Nevertheless, owners opposed granting women concessions simply because they asked. Slaveholders believed that slaves engaged in deception and attributed the tendency to an inherent character flaw. They thus discounted the complaints of slave women—and slave men for that matter—about physical exhaustion or other health problems as a matter of course. When slave women reported fatigue, nausea, or other symptoms of pregnancy, their owners often ignored them or, worse, castigated them for shamming to avoid work. In addition, they enacted measures to ensure that women did not feign pregnancy as a means of gaining time away from the field. This attitude forced slaves to renegotiate with owners each time a woman became pregnant in order to secure conditions of work favorable to the successful conclusion of the pregnancy.

The fact that some slave women who claimed special consideration because of pregnancy never bore a child within nine months of making the claim complicated negotiations over the treatment of pregnant women. One of Pierce Butler's slaves received extra rations during a "pseudopregnancy" that lasted so long both he and Fanny found it comical. A proportion of these women no doubt falsely claimed a pregnancy to obtain lighter or shorter tasks or possibly extra rations from those owners who supplied them; however, others probably miscarried without reporting the fact or suffered from health problems that mimicked some of the signs of pregnancy. Owners excused their own callousness in responding to pleas for relief by citing the slaves' supposed tendency toward deception. Pierce shrugged off Fanny's criticism of plantation policies related to pregnancy by claiming the women "were *shamming* themselves in the family way in order to obtain a diminution of labor," and Fanny had to admit there was some truth to his claim. Such deceptions may have occurred less often than owners believed, however. The slave woman Sary received a whipping for feigning illness, then five months later gave birth to a son in South Carolina.[15]

To ensure that women were actually pregnant as they claimed to be, South Carolina planter James Richie Sparkman kept records indicating the exact date women reported quickening—the time a woman first perceived movement of the fetus, usually around eighteen to twenty weeks in a forty-week gestation.[16] He later added the date the woman gave birth, presumably so he could identify women who claimed the benefits of pregnancy without producing a child or whose pregnancies were longer than normal. The charts he made confirmed planters' suspicions that not all women who claimed pregnancy were expecting. The slave woman Bella, for example, convinced Sparkman that quickening had occurred 263 days before she actually gave birth to a boy on June 20, 1860—a physical impossibility. Two months and two days following the baby's delivery, Bella convinced Sparkman once again that she was pregnant, only this time her pregnancy ended in miscarriage, if indeed there was one. Bella probably gained concessions from Sparkman, who must have felt duped. Such experiences no doubt figured in his determination to disregard Sally's pregnancy until thirty-six days before her child Balinda's birth.[17]

Women like Bella worried slaveholders, who by mid-century increasingly demanded proof of pregnancy by physical examination before granting concessions. By the late antebellum period, advances in medical knowledge and training had improved the physician's ability to verify pregnancy, which provided slaveholders with a means of preventing women from claiming privileges to which they were not entitled. Whereas previously an owner might have exhibited doubts about whether to press women into performing heavy work for fear that some or all might be pregnant, now an owner might insist on heavy work from all but those with medically verified excuses. Some women found themselves subject to invasive examinations without gaining additional benefits, but the difficulty of pinpointing an exact due date and the high rates of miscarriage and stillbirths encouraged owners who verified a pregnancy through physical examination to continue refusing accommodations until late in the pregnancy. In addition, many slaveholders and physicians alike continued to believe that the only "certain mode of knowing whether a woman be pregnant or not, is by waiting till the term of nine months is completed, when . . . if the uterus contain an ovum, it will be expelled!"[18]

A slaveholder could justify the expense of a physician by calculating the savings that ensued from excusing from field work only those women actually pregnant, rather than all those claiming to be. Women, desirous of decreasing their work loads, could not be relied upon to report accurately other signs of pregnancy, including quickening, cessation of the menses, food cravings, or even swelling of the abdomen. With much at stake, some slaveholders called in doctors to perform cervical examinations, inspect the areola, and make other observations that might confirm or deny the existence of a pregnancy. When Virginia planter James Olds observed a slave woman acting "in a strange way," he paid a physician to determine whether she was pregnant. At a time when physicians were meeting resistance to their management of pregnancy and childbirth among free women in the United States and Europe, doctors in the South found a way of garnering fees for these medical services by convincing owners to let them attend slaves. Southern physicians cited among their credentials for treating slaves a supposed understanding of the slave's character and perceived habits of deception. A knowledge of medicine, coupled with a readiness to detect malingerers, made them suitable allies of slaveholders concerned with protecting their own economic interests. The rhetoric of southern physicians both reflected and reinforced negative stereotyping of the enslaved.[19]

A large number of masters saved the expense of hiring a doctor by entering the medical profession themselves or by asking relatives in the profession to treat their slaves' health problems.[20] Robert F. W. Allston's mother advised him to study "Phisic" specifically to "save yourself the expence of Doctors Bill on your [rice] Plantation, and in your Family." Owners with no medical training could follow advice on verifying pregnancies published in medical books for home use or have their overseers do so. John G. Gunn specified that his popular *Gunn's Domestic Medicine,* which described how to verify pregnancy by cervical examination and discussed other aspects of pregnancy and childbirth, was intended for use in the slave states. As part of a written agreement dated 1853, the rice planter Charles Manigault required that his new overseer, S. F. Clark, secure a "good book of Medical instruction" so as to enable him to administer to the slaves as their health required; he no doubt expected Clark to become familiar with the sections on pregnancy and childbirth along with others. Robert Beverley's plantation manager in Alabama kept him informed of changes in the slave woman Barbara's pregnancy, as well as in her productivity, soliciting advice on how to treat her. Mariah Bell's master, a Virginia physician, trained her as a midwife.[21] He no doubt monitored his slaves' pregnancies himself until she could assume the responsibility.

Owners avoided pecuniary losses by waiting until the pregnancy was clearly visible to excuse pregnant women from heavy labor. Even then they did not release women from the field to live a life of ease, however. Instead, in the month or months before the expected due date, they kept expectant mothers busy at tasks regarded as light. A seemingly endless number of chores could substitute for field work or other demanding duties when a woman's confinement drew near. In fact, having a large slave force whose members specialized in different types of tasks encouraged owners to reassign female field workers to other, less taxing chores. Agricultural journals recommended that planters undertake a "general patching" of clothing "for all hands" whenever "a breeding woman gets too heavy to go to the field." The overseer on one Alabama cotton plantation had pregnant women and nursing mothers shuck seed corn and thrash oats, while other hands performed the more arduous chores of picking cotton, gathering corn, plowing, splitting rails, fixing fences, and chopping corn stalks. *DeBow's Review,* a journal popular among the planter class, specified that "pregnant women are always to do *some* work up to the time of their confinement, if it is only walking into the field and staying there." The journal recommended leniency only for women who required medical care, reflecting planters' worries that they might accommodate pregnant women too readily. Robert Beverley's manager in Alabama reported of Barbara: "She is fine cooking, and grows I think very fast," but she "pretends to be more afflicted than I think she is." Barbara's health problems related to pregnancy and childbirth continued to be a subject of correspondence and concern between plantation manager and owner into the following summer.[22]

Despite a need for other types of labor, the owner's desire to keep pregnant women in the field as long as possible forced some women to work beyond the limits of endurance. James Williams, a former Alabama slave, reported whippings of pregnant women who were unable to complete assigned tasks. He maintained that slaves in an advanced stage of pregnancy not only went to the cotton field each day, but also completed the same tasks as other hands. When one woman miscarried after she was punished for failing to complete her assigned chores, Williams attributed the infant's death to the beating sustained by the mother rather than to the strenuous nature of her work, which suggests that he viewed the punishment as more unusual or unsuitable for a pregnant woman than the work routine. When Lucy, a Virginia slave, told the overseer that she was in labor, he tried to force her into the field with a whip, believing that Lucy's "time was way off an' dat she was jes' stallin' so as tuh git outa wukkin." Lucy died within days of the incident, following the birth of a daughter. Former slave Mandy McCullough reported an Alabama case in which a severe whipping resulted in the death of a pregnant women and her unborn child. One Charlestonian mistress became so angry at her pregnant laundress over the way she washed the clothes that she threw the woman out of the door, whereupon the laundress miscarried. Distressed at her loss and the manner in which it was inflicted, the grieving woman asked to be sold, at the same time threatening to kill the mistress if she remained under her authority. She was whipped and her request denied. Such stories circulated throughout the nation in the antebellum years. Slaveholders denied the truth of the tales, but some were no doubt accurate. Although slaveowners discredited Williams's account when it appeared in print in 1838, its publication— along with other, similar narratives—fueled criticisms of slavery and probably dissuaded some owners from exposing pregnant women to especially harsh disciplinary measures.[23]

Slaves sought more from owners than the cessation of pregnant women's labor in the field and their relief from harsh discipline. They wanted additional and better food for expectant mothers. Slaves thought it was important to indulge women's longings or cravings for special edibles during pregnancy for fear that the child would be born with a birthmark in the color or shape of the thing longed for. Accounts of food allotments dispensed to slaves by their owners indicate that slaveholders did not usually provide pregnant women with extra rations or a special diet, expecting that the women could make do with their usual fare.

Slaves disputed this regimen. Everyday experiences at heavy labor taught them that pregnancy should be accommodated as soon as it was known by the provision of more or better food as women requested. Owners were reluctant to expend plantation resources to satisfy their slaves' dietary cravings, and during the antebellum years they found their position justified by medical authorities who spurned such indulgence. Gunn's medical advice book advocated a "simple and plain" diet for pregnant women. William P. Dewees, a physician and professor of midwifery at the University of Pennsylvania, published a popular book entitled *Treatise on the Physical and*

Medical Treatment of Children in which he assured readers that pregnant women could successfully nourish a child in the womb without increasing their daily intake of food or appeasing dietary cravings. The physician Alva Curtis, who lectured on midwifery at the Botanico-Medical College of Ohio, warned pregnant women: "DON'T EAT TOO MUCH . . . confine yourself to what is generally considered a small portion."[24]

The limited resources available to slave women restricted their ability to indulge the food cravings associated with pregnancy, and many no doubt suffered as a result. Others consumed food, in addition to their usual fare, obtained surreptitiously by their own efforts or through their husbands or other slaves. The slave Jim Bell of Virginia helped satisfy his pregnant wife's yearning for meat by stealing and butchering a young pig, for example. Generally, slave women encountered more difficulty securing special foods to satisfy cravings than a sufficient quantity of food to meet nutritional needs. Though an inability to satisfy cravings did not have the same dire consequences for the health of mothers and infants, slaves nevertheless worried that it would. Many people, black and white alike, believed that expectant mothers risked disfiguring their children when their cravings for certain foods went unsatisfied—despite modern medical opinion to the contrary. Emma Coker of Georgia attributed her child's birthmark to her unappeased yearning for rabbit while she was pregnant. She also thought her sister had marked her baby through an unexpected encounter with pig's feet. The need to satisfy longings by pregnant women no doubt helped justify in the minds of slaves the appropriation of certain foods from owners without authorization. Owners labeled the act theft, but slaves called the behavior "taking."[25]

The tension between owners and slaves over the needs of expectant mothers increased as the pregnancy advanced. Owners conspired to prevent pregnancy from significantly altering a slave woman's daily life and straining the plantation's finances. They neither provided special maternity clothing to women nor granted women the time or the resources to fashion such clothing for themselves. Instead, pregnant women adjusted their everyday clothing as best they could to accommodate their swelling abdomens. Most slave women wore two-piece outfits which they could easily adapt to changing body shapes. Loose blouses simply expanded, while skirts were hiked above the middle and drawstrings loosened to conform to a thickening waist. Some owners provided extra clothing as a reward for giving birth and increasing their slaveholdings, but this almost always occurred after the woman produced a living child.[26]

Although owners rejected the idea of spending extra money to accommodate pregnant slaves, they—along with many slaves—did not hesitate to provide slave women with detailed advice on appropriate behavior during pregnancy. The son of one Alabama planter recalled that expectant mothers received "a store of cautions" from the mistress. Slaves, for their part, drew on their own knowledge of pregnancy, adding to or countering the "store of cautions" provided by owners. They widely believed that expectant mothers risked disfiguring their babies or injuring them by being surprised or frightened. Expectant parents even worried that everyday actions might threaten their babies' lives. Anyone who planted a vegetable garden at the time of a child's birth and walked through "it befor' de chile is growed like it oughter" risked the child's life, Emma Coker said.[27]

Owners who thought themselves entitled to control the conditions of pregnancy for slave women also expected to determine the course of childbirth by offering their own observations about proper procedures and suitable birth attendants. Many slaves—uncertain as to the best course of action and having little choice in the matter—accepted the attention of masters and followed the advice of mistresses, but others maintained faith in their own ideas about childbirth. This latter group turned to other slaves for advice: lay midwives (called grannies), mothers, other relatives, and friends. Still others drew on both traditions, with the result that their birth experiences had origins in both Africa and Europe, although they took on new meaning within the context of everyday slave life.[28]

The inability of owners to predict the exact date of delivery aided slave women who wanted to maintain control over childbirth. Slaveholders who wanted to orchestrate the events surrounding childbirth could hope to do so only after a slave woman reported the onset of labor. Slaves and slaveholders understood the physiology of human reproduction, one as well as the other. Both knew gestation lasted nine months. A slave named Sarah attempted to assuage her husband's doubts about the paternity of her child by reminding him of a sexual encounter that occurred nine months earlier. "You kno' jes as well as I kno', de mornin' I sent ya to Aint Manervia's to git dat buttermilk," she argued, apparently to the satisfaction of her skeptical husband. Slaves could calculate the progress of their pregnancies using a "notchin stick," a long stick in which notches were made with a knife. The entire calendar could be carved into the wood, including notations of special events and time periods. Slaves could record months as they passed or count the months since conception.[29] Whether slaves reported expected birth dates accurately depended on their assessment of whether telling the slaveholder would help or hinder the birthing process.

On the majority of plantations and farms, owners and slaves alike preferred midwives as attendants, unless complications arose. Only those births that took an "unnatural" turn required medical attention, according to popular opinion of the day. Slaveowners did not like the extra expense of calling in a doctor, which reinforced this folk wisdom. The slave trader Thomas Burton bragged that one of the women he peddled had borne a child for only a trifling cost. "I had no physician with her at all," he said, only "an old negro woman that lives in this place." On the other hand, owners welcomed the positive results that physicians sometimes brought to childbirth. By the late antebellum years, southern physicians were beginning to use forceps and other instruments in difficult deliveries. They also prescribed medications, manipulated the perineum during birth, and took extreme measures such as bloodletting. Perhaps even more important, they identified themselves with modernity and science, thereby increasing confidence among slaveholders that they might rescue valuable slave women from debilitating birth experiences. When planters heard that a local physician had helped with a difficult birth, it encouraged them to secure his services for their own slaves. However, most planters obtained the services of physicians only when the difficulty of the birth seemed to require it. This held true for the births of their own children, as well as those that occurred among their slaves. The preference for midwives remained so strong among slaveholding women living in the South Carolina low country that even women married to physicians continued to rely on midwives when giving birth.[30]

When physicians attended slave births, black midwives assisted, which suggests that slaves and their owners continued to put their trust in traditional childbirth practices even as physicians increased their presence at the childbed. In January 1857, *DeBow's Review* published rules for plantation management that assumed the need for a midwife, as well as for slave nurses to care for the new mother. When the slave woman Betsey gave birth to a boy on John Gavin's rice plantation in South Carolina, two midwives and a doctor attended her.[31]

Whether or not a doctor's services were engaged, owners wanted to be consulted. They maintained a suspicion of the folkways of their slaves, preferring that their bonded men and women look to them for direction in all aspects of life. Slaveowners who did not observe slave births firsthand or call in a physician at least wished to approve the choice of midwife. Many planters arranged in advance for particular midwives to attend slave births.[32] When the midwife belonged to another slaveholder, the owner paid for her services, which increased the expectation that the midwife would adjust her practice to meet the owner's wishes.

Many slaves preferred to manage childbirth without interference from their owners or their owners' agents, and uneventful pregnancies and uncomplicated childbirth usually left slaves free to assume sole charge of the birth process. Owners might choose attendants in advance, but normally they did not know when to come unless summoned by some slave. Even when slaves complied with their owners' directives to call a particular attendant, they could wait so long that the doctor or midwife arrived after the baby's birth.[33]

Although some slaves resigned themselves to or welcomed the attention of their owners, others kept the progress of their pregnancies secret to avoid interference, perhaps with good reason. When an Alabama slave in 1838 suffered complications of childbirth, her master, mistress, and attending physician each gave her quinine, not knowing that the others had done the same. When she lost consciousness, the three attendants attempted to revive her by dousing her with buckets of cold water, firing pistols about her head, and sticking her with pins. Poor outcomes such as this, even if rare and not resulting in death, discouraged slaves from trusting procedures recommended by owners and their representatives. Moreover, racist attitudes on the part of physicians meant that many of them proved insensitive to a slave woman's pain, believing that black women gave birth more easily than white women. With callous disregard for slave sensibilities, some physicians carried out medical experiments on their slave patients, and they sometimes dissected stillborn infants. Slaves found these acts abhorrent. Instances in which overseers or owners learned of births days after they occurred suggest that many slaves, perhaps most, succeeded in managing childbirth for themselves. Owner James M. Torbert apparently did not learn of the infant Lewis's birth on Christmas Day, 1856, until two days later, although he was in residence on the estate. Other slaves on Torbert's plantation had their deliveries attended either by a physician or a granny, which suggests that Lewis's mother made her own arrangements for help with his delivery. Fear of meddling by her overseer probably explains why Matilda, a slave on the Mississippi cotton plantation of President James K. Polk, withheld knowledge of her pregnancy from the overseer "until a few minets before the burth of the child." The overseer blamed the infant's death on Matilda's reticence about her condition, explaining in a letter to his employer that her last-minute announcement left him no time to engage the services of a midwife. One low-country South Carolina physician waited beside a slave woman's childbed for several hours before learning "to his astonishment there was no child." Her baby had been stillborn earlier while she was in the field, a fact she chose to conceal. The doctor discovered the deceit when—having grown tired of waiting for the labor to progress naturally—he insisted upon examining her.[34]

When complications of birth arose, owners ordered midwives to seek the assistance of a physician. Some summoned the doctor through their masters, others under authority already delegated to them by their owners. When the slave woman Barbara endured a long and difficult labor, she received what many physicians considered standard medical treatment: "copious bleeding in the arm and Temples." Master William Gilmer sent for a doctor to attend Mirey when her labor proved "hard and slow." When the slave Mahala appeared near death following the birth of her child, two doctors hovered at her side, along with her master and mistress. In Virginia, the pioneering physician John Peter Mettauer treated slave women for complications of pregnancy and childbirth, as did the noted doctor J. Marion Sims in Alabama.[35]

One physician observed that slaveowners allowed slaves to manage childbirth for themselves "as long as they can. When they can't go further they call for help."[36] When complications threatened the life or health of the mother or child, both midwife and mother were less likely to oppose the physician's presence. In fact, many midwives welcomed the opportunity to call in a physician for a complicated birth, since it meant they could shift blame for any unfortunate outcome, and mothers (as well as fathers and other relatives) became more willing to accept assistance from anyone who held out hope for a live birth and the mother's successful recovery.

Physicians, for their part, valued the fees awarded them for treating the health problems of slaves, but obstetric cases were less desirable than others. Childbirth was time-consuming for the doctor, and the fees paid to physicians for attending black women tended to be lower than those paid for attending white women under similar circumstances. A schedule of fees published by one South Carolina medical society in 1819 revealed that fees for attending white women during labor ranged from thirty to fifty dollars, while similar attendance at the birth of black babies drew fees ranging from fifteen to fifty dollars. Although slaveholders willingly paid doctors as much for attending exceptionally complicated slave births as for similar births involving their own families, they were unwilling to pay the same amount when more routine problems arose. The notion that black women gave birth more easily than white women no doubt served to justify less attention on the part of the doctor, as well as the lower fees.[37]

Of course, some planters only reluctantly called in physicians under any circumstances, preferring to avoid such expenses whenever possible. This could appear callous to women in labor, as well as to the woman's loved ones, especially if the labor was difficult. A slave woman near Beaufort, South Carolina, suffered labor pains for three days and nights before her owner authorized the expense of a physician. By then she had grown too weak to push, and the doctor "hab to use force" in delivering the baby. The high fees that doctors charged for attending births, necessitated by the time-consuming nature of obstetrics, no doubt helped account for this slaveholder's reluctance to send for the doctor earlier.[38] Childbirth represented another instance in which owners weighed a concern for slaves' welfare against the financial price of solicitude.

As the time for birth drew near, anxious women watched the moon, knowing that "on the change of the moon, water come more freely." If the moon proved unfavorable, a midwife might brew herbal tea or another special drink to stimulate labor, but most midwives let nature do its work, simply "catching" the infant for the mother. They also helped in managing pain, most often by placing an ax or a "rusty piece of tin" under the bed to cut the pain of childbirth. A few tried more drastic methods to aid in desperate cases. Fanny Kemble Butler reported the actions of one midwife during "one or two cases of prolonged and terribly hard labor." The midwife tied "a cloth tight round the throats of the agonized women, and by drawing it till she almost suffocated them she produced violent and spasmodic struggles, which . . . she thought materially assisted the progress of the labor."[39] The process described by Butler was unusual. Most slave women endured the pain of childbirth without taking such drastic measures.

The midwife's attention to the mother did not end with the baby's appearance. Following the birth, the midwife placed an ax or another object with a sharp surface under the bed to ease the pain associated with the afterbirth, if she had not already done so to cut the pain of childbirth. Although the practice was widespread, not everyone relied on this method of managing pain. Emma Coker claimed that her sister avoided after-pains by placing "a meal bag . . . in de span o' her back" as she lay down. Coker maintained that it took "off all the hereafter pains."[40]

Even when a physician attended a birth, responsibility for the new mother returned to the midwife once any immediate danger to her health subsided. After the birth, the attendant cleaned the room, burned the after-birth in the fireplace, and took care not to sweep under the bed or disturb the ashes in the fireplace—actions thought to bring bad luck. The midwife also took charge of the baby's needs. Immediately following the birth, she cut and tied the navel cord, then browned a bit of linen or cotton from the gin house in a skillet of grease. She or her helper placed this on the new-born's navel, next wrapping a band of cloth around the baby's middle. Parents, slave and free, considered the belly band necessary for supporting the infant's back and abdomen. It could be made of linen, possibly torn from a tablecloth or bedclothes "donated" by the mistress. Ideally it was made of flannel, a material thought especially suitable for newborns. This part of the after-care was important, for improper handling of the umbilical cord could introduce the bacterium responsible for neonatal tetanus (lockjaw), with deadly results. Fanny Kemble Butler, struck by the high disease rate among infants on her husband's Georgia plantations, attributed many deaths that occurred during the first or second week of life to this disease, which claimed the lives of nearly twice the number of slave babies as white infants. The navel cord usually fell off after three days, and that too needed to be burned in the fireplace.[41]

Enslaved women, whether giving birth or assisting as midwives or help-ers, believed in signs. Events that occurred during pregnancy and child-birth had meaning and required interpretation and, in some cases, action. The midwife helped parents understand and respond to such unusual de-velopments as the birth of twins or the presence of a caul (the amniotic sac) over the face of the newborn. Many slaves believed that twin births indi-cated a baby with supernatural powers and called for special rituals, while an infant born with part of the amnion covering the head supposedly saw spirits invisible to others. Maum Hagar Brown, who acted as a granny in the Georgetown District of South Carolina, brewed and fed newborns as needed a special tea made of the caul. She did this to prevent children from seeing ghosts, which she said frightened them. First, she would have needed to gain the confidence and permission of the parents. "Maum Hagar" and other midwives played crucial roles in the slave community by injecting a sense of understanding and control into the everyday experi-ences of a people unable to direct much of their own lives.[42] No profession-ally trained physician—no matter how skilled—could substitute for the midwife, because he lacked basic understanding of the folk beliefs that guided slave behavior.

The length of a midwife's attendance varied from plantation to plantation, but she usually remained nearby for days and continued to consult with the new mother over a period of weeks. Sam Polite, who had been a slave on St. Helena Island, South Carolina, said that midwives cared for mothers and babies for nine days, although the mothers remained out of the field for a month.[43] Customs varied, but this corresponded with the practice of some slaveholding women who remained in bed for nine days after the birth of a child, followed by weeks of curtailed activities. A general cleaning of the slave cabin took place under the supervision of the midwife a month after the birth. The room was swept and bedclothes removed and scrubbed. The mother's clothes, too, were scrubbed, and the mother herself washed. Slaves observed a variety of precautions during this time to protect the mother and baby from bad luck, ill health, and even death. Throughout the South, babies, as well as older children, wore bags of a foul-smelling plant resin (asafetida) around their necks to ward off disease. Family members refrained from rocking an empty cradle and guarded against allowing infants to see themselves in a mirror. They rubbed various objects representing different trades on the palm of the baby's hand in the hope that the child would grow up to excel in a particular occupation. The many prohibitions committed to memory by midwives and observed by new mothers prompted Alabama midwife Carrie Dykes to exclaim that "there's a heap to midwifin," although by the time she talked about her practices in the 1930s, many if not most of her contemporaries spurned the "old-timey remedies" as foolishness.[44]

Slaves measured the success of midwives using standards that differed from those of owners. Both slaves and slaveholders wanted mothers and their infants to survive, but slaves also wanted women to experience birth according to their own notions of proper procedure. Whether midwives met the expectations of either depended in part on the amount of time they could spend with each case and on how closely owners supervised their practices. On some plantations, heavy case loads prevented midwives from performing adequately because they were expected to care for sick slaves in addition to mothers and newborns. The midwife on Pierce Butler's rice plantation attended to everyone housed in the plantation infirmary, including women in labor, those who had just given birth, and those who had suffered miscarriages, along with any slaves too ill to go to the field.[45] The situation left little time for her to devote to expectant and new mothers. Perhaps more troubling, it left the women vulnerable to the oversight of the owner. Fanny Kemble Butler did not hesitate to tell the mothers how to care for their newborns.

Decisions about who made the best birth attendants were not clear-cut.

Not all midwives who followed the dictates of owners were rejected. A midwife well respected by members of the owning class could act effectively as an advocate, soliciting time off from the field or other benefits for the women she served. Midwives whose loyalties clearly lay with slaves to the exclusion of owners would have encountered difficulty in securing equal consideration for the recipients of their services. For many, the ideal midwife was one who could satisfy the expectations of both owners and slaves.

Most grannies learned what to do by assisting friends who gave birth or who acted as midwives. As they became experienced, the best assistants would gain a reputation as able grannies. This meant that the majority of midwives were older women—mothers themselves. Midwifery involved more than simply knowing the physiology of childbirth. It also called for maturity of judgment. Knowing when to let nature take its course and when to call in a physician called for wisdom, as did the need to satisfy both the slave and the slaveholder.

Slaves imparted knowledge of folk medicine, including midwifery, from one generation to another. Jeanette Chaney, who practiced midwifery in Alabama, bore thirteen children and possessed a knowledge of herbal medicine, which she may have learned from her husband's family. Born in another country, probably Africa or the Caribbean, her husband's grandmother enjoyed a reputation for wisdom and for doing "a plenty good while she was livin'." Her great-grandson Ned Chaney recalled later that much of the older woman's learning had followed her to the grave. "All dem little bags she had, had ter be buried wid her," because "couldn' nobody use 'em but her." Nevertheless, Ned's mother practiced midwifery, and her healing concoctions probably represented at least a truncated version of the older woman's store of folk knowledge. Ned knew something of the art, for as a boy he had gathered herbs for his mother to use in her work.[46] Ned never took up midwifery, an occupation restricted to women, but he surely became a conduit of knowledge to a new generation of women or men engaged in folk medicine or even conjuring. In this way, some of his mother's and great-grandmother's knowledge of folkways could have passed from generation to generation, changing content and purpose as older members of a family died and younger members put their knowledge to different uses, depending in part on the sex of the child involved.

The midwife Elsey, like Jeanette, was a mother herself when she practiced midwifery in Georgia in the 1830s. Elsey acted "as midwife, to black and white in the neighborhood who [sent] for her," with her owner's permission, probably bringing home fees to her owner from other slaveholders in the area. Her master approved her midwifery practice, arranging with the overseer to ensure that Elsey's older daughter cared for the woman's younger children and household affairs whenever her mother had to attend a birth. Her owner expected Elsey to act as "Doctoress of the Plantation" as well as midwife. He authorized Elsey to call in a physician for any case of sickness she could not handle alone. In a set of written directives, the master tried to make certain that his overseer followed Elsey's instructions: "In the case of extraordinary illness, when she thinks she can do no more for the sick, you will employ a Physician."[47] Elsey also fed her master's poultry when she was at home. Her combined duties meant that Elsey continued to augment her owner's fortunes as she grew older, even as she enhanced his image as a kindly slaveholder who met the health needs of his slaves and also of the white women of the neighborhood. For their part, the slaves probably accepted Elsey's assistance, relying on her to accommodate their own wishes with regard to birthing practices while assuring her master that his were met as well.

Owners made judgments about the trustworthiness of midwives who visited their plantations, encouraging some more than others. However, some owners looked with suspicion upon all midwives' activities, blaming them for poor outcomes of birthing practices or worse. The life of Lou Russeau, who combined a midwifery practice with fortune telling in Alabama, reveals a link between magic or conjuring and midwifery that worried slaveholders. The Alabama midwife maintained she could not explain how she learned her art, except that she knew she "was born with a Skain over my eyes," by which she meant a caul. Since her mother was a Creek Indian, Russeau doubtless employed some skills handed down from Indian forebears. If so, she and other slaves of similar backgrounds must have incorporated into their store of knowledge ideas about pregnancy and childbirth drawn from Native American as well as African and European traditions.[48]

Although slaveholders generally accepted the need for midwives, they feared their authority. Owners worried about the powers grannies had to heal and harm. If left unsupervised, they could induce abortion, thereby reducing the number of slave births. The physician John Morgan gave voice to these fears before the Tennessee Medical Association in 1860. Some slave women, he said, were "willing and even anxious to avail themselves of an opportunity to effect an abortion," using tansy and other plants "commonly cultivated in our gardens." In South Carolina, the slave Lucy denied her pregnancy, then delivered the child (whether stillborn or alive was not known) and hid it. Lucy was imprisoned for eight days and given ninety lashes over a period of time. The midwife who attended her and other slaves implicated in the affair also received punishment.[49]

Physicians, as a group, tended to be highly critical of midwives, in part because this allowed them to shift the blame for infant deaths resulting from tetanus or other common neonatal problems. Mary Frances Brown, a former slave who spent her life in northern and coastal South Carolina, reported that her grandmother, the plantation midwife and nurse, was held responsible by her owner for any infection that set in even when a physician attended mother and child. Although physicians did not understand the cause of tetanus, they could see inflammation in the area of the umbilical wound and related this to the disease. The Alabama physician William O. Baldwin argued that black midwives did not know how to care for the umbilicus following birth. He further complained that slave women could not properly care for infants because of the filthy conditions of their cabins. In addition to better sanitation, he urged that soft dressings applied to the navel be changed often as a means of preventing tetanus. Nonetheless, most doctors left decisions about the treatment of the navel to the midwife, probably because both owners and slaves wanted it that way, though for different reasons: slaveholders to avoid more expensive services offered by doctors and slaves to maintain control over the culture of childbearing. Greater involvement of physicians probably would not have led to more successful outcomes. Southern doctors failed to understand the needs of slave women, and the evidence suggests that the postpartum techniques of physicians were no more effective than those of grannies. One doctor recommended cleaning the navel with turpentine and olive oil; another recommended poultices made of garlic; yet another preferred mustard baths.[50]

AFTER the birth of a child, owners kept up their meddling. On a visit to the infirmary where new mothers were housed along with slaves too sick to perform their work in the field, Fannie Kemble Butler ordered the mothers to bathe their new babies in a tub of warm water. Exhibiting doubt as to the wisdom of doing so, the women cooperated only reluctantly. One of the mothers threw her baby's clothing into the water instead of her infant, and Butler immediately had the clothing retrieved and hung by the fire to dry. She admitted that the clothing was "quite as much in want of washing as the baby," though she declined to undertake this task because the infant had only one set of clothes.[51]

Part of the mothers' reluctance must have stemmed from their practice of swaddling their infants. Not all slave mothers swaddled their babies in this period, but apparently some did, at least along the rice coast where Butler encountered them. African Americans made up a substantial portion of the population in the region (about 70 percent throughout the antebellum years), and African customs are said to have survived longer in this region than elsewhere. However, no other evidence suggests that the practice was African in origin, as a minority of white women—mostly recent immigrants and those living in rural areas—continued to swaddle children beyond the end of the eighteenth century. Indeed, the physician William P. Dewees found it necessary to warn more wealthy parents against swaddling when he published his *Treatise on the Physical and Medical Treatment of Children* in 1826. Fanny Kemble Butler, like other members of the ruling class, disapproved of the practice and complained that "these poor people pin up the lower part of their infants, bodies, legs, and all, in red flannel as soon as they are born, and keep them in the selfsame envelope till it literally falls off." She found swaddling "most absurd and disgusting," but had to admit that inhabitants of her native England had practiced the custom until recently.[52]

Slaves followed their own customs in caring for newborns. Indeed, the material conditions under which slaves lived would have prevented their imitating the child-rearing practices of the owning class, which had abundant resources to devote to children's care. Dr. Dewees recommended against deliberate "hardening" of children by bathing them in cold water or exposing their limbs to cold. For him, the high mortality rate among poor children, whose parents routinely exposed them to the elements, offered proof that such a strategy did not work to promote health. Slave parents, however, with little time and few resources, dispensed with heating bath water (which used precious fuel) and kept their children wrapped (to ensure that they stayed out of harm's way). Dewees's additional advice to change diapers (rather than to let the infant remain in wet clothes) and to wash the diapers (rather than simply drying them after they had been soiled) would not have influenced slave mothers had they encountered it (which they did not) because they lacked soap, extra cloth, and the time to implement the doctor's suggestions.[53] Slave mothers, of course, had a special incentive to "harden" their children. They knew they must prepare their children to survive the years of hardship and deprivation that awaited them.

Slave mothers must have worried about their ability to nurture their newborns, given the limited resources at their disposal and the high rates of mortality that characterized the slave population. Pregnant slave women knew, as did other expectant mothers, the hazards of childbirth, which claimed the lives of many women and infants. One reason the choice of midwife was so important was that she would assist a woman in facing the dangers of childbirth, emotionally as well as physically. Those women who had entered into forbidden sexual liaisons, willingly or unwillingly, had special reason to worry about the impending birth. A living child—especially one with light skin—could raise troublesome questions that called for answers. Mack Brantley described himself as a "stole chile," by which he meant he was born of a relationship forbidden by the master. "Ma had a husband the master give her and had children," the former slave explained. "My pa lived on a joining farm. She wasn't supposen to have children by my pa."[54] Births such as Mack's revealed clearly the way slaves challenged the prerogative claimed by owners to approve personal relationships among their slaves. Unable to control sexual relationships among their slaves, most owners feigned ignorance of the matter and accepted the addition to their slaveholdings of a child born of a forbidden alliance.

When childbirth produced a baby of mixed race, the situation was further complicated. No immediate celebration of life ensued; instead participants and witnesses negotiated the moment gingerly or angrily, depending on their ideas of who had been victimized and who had been betrayed, who had the power to punish and who was vulnerable to punishment. Children of mixed race were often the result of forced sexual encounters by masters, the masters' sons, overseers, or other whites living or visiting in the neighborhood. The practice of white men forcing themselves upon slave women was so widespread that Reverend C. C. Jones accused a guest in his home of debauching one of his chambermaids and continued to believe him guilty even after an official investigation exonerated the man. Slaves discussed the matter frequently, although not before owners or children. The slave woman Ethel Jane became the object of sexual gratification for a father and his son. "Both took her," a friend later explained, "the father showing the son what it was all about—and she couldn't do nothin 'bout it."[55]

Knowing the frequency with which men of the owning class forced sex upon slave women, mistresses, often present at a slave baby's birth, must have entered the birthing room with trepidation, as much for themselves as for the welfare of the slave mother and infant. When former Alabama slave Henry Green was born with light skin, straight hair, and blue eyes, his mother received a whipping at the hands of her mistress, apparently in retaliation for what the mistress assumed was a sexual liaison between her husband and the young slave mother. Upon his birth, the "old mis . . . so mad dat she gib mammy er good stroppin," Green recounted later. The mistress eventually forgave and forgot what happened, in part because she observed Henry's skin darken as he grew. All involved in the matter agreed to subscribe to the myth that neither Henry nor his sister "neber hab no pappy, jes er mammy whut wuz name Emily Green," and well into old age the former slave continued to insist that he had no father.[56]

Candis Goodwin knew her father to be her master from the time she was a little girl, but she learned to respond to questions about his identity by explaining that "tuckey buzzard lay me an' de sun hatch me." Former slave Annie Wallace of Virginia also knew that her master was her father, but she refused to acknowledge this fact into old age. Another mother who told her daughter of her white father's identity was able to avoid problems with the mistress until the girl grew old enough to answer truthfully a question about her parentage. Upon hearing the girl's response, the mistress ordered the child permanently out of the back yard, which made the child grieve because the mistress periodically dispensed treats to the slave children who gathered there.[57] Identifying fathers of mixed-race children could prove dangerous for the youngsters, and parents who denied children knowledge of their paternity hoped to shield them from reprisals.

Mothers who denied children information about their fathers also hoped to protect themselves from reprisals by angry mistresses who, unable to prevent their men from seeking sexual gratification in the slave quarters, often took out their frustrations on the slave women—thereby victimizing them twice, once when they were raped or coerced into having sex and again when they were punished for bearing children as a result. Even when the male offender was not a family member, mistresses took offense at the situation. Alabama slave Annie Burton learned her father's identity from her mistress, who stood on the porch with Annie and shouted to the neighboring planter whenever he came in sight to stop and meet his "darling child." Annie understood that her mistress wanted "to humble and shame" him. Annie's mother had run away while Annie was still young to avoid her mistress's acrimony, leaving Annie under the care of her antagonist.[58]

Slave pregnancy and childbirth complicated plantation life and raised disturbing questions of authority, family, and identity. Annie's mother was unusual. Few slave mothers abandoned their children, no matter what the circumstances of their birth. Mixed-race children generally were accepted into the slave family and taught the ways of slaves, rather than the customs of slaveholders. This practice helped ensure that the sexual exploitation of

slave women by men of the owning class did not create chaos in the family
or in the community. By maintaining family relationships flexible enough to
include children of coerced sex, the slave family proved itself adaptable,
even to the most sordid aspects of servitude.

Very rarely did children of mixed race attain a status other than that of
slave. Slaveowning men spurned their children born to enslaved women.
On rare occasions white fathers provided mulatto children with educational opportunities, sheltered them in their homes, or favored them
through other means; much more frequently such children were ignored,
sold, or barred from their father's presence. Southern society discouraged
recognition of mulatto children, and a father's flagrant favoritism toward
sons or daughters of mixed race could serve as grounds for divorce.[59] The
practice among slaveholders of ignoring mulatto sons and daughters earned
the disdain of slaves, who believed men should assume responsibility for
their children. Decades later, former Virginia slave Ishrael Massie still felt
his "blood . . . bilin'" at the thought. "When babies came dey ain't
exknowledge 'em," he complained. "Treat dat baby like 'tothers—nuthing
to him."[60]

Slaves accepted that circumstances prevented some slave fathers from assisting their families to any great extent, as occurred when children were
born of unions forbidden by owners. But when fathers—white or black—
deliberately shirked responsibilities they could have assumed, their children suffered humiliation and anger. Overseer Roswell King of the Butlers'
Georgia estate fathered Renty, who learned his identity from the children of
a neighboring planter. As a boy, Renty never asked his mother to name his
father because he felt "ashamed to ask her." Despite this, the mulatto youth
thought his father owed him recognition of some sort. When King left his
owner's employ, Renty tried to claim the gun his father had left behind, and
he expressed resentment that King did not think of doing so himself as a
"token of parental affection."[61] Renty never expected King to treat him as a
son, but he believed he was entitled to some form of acknowledgment.

Despite such complications, masters and mistresses attached great importance to the addition of slave children to their holdings. Lists of slave
births, as well as notations in farm journals, diaries, and memoirs, testify to
this. Charles Heyward's homecoming to his South Carolina Rose Hill plantation in November of each year, following a warm-weather sojourn to
Charleston, was marked by an elaborate ritual that included a meeting with
his overseer. The occasion called for the overseer, among other things, to
announce the names of children born since the owner's departure the pre-

vious May. These were duly recorded by Heyward in his plantation journal. Like Heyward, James M. Torbert of Alabama kept a list of slave births. He also recorded the names of the babies in his diary as the births occurred and tallied the number born each year in his annual summation of assets and debits. So important was this category of assets to the calculation of his financial well-being that he entered a notation even for years in which there were no births to report. "I have no negroes born this year," he lamented in 1860.[62]

The well-wishers and onlookers who crowded around a slave mother as she gave birth to her child viewed the event differently from one another, depending on their social status. Members of the owning class congratulated themselves on the birth of the newborn because the infant represented a new financial asset and attested to the humane values they associated with southern slaveholding, which allowed slaves to enjoy some form of family life. The mother would lose some working time because of the pregnancy and childbirth, but the baby represented an investment in the future. When the child reached adulthood, he or she could be put to work, perhaps by the owner's son or daughter, and thus the slave child's birth would help ensure the perpetuation of the slave system.

Slaves viewed the birth of the infant quite differently. The survival of the child might perpetuate slavery, but it also promised the continuity of a people. Slaves knew that life under the slaveholder's regime was fragile; the newborn would need help to survive under precarious circumstances. Slave families had struggled to ensure the healthy birth of an infant and to maintain cultural customs important to the baby's development. They now were determined to see that the owner's demands for the mother's work would not compromise her efforts to care for the baby.

2

NEW MOTHERS
AND FATHERS

TOM AND VINEY, slaves in Alabama, had a child in April 1835. Although they lived on the same plantation, they did not move into their own cabin until November of that year. Still, their overseer did not acknowledge the couple's union as a permanent alliance. Not until early in 1837 did John G. Traylor note tersely in his farm journal that "Tom an Little viney got maried last night."[1] Prior to this, he must have viewed Viney as husbandless, despite the presence of Tom and the child. He probably regarded Tom, too, as having no spouse. Traylor's attitude typified that of the owning class. Only those family relationships of which owners approved were acknowledged and accommodated. Young slaves—like Tom and Viney—lived apart, even after they began having children, until their owners allocated separate housing.

Obtaining housing was only one of many obstacles that Tom and Viney had to overcome in establishing a family and caring for their child, if their experience was typical of other slaves. The young parents would have needed time away from their owner's work to maintain a home and care for their infant. Slave babies, like all infants, had to be fed; kept clean, warm, and dry; and protected from danger. Securing time for nurturing babies and ensuring their safety could prove as difficult as obtaining a cabin and household furnishings. Slaveholders were reluctant to allot any of the slave's time to private matters, preferring that men and women devote undivided attention to fulfilling their owners' labor needs, but they recognized that infants had to survive if southern society were to continue. The law declared slaves property, but the birth of a slave child exposed the contradiction inherent in declaring humans chattel. Unlike other property, infants required nurturing. Tempering the owners' willingness to designate time for infant care was their knowledge that many babies would not survive to adulthood, and those who did would require years of economic support before they began to pay a return on any investment in their care. Slaveholders knew they could not turn their backs on slave infants, however. Cruelty toward slaves' sons and daughters, nieces and nephews—or any helpless infant for that matter—would alienate the work force and destroy any semblance of cooperation between owners and slaves. Consequently, most owners conceded the needs of infants but exercised caution in allocating plantation resources for their benefit.

Slave parents did not allow the economics of child rearing to restrain their desire to care for children. They knew that not all infants survived childhood, but they did not believe this fact should diminish the emotional and material support of the adults responsible for them. This held true for mothers and fathers alike, who hoped the arrival of children would encourage owners to recognize the authenticity of slaves' personal relationships. A parent's prolonged, loving attention, especially that of the mother, helped ensure an infant's survival, they pleaded before planters. It also fostered the child's loyalty to family and community, slaves acknowledged among themselves.

Parental resolve helped persuade owners to organize agricultural routines around the nurture of infants and to provide plantation resources for them. Not all couples who had children succeeded in gaining separate housing, however. Owners frequently denied young parents cabins, and many a new mother and infant lived with her parents while the couple awaited the owner's approval for a home of their own. This was especially true for couples who belonged to separate slaveholders and lived on different estates, although first-time parents living on the same plantation might occupy different households as well. The promise of a growing slave population enticed many owners to recognize new family units. The majority of slaves throughout the South eventually procured housing and household furnishings for growing families, even if their owners did not allocate them following the mother's first birth. Though the practice was far from universal, the majority of slave children while young lived in homes with two parents.[2]

By persuading owners to allocate resources for their households, slaves gained for their families a certain legitimacy in the eyes of the ruling class, which helped to foster stability. Slaveholders were more reluctant to separate family members whose relationships they acknowledged than those they did not. Slave marriages had no legal standing, but many slaveowners recognized certain couples as married through their designation of cabins and the granting of other accouterments of married life. Couples wanted whatever material advantages the slaveholder would give families, but perhaps even more, they wanted the opportunity to define "family" for themselves. If parents could establish private housing and secure time to care for their infants, their children could grow up learning at a parent's knee about the South's peculiar social relations and how to negotiate them.

When owners refused new families access to cabins, three generations of slaves lived together for better or worse. The arrangement did have its benefits: a new mother could count on help with infant care and housekeeping, and she and her child could depend on her parents and other relatives to intercede with owners or take other action to secure food and protect them from danger. The high infant mortality rate meant that many mothers would suffer the loss of a child, and the presence of parents could be comforting under these circumstances. Nonetheless, young couples wanted their owner's recognition of their marriage and the privileges this brought. Privileges extended to family households involved more than the allotment of cabins and furnishings. Slave householders were usually given small patches of land for gardening, opportunities for raising poultry, and in some places hogs or, more rarely, cows. The knowledge that a variety of family and household configurations had existed in Africa among their ancestors may have helped make other arrangements acceptable to antebellum slaves, but their goal remained a home of their own.[3]

The situation grew fraught with tension as each side—slave and slaveholder—waited to see who would triumph. Pleased about the growth in the slave population, the owner gave in at times and designated a dwelling for the new family's use, even if the husband lived elsewhere. At other times, the mother—yielding to her owner's wishes—gave up her endeavor to marry her child's father or agreed to postpone marriage or to marry a man more to her owner's liking. Sometimes the issue was settled by the disapproval of the father's owner or by the disappearance of the father from the vicinity, a victim of his owner's decision to relocate labor. The births of additional children to a couple increased the likelihood that the owner would recognize a family by allocating a cabin for its use.

Any decision by a slaveholder to allow a couple to set up housekeeping obligated the slaveholder to undertake certain expenses, which further inhibited owners from recognizing new slave families. Each household needed a room for sleeping, furnished with bedding, a table, chairs or benches, a few tin plates and cans, a small iron pot for cooking, baskets, tools, and other household items. The expense was not inconsequential. In the 1820s, one Virginia planter regularly paid $53.00 for a bed, bureau, and other furniture for each female slave who set up housekeeping. If planters did not spend money purchasing the items, they arranged for their construction, which drew workers away from the crop.[4]

Owners who agreed to build cabins for young couples timed the work to avoid disruption to plantation routines. Slaveholders, who controlled access to building materials and labor, were reluctant to authorize the construction of housing for new families as long as the crop needed attention, and most of them authorized the building and repair of dwellings only during slack seasons. Louis Manigault of Georgia put slaves to work constructing cabins as the winter of 1854 drew to a close and before rice planting began. Other slaveholders considered the construction of dwellings summer work, ideally undertaken only after crops were "laid by," a term describing a period when the crop in the ground required relatively little attention. John G. Traylor preferred that slaves build or repair dwellings at the end of the cotton-picking season or during the winter months before spring plowing, although he authorized emergency repairs at other times.[5] Neither he nor other planters considered the birth of a baby an emergency, however, and new families, such as Tom and Viney's, waited for a cabin until a slackened work schedule made its construction feasible. The waiting occurred whether the owner approved the construction enthusiastically or only reluctantly.

The construction, repair, and maintenance of cabins were viewed as men's work, and slave men negotiated with owners over the need for new cabins. The majority of houses, constructed of logs or hewn wood, consisted of one room, although larger families sometimes occupied buildings

of two rooms. Some had wooden floors, others only a bare earth floor. Former Virginia slave Joseph Holmes recalled that men built cabins "out ob
logs an' ceiled or chinked" them, positioning them in rows along the
"streets" and insulating them by throwing "dirt up under de house tuh
keep de snow an' cold out."[6]

For furniture, slaves relied mostly on hand-hewn pieces, which took time
to construct. Homemade bedsteads, chairs, tables, and benches varied from
cabin to cabin and from slaveholding to slaveholding, but most were made
by slave men from wood found on the plantation or farm. A slave carpenter,
whether highly skilled or a crude craftsman, had to gain the owner's approval to begin work on a piece, for slaveholders wanted to approve the use
of any wood, and many objected to the construction of furniture styled to
conceal forbidden items. While some owners allowed or even provided
chests or boxes for storage, others insisted that there be "no place to stow
away anything."[7] The type and quantity of furniture fashioned for new families could involve owners and slave men in prolonged bargaining. Slave
men, who hoped to be granted as much time and material as possible for
manufacturing furnishings for their families, took pleasure in crafting not
only tables and chairs but also smaller household necessities such as baskets and mortars and pestles. A husband or father gained satisfaction from
knowing that the fruits of his labor belonged to himself, his wife, and his
children, and the act of craftsmanship offered relief, if only temporary, from
other, often grueling, labor that benefited owners rather than slaves.[8]

Slaves did not find communal efforts to construct housing and furnishings objectionable, especially in areas where husbands and wives lived on
separate slaveholdings and children lived with their mothers. Men, under
these circumstances, could not easily work on behalf of their families, a situation that occurred most often in the states of the upper South where
small slaveholdings predominated.[9] The willingness of slaves unrelated by
blood or marriage to build and maintain the slave quarters helped ensure
that all slaves achieved at least a minimum standard of shelter, restricted by
the availability of materials and the time allotted for home construction and
maintenance. Such activities fostered notions of community among slave
men, an outcome hardly intended by the owners who made decisions about
how, when, and where to construct and furnish slave dwellings.

When couples lived apart, slave men and women generally relied on the
assistance of the larger slave community. When a single father needed a
quilt for his children, the women of the community might pool scraps of
material and labor to construct one. A community of slave men would share

the fish they caught and the wood they chopped with women and children whose husbands and fathers lived too far away to complete these chores for their families. Women did not dominate the family, nor did family life center on women's activities. Rather, men and women cooperated as best they could to ensure the survival of children. Slaves did not equate the idea of family with a particular form of household composition or domestic unit because the capriciousness of slavery made this impossible, with marital ties frequently sundered and husbands and wives often living on separate estates. Absent fathers or mothers were sorely missed, in part because men and women shared the rights and responsibilities for the maintenance of the household and care of the family, but the involvement of extended kin and community members ensured that adults of both sexes played important roles in the lives of children.[10]

Infants were partly dependent on people other than parents even when the parents remained together. Their owners' work kept mothers and fathers from devoting much time to their families. Work routines regularly required women and men to labor in the field six days a week and to work at other duties into the night. Workdays lasted eleven or twelve hours, and some planters worked their hands longer, from thirteen to fourteen and even up to sixteen hours each day during busy periods. Such long hours played havoc with a mother's or father's ability to carry out basic child care and household chores in the slave quarters. Even owners expressed concern that children lacked necessary care. A popular agricultural journal carried this warning concerning slave children: "They are suffered, by not having one to attend to them."[11] Thus, slave babies remained vulnerable to neglect even when parents resided in the same household.

Owners got around the dilemma of wanting slave parents busy in the field and infants cared for in the quarter by turning over chores traditionally associated with parenting to people who by virtue of their status, skills, age, or disability would not be expected to devote time and attention to the crops. Well before the mother's labor pains began, slaveholders planned how to meet the needs of infants without taking the mother from the field. On smaller farms, the labor of the mistress or a slave whose labor was marginal to agricultural production might make up a layette, or "baby bundle," for a newborn. On larger plantations where slaves specialized in different jobs, seamstresses spent considerable time sewing baby bundles, along with the mistress who considered their ongoing construction part of her regular work routine. Fanny Kemble Butler, within a month of her arrival in Georgia, reported having already "run up some scores" of baby bundles, and she continued to make "innumerable" others "for the use of small newborn slaves" throughout her stay in Georgia. On Butler Island, the baby's layette consisted of "coarse cotton and scarlet flannel," a material commonly used in the South for slave infants' clothing. South Carolina planter James R. Sparkman prepared to give each infant at birth "two entire suits ready made of flannel etc., and a blanket of small size." Colored flannel was ideal for baby clothes because it absorbed water well and did not show dirt easily.[12]

The arrangement whereby infant clothing was constructed in advance by people who were not expected to labor in the field represented an efficient use of workers from the slaveholder's perspective, although slave women may have viewed it differently. The overseer of a plantation arranged for a slave woman named Dolly to make up the layettes for Linder's and Bess's babies. Dolly had been dispatched by Charles Manigault from his Charleston home to care for the infants at his rice-growing Gowrie plantation, but neither infant had been born yet. Sewing would help keep the slave nurse occupied until the babies' arrival. The owner's involvement in the construction and distribution of baby bundles was needed to help clothe infants, since the mothers had neither the time nor the resources to make the layettes. But mothers everywhere must have recognized—and worried—that the owner's provision of clothing and other material goods added legitimacy to their claims to be in charge of slave children, even as they welcomed the items and encouraged owners to do more to keep their babies warm and dry.[13]

Although most slaveowners distributed baby bundles at the time of birth as a matter of course, babies grew and clothing became soiled or torn or worn beyond repair. When clothes grew inadequate, mothers had difficulty obtaining others. Their impoverishment and long hours of work left them little choice but to approach their owners for additional layettes, or the cloth and time necessary for making them. On Butler Island, slave mothers individually or in small groups begged the mistress for extra baby bundles, along with bits of cloth, food, or other goods for their children. A ritual whereby slave mothers pleaded with mistresses on their children's behalf played out on plantations throughout the South. Mothers claimed a right to the mistress's help in nurturing their babies by arriving at her door bearing small gifts, usually something home-grown or handmade. Mistresses were expected to return the favor by granting goods or other assistance. One South Carolina house servant had not even left her childbed before staking a claim to her mistress's largesse. On the very day she gave birth, the new mother sent a gift of eggs to mistress Mary Chesnut.[14] The slave woman must have expected in return a kindness or, more likely, a material reward for her child. In this way, she pushed Chesnut to act maternally toward the infant. Mistresses, who cultivated reputations as caring parental figures, would hardly have accepted a token favor from a slave without bestowing gifts of their own.

Mistresses proved sympathetic to slave mothers' pleas at times, but they expected to influence the way mothers cared for their newborns in exchange for whatever goods they donated toward a child's welfare. Fanny Kemble Butler objected to the common slave practice at Butler Island of putting caps on newborns, so she "bribed" one mother to keep her baby's head uncovered by promising her a pair of socks for the infant. She even prevailed upon her "to forego the usual swaddling and swathing." Her success astounded her. When she arrived on St. Simons Island, another of her husband's plantations, shortly after this incident, she was greeted by mothers who presented their babies for her inspection "without caps."[15] Disagreements over such mundane child care practices had the potential to roil relations between slave and slaveowner. No doubt Butler and the many other mistresses who advised slave mothers about how to nurture newborns meant well, but slave women understandably were wary of changing customs to please slaveholding women. The impoverishment of the mothers and their desire to secure material goods and time to care for infants enabled mistresses to influence baby care by shaping the behavior of the mothers.

Despite efforts to enlist the labor of unrelated slaves and mistresses in meeting some of a baby's needs, it seemed natural to nineteenth-century Americans of both African and European descent that mothers should assume primary responsibility for newborns. Slaveholders knew that women needed time to recover from childbirth and that babies benefited from a mother's close attention. Following birth, they released the mother temporarily from her work in the field or elsewhere to enable her to nurture her baby, but they expected a mother to "return to the field as soon as she was able."[16] After mothers returned to their regular work sites, the owners or overseers also lightened their tasks until they deemed the mother and infant hardy enough to survive without the concession. Following this brief respite, mothers were held accountable simultaneously for caring for their babies and completing their owners' work, a heavy burden by any measure. Tensions between slaves and slaveholders surfaced over when concessions should cease. When owners pressed new mothers into returning to the field too quickly, both mother and infant suffered, but owners would not tolerate more hours of labor lost than absolutely necessary.

Owners had two major concerns. The first was getting the crop planted and harvested, work that taxed a new mother's health. At the same time, owners wanted women to recover their physical strength and the good health necessary for bearing more children. Many planters believed they could achieve both ends by granting new mothers a reprieve of one month from the most taxing agricultural labor. The month-long "lying-in" corresponded to the practice common among elite white women of confining themselves to the bedchamber and nursery for a month after childbirth. Alabama planter James H. Ruffin expected that new mothers would return to picking cotton about a month after giving birth. The slave woman Charity, who had her child on September 4, 1844, returned to the field on October 4. Fanny, whose infant was born on July 30 of the same year, commenced picking cotton on August 29. After a month's recuperation "at the negro houses," many mothers still were not ready to return to the levels of production they had achieved prior to their pregnancies, so a liberal owner might permit them two or more additional weeks of duties less burdensome than normal. One plantation manual recommended several months of only "the lightest labor" following childbirth, but usually such catering continued beyond the customary month only if warranted by the mother's health.[17]

When prices paid for staple crops increased or when a planter was short-handed, some slaveholders sought to shorten the period of recuperation from childbirth and extract more work from mothers, convincing themselves that women could return to work sooner than one month with no ill effects if they were in good health. Years after emancipation, former slave O. T. McCann recalled that the confinement of new mothers in Alabama lasted from three to four weeks, depending in part on their health. Owners could justify the decision to shorten the period of recuperation to their own satisfaction—although not to the slaves'—by imagining that black women gave birth more easily than white women, who were supposedly more civilized.[18]

Planters who reduced the customary period of recovery for new mothers could expect slaves to protest. When Fanny Kemble Butler visited Georgia in 1839, she heard a chorus of complaints from women that they were expected to return to the field too soon after giving birth. Molly explained the hardship of the women in this way: "Missis, we hab um pickanniny—tree weeks in de ospital, and den right out upon the hoe again—*can we strong* dat way, missis? No!" Many of the women Butler encountered had health problems, which she agreed were probably due to their early return to field labor. Women on the Butler cotton plantation returned to field work only three weeks after giving birth, whereas women on Butler's rice plantation regularly spent at least four weeks in recovery, the difference reflecting the difficulty of the work associated with the two crops. The slave women Charlotte and Judy visited Fanny in February complaining about vaginal bleeding that they attributed to the brief time for recovery. The mistress offered them sympathy, in addition to the menstrual "bandages they especially begged for." Other women visited as well, pleading for Fanny's help in persuading Pierce to extend the period of confinement by one week. The women sought no new privileges, but rather a return to the practices of an earlier day when the Butler slaves routinely had been allowed four weeks' confinement on the cotton plantation and five weeks for postpartum recovery on the rice estate. The usual period of confinement on the Butler plantations had been shortened after Roswell King, Jr., assumed the job of overseer in 1819. Though twenty years had passed since the implementation of the current policy, slaves continued to plead for adherence to the previous "customary" practice.[19]

Virginia planters, who grew mostly tobacco and wheat for market, generally proved more willing to accommodate new mothers than their counterparts in the lower South who grew cotton and especially rice. Economic dislocations and trends from 1812 to the early 1850s favored the latter group over the former. As a result, slaveholders in the upper South placed greater emphasis on the births and sales of slaves as an important source of revenue. The writer J. S. Buckingham detected this tendency as he traveled through Virginia, where he found planters in Augusta County relying, at least in part, on increasing "their live-stock—little negroes included" to secure their financial positions.[20] The same economic trends made the owners of cotton and rice plantations less willing to accommodate the needs of mothers and infants, particularly during boom years.

Although the majority of new mothers returned to field work about a month after childbirth, mothers of newborns occasionally were excused from field labor for longer periods on large, well-established plantations. Larger estates afforded opportunities for some women to work full-time at tasks outside of the field, and these jobs could rotate among pregnant women or new mothers. Women who gave birth early in the cotton-picking season sometimes withdrew entirely from the fields during that year's harvest. On the Lewis plantation in Alabama, Winnie, whose child was born at the start of the 1859 picking season, did not pick cotton at all that year. One of more than fifty adult hands on the Lewis estate, Winnie could have been put to work easily elsewhere on the plantation, spinning, sewing, cooking, or caring for infants. The following year, plantation records listed Winnie as back in the field picking cotton. The name of Caroline, a woman who delivered a daughter near the beginning of the picking season, no longer appeared on the roster of field hands, however.[21] When the number of pregnant women and new mothers exceeded the number of jobs available outside of the field, the women could expect no special assignment lasting more than the customary month.

Whatever the intentions of owners, complications of pregnancy and childbirth could leave a slave woman so incapacitated or permanently disabled that any plantation rules governing the return of new mothers to the field became meaningless. Following a difficult pregnancy and labor in Alabama, the slave woman Barbara remained "very weak" and unable to use her arm even to nurse her infant, despite having had ample time for recovery in the plantation manager's opinion. Although Barbara prevailed in her battle to avoid her work assignment, her overseer did not yield without a struggle. "Various stimulants" were administered, "to no avail." Owners who sent women back to the field despite their health complaints assumed a risk that the mother might die or suffer complications that would render her unable to care for her infant.[22]

Pregnancy left women vulnerable to various illnesses, disability, and death, especially in the coastal areas of South Carolina and Georgia where climatic conditions posed special health risks. Some owners went so far as to remove slaves from the area during epidemics. A cholera scare forced the removal of slaves from Charles Manigault's low-lying Gowrie plantation to higher, more healthy ground in August of 1849. After the crisis passed, the slaves returned, except for new mothers and pregnant women who remained a while longer at the high-land encampment, along with children and their designated caretakers. Successful rice planters like Manigault found the situation frustrating. Unlike their counterparts in the tobacco and grain-growing region of the upper South, rice and cotton planters depended more on profits from agriculture to enhance their financial condition than on the growth of their slave forces. Consequently, they resisted granting concessions to new mothers more than their counterparts who grew tobacco and wheat to the north. New mothers might have to undertake even the most difficult jobs soon after giving birth in rice country. Recent childbirth only *sometimes* rendered a slave woman "unfit . . . to work in water," according to rice planter Plowden C. J. Weston, a self-proclaimed authority whose rules for plantation management appeared in the popular periodical *DeBow's Review*.[23]

Financially strapped planters worried more about the potential for childbirth to disrupt farming operations than did more established slaveholders because they depended on short-term profits to pay off pecuniary obligations. They might increase their assets with the births of slave children, but the benefit would be realized only if the child grew old enough to return a profit, through either work or sale. Meanwhile, the loss of the mother's work, even briefly, could spell disaster for the crop and the slaveholder's pocketbook. Smallholders who sought economic opportunity in newly settled cotton country risked not having enough workers to ensure their success. During his first year in Alabama when he had only a small number of slaves, planter John S. Haywood worried about being short-handed in the field. The young man, native to North Carolina, hoped to pay off old debts and begin a new life. He found himself with only "5 or 6 effective hands" in the field in 1835, in part because Sarah Ann was "far advanced with family way" and Charlotte had "a young child to suckle." To avoid financial disaster, the young man resorted to picking cotton himself and foregoing all clothing purchases. A more secure financial position reduced a planter's anxiety over how childbirth would affect production on the plantation. One Alabama planter with holdings near Cahaba made fewer notations concerning the births of slave children in his plantation journal for the 1850s than the 1840s. His acquisition of more land and slaves reduced his worry that childbirth would have a detrimental effect on his cultivation of cotton; consequently, he did not maintain the keen interest he had shown about slave births in earlier years.[24]

The need to excuse women from field work to fulfill their reproductive roles—sometimes at the most inopportune times—explains why some planters preferred to purchase male slaves. A disproportionately female work force could leave a slaveholder short-handed during the busy season, and planters tried to avoid such an imbalance by taking into account the sex of any hands they purchased. Virginia planter Robert Beverley experienced firsthand the folly of establishing a predominantly female work force on a plantation he owned in the Alabama black belt. In August 1835, with the cotton-picking season at hand, the planter learned that "nearly all" the hands on his Alabama plantation were pregnant. "I fear too a great deal of time will be lost when it is most wanted," lamented Beverley's nephew and overseer. The younger man must have had the next picking season in mind

that spring when he urged his uncle to send young men or older boys from
Virginia as soon as he could make the arrangements.[25]

ALTHOUGH slaveholders excused new mothers from performing the most
difficult farm chores, they expected them to keep busy at alternate tasks, in
addition to caring for the baby. Mothers frequently spun or sewed while
watching their infants. Betty Simmons reported that in the area of Alabama
where she lived, women stayed "in de house for one mont'" before returning to the field. During that time "dey hab us card an' spin." Most new
mothers managed to fulfill daily work quotas, which might consist of spinning seven or eight cuts of thread, but the requirement was "consid'ble
hard on a woman when she had a frettin' baby."[26]

From the owner's perspective, breastfeeding provided the biggest obsta-
cle to sending new mothers back to the field to work at full capacity. Infants
did not thrive when denied access to a mother's breast in the days before
sterilization made bottle feeding practical. Keeping nursing mothers near
their infants was often the only practical solution to the problem of maintaining the mother's productivity while meeting the nutritional needs of
the baby. Allowing mothers to work near their infants enabled infants to
suckle, while mothers maintained an acceptable pace of work. Mothers who
worked too far away from their babies lost time journeying to and from the
field. Generally, efforts by owners to extract as much work as possible
from nursing mothers concentrated on improving the efficiency with which
mothers breastfed infants, rather than on reducing the mother's responsibility for breastfeeding. Women either took their babies to the field or left
them in the slave living quarters where they returned periodically to breastfeed. So great was concern over efficiency that owners in deciding the location of slave cabins considered in part the site's convenience for breastfeeding women.[27]

Some owners preferred the arrangement where infants accompanied
mothers to the field because it saved the mother "the time of going to the
house to nurse." For mothers, attending to infants at the side of the field
broke up long and grueling work regimens and offered reassurance that
their babies were safe and well. They could respond quickly to their infants' needs in an emergency, even though they might not stop work to
suckle them until they reached the end of the row or until the other hands
stopped to rest. Charles Ball, recalling slavery days in cotton country, said
that mothers suckled their infants when the other hands stopped for water.

They depended on family and friends "to bring them water in gourds, which they were careful to carry to the field with them."[28] In this way, fathers and other slaves helped care for the infants, while stretching out their own rest periods.

In agreeable weather, infants taken to the field usually slept most of the day in a basket or box or on a quilt or pallet at the end of the row, where mothers or other slaves—sometimes an older child brought for that purpose—kept an eye on them. Mothers who swaddled or wrapped their babies restricted their movements so they could stay out of harm's way. If a tree grew nearby, a basket or quilt could be suspended from a branch to hold the child, a practice that offered some protection for infants from the ants and insects that populated the fields. As an infant, Oliver Bell went with his mother to the field each day in Alabama. She plowed, leaving Oliver, who was too young to walk, under a big oak tree, drolly described by the former slave in later life as "my nurse." In Virginia, Sara Colquitt's youngest baby swung from a tree limb as her mother hoed in the field. A South Carolina mother kept her child in a knapsack on her back while she cultivated cotton.[29]

Inclement weather could prevent women who worked outdoors from bringing infants to the work site. When winter temperatures fell below freezing, as happened occasionally even in the lower South, babies remained in the cabin alone or with slightly older children to care for them. Often their only supervision came from visitors, usually mothers who returned at appointed times to breastfeed their youngest babies. At times owners sent other adults to check on the babies, although sometimes they looked in on the infants themselves, which allowed all hands to keep busy tending the crop. Infants left in the slave quarter on Sherman Varner's Alabama plantation had only older brothers or sisters to mind them, but the master visited the quarter regularly to check on the children and bring them milk.[30]

When infants stayed in the slave quarter, owners and parents alike preferred that mothers labored nearby. Sometimes nursing mothers worked as a separate group or joined so-called "trash gangs" composed of workers who could not keep pace in the field with other hands. On an Alabama estate in early December 1858, "sucklers" and women in an advanced stage of pregnancy shucked corn, while other slaves picked cotton and gathered corn. Later that month, six breastfeeding mothers worked with a man to repair plantation fences, while other women performed the more arduous work of "pulling and trashing cotton Stalks in the field over the road." Such

assignments not only kept mothers working near their infants but also prevented infants from disrupting the work of other hands, as would have occurred if they had been taken to the field. Another Alabama owner assigned
nursing mothers Rachael and Lucy to "chopping in Mill Field . . . as it is
convenient for sucklers."[31]

Arrangements for keeping mothers and babies close to one another did
not always prevail. Owners objected to leaving work undone simply because it lay some distance from the slave quarter. Advice by James M.
Towns in an agricultural journal popular among southern planters reflected
the dilemma created when the demands of crop and baby conflicted: "A
woman nursing is allowed ample time to attend to her child, and I avoid *as
much as possible* sending them to a distance from the house to labor." Alabama slaveowner Willis P. Bocock advised his plantation manager to have
"suckling women" work near the house, but only *"if possible."*[32] Doubts
about the best course of action left room for slaves to manipulate the situation by pressuring overseers and owners to keep mothers and infants together.

When infants remained in the slave quarter while mothers worked in the
field, the women returned periodically to breastfeed them. Regimented
feeding schedules were more typical of large plantations than smaller farms,
and their importance was reflected in discussions of the topic in agricultural journals and plantation rule books. The *Southern Cultivator*'s "Rules
of the Plantation" recommended that nursing mothers "visit their children,
morning, noon and evening until they are eight months old, and twice a day
from thence until they are twelve months old." Other planters stated similar
policies in writing for fear that overseers might neglect the needs of nursing
infants in the interest of bringing in a crop. "Sucklers must be allowed time
to suckle children," one planter insisted. Another directed the overseer to
allow nursing mothers an extra half-hour to get to the field in the morning,
so they could attend to their infants. Rules for overseers reiterated the expectation that mothers should have time to breastfeed even during harvest.[33]

In addition to specifying the number of times a mother could breastfeed
her baby each day, some slaveholders attempted to impose other restric-
tions that reflected prevailing ideas among whites about breastfeeding. One
planter not only specified that women on his plantation should come in
from the field to nurse their babies four times each day, but he also insisted
that they wait "until they become properly cool" before nursing their babies. Such warnings against breastfeeding when "overheated" were com-

mon.[34] Hungry babies surely wailed in protest, but mothers may have welcomed the respite from work offered by the requirement to cool down and insisted on prolonging their absence from the field accordingly.

A few slaveholders held bizarre ideas about breastfeeding and tried to impose them on their slaves, but mothers resisted implementing them. The physician and planter W. C. Daniell of Georgia recommended that owners withhold mother's milk for the first ten days of a slave baby's life, substituting as nourishment "sweet oil and molasses in such proportions as will keep the bowels loose." During this time the mother's milk was to be drawn off "by the nurse, the midwife, another and older child, or by a puppy." Touted as a preventive for lockjaw, the scheme in all likelihood was never adopted by anyone. In fact, slave mothers on the doctor's own plantation apparently refused to abide by his instructions, for he found it necessary to hold another slave woman responsible for the distribution of the oil and molasses and the "faithful execution" of the plan. Despite this effort, mothers still did not carry out his instructions, and the woman charged with implementing the plan apparently appropriated much of the oil and molasses for her own use.[35] The advocacy of this scheme in a major agricultural journal illustrates the bewildering medley of advice owners confronted when making decisions about breastfeeding routines, as well as the difficulties they encountered in ensuring that the slaves complied with them. An owner's doubts about the best course of action enhanced the mother's ability to breastfeed as she liked.

No matter what slaveholders commanded or slaves desired, the nature of the work system determined breastfeeding regimens, at least in part. Women working in the field on plantations employing a gang labor system—in which groups of slaves worked at a common task for a specified period of time—generally adhered to a fixed schedule for nursing their babies, at least during working hours. This situation prevailed wherever slaves grew cotton for market. Consequently, mothers in Alabama's black belt often exercised little control over daytime feeding schedules. Betty Simmons described the practice of calling mothers from the cotton fields to nurse their children: "Dey hab a ho'n up in de house an' dey blow it in de middle of de mawnin' an' atternoon for de mammies to come up an' nuss dey li'l babies." On large tobacco and wheat plantations of the upper South, breastfeeding was similarly regimented when crops demanded extra attention. Virginian H. C. Bruce described women breastfeeding babies "during the crop season" in the same manner as in the Alabama black belt. According to the former slave, "sucklings were allowed to come to [their infants] three times a day between sun rise and sun set, for the purpose of nursing their babes, who were left in the care of an old women." Even women along the rice coast sometimes encountered the need to conform to rigid patterns of breastfeeding if their work took them far from their infants. The son of a Combahee River rice planter recalled that new mothers left the field as a group at designated times to perform "their maternal duties."[36]

Slave women who labored under a task system—in which individual slaves were expected to complete a given amount of work in a day—generally enjoyed greater flexibility in deciding when to feed their infants. Rather than calling women in from the field at appointed intervals, owners who assigned slaves specific tasks provided time for women to breastfeed by reducing their workloads. One advantage of the task system, which operated more commonly along the rice coast than elsewhere in the South, was that fathers, friends, and kin could assist women in completing chores so they could spend more time with their infants. Of course, owners knew this and may have refused to reduce the mother's workload accordingly. One former slave reported that the husband assumed responsibility and received the blame for failing to complete his wife's task when she stopped to nurse her crying child and fell behind in her work. Generally new mothers—whether they labored in cotton, tobacco, wheat, or rice—were expected to complete less work than others if they were breastfeeding, and some owners in all areas of the South expressed the reduction with reference to a specific task. The overseer on George Walker's cotton plantation in Alabama apportioned work so that mothers of nursing infants hoed 55 rows, each 70 yards long, while other women were held responsible for hoeing 60 rows of the same length.[37]

On large estates where slaves specialized in particular types of jobs, not all women worked in the fields, which gave them greater opportunity to breastfeed babies as the need arose. Weavers, seamstresses, and cooks usually kept their children at their work stations, for example. Ned Chaney stated that his mother, an Alabama slave, kept her infants with her as she wove cloth on a loom and performed other chores: "She nuss 'em, totin' 'em around if she was busy." Levi Pollard's mother, a seamstress in Virginia, tended to the needs of her babies while she did her owners' sewing, spinning, and knitting in her cabin. The cook on the Meadows plantation in Alabama managed to fulfill her parenting and work obligations with the help of the young master, who devised a swing for her baby. The infant hung suspended from a tree while her mother cooked in the kitchen, no doubt stopping from time to time in response to the baby's cries. Swings, jumpers, and other contraptions that kept babies off the floor or the ground and offered amusement and exercise appealed increasingly to elite families in antebellum America, but in this case the swing served the practical function of keeping the infant occupied so the mother could work.[38]

On small slaveholdings where only one or two babies lived, there was no need for elaborate routines for nursing infants, and owners and slaves improvised as best they could to feed babies. Because women on small farms worked near their infants, breastfeeding mothers could return to their babies from work sites without losing much time in traveling. This situation helps explain why many slaves in the upper South, where small farms predominated, dreaded being sold to cotton country. They preferred the more casual arrangements for child care found on smaller farms, even though the size of the slaveholding forced most spouses to live on separate plantations or farms. The anxiety felt by mothers at being separated from their infants while they worked in the fields found poetic expression in the words of former slave William Wells Brown:

> The morn was chill—I spoke no word,
> —But feared my babe might die,
> And heard all day, or thought I heard,
> —My little baby cry.
>
> At noon, oh, how I ran and took
> —My baby to my breast!
> I lingered—and the long lash broke
> —My sleeping infant's rest.[39]

Tensions between owners and slaves over child care increased in periods of peak labor demand—especially during planting and harvesting—in part because owners pressured mothers to spend more time in the field and less time caring for their infants. Owners who otherwise granted women "ample time to attend" their children looked for ways of supplementing the diets of infants to stretch the time between feedings. Some slaveholders who normally had mothers leave their infants in the slave quarter required mothers to carry their infants to the field, even in severe weather, if they needed the women's labor. One Virginia slaveowner provided brandy to slaves to fortify them against extremely cold temperatures in such circumstances, and they shared the brandy with all who went to the field, infants included. The temperance movement that developed in the antebellum years discouraged giving alcoholic beverages to babies to make them quiet, as had been the custom previously. Even so, many elite parents continued to give their babies alcoholic drinks or medical concoctions containing a high percentage of alcohol or other types of drugs, and apparently some slave children were fed the elixirs as well.[40]

Although the majority of mothers left their work to breastfeed their babies or kept their babies with them throughout the day, other arrangements were possible when a planter could not spare a woman's labor. An Alabama slave whose disability prevented him from working in the field drove babies there in a cart so their mothers could breastfeed them with minimal disruption to their work. A South Carolina slaveholding couple did not even allow the wet nurse they used for their own child to come in from the field to suckle it. Instead, a young boy carried his owners' infant to the field every four hours for a woman to nurse. Some slaveholders theorized that infants could nurse at an animal teat, but few tried to implement this practice. Slave infants who fed regularly at the breast of their white mistresses were uncommon but not unknown. When Mack Brantley's mother died in Alabama, his sister tended to his other needs, but his mistress suckled him along with her own daughter. Former Virginia slave George White reported that his mistress nursed him along with her own child whenever his mother had to be in the field. "An abundance of nourishment" following the birth of her child encouraged a Georgia mistress "to nurse one of the little Negroes" to alleviate the soreness in her breasts.[41]

Men—masters or overseers—usually made the final decision about where nursing mothers worked and when they left the field to feed their babies; they even advised their own wives on breastfeeding infants. But whatever policies men formulated, they designated women to oversee the process. One popular plantation manual recommended having the overseer's wife see that the "children are well nursed and taken care of."[42] More often, another slave woman assumed this role. Mistresses involved themselves with nursing arrangements mainly on smaller farms or under unusual circumstances on large estates. When slave mothers died in childbirth or were unavailable for breastfeeding for other reasons, mistresses helped decide the best solution to the problem of feeding the infants.

Circumstances beyond the control of either slave or owner complicated nursing arrangements. Even when planters adopted rules conducive to breastfeeding, the poor health of the mother might undermine success. "Rachel's child from sucking has become almost as sick as she is, and I fear will die," warned her overseer. Barbara, whose difficult pregnancy and labor threatened her life, remained in such poor health that she could not lift her child to her breast for nursing. The need for a wet nurse by the white family put an additional strain on a breastfeeding mother, who might find herself nursing another child in addition to her own. According to one estimate, about one-fifth of mistresses relied on a wet nurse at least part of the time. Although some of the wet nurses employed by planter families were white, it appears that a significant number of slave mothers must have been recruited for this purpose, at least from time to time, and slave mothers could be called upon to serve as a wet nurse to slave babies as well as to infants of owners. Henry Baker's mother died when he was only two weeks old, and the young Alabama slave was given to a wet nurse "til' I could eat an' git about."[43]

The preferred practice was to provide infants, whether black or white, with wet nurses when the mother could not breastfeed the child. Slave babies only rarely received nourishment from a bottle, a dangerous practice in the days before bottles were commonly sterilized. Although the dangers of bacteria in milk were little understood, everyone knew the results of hand-feeding infants—high rates of illness and mortality. Giles Smith's experience in Alabama was exceptional. The slave infant became a wedding gift for the young mistress when he was only a few months old. Weaned precipitantly from his mother's breast, the infant resisted the bottle so long that his mistress considered returning him to his mother. As an adult, Smith explained that he would have been given to a wet nurse, but there "was no cullud women on de Missy's place dat could nurse me." Smith survived, but others did not. Despite the best efforts of another woman to feed Mary Montgomery's baby "by hand," the infant died shortly after her mother apparently took the unusual step of fleeing her Virginia plantation for freedom. Slave mothers who abandoned infants as Montgomery did were rare. Their disappearances are usually explained by a desire to escape egregious abuse, as was the case with Montgomery.[44]

Owners wanted infants weaned as quickly as possible, so they interfered with weaning, just as they did with breastfeeding. Most children were weaned gradually, as mothers' trips in from the field became less frequent as their infants grew. The *Farmer and Planter* called for mothers to feed infants before leaving for the field in the morning and on arriving in the quarter at night, and three times in between. This was to last until the babies were eight months old, when one of the feedings could be eliminated. Another set of rules for plantation management published in a different agricultural journal also recommended reduced feedings at eight months, and weaning at one year old, at least between dawn and dusk. Thus, weaning occurred incrementally for slave infants, who received more and more foods meant to supplement breastfeeding as they grew older. The babies left under the care of former slave Vicey Williams were suckled by their mothers at ten o'clock each morning, when the women came in from the field. In the afternoon, they had to make due with "potlicker" (the broth left in a pot after greens are cooked). Later in the day, babies joined slightly older children in downing a meal of "mush and skimmed milk." Other common foods for infants included clabber and "cush" (bread mashed into gravy). Despite such supplements, patterns of childbearing among slave women suggest that they breastfed their infants for at least a year.[45]

Feeding older babies presented problems for women left in charge of groups of slave infants, because babies began receiving supplemental foods before they could feed themselves. Many caretakers, short-handed, oversaw a system in which very young children fed at troughs like so many farm animals. Former Virginia slave Nannie Williams, who as a girl helped "Ant Hannah" feed fourteen black babies left in her charge, prefaced her explanation of the procedure with a declaration that "you ain't gonna believe dis, but it's de gospel truf." The young girl watched Aunt Hannah "po' dat trough full of milk an' drag dem chillun up to it. Chillun slop up dat milk jus' like pigs."[46]

Nursing and weaning regulations applied only to daylight hours and only to those mothers who left their babies in cabins or nurseries. Mothers who kept their infants with them as they worked breastfed their babies when they wished. Even mothers who worked in gangs and who left their babies in the slave quarter exercised some discretion in when they weaned infants. They could breastfeed infants before leaving for the field in the morning or after they returned each night. Plantation rules intended to ensure that field hands received a good night's rest so they could work at full capacity the following day applied only to fathers, not mothers. A mother was expected to be "up with her child" at night.[47] Owners encouraged or acknowledged prolonged breastfeeding by denying infants under age two the weekly food rations they distributed to other members of slave families. Some of these children ate meals prepared for them by a caretaker or children's cook during the day, but the policy of withholding rations from babies under age two meant that many—probably most—mothers found it desirable to continue breastfeeding a baby through the child's second year of life during the evening and nighttime hours, when mothers exercised greater discretion as to their own behavior. In this case, the mother's preference for prolonged breastfeeding—noted in other slave societies of the Americas and attributed to African cultural preferences—did not pose a problem for slaveholders. They contracted no extra expenses by allowing the women to breastfeed their infants as long as they wished.[48]

MOTHERS no doubt thought that breastfeeding beyond a baby's first year helped children get a good start in life, but they knew this would not be enough to ensure their health and safety. They objected to leaving their infants unsupervised or exposed to the elements as they completed their owners' work. The designation of one slave to care for infants of working mothers in a day nursery offered a solution to the problem of supervising infants when mothers worked at some distance from their cabins. Slaveholders adopted this practice only if a slave marginal to the production process was available to assume this chore, however. And slaves accepted the practice only if they believed that the health and safety of their infants required it. Consequently, plantation nurseries functioned only on the largest estates and only when winter weather or heavy demand for labor made them necessary. Their use grew in the antebellum years among the South's largest planters, who hoped to make infant care more efficient and less costly. Slaves who were transferred from smaller slaveholdings in the upper South to cultivate cotton in states farther south could find themselves adjusting to a new pattern of child care. Instead of keeping infants with them as they worked, mothers might be expected to drop their infants off at a nursery before leaving for the field each morning.

The presence of a slave who was not crucial to the production process, especially an older woman no longer productive in the field, increased the likelihood that an owner would establish a nursery for infants. Women who were mothers themselves—especially those who had given birth to a large number of children—were rewarded with the opportunity to serve as child minder. Such slaves were not always available for child care, however. Sparse population, combined with a general absence of older slaves, meant that some slave children grew to adulthood without ever encountering an elderly black face, especially in the frontier regions of the South during the early years of planter settlement. In Alabama's early years of statehood, no more than 3 percent of slaves in Greene County—located in the heart of the black belt—were older than age forty-four. In contrast, nearly 14 percent of slaves in the rice counties along the South Carolina and Georgia coasts were in this age group, as were 10 percent of the slaves in central Virginia.

Even where elderly slaves could be found in the population at large, older women did not live on every farm or plantation. This was particularly true of small slaveholdings, where owners were unlikely to establish a special nursery for only one or two infants anyway.[49]

Given the scarcity of older slaves, owners who wanted to establish a nursery turned to any slave unable to engage in sustained physical labor. A disability or an illness that prevented a young woman from working at full capacity made her a likely candidate for the job of caring for infants. When Emma, an Alabama slave, failed to recover fully from a bout of sickness that began about six weeks into the cotton picking season, she assumed the job of tending babies for the duration of the season. At times new mothers suffered from complications of pregnancy and childbirth that left them unsuited for other types of work, and some may have exaggerated their complaints following childbirth to win the job of child minder. Charlie Van Dyke, a boy of eleven whose injured leg rendered him unfit for a more arduous assignment, was put in charge of youngsters on another Alabama plantation. Men unable to perform field work or other strenuous outdoor chores also tended children. Planter Edward Carrington Cabell took Abraim, a slave, from the family plantation in Virginia to his new home in Florida, because the older slave proved "chiefly useful on the plantation as a nurse." Older girls represented another source of potential caretakers who might easily relinquish field duties without jeopardizing the crop. Former Alabama slave Jennie Bowen recalled that either an older woman or a "half grown girl" looked after the young children, who no one thought required a great deal of individual attention.[50]

Supervision in nurseries tended to be minimal. Owners expected adult slaves left in charge of infants to perform other chores, such as spinning, sewing, or cooking, while they minded the babies. Former Alabama slave Vicey Williams, for example, had to prepare food and spin while she watched her little charges. Some child minders found themselves responsible for attending ill slaves as well. D. E. Huger Smith considered the so-called sick house on his father's rice plantation near Charleston misnamed, because it mostly served as a nursery for babies and small children.[51] Such arrangements had the unfortunate disadvantage of exposing youngsters to disease. Despite the shortcomings of this system, many owners and some slaves preferred using nurseries to leaving infants home alone or with brothers and sisters only slightly older than their charges.

The quality of nursery care depended on the abilities of individual caretakers, the number of infants left in their care, and the types of resources at

their disposal, as well as the other demands placed on them by their owners. Vicey Williams no doubt succored the young infants assigned to her
care. Even though she had other duties to complete while she watched the
infants, she could count on help from their mothers, who arrived from the
field to nurse their babies at about ten o'clock. Children, barely past infancy themselves, also helped care for babies in the nursery. Possibly even
more important for the infants' safety was the fact that each baby left in Williams's care slept in a "little home-made cradle," which furnished some
protection for babies who could not yet pull themselves up and risk top-
pling over the side. Sturdy cradles, which could have been fashioned by
slave men with only rudimentary woodworking skills, were the exception in
most nurseries, perhaps because the use of cradles among the elite class
had declined by the nineteenth century, reflecting a growing belief that children might be injured by too exuberant rocking as child minders tried to
quiet a fussy baby.[52] What former slave Mandy McCullough remembered
most about infant care arrangements on her Alabama plantation was the
way the "chillun roll aroun' in de big nurses room." Each baby slept on a
"pallet," which made it easier to keep the room and its occupants clean but
also exposed the babies to certain dangers, especially in winter when a fire
burned in an open fireplace. On rice plantations, caretakers placed infants
in "fanner-baskets" otherwise used in separating the rice from the husk. In
good weather, these baskets sat outside the nursery, with a folded blanket
and a baby in each one. "Near each baby sat or played a small boy or girl
who had been detailed to care for that especial baby," under the somewhat
lax supervision of a nurse. The younger caretakers were little children incapable of performing other work.[53]

Any children old enough to walk and talk stayed in the nurseries to help
care for the babies. Nannie Williams, who helped "Ant Hannah" care for
fourteen babies in Virginia, was herself so young that her mother had to accompany her to Hannah's house each morning. Julia Baker also was very
young when she helped to watch the plantation's infants while their parents
worked. Children as young as two or three rocked babies or protected them
from wandering off or getting too near the fire. A Mississippi planter's
boast of his successful nursery in *DeBow's Review* offers evidence that nurseries catered to infants rather than to older children. The babies were kept
dry and clean and allowed to suckle four times each day when their mothers visited the cabin for this purpose. The types of accidents and deaths
believed to have been prevented by the establishment of nurseries further
suggests the youthfulness of the nursery population: deaths or accidents

caused by burning, teething, and "summer complaints," to which the youngest children were especially prone. Some nurseries served infants only for a brief period. Writing in *DeBow's Review*, South Carolina slaveowner R. W. Gibbs explained that the nursery on his plantation cared only for infants of two and three months. Mothers tended babies younger than this in their cabins, and after three months the children were considered hardy enough to accompany the mother to the field.[54] Thus, the establishment of nursery care reflected prevailing ideas about infant development and vulnerability to the elements, as well as the need for labor.

Slaves wanted their babies supervised, but they also preferred that distressed babies receive immediate attention. Owners expected infants to await the regularly scheduled work breaks planned for mothers. Caretakers and their child helpers usually tried to mollify fussy babies until their mothers returned from the field at the scheduled times. Louise Jones, who as a young girl assisted with slave babies in Virginia, provided them with pacifiers made out of meat skins. The skins kept the babies sucking and quiet but posed a danger of choking, necessitating constant vigilance on the part of the child in charge. "Durin' slavery time us nurses uster keep de babies from hollarin' by tying a string 'roun' a piece of skin an' stickin' it in dey mouth. You see if dey got choked, we pull out de meat skin wid dis string. Lord, yes! I've done it many time," she recalled in later years. Overworked caretakers sympathized with the babies, however, and they sometimes called mothers in from the field to quiet their fussy infants whenever they could not be placated, especially when mothers labored nearby. "Mammy Larkin," who cooked for the hands and who also watched the babies while their mothers worked in the field, found it easier to do both if mothers returned to suckle any wailing children. She would dispatch a young child, also left under her supervision, to the fields to fetch a mother when an infant cried.[55]

However much an owner wished to minimize the time mothers spent away from field or other chores, the necessity of caring for an infant decreased a mother's productivity. The dramatic decrease in the amount of cotton picked by new mothers on the Mary Foreman Lewis plantation in central Alabama serves as evidence. Mothers of infants under six months old picked substantially less cotton than they had the year before, or even than they did the year after when their children were older than one year. Elizabeth, who managed to keep pace with some of the best hands in 1858 before she had a child, picked an average of 219 pounds of cotton each day. One year later, with a six-month-old child to tend, she averaged only 127 pounds, a decline of more than 42 percent.[56] Once babies passed their first birthdays, the amount of cotton picked by their mothers on the Lewis plantation increased, but not to the levels achieved before the births of their children. Thus even during the second year of life, babies placed demands on slave women that kept them from keeping pace in the field with childless women or women whose children were older.

Although women withdrew from the fields during the day to care for infants, evidence from the Alabama black belt suggests that at the busiest times of year the work routines of mothers remained rigorous enough to jeopardize the health of slave infants. Deaths of infants under one year of age peaked in September and October of 1850, the height of the cotton-picking season. As the harvest drew to a close in November and December, the number of infant deaths fell to their lowest levels. Infant deaths increased sharply in January, clearly the result of increased congestive ailments described in the records as whooping cough, pneumonia, and croup. A drop in the infant death rate followed in February that cannot be explained solely by the shortness of the month. As plowing began in March, infant deaths rose again to January levels as children continued to succumb to congestive disease, as well as a variety of other ailments. The mortality rate tapered off through the spring as planting was completed, remained low as crops were "laid by" (a period between planting and harvesting when crops demanded comparatively little attention), and rose only slightly during the summer months before harvest began the cycle again.[57]

The situation differed along the seacoasts of South Carolina and Georgia and in central Virginia. Infant mortality remained high year-round on rice plantations. The unhealthy conditions associated with rice cultivation meant that infants remained at high risk for death even during less busy times of year. Infants living on cotton plantations along the Atlantic coast apparently experienced cycles of mortality similar to those just described for Alabama, however. On the Gaillard cotton plantation in South Carolina's St. John's Berkeley parish, babies died in greater numbers during the peak labor season when mothers would have had less time for their children.[58]

Whereas cotton production placed heavy demands on laborers for months at a time in the late summer and early fall, Virginia's mixed farming economy tended to spread the need for labor more evenly throughout the year. Intense periods of labor involving large numbers of slaves occurred during wheat harvests, but they were of short duration compared with cotton harvests. Thus, when mothers were forced to neglect infants during Virginia's harvests, the consequences were less catastrophic.

High mortality rates among slave infants served as an indictment of slavery that stood at odds with slaveholders' claims that slavery benefited both owners and their slaves. Slaveowners shielded themselves from the logic behind the numbers by blaming the atrocious death rates on poor parenting on the part of slave mothers and by arguing for reforms that would place more of the responsibilities for infant care under their own control. The trend in the antebellum years was for owners with sizeable slaveholdings to turn child-rearing tasks over to unrelated slaves in a nursery, thus freeing mothers to work longer hours in the field growing staple crops.

As slaveholders assumed greater responsibilities for infant care in the antebellum era, slaves confronted a dilemma. On the one hand, they welcomed any material goods or attention that improved an infant's health, welfare, and chance for survival. On the other hand, having owners make arrangements for infant care made it more difficult for slave parents to define their families apart from their owners' plantation households. Slaves were reluctant to concede to owners the right to determine how babies were cared for, but they lacked the resources necessary to counter their owner's claim to do so. Antebellum slaveholders used the language of kinship to discuss and disguise their relationships with slaves. They referred to the black and white residents of their plantations as one family, whose members were united by sentimental ties as much as by common economic and social interests. They discounted the desire of slaves for separate housing for their families and appropriated the slave mother's time for their own use because they recognized no need for slaves to maintain a separate family identity. This situation made it difficult for slave parents, who were committed to their own concept of family, to define family relationships and responsibilities for themselves. Weaning marked the end of infancy, but not of the struggle by enslaved mothers and fathers to gain recognition of parental rights.

3

YOUNG CHILDREN IN THE QUARTER

THE SLAVE GIRL Harrette fell into James M. Torbert's well and drowned on August 30, 1855. The Alabama planter noted the loss in his farm journal: "She was four years three months and 3 days old Anthony Come to the plantation after Me. I Come home Made a Coffin and buried *My* little negro I am Sorry *my* little negro is dead, but I Cant help it." In July Torbert had fashioned a coffin for another slave child and recorded the event in his journal. One of his father's slaves, a little boy named Artur, had died, and Torbert oversaw his burial. No one recorded the reactions of the children's parents or told what, if any, role they played in making the funeral arrangements. Perhaps they took comfort in knowing their children were at peace and would not experience life in bondage. More likely, they grieved and considered the loss to be theirs—not Torbert's. When the slave Cissy's young son died in Virginia, she, too, used a possessive pronoun to describe what happened: "*My* little chile is gone to Jesus."[1]

Slave parents and slaveowners both staked claims to slave children and experienced a loss when children died. The infant and child mortality rates were appallingly high among the slave population, especially in the coastal rice-growing area. Everyone knew it. Black babies born in bondage died at twice the rate of white infants, and slave children continued to experience higher rates of mortality than white youngsters beyond infancy. Yet slaves and slaveholders both put their hopes for the future in the survival of the children, which they could not take for granted.[2]

Early childhood—roughly between the ages of two and five—was considered by owners to be a crucial time in a slave's life. Slaveowners understood that the quality of care provided children affected their survival, and their understanding of child development led them to conclude that slaves in their early years formed lasting habits of mind and behavior: attachment or animosity, diligence or dereliction, complacency or discontent. They continued to want mothers and fathers in the field or working at other tasks that benefited the owners rather than slave families, but by helping to ensure the children's survival, they might "prove" slavery a benevolent institution and themselves "good" masters and mistresses.

Slaveholders were keenly aware that critics of slavery, whose voices were growing louder in the antebellum years, accused them of mistreating their human property, hence Torbert's rejection of any responsibility for Harrette's death: "I Cant help it," he wrote. Most owners were eager to do more than merely deny responsibility for tragedy. They wanted to disprove abolitionist allegations of cruelty toward slaves by collectively adhering to community standards for slave treatment that were either codified in law or established more informally through discussions among neighbors, in the pages of farm journals, or at meetings of agricultural societies. Although some owners failed to meet the community standards, "good" slaveholders did not ignore the needs of slaves in early childhood. They took an interest in the health and welfare of children and allocated minimal resources for their benefit. When children survived, they credited their own humane stewardship. When children died, they attributed the situation to fate or cast blame upon parents. This allowed slaveholders to maintain an image of themselves as enlightened managers, or even parent figures—in their own eyes if not in those of their slaves.

Plantation policies that gave children a chance to survive, even when this meant reduced short-term profits from crops, held additional advantages for owners. Slaves raised properly on the home place from infancy proved more loyal and obedient than slaves purchased on the auction block, they thought. Those "born and reared up in the master's household, or [who] have long been members of his family," think of him "as their father," opined one group of planters, who believed the "strong attachment" link-ing owner and slave lasted a lifetime. The best defense against slave disobe-dience, disrespect, even insurrection, they thought, was the little children raised in the yard behind the "big house." Thus, the goals of slaveholders extended beyond keeping children alive. They hoped to transfer the love and allegiance of the children from parents to themselves. They knew this would prove difficult because parents bonded with their children and would resist strenuously any attempt to disengage youngsters from their families. But slaveholders were confident of their right to interject them-selves between parent and child. Racist attitudes coupled with class con-sciousness convinced them of the slave's inability to act independently and of owners' responsibility to care for their dependents, especially slave chil-dren. They intended to teach boys and girls that they—not parents—headed the plantation household. As the slave population grew through hu-man reproduction, owners accepted the large numbers of children who peopled the plantations of the South as "evidence" of their own benevo-lence and proper handling of their bonded population. Many took such pride in their black children that they showed them off before visitors, ex-pressing some degree of affection for them as they would for pets. Mistress Matt Ross brought visitors to the back door of her house so they could peer out at the yard "black wid us chillun," one of the youngsters later re-called. The mistress customarily distributed bread to the youngsters, after bragging about her "pretty crop of little niggers."[3]

The situation in which owners expressed an interest in children's wel-fare held some benefits for individual boys and girls, but it also threatened the fragile existence of the slave family. On the one hand, parents welcomed better supervision or special favors for their sons and daughters. On the other, the owner's attention to the details of child rearing curtailed the ca-pacity of the slave family to create a cultural space where slaves could be critical of servitude and slaveholders and could teach their children stan-dards of behavior that differed from those of owners. Little doubt existed in the minds of slave parents as to who should be in charge of their children. Their experience of nurturing sons and daughters taught them that chil-dren did not thrive without parental care, particularly the mother's. They believed that children who survived years of neglect might never recover from the deprivation. Josephine Bacchus, who had been enslaved in South Carolina, blamed her inability to carry a child to term in adulthood on her lack of mothering in childhood. She had been a small girl when her mother died, and Josephine attributed her lifetime of poor health to that cause.[4]

Certain of the rectitude of their position, parents struggled to impress upon children that they—not owners—headed the slave family.

The task of maintaining their children's allegiance was daunting to slave couples, whose resources were meager, especially when contrasted with those of their owners. Slaves needed to cooperate with masters and mistresses and to teach children the day-to-day deference owners considered their due while at the same time securing the youngster's loyalty to his or her family and the larger slave community. Life in the quarter was already precarious, and slaves relied on one another to keep secrets from their owners and to assist each other in times of trouble. Maintaining a cultural space within the family, defined separately from their owners' plantation households, gave slaves a means of creating identities for themselves other than those of master's field hand or mistress's seamstress. Parents wanted children to comply outwardly with owners' expectations concerning behavior; to do otherwise would have invited disaster upon themselves and their youngsters. But they confronted this dilemma: how could they teach the rituals that passed for racial etiquette in southern society, without imparting to their children a sense of inferiority and without diminishing their own worth in the eyes of their sons and daughters?

For their part, children had to learn how to negotiate a dangerous world, which entailed pleasing two sets of adults with very different expectations. Their dependence encouraged them to respect whatever adults looked out for their interests, but children in their early years had difficulty determining who had their best interests at heart. An owner's special treat or favor could serve as evidence of love, in a young child's estimation, but boys and girls were fearful of the slaveholder's power to separate them from loved ones and of the punishments regularly inflicted upon slaves. Consequently, owners found themselves competing with parents for the children's loyalty by mitigating slavery's brutality for the youngsters and instituting activities that children regarded as fun. The presence of small children on the plantations of the South thus encouraged paternalistic practices among slaveholders, which in turn challenged parental authority over the youngest children. For slave parents as for owners, early childhood was a critical period in the slave child's life.

Both slaves and slaveholders agreed that youngsters needed supervision beyond infancy, but they had different ideas about how to provide it. Parents preferred to devote more time to their children and less time to their owners' work. Owners wanted to relieve parents of the need to supervise young children by turning the responsibility over to other, often unrelated, slaves. Better supervision could protect children from dangers and prevent tragedies such as the one that befell little Harrette when she tumbled into Torbert's well. Decreasing the responsibilities of slave mothers for child care simultaneously increased efficiency by getting children out of the way, so that mothers could remain longer in the field or perform more chores elsewhere. Owners thought that the presence of sons and daughters in the field with mothers and fathers, when the children were too old to sleep most of the day and too young to work diligently alongside adults, distracted parents from their work, and removing them would make everyone more productive. Assigning duties traditionally carried out by parents to specially chosen slaves would also teach youngsters that they could turn to someone other than a parent for sustenance.

Changing attitudes toward children's health and welfare aided slaveholders in shifting traditional parental responsibilities for supervising youngsters, including feeding and clothing them, to other designated caretakers. In colonial days, parents had comforted themselves over the death of a child by attributing infant and child mortality to God's will. They felt the loss of a child keenly, but they reconciled themselves to providence. By the early years of the republic, adults were acknowledging the important role played by child-rearing practices in keeping children alive and healthy. Society as a whole increasingly viewed high infant and child mortality rates as unacceptable, the result of neglect or ignorance rather than providence.[5] Slaveholding grew more profitable and the need for healthy slaves increased as people became less resigned to high incidences of death and disease among children. Indeed, critics of slavery—who noted the high mortality rates—pushed slaveholders into addressing child-rearing practices.

Early in the nineteenth century, many slave children past infancy but too young to be of help to working adults stayed by the side of a parent or other relative during the day or fended for themselves as best they could alone in the slave cabin. Supervision came mostly from mothers and other adults working nearby, who checked on the children periodically to make sure they were safe and staying out of trouble. This continued to be the case in the late antebellum years on smaller slaveholdings, many of which were located in the upper South. Large holdings complicated arrangements for children's supervision, however. Adults could not as easily leave and return to the fields, and owners objected to the additional loss of time when they did so.

In the antebellum years, plantations expanded into newly settled territory, and the size of slaveholdings increased as the center of the slave population shifted westward. Mature cotton plantations tended to be larger than those that produced tobacco and wheat, and by 1860, approximately 61 percent of slaves lived on them. In many cases they rivaled in size the large, well-established rice plantations of the South Carolina and Georgia coasts. By 1860, about three-quarters of all southern slaves lived on plantations with at least 10 slaves, nearly one-half lived on slaveholdings that numbered from 10 to 49 slaves, and roughly a quarter resided on plantations with 50 or more. Only 11 percent of slaves in the upper South lived on plantations with at least 50 slaves, but approximately 30 percent of slaves in the deep South did so.[6]

Certain adults—particularly breastfeeding mothers and older men and women—continued in the antebellum years to work near the slave quarters to oversee children. Supervision was often minimal; the children at the quarter frequently outnumbered the adults in the vicinity by a sizeable margin. A traveler through Alabama's cotton country early in the century remarked that rows of slave cabins had "very few but children in them," and the situation still held true in many places on the eve of the Civil War. Former Alabama slave W. B. Allen, for one, recalled staying alone in a cabin as a young child, rising late to eat the breakfast his mother had prepared for him before leaving for the field.[7]

Under such circumstances, parents devised strategies to ensure their children's safety. Mothers and fathers taught children to look after one another and not to go anywhere alone. Former Virginia slave Joseph Holmes recalled that parents raised brothers and sisters "in pairs," by which he meant that mothers and fathers held two children responsible for keeping each other out of trouble. Jeff Nunn, of Alabama, wore bells around his neck, which enabled adults to know his whereabouts even when he meandered out of sight. (Owners used bells in a similar fashion to keep track of those adult slaves who habitually attempted to run away.) Slave parents also controlled their children's activities by playing on their fears, as did many other nineteenth-century parents. To frighten her children, one mother recited a chant about the night watchmen (called patrollers) who roamed the countryside looking for errant slaves: "Run nigger run, run nigger run, the 'pat-er-rollers' will get you if you don't look out." The mother had found it necessary to leave her children to fend largely for themselves under a big tree in the slave quarter, and she probably hoped to prevent their wandering off where no one could find them. Slave children throughout the South learned to fear the make-believe characters Raw Head and Bloody Bones. Former slave Sallie Paul remembered that adults tried to keep the children

from doing mischief with stories of the fearsome pair "to spare de punishment" that would follow misbehavior: "Tell us Bloody Bones would jump
out dat corner at us, if we never do what dey say do."[8]

Slaveholders increasingly viewed these methods as inadequate for ensuring the health and safety of children. Children represented a substantial
part of an owner's future profit. Yet accidents, particularly fires, claimed
lives or left youngsters disabled. Stories of disaster circulated among slaves
and slaveholders, reminding them that very young children should not be
left alone. One tale recounted the tragedy of two slave children who died in
a fire after their mother locked them in a cabin to make sure they would not
wander about in her absence. Supposedly, she returned to discover two
hearts beating in the embers.[9] However fantastic its ending, the story conveyed adult concern about leaving children unsupervised.

Planters with sizeable slaveholdings argued increasingly that specially
designated caretakers could watch youngsters more closely than parents,
reducing the danger of accidents and improving children's chances of survival, but slaveholders held more complicated concerns too. Injuries that
interfered with a slave's ability to work, or, in the case of young females, affected their beauty, would damage a slaveholder's finances if they reduced
the size of the labor force or the price realized from the sale of a slave. Such
injuries also tarnished the image of slaveholders as benevolent. Moreover,
taking proper care of children deflected criticisms of slavery. Efforts to reduce child mortality and improve children's health bolstered the slaveholder's contention that the enslaved benefited from slavery as well as the
enslavers.

Slaves worried about harm to or death of their loved ones, but parents
resisted entrusting their children to others, in part because this pushed
mothers and fathers at a more ruthless pace than would have been possible
if they maintained major responsibility for caring for their children. If they
kept sons and daughters nearby as they worked, the children's activities
would likely interrupt the work routine. If slaves fed their own children,
mothers would need to leave the field daily in time to cook the evening
meal and fathers would need to tend their own crops from time to time, instead of their owners'. To meet their children's clothing needs, mothers had
to be excused occasionally to sew or do laundry. Just as important, performing such chores within the slave household had the effect of enhancing
the importance of family relationships and teaching children how to endure
conditions of oppression.

When children stayed near parents, mothers and fathers could demonstrate how adults kept enslavement from taxing them to exhaustion. Slaves needed to work at a pace slow enough to preserve their health but fast enough to avoid the ire of an owner or overseer. Slaves also had to know how to interact with supervisors who faulted their work. Many youngsters witnessed parents agreeing deferentially with the master, mistress, or overseer on the need to speed up or improve work habits, only to resume the accustomed pace and methods as soon as the owner was out of sight. Such scenes, played out repeatedly, required no explanation. Indeed, the fact that adults did not discuss them sent an important message to children, who had to learn at an early age that certain topics could not be addressed openly. As children grew, parents gradually incorporated them into work routines by showing them how to clear fields of rocks, hoe, or harvest crops according to the most minimal standards an owner might tolerate.

When children spent their days in a distant location under someone else's supervision, the responsibility for educating them about behavior at work and elsewhere fell to others. Child caretakers almost always came from the slave community and might have been expected to share the parents' goals for their children, but owners could supervise them more closely than parents and pressure them to teach the children behaviors and attitudes contrary to those of mother and father. The role of the child caretaker, in the words of one former slave, was to see that the plantation children did "what de Missus look for dem to do."[10]

Parents found this situation worrisome and often preferred to leave young children with older siblings. At least under these circumstances, no one usurped parental authority. Slightly older brothers and sisters could watch youngsters under the supervision of mothers, who could check periodically when they returned to breastfeed the youngest baby or to prepare the noonday meal. Upon their return from the field in the evening, mothers or fathers could note chores left undone or other evidence of misbehavior and render punishments accordingly. The appointment of another caretaker deprived parents of this right. It might even deny them access to their children's rations, because owners preferred to turn them over to a woman who cooked for all the young slave children.[11]

BECAUSE parents and owners could not or would not devote much time to the care of children, they kept child-rearing tasks simple. Youngsters ate plain foods that could be prepared easily. Parents liked milk mixed with bread, or mush, for younger children, who preferred it flavored with molasses. Another food thought especially suitable for small children was corn bread with potlicker, possibly served with the greens. The simplicity of slave children's dress and the informality of toileting arrangements indicate that children could be kept dry and toilet-trained with minimal effort. Children of both sexes old enough to walk or crawl about wore one-piece garments with no underclothes, although leggings of some type might be provided in winter. They learned to relieve themselves outdoors in imitation of parents and other adults. The simplicity of bedding helped ensure that bed-wetting was more of a nuisance than a transgression. Mattresses usually consisted of ticking stuffed with grass, corn shucks, hay, or pine needles. They dried quickly outdoors or in front of the fireplace, and parents could easily replace their filling. The pallets used by many children for sleeping could be washed or aired readily.[12]

When planters did not set aside adequate time for even these tasks, mothers resorted to bathing youngsters and caring for their clothes at night or during the noon rest period that many owners provided for slaves and work animals. Most mothers bathed children no more than once each week. Former slave James Williams of Alabama said that the slaves he knew rolled their children's hair or kept it cut short, because they could only dress it on Sundays. Plantation rules required slaves to turn in by a certain time each night so that hands would be well-rested for work the next day, but mothers could not always finish their cooking and washing before bedtime. In such cases, adults doused the fire and ate their supper or completed household chores quietly in the dark.[13]

Mothers, short on time, understandably grew unhappy when their children created extra work. Youngsters wore out their garments quickly, in part because they were made of cheaper, less durable fabric than the clothes of working adults. They tore and dirtied clothes in work and play. Women had little time or resources for mending, washing, or replacing clothing. Gus Feaster's mother reacted typically when he stained his shirt while eating peppermint candy, a rare and unexpected treat. She had warned her young son to keep his shirt clean as he ate. When he did not, the mother confiscated the candy and harangued him as "good-fer-nothing."[14]

Gus's mother would not have wanted her owners to see her son wearing a dirty shirt, because slaveholders were quick to cite such incidents to prove that slave mothers did not care properly for their children, reinforcing the view that the tasks of child rearing should be turned over to others. On Sunday mornings, masters and mistresses customarily called all slaves to the big house for inspection. Mothers came with children bathed and dressed in their best and cleanest clothes. This ritual—enacted on plantations throughout the South—implied the mother's sole responsibility and the owner's lack of culpability for any child neglect. Susan Hamlin was one of many little children who filed past their mistresses and masters each Sunday before going to church. "We had to be dressed nice," she later recalled. "If you pass [the master] and you ain't dress to suit him he send you right back and say tell your ma to see dat you dress right."[15] Susan's master probably worried about what his neighbors would think of him if he sent a child to attend church looking like a ragamuffin, because southerners expected "good" owners to ensure that their slaves dressed adequately for the weather in clean clothing. No doubt he also wanted to assert his authority over the youngster.

Slaves, too, worried about children's grooming. Slave mothers and fathers approached the back doors of their owners' homes with trepidation. When children did not show up properly attired and groomed, the owner might appoint another woman to sew the children's clothing, do their laundry, or even take charge of them throughout the day. Planters with large slaveholdings could afford to appoint someone to specialize in certain occupations, including those of children's cook or child minder.[16] This created a vicious cycle: mothers who worked long hours in the field could not properly care for their children, which gave owners an excuse to shift childcare responsibilities to other slaves. This, in turn, freed mothers to work yet longer hours in the field.

Mistresses pointed out the personal shortcomings of slave mothers rather than identifying or attempting to rectify the conditions that left them little time for children's care. By joining their husbands in blaming child neglect on the ignorance or laziness of black women, they demonstrated their belief in racial difference rather than gender solidarity. Exceptions did occur: some mistresses, such as Fanny Kemble Butler, petitioned their husbands to grant more time for slave mothers to care for children. However, most women of the slaveowning class contented themselves with appearing at the back door each Sunday, where they dispensed meager gifts to mothers who arrived with their children in an acceptable state of cleanliness and blame to those who did not. The mothers, desperate for any help in meeting the material needs of their children, complied with the ritual, accepting whatever gifts the mistress offered and simultaneously encouraging her to assume a degree of responsibility for their children's welfare.

A planter's success in reassigning child-care duties from parents to other slaves depended on the number and ages of youngsters living on the planta-

tion, the availability of slaves to serve as caretakers, the trust placed in potential caregivers by owners and parents, the perceived dangers of leaving
children unattended, and the cycle of cultivation associated with the market
crop grown on a particular plantation. As a result, the child-rearing duties
assumed by caretakers—where owners succeeded in appointing them—varied from one slaveholding to another and from season to season. Among
large slaveholders, rice planters proved the most successful in shifting parental responsibilities to other slaves. They were aided in this endeavor by
the high prevalence of disease that characterized the South Carolina and
Georgia coasts. Neither owners nor parents understood the cause of ma-
laria, which plagued slaves on rice plantations, but both understood that
mortality rates rose for children who stayed in swampy areas during the
warmer months of the year or any place during epidemics. Consequently,
wealthy rice planters sent young children for weeks or months at a time
to "pineland camps," which they rented or purchased for this purpose.
Toward the end of the antebellum period, they sometimes sent children
away to the pinelands for as long as five or six months—a period that
corresponded to the time they sent their own families to Savannah and
Charleston to avoid contagion on the plantation. Unlike owners, slave parents did not usually accompany their children on these removals, so they
watched their children leave home literally by the cartload.[17] Most parents
probably took comfort in knowing the camps reduced their children's exposure to grave risks. The children, particularly those too young to anticipate their parents' visits or their return home, must have agonized over the
separation.

The child care available at the summer camps did not consist of around-
the-clock adult supervision. A few older women cooked for as many as
eighty to one hundred and fifty children at a time at Stroyer's camp. Jacob
and the other little boys and girls usually fell under the supervision of

Unable to prevent their children's removal, in part because they feared
for their children's survival, parents did their best to ensure that their children did not forget their families. They visited periodically and counted on
slaves working in the camps or at sites nearby to care for them and remind
the children of home. Jacob Stroyer, when a child at such a camp, knew he
could count on visits by his parents and other relatives every Sunday. They
brought him food, and Jacob looked forward to breaking the monotony of
the bland weekday fare of mush and molasses or clabber. He much preferred the "hoppin john" (field peas, rice, and bacon) his mother cooked
for him.[18]

slightly older boys like Gilbert, who whipped his charges for no apparent reason other than that he considered this appropriate to his role. Adults worked nearby and could come quickly if needed, however. Jacob, in an attempt to avoid one of Gilbert's whippings, ran for help to adult carpenters working in the camp's vicinity, one of whom was his uncle.[19]

Not many slaveowners succeeded in separating children and parents to the extent that wealthy rice planters did. Planters with sizeable work forces—whether they grew cotton, tobacco, or wheat—often established day nurseries for infants during picking season or during other busy times of year or periods of inclement weather. Young children could help care for the babies and simultaneously receive supervision themselves. Rice planters who did not send children to pineland camps made similar arrangements, but on smaller farms slave children continued to stay near parents as they hoed, harvested, or plowed.

Masters and mistresses with large slaveholdings that included slaves of marginal help in the field were most likely to assign an adult to oversee children past infancy, mainly during planting and harvesting, but child care, even for children as young as three and four years of age, rarely entailed direct or continuous adult supervision. In fact, boys and girls of this age had sufficient physical strength to lift a baby, the only requirement deemed essential for the job of nursing assistant. The adult in charge mainly checked to see that the young helpers cared for the babies according to accepted plantation practices. One witness described the child nursery on a rice plantation: "Near each baby sat or played a small boy or girl who had been detailed to care for that especial baby, and at the door of the house sat Maum Judy, or later Kate, the nurse." Slaveholders held the adult nurses responsible for supervising both the infants and their young nursemaids.[20]

Owners expected caretakers not only to keep the youngsters under constant watch but also to complete domestic chores, such as cooking, sewing, or gardening. Sometimes the caretakers did not perform the chores on behalf of children, but rather supervised the youngsters' completion of the tasks. On some estates boys and girls routinely washed and mended the clothes they wore, waited on one another when they were sick, and aired out or refreshed their own bedding, under the caretaker's supervision.[21]

Most slave overseers of children probably sympathized with their young charges and did their best to carry out their responsibilities toward the children. They monitored the youngsters' whereabouts and tried to keep them away from fires and other dangerous places. They frequently fed children at midday and sometimes provided an evening meal as well. Caretakers also oversaw the children's health, dispensing various concoctions to prevent or cure disease. They sometimes mended children's clothing and almost always assumed authority for disciplining the youngsters.[22]

Some children probably fared better under their jurisdiction, particularly if the only alternative consisted in leaving the youngsters home alone. But many caregivers found it impossible to keep up with the large numbers of rambunctious children left to their supervision, especially when they had to cook, sew, or perform other chores in addition to overseeing the children, which most did. In fact, many children received no more adult attention after their assignment to a caretaker than they had previously when they were taken to the field with parents or left at home with older siblings.

The majority of planters who shifted responsibility for child care from parents to caretakers relied on a variety of adults to help rather than one specially designated person, which kept any one slave from assuming charge and challenging the owner's power to make decisions about children's care. The dairymaid or even the mistress could lend a hand as needed. The dairy woman on one South Carolina cotton plantation fed the children clabber each day after she finished the churning. She poured the leftover clabber in a big wooden tray kept under a tree near the dairy for this purpose, and then called the children to come and eat. One Alabama mistress checked on slave children each morning, giving them a dose of oil and turpentine, which she believed kept the youngsters well. A girl named Agnes James went with the other slave children "up to de big house" to "get somethin to eat twixt meals." The children saw the mistress each morning. She talked and prayed with them, then fed them medicine she had concocted for preventing worms.[23]

Long workdays for parents, coupled with early bedtimes for children, meant that youngsters saw little of their parents during the six-day work week typical of most plantations and farms, at least during periods of peak labor demand. George Coulton's father, a slave in Virginia, assumed responsibility for curing his master's tobacco, an around-the-clock job during part of the year that left him little time even for sleep. Former Alabama slave Maugan Sheppard rarely saw his mother or father "cept upon a Sunday." Both parents left for the cotton field before sunup, and Maugan ate his supper and fell asleep before they returned in the evening. An Alabama physician noted that exhausted field hands in his region tended to fall asleep soon after returning to their cabins in the evening, napping until nine or ten o'clock at night.[24] By this time, most young children had gone to bed.

Children regretted having so little time with their parents. If mothers never returned to the cabin to fix meals or check their youngsters, children might go a whole day or even longer without seeing a parent. Although they interacted with them infrequently, children held their parents in esteem and struggled to stay awake to see them in the evening upon their return from the work site. In Virginia, the slave Duncan Gaines remembered listening for his mother's singing, which signaled her return from the field. A sleepy Henry Barnes, who ate supper with other slave children on a plantation in Alabama, somehow forced himself to remain awake long enough for his mother to arrive home and tuck him into bed for the night. Charlie Grant considered his South Carolina overseer "pretty rough." Among other things, he prevented children from going "over to see your mama and papa" while they worked. Children whose parents lived on separate slaveholdings usually lived with their mother and saw their father only on weekends and perhaps once during the week.[25]

THE CHILD-CARE system that developed on large plantations in the antebellum years had an insidious outcome, unintended perhaps by the men and women who first designated slaves to carry out domestic chores for children: it enabled planters to purchase individual children too young to fend for themselves. Young children had always been bought and sold as part of family groups, but planters who arranged for child care outside of family settings could purchase them alone because they could be assured that the children would be cared for. Often the cooks assigned to feed children the midday meal extended their oversight to mend children's clothes and to keep them out of danger, all with their owner's blessing. Owners thought child care meshed particularly well with cooking duties. Preparing meals for all hands did not engage a plantation cook for the entire day, leaving her (or him) free to perform other duties. One advantage of designating a particular slave as cook, some slaveholders argued, was that it not only increased efficiency in feeding slaves but also offered planters an opportunity to increase their slave populations by purchasing youngsters who could be raised on the plantation. In the pages of the *Southern Agriculturalist,* one planter proclaimed that even if the designation of an old woman as cook made it possible to raise only "one little Negro extra," the addition of this slave to the plantation population alone would compensate for the loss of a hand taken from the field and placed in the kitchen.[26] In early childhood, boys and girls lacked coordination, strength, endurance, and judgment, which prevented them from performing many farm and household chores, but owners who purchased children of this age were more interested in instilling habits of obedience and subservience for the future than in obtaining useful services right away.

Abolitionists called attention to the separation of parents and children in such popular accounts of slave life as the *Narrative of the Life of Frederick Douglass: An American Slave* and the *Narrative of William W. Brown, A Fugitive Slave.* Harriet Beecher Stowe's powerful indictment of slavery, which appeared in 1852 under the title *Uncle Tom's Cabin,* included a direct appeal to end slavery on the ground that it separated parents and children: "I beseech you, pity those mothers that are constantly made childless by the American slave trade!"[27] Partly to stave off critics but also because many slaveholders truly believed that young children should be raised in families, some state legislatures enacted laws barring the sale of children under certain ages without their mothers.

Laws restricting the sale of children may have retarded such sales in some places, but because the number of young children sold apart from parents was never large, trends are difficult to discern. One study estimates that in the upper South fewer than 1 percent of children under age eight were sold separately from parents in the antebellum years; another suggests that from 5 to 7 percent of children under age ten were sold apart from their families. At any rate, laws ostensibly protecting children from sale did not always achieve that purpose. Legislation passed in Alabama in 1852 prevented the separation of children younger than five from their mothers through sale, but the same law permitted the sale of children of ages five through nine if keeping them with their mothers would impinge upon the owner's financial interests. Motherless children of any age were not covered by the legislation, leaving open the possibility that unscrupulous slaveholders would falsify documents declaring certain children orphans or older than they were. With these loopholes and the absence of any effective enforcement mechanism, the law protected few youngsters from separation and stands only as a reminder of the large-scale disregard by slaveholders for slave family ties that prompted legislators to pass such a law in the first place.[28] On the other hand, legislation passed in Louisiana appears to have had some effect. A law of 1829 prohibited the sale of children under the age of ten into the state without their mothers, unless traders could vouch for the child's status as an orphan. Anyone charged with violating the law had to prove his or her innocence, rather than the other way around. This law reduced significantly the number of children under age ten sold in the state, particularly from Virginia, and the traffic in young slaves sold without mothers all but disappeared. Whereas children had once constituted 13.5 percent of the trade from Virginia to Louisiana, after the law's passage the proportion fell to 3.7 percent.[29]

When the supply of slaves exceeded the number needed by residents of a state, legislatures generally imposed prohibitions on the importation of any slaves from outside the state's borders. Alabama attempted to control the sale or purchase of slaves of all ages during the late 1820s and again in 1832, but the prohibitions, prompted by economic panics and fears of slave insurrection, apparently were not only short-lived but largely ignored. Georgia enacted legislation to ban outright the importation of slaves for much of the antebellum period, but its citizens complied only with the letter, not the spirit, of the law by completing slave sales outside the state's boundaries. Virginia barred the importation of slaves during the antebellum period, but with little consequence, since its slaveholders primarily sold slaves rather than purchasing them. In 1838, the state legislature approved a provision making clear that all slaves—even those "quite young"—could be sold. The existence of this law suggests a reaction in the upper South to legislation in states farther south barring the sale of children. The Virginia legislation also indicates that the trade in children did not cease, as the Louisiana case suggests, but merely decreased or shifted from one location to another.[30]

Although few children were sold separately from parents, the possibility of separation haunted the minds of children and parents from the child's early years. The chance of sale increased with age. Adolescents and young adults were particularly vulnerable, and owners sold parents away from children, as well as children apart from parents. Young children knew of sales either because they witnessed them firsthand or because they heard about them from other slaves. Nancy Williams feared seizure by slave traders after she saw a mother sold and forced to leave Virginia without telling her husband or baby goodbye. "Ise so fraid dey gonna tek me!" she recalled in later life. Samuel Walter Chilton, also of Virginia, knew slavery as "a sad partin' time." He feared being sold, but he also feared being left alone. "Sometimes dey sell your mother an' leave you," Chilton later recalled. Patience Avery, another Virginia slave, remembered long after the end of slavery the agony of mothers parted from their children by sale: "All de time de sale is goin' on you hear de mos' pitiful cries o' mothers bein' part from dey chillun."[31]

Children who lived near roads traveled by slave traders witnessed the movement of slaves headed for new homes. Droves of slaves that included children of all ages commonly traveled through parts of central Virginia. Slaves along these routes feared for the welfare of children, especially infants, who had difficulty sustaining the rigors of the journey. Stories about abandoned babies circulated. Fannie Berry, as a child in Virginia, heard of mothers forced to leave their precious babies "on de groun' . . . to live or die," depending on whether poor whites found them and raised them to work on their homesteads. These tales, real or imagined, reflected and engendered fears among children and parents, who worried about the likelihood of their own separation in the years to come.[32]

Tales of child snatching exacerbated the fear slave families had of separation. Bettie Tolbert believed that slave traders roamed neighborhoods "stealin the nigger children and takin them off no telling where at, and sellin them same as they's cattle." The kidnappers reportedly enticed little children to their wagons by offering them "apples and oranges, and all kinds of pretty little red trinkets," according to Tolbert, who offered this explanation for why some former slaves she knew could not remember their parents or where they had come from. Tim Thornton heard similar stories in Virginia. Parents added to worries of kidnapping by telling stories of their own; images of child snatchers kept youngsters from wandering too far from home. Former slave John Wesley lived in Kentucky as a boy when Indians remained in the vicinity. His mother made clear her fear that Indians would snatch her children, although as an adult Wesley could not be sure whether they actually posed a threat or whether he just believed they did. Tolbert's description of speculators' wagons contains an element of truth, for slave traders carried food and supplies in wagons as they plied their trade throughout the countryside. Kidnappers captured and sold slaves of all ages, including adults, which added to the anxiety felt by parents and children. Although they did not carry off slaves on the scale these former slave children believed, enough stories circulated to keep everyone—slaves and slaveholders—concerned.[33]

WHETHER small children were purchased or raised at home, they performed duties expressly chosen to cultivate in them an awareness of the southern social hierarchy and their subordinate place within it. Many planters stationed little boys and girls at a gate, ready to open and shut it as members of the white family or their guests came and went. Although she was no larger than her charge, Louella Holmes Williams became a companion to "Miss Lucy," her owner's daughter. Master and mistress held the slave girl responsible for Lucy's wearing her bonnet outdoors. Louella would run after Lucy while the white girl played to "pick de bonnet up an' put it on her head" if she shook it off. Jeff Allen's Alabama mistress wore dresses with long trains. Possibly as young as age two, but no older than three, Jeff trailed her on excursions through the yard, holding her skirt off the dirt, a chore he shared with another boy. As a serving girl, Susan Broaddus stood behind her Virginia mistress during meals ready to pass her salt, syrup, or anything else she wanted. Emma Howard's chores included brushing flies away from her mistress in Alabama, and Isaac did the same in South Carolina while his owner's family ate. Little Mike Lawrence carried a hot coal to his master when he wanted to light his pipe.[34] White children who watched the black youngsters performing such acts learned to expect similar services from boys and girls who otherwise might have been viewed merely as playmates.

All members of the white family, as well as the overseer and his wife, enjoyed personal services performed by slave children. Girls usually waited on women and their daughters, boys on men and their sons. Slave children fetched items ranging from shoes and desserts to mail from town. One girl carried the basket of medicines used by her mistress when she visited sick slaves in the quarter. The overseer on Charles Manigault's Gowrie plantation had a small boy to "run with his umbrella & great coat in case he should be caught by rain in the field."[35] Simply completing the job did not suffice, however. Rather, each child had to perform the job in such a way as to emphasize the unequal relationship between servant and served.

Small children knew about the cruelties of slavery and harbored fears that owners would mistreat them; consequently, they did not learn easily the roles owners assigned them. To obtain their devoted service, owners understood they would have to help children overcome their apprehensions. "Young servants," warned a Virginia planter, "should not be suffered to run off and hide when the master comes up, or any other white person."[36] Slaves too fearful of the owner challenged the notion of the benevolent father or mother figure that most owners hoped to display for guests. Yet young slaves tended to avoid whites. When William Howard Russell visited the Pringle plantation near Georgetown, South Carolina, at the start of the Civil War, the English correspondent found the slave children so frightened "that they generally fled at our approach." He called them "shy," rather than scared, probably echoing the explanation offered by his host. The master, in particular, terrified youngsters, who often ran from him as he approached, especially if they lived where they did not encounter him often. Young Perry Madden spent most of his days in Alabama under the watchful eye of an older brother, whom he helped tend livestock. When Perry heard his master coming, "I'd be gone, yes siree."[37]

Slaveholders employed several strategies to overcome such fears and teach children to bow and curtsy rather than to run and hide. Some had children live or work in the owner's home so they could learn to serve the white family gradually as part of everyday routines. Others went out of their way to solicit the cooperation of children, offering them special treats and privileges in order to win their affection. Still others capitalized on the youngsters' desire for play to cement relationships between their own children and their young slaves. Owners also avoided imposing harsh penalties upon children for misbehavior when they thought the perpetrators too young to know better and turned over to parents the responsibility for disciplining children as they grew old enough to understand the consequences of their actions. Such strategies helped diminish fear of owners among children, who often enjoyed extra food when visiting the big house or played games there, particularly if the master and mistress had young children to serve as playmates.

Owners emphasized to slave children that they "belonged" to someone other than their parents. They attempted to influence the child's perception of family to include themselves, a few even insisting that slave children refer to them as their fathers and mothers. Hannah Scott learned to call her owners "White Pa and White Ma." Virginia slave Henry Johnson heard repeatedly that he was born one hour before the master's youngest son. Henry served as companion and waiting boy to the young master, so his owner by his continued references to the coincidence of their birth probably intended to forge a link between the slave boy and the child who would one day become his master.[38]

Attempts by slaveholders to stress that slave children did not belong to their parents sometimes took the form of "giving" particular slave children to their own sons and daughters who were close in age to the slave youngsters. The slaves became the white children's playmates. Sometimes the slave children lived in their owning family's home; at other times they remained in the slave quarter with their parents. Either way, the gift-giving custom helped to separate the children psychologically from their immediate families. The youngsters knew that when the young mistress or master married, they would accompany their owners to new homes. The young masters and mistresses customarily gave special treats to their slave playmates to help the children form new loyalties and allay the distress they must have felt at the thought of being apart from their families—even if the actual separation lay years into the future. Special treats brought positive results, at least while the children were still young. Callie Williams of Alabama, "given" to her owner's eldest daughter when Callie was only six years old, was "proud as ah peacock" in her first calico dress, a present from her new owner. Older slaves understood the situation differently and expressed their disquietude in song: "This is a hard world, Lord, for a motherless child."[39]

Some of the relationships that developed between white and black children produced friendships that lasted a lifetime, but they also reinforced in the minds of children the idea that blacks served whites and held inferior positions in southern society. Through play, slave children learned to obey, slaveowning children to command. J. G. Clinkscales, the son of a South Carolina slaveholder, play-acted funerals with his siblings and the slave children on his father's estate. The owner's children led the procession and took the major roles. As a young boy, J. G. had grand times playing with two slave companions, Jack and Peter, whom he hitched to a small wagon. His baby sister rode in the wagon, while he whipped the human "horses" to make them go. Long after slavery ended, Clinkscales remembered the "division of labor" as amusing, rather than as exploitive of the slave boys. Owners took action to ensure that slave children understood they had access to special toys only through the whims of the owner's children. A rice grower's son who spent the warm-weather months in Charleston received assurances from his father that his rocking horse had been packed away for the season so his black playmates, who enjoyed riding the horse when he was home, would not continue the pleasure in their young master's absence.[40]

Games and other pastimes could bridge the gulf of race and class that divided black and white children or could emphasize it. Hunting, engaged in by almost all white men and boys, frequently cast slave boys in the role of attendant. The little slave boys who went along on dove hunts kept up a commotion intended to send the birds into the air so the young master could shoot them. Pretend games of "soldiers and Indians" (transformed to "Yankees and Confederates" during the war years) reinforced notions of difference, when the owner's children assumed the preferred roles of "soldiers" or "Confederates" and cast slave children as the enemy.[41]

Not all owners had children of an age to play, and those who did wanted slave youngsters to exhibit proper demeanor around themselves and their adult guests—not just their children. Consequently, they arranged for slave children to visit periodically with adults in the big house. Visits mandated by the master or mistress helped establish ties between children and owners, while reinforcing the ideal of plantation hierarchy held by white southerners. Owners enjoyed the presence of children as entertainment both for themselves and for their guests, for most adults found little children "cunning," by which they meant cute. Such visits in the owner's house served to mitigate the fear many slave children had of their owners.[42]

Just as slave children visited the big house, owners went periodically to the slave quarter, where children learned to welcome them. Children engaged in ritual behavior to greet owners arriving home from a holiday or business excursion. The ceremonies that marked such occasions were intended to inspire in children awe for their owners. Jacob Stroyer and the other slave children in the summer camp in the pinelands cleaned in anticipation of the owners' visit and learned how to greet the master and mistress: boys bowed and girls curtsied. Before their owners arrived, the children would line up to welcome them, boys on one side of the lane and girls on the other. After the Civil War, former rice planter Charles Manigault regretted deeply the passing of the practice whereby slave children learned "to watch for my coming."[43]

Youngsters anticipated efforts by owners to bestow favors upon children and did their best to extract whatever treats they could. Each time one Virginia wheat farmer left for town, slave youngsters hung onto his coattails, begging him to bring them back cakes. Upon his return he stood on the porch and tossed the cakes out to the children, who came up to the big house as soon as they saw him arrive home. Such small indulgences of children's taste for sweets encouraged youngsters to flock around the master, which in turn rewarded the master for his actions and allowed him to sustain his image as a beloved father-figure. The mistress on this same plantation was much more "sedate" than her cake-tossing husband and expressed openly her distaste for being touched by the slave children. Nevertheless, she earned a reputation equal to her husband's for being "fon' of de colored chil'en" by sending them to the dining room from time to time where a servant fed them bread and sugar. Another Virginia mistress sent biscuits to the children in the quarter each Sunday morning by way of a servant. She, too, earned a reputation as "good to me" among the slaves.[44] All slaves hoped that owners would live up to any praise they heaped on them.

Owners tried to win children's affection with offerings of food and other privileges that parents could not give. Mistresses frequently visited any nurseries on the plantation, bringing the children who tended babies something to eat. Slave children did not conceal their preferences for certain foods usually reserved for the white family, especially prized candy and biscuits made with white flour. They coveted other privileges too, along with affection. Planters could authorize rides in the carriage beside the driver and hold children in their arms. One plantation mistress customarily rode about her plantation carrying a silk bag filled with trinkets, which she threw to the slaves along her route. Her comings and goings drew slaves, presumably young and old alike, who looked "upon her as a great personage . . . and greeted her with profound courtesies." Giving out shinplasters or other small tokens was an important way of cementing paternalistic feelings between owners and slaves, as rice planter Charles Allston knew. When Union forces appeared in the vicinity of his family's Chicora Wood plantation after the start of the Civil War, he urged his mother to come to the plantation to "give out clothes and any little thing you may have for them even if you do not stay" in order to maintain the loyalty of the family's slaves.[45] Because of their impoverishment, slaves welcomed presents, however small, and some may have considered them a sign of an owner's genuine benevolence. Everyone knew such gifts did not guarantee an owner's kindness, but the fact that owners did or did not bother to distribute them counted for something. Slave children thought so especially. By expecting treats, children influenced the behavior of owning adults, who acted to prove themselves the kind-hearted parent-figures they said they were.

Children, fearful of slavery's capriciousness, wanting attention, and subject to the monotony of their daily diets, accepted small favors as confirmation that their owners cared for them. The prospect that owners might separate them from their families or whip their parents made children so afraid that they looked for any kindness on the part of owners, no matter how small, and extrapolated from that a belief that they were safe and cherished. Some even exaggerated their owners' powers to protect them. Edward Taylor, a young slave boy in Louisiana, remained calm when the "stars fell" in a meteor shower that frightened adults because he trusted his owners to shield him from any harm.[46]

The paternalistic bargain that slaveholders and slaves struck required each to give something to the other. Slaves displayed loyalty to their owners, at least outwardly, and slaveholders rewarded this with better treatment. This could take the form of an actual exchange of goods on both parts. For example, slaves often took eggs or other home-grown produce to their owners, expecting in return gifts ranging from extra rations to toys for their children. Children understood and enjoyed playing this game to their advantage. Although very little, Agnes Ames rushed ahead of her grandmother each morning on her way to the big house. She liked to pick a pretty flower along the way for her mistress. Agnes looked forward to the visits because she knew that after greeting her mistress with the flower, she could eat her fill of milk and bread.[47] Paternalism in the minds of children like Agnes was not an abstract idea, but a ritual of reciprocal exchange that had meaning in their everyday lives.

Both slave and slaveowning children had to learn their parts on the paternalistic plantation. Adele Allston, like many other southern mistresses, helped to see that they did. She met with the plantation's slave children once a week in Sunday school, which closed with a ceremony that emphasized both the mistress's authority and her benevolence. A big cake, baked especially for the occasion, was brought out in a wheelbarrow following the lesson. To obtain a slice from the plantation cook who served it, the children first curtsied in the mistress's direction. After receiving the cake, they curtsied to her again. The white children received pieces of the cake, too, which the slave cook saved for them, but not until the black children had been served.[48] This ritual imparted a lesson to the owner's children, as well as to the slave boys and girls: they might have cake during the rest of the week, as long as they allowed the slave children this special treat on Sundays.

The myth of southern paternalism rested on the ability of both owners and slaves to play particular roles in everyday life. Slaveowners pretended to oversee a labor system that worked to the advantage of all members of the working class, including people too young or old to work in the field. In return, they expected slaves to exhibit respect, obedience, and love toward all members of the slaveowning family. Slave parents foresaw the harsh consequences for children who did not learn their parts and did their best to teach children how to behave as owners wished, at least when the owners were present. One young mother who spotted the master coming up the road dropped the package she carried in order to curtsy, then ordered her son to "git dat hat off dat head and bow your head fo' he git hear!" Amos Gadsden learned to "step aside at all times for white people" while living in the big house with his owning family.[49] Such regulations emphasized the slaveholder's power, which could be frightening to children, but the knowledge of how to act in specific situations related by mothers and other trusted slaves helped to reduce anxiety that inadvertent behavior on the part of children would draw the wrath of the slaveholder.

Despite instruction in racial etiquette, many youngsters remained fearful of owners. To alleviate their fears, slaveholders tried to exercise leniency in their dealings with children, excusing inappropriate behavior if they thought the perpetrator too young to demonstrate better judgment. Forest Gibbs avoided a whipping once while being trained as a house servant in Charleston because of his youthful inexperience. The youngster thought his master had told him to eat some hoppin' john, but his owner had actually said "heat it." The master wanted to punish him, but the mistress dissuaded him from doing so by pointing out the boy's age and explaining that he knew no better. Misdeeds by youngsters often invoked only mild chastisement, in part because harsh criticism or punishment of young slaves could have unintended results, causing frightened children to act worse rather than improving their behavior. Small girls and boys already feared the possibility of punishment for themselves and their loved ones, and they worried about being separated from parents and other relatives and friends. Too frightened to sleep, little David Holmes lay awake each night in Virginia listening to or imagining the cries of slaves on other plantations. Even gentle admonitions from his mistress brought tears to young Amos Gadsden's eyes, along with his efforts to do better.[50]

Owners did their best to persuade youngsters that only bad slaves deserving of punishment were ever whipped. Some children observed this to be true, but most came to realize that owners set the rules and whippings occurred when slaves did not follow orders. Amos Gadsden, thinking back on slavery days in South Carolina, said that bad slaves "had to be punished; they got a few lashes on 'um." Louisa Gause, though, knew that her mother, grandparents, and other slaves had been whipped for not doing "what dey tell dem to do," rather than for violating a moral principle.[51]

Rather than discipline young slaves themselves, owners pressured slave parents to teach their children their parts in the paternalistic drama of southern race relations. This was necessary especially for the children of field hands, who encountered owners only rarely. Because these children spent their days almost exclusively with slaves, owners had little choice but to enlist the slaves' help in socializing children. Owners recognized the influence parents had over their sons and daughters and urged them to subdue children and turn them into dutiful and submissive servants. They impressed upon children the necessity of obeying mother, father, other relatives, and caretakers, just as slave parents impressed upon children the necessity of obeying master and mistress. One Virginia master, who became annoyed with the noise coming from the children in the slave quarter one Sunday afternoon, threatened to sell some of the children if all of them did not quiet down.[52] He counted on the parents to heed the warning, and his threat had the desired effect. In this case, the master used the cohesiveness of the slave community to his own advantage, while at the same time—perhaps unwittingly—he reinforced it.

Owners preferred not to use physical punishment to shape the behavior of young slaves, but parents—both mothers and fathers—resorted to physical chastisement often. Owners encouraged this. At times, masters and mistresses ordered or persuaded parents to administer a switching, rather than doing it themselves, but parents believed that they had the right and duty to chastise their own children, so they usually punished their sons and daughters themselves to prevent their owners from taking over this responsibility. When parents punished children on their own accord for offenses that aroused the ire of owners, they denied outsiders the opportunity to discipline their children. They also taught the youngsters how to stay out of trouble. One Alabama mother whipped her young son for refusing to participate in races organized by the overseer at a watermelon feast. She may have worried that the overseer would punish her or her son for his failure to show proper gratitude for the festivities. She probably wanted to teach the boy to cooperate with the overseer, at least outwardly, to avoid disciplinary action. Jacob Stroyer's parents often reminded him to submit to the will of his owners and their overseers.[53]

When a parent or another slave punished children for behavior offensive to owners, the action could reflect the slave's own understanding of the situation, rather than that of the slaveholder. When her Alabama master tried to punish Eliza Evans for sassing him, the young girl ran to her grandmother for protection, only to be whipped by the older woman. The master left satisfied that Eliza's insolence had been suitably punished, but the grandmother probably acted to ensure that Eliza learned to distinguish among the people to whom she spoke. Evans in later life explained the lesson she learned from the incident: "I jest said dat to de wrong person."[54] She could denounce her master, but only to a trusted slave—a lesson all slave children needed to learn.

Slave parents wanted to make sure their children exhibited proper demeanor before owners and their guests for fear that their children would be ill-treated or taken from them. Incorrigible youths were more likely to be sold than those who proved tractable. As a result, parents felt bound to instruct children carefully in the intricacies of racial etiquette. Children learned not to stare at whites engaged in conversation so they could not be accused of listening. Julia Woodberry called this "listenin widout no ears en seein widout no eyes."[55] Parents also taught children from a young age to avoid certain topics in conversation. Some youngsters did not dare inquire about their own parentage. Fantastic stories explaining human reproduction with references to reptiles and buzzard eggs served to deflect questions by young children about the identity of fathers, some of whom preferred to remain anonymous. When Patience M. Avery's mother and grandmother introduced a Virginia planter's son as her father, probably following the Civil War, the young girl rejected the idea outright. Frightened by the revelation, Patience kept repeating "I ain' got no father," explaining that the "buzzards laid me an' de sun hatch me; an' she [mother] came 'long an' pick me up."[56]

Slave parents disciplined children for violating the rules of the slave community, as well as those of their owners, but most of their efforts went toward ensuring that they and their children avoided trouble. Adult slaves worried about the tendency of young children to blurt out information to the white folks that would prove detrimental to their interests. Penny Thompson told her master of a plot to help slaves escape from his plantation in Alabama.[57] No wonder parents insisted on exercising their right to exert authority over their children! It is significant that neither mothers nor fathers appealed to the master or mistress for help in controlling a rambunctious son or neglectful daughter. Both understood that doing so would have undermined whatever authority they maintained over their sons and daughters.

Slaves maintained a cultural identity apart from owners by creating a world of their own beyond the scrutiny of slaveholders. To ensure their privacy and to protect their children from interrogation by owners, adult slaves withheld important information from children, creating a clear dividing line between the generations. "De olden people was mighty careful of de words de let slip dey lips," according to former South Carolina slave Lizzie Davis. Jane Simpson of Kentucky listened to adult conversation while she played, but she claimed later that she did not know the subject of their conversations because they spoke using metaphors. Slaves sent children to bed early, then sat up to talk after their children fell asleep. Bettie Tolbert recalled that children were sent out to play as "soon as somethin happen what warn't regular." Adults held meetings at night in houses where no children resided. May Satterfield said important conversations waited until the children fell asleep "so dat ef de white fo'ks axe us 'bout it we wouldn't know nothin'."[58]

These methods generally proved effective, but young children occasionally learned inadvertently of clandestine activities on the part of slaves. Moreover, older children eventually had to be incorporated into the adult community and entrusted with its secrets. Under these circumstances, adults acted to ensure that a child kept certain activities concealed and remained loyal to the slave community. Slaves threatened reprisals or took stringent measures to make sure that children did not inform owners if they learned by chance of irregular events in the quarter, such as thefts. When one little girl in Virginia accidentally came upon some adults preparing to eat lamb, a food normally unavailable to slaves, an old man took her "out back of the quarter house" and whipped her severely, explaining: "Now what you see, you don't see, and what you hear, you don't hear." She eventually realized that the slave feast consisted of stolen food, and the whipping was intended to warn her of the consequences if she ever told what she had seen. Henrietta Williams, born in Georgia's cotton country, lived in the big house from a young age. When she mentioned before other slaves that her mistress had raised her, they responded yes, but we will "kill you."[59] They meant to impress upon Henrietta their willingness and ability to retaliate if she proved disloyal to her fellow slaves.

When children did not absorb the lesson that some information must be spoken "in their sleeves," or kept within the slave community, the reactions of owners served to instruct them. As a young girl, Susan Snow had difficulty understanding the necessity of choosing her words carefully in front of the master. She learned this lesson the hard way, when her mistress hit her with a broom for singing a song favoring the Union during the Civil War. Most children learned the importance of discretion more easily than Susan did. As a young girl in Virginia, Julia Frazier knew she could not sing a song making fun of the master in his presence, but she could sing the same song "all roun' de cabin."[60]

Children had to meet the conflicting expectations of owners and parents, but not all did so in the same way or with the same success. Some children learned "manners" and "to mind." Others learned instead to modify their behavior to include a degree of subterfuge. Allen Sims knew as a young tyke in Alabama how to behave when Aunt Mandy punished him with a brush for some infraction. "It didn't hurt much," he later said, "but us cry lak she killing us." Whipped by her Alabama master for wading too far into the river, Annie Davis learned to make sure no one was around before she ventured into the water, rather than to avoid the deeper areas of water as her master intended. Jacob Stroyer, confused about the reasons behind his punishments, did not know how to modify his behavior to avoid them.[61]

Slave parents had to exercise care to avoid offending owners, while making sure that their children understood the superiority of their own claim to the children's loyalty. By subtle means, they taught children the difference. One slave mother had her daughter say the following prayer before going to sleep for the night:

> Now I lay me down to sleep,
> I pray the Lord my soul to keep.
> If I shuld die befo' I wake,
> I pray de Lord my soul to take.
> Bless pappy, bless mammy,
> bless marster, bless missie,
> and bless me. Amen![62]

The child remembered her master and mistress in the prayer, but placed the parents at the head of the list, where mothers and fathers thought they rightfully belonged.

While regular visits with owners, ceremonies, and treats lessened the fear children felt toward occupants of the big house, the same activities also reinforced notions of separateness between white and black, for black children observed the differences between the content of their daily lives and the lives of their white owners, even if they did not understand the institution of slavery that divided them. Annie Burton, who grew up in Alabama, admitted that as a child she did not understand "the great chasm" that separated the children of owners and slaves, "only that they had dainties and we had crusts." The white children slept in "luxurious bedrooms," while Annie and her brother lay down on the floor. Alabama slave Sarah Fitzpatrick spent much of her time at the big house, playing with the white children, eating at their table, and even sleeping in their beds. From a young age, she understood her position as different from that of the white children, for she bathed in a different tub, used a separate toilet, drank out of her own cup and glass, and waited on the other children when they ate. "We all et right at de same table," Fitzpatrick later recalled, but not at the same time. First, owners had slaves put away some of the delicacies; only then did they allow her and the slaves to "eat jes' lack dey did." Slaves on the Smithfield plantation in South Carolina ate the leftovers after the white family finished Christmas dinner.[63]

Giving curious young children accurate explanations of why the lives of black and white children diverged could prove dangerous. Biological and religious explanations appeared logical to children and had the added advantage of satisfying owners, who preferred telling slave children that they ate crusts while their own children got dainties because nature or God ordained it rather than that slaveholders wielded enough power to make it so. Katie Sutton's mistress told the young slave a fanciful tale about the different origins of white and black children: storks brought the owner's children, but slave children emerged from buzzard's eggs. Slave parents hesitated to challenge their owners overtly, particularly with children too young to understand human reproduction. Instead, they tried to teach their children to accept such differences, without accepting the racist notions that lay behind them. They insisted they loved their children just as much as white parents loved their own sons and daughters. One mother expressed this sentiment in a lullaby:

> A snow white stork flew down from the sky,
> Rock-a-bye my baby, bye:
> To take a baby gal so fair,
> To young Misses, waitin' there;
>
> Dat little white gal was borned rich and free,
> She's de sap from out a sugah tree;
> But you are jes as sweet to me,
> My little colored chile.
>
> To a cabin in a woodland drear,
> You've come, a mammy's heart to cheer;
>
> Don't be ashamed my chile I beg;
> 'case you was hatched from a buzzard's egg,
> My little colored chile.

The anonymous singer of this lullaby challenged the demeaning message of the mistress's explanation without directly assaulting its veracity. Adults throughout the South told slave children similar tales to explain the birth of babies.[64]

The division of authority for disciplining slave children could be confusing to some youngsters, but it provided others with a means of manipulating adults to their own advantage. Anna Baker earned dolls, candy, goobers, and other treats from her Alabama master while staying on the good side of the slave community by reporting the activities of one to the other. Anna hung around adult slaves while playing. "All de time I'd be a-listenin'," she admitted. "Den I'd go an' tell Marster what I hear'd." Anna's tattling did not always benefit her owners. "I mus' a-had a right smart mind," she said later, "'cause I'd play 'roun' de white folks an' hear what dey'd say an' den go tell de Niggers."[65] Anna's situation illustrates that slave children were often caught between slave and slaveholder. Tattletale Anna may have been cunning enough to move comfortably between two sets of adults, but most children realized soon enough that they had to choose one or the other.

At some times and in some places, owners succeeded in gaining the loyalty of slave children. Most were children raised from a young age in the big house by their owners with no close relationships with kin or other slaves—children dependent on close attachments to the white family for their survival. These children most often expressed genuine affection for their white families, which they believed to be mutual. After the Civil War, they sometimes had difficulty accepting the idea that they should live with their black families whom they had never known. Daphne, a motherless child raised in Virginia by her mistress and later claimed by her biological father and stepmother, made clear her preference for living with the white folks. "You see Daphne knew no other parents but dese two white folks," an acquaintance explained.[66]

Daphne was atypical. Most children learned to identify their own interests with those of other slaves, rather than with their owners. Certain slaves succeeded so well in maintaining control of youngsters that their children throughout early childhood did not understand their slave status until a startling incident revealed it. Some youngsters first grasped their status as slaves when they learned about the chain of command that denied parents the right to protect their own children from punishment by owners. When Emma Howard's master used a switch on her for her tardiness in carrying a message to town, Emma threatened to tell her mother. The master turned to the mistress, saying "that little devil don't know I'm her Master." The incident amused rather than angered her owners because of her youth, but Emma was taken aback to learn of her mother's inability to insist that no one "whip me but her."[67]

Harsh treatments meted out to slave men and women, often in front of children, confirmed in stark terms the very different positions of owners and slaves. Children witnessed or heard about cruelty to slaves by owners and overseers, if not regularly, at least from time to time. Assaults against parents, whether verbal or physical, upset sons and daughters, most of whom stood helplessly by as parents suffered the indignities that passed for discipline under slavery. Oliver Bell's earliest memory was of his master beating his bare-breasted mother with a leather strap. When the Alabama boy cried, his mistress directed someone to "go get that boy a biscuit" to allay his distress. Allen Wilson could only seethe with rage at the sight of his mother being whipped in Virginia, silently planning, after he grew to manhood, to kill the overseer who inflicted the blows. Former Alabama slave George Brown once tried to prevent his mother's whipping by hurling bricks at the overseer ready to inflict it. Owners, for the most part, accepted these occasional outbursts of anger from children, even after they grew older, as expressions of a natural affection between mother and child. In this case, George avoided punishment for the brick-hurling incident because, in the owner's words, "a calf loves the cow."[68]

Violent responses by slaves to brutal treatment were rare, but well known within the slave community. The circulation of stories about such events on other plantations provided a safe avenue for discussing the injustices of the slave system with youngsters. Parents or other adults could avoid direct criticism of their masters and mistresses, even as they taught children a view of right and wrong that differed from that of owners. One story circulated among slaves in Sumter County, Alabama, that a slave woman had extracted revenge for her beating at the hands of her master by flinging his young child into a pot of lye.[69] Children listening to such accounts understood them as critiques of slavery and shared in the anger adults felt upon hearing of the initial outrage.

The outcome of the contest between slaveholders and parents over the love and loyalty of slave children was not decided entirely by adults. As they grew, boys and girls learned from members of the older generation, but they also forged new paths for themselves based on their own understanding of the situation. This process began in early childhood, when children learned to manipulate the adults around them to gain the advantages and treats they desired. As did Anna Baker, they made themselves readily available to any adults, black or white, who had special foods to give away. Sabe Rutledge realized from an early age who could dispense sugar on the plantation, so he begged for his mother to take him to the master, who gladly supplied the sweet as a reward for the youngster's wish to see him. Prince Smith asked his master for money to purchase treats from the peddlers who sold ginger and other goods to people on the plantations from time to time. Little children hung around slave cooks "so as to git to lick de spoons and pans," and it required more effort than the house servants could sometimes muster to keep black youngsters away from the dining room while the white family ate. Children cunning enough to elude the servants who guarded the dining room doors and stand politely by the master's chair as he ate might be rewarded with a plate of leftovers after he had finished his meal.[70]

In the end, increased interference by owners in child rearing did not result in better health and welfare for children, nor did it gain for owners increased industry, loyalty, and affection from slaves, at least not among the great majority. Child mortality rates were not falling. Indeed, some evidence suggests that they were rising, at least until the 1850s.[71] A major reason appears to have been the owners' lack of commitment to meaningful reform. The child care offered by substitute caregivers was of no greater quality than that provided by parents, who continued to be driven to do their owner's bidding while neglecting their children. Any favors extended to children were short-lived and temporary in nature. Owners might dispense tangible treats to win temporarily the affections of the youngsters, but it was the slave family, with support from the larger slave community, who would teach children how to endure the conditions of oppression in which they lived. Slaves of all ages knew only too well that slaveholders eventually would push young children into the workplace, where treats were rare, toil routine, and castigation commonplace.

4

❀

EDUCATION IN THE
MIDDLE YEARS

THREE Virginia slave boys—Robert Williams, George Martin, and Wyatt Steptoe—went fishing one Sunday afternoon, after completing their regular chores. The day ended in near disaster when Wyatt slipped and fell into the river. Robert watched his friend bob up and down in the water, expecting he would drown, but George managed to throw Wyatt a line and pull him to shore. Wyatt had taken in a considerable amount of water and struggled for life on the river bank. As he did, Robert and George planned how to dispose of the boy's body. "If Wyatt had died we was goin' to say he went away and we never did see him again," Robert explained later. The seeming insensitivity of the two comrades was rooted in fear. By the time slave children reached the age of five or six, they faced harsh consequences for any misbehavior, and they contrived to avoid punishment as best they could. An Alabama boy hid out in a hollow tree stump, despite freezing weather, rather than return from the pasture without all the cows he had been sent to fetch.[1]

Slave youths in their middle years (from about age five to eight or ten) were no longer petted or excused for their shortcomings by masters and mistresses who cultivated their love and loyalty more than their labor. Children as young as five or six could perform tasks of tangible economic benefit to owners, even though they might not be classified as working "hands" for another half-dozen or so years. The largely self-sufficient cotton plantations characteristic of the lower South, the smaller wheat and tobacco farms located in the upper South, and the large and lucrative rice plantations along the Atlantic coast presented many opportunities for putting children to work in ways that benefited slaveowners. The tasks necessary to produce a cash crop, feed and clothe a labor force, and provide a comfortable home for the owning family and its guests included scores of jobs within the capabilities of children. Both girls and boys drove the master's cows to pasture, fed his chickens, and gathered eggs. They fetched water and wood for the mistress from the spring or well for use in cooking, cleaning, laundering, bathing, and gardening. Girls and boys also fetched wood and water for the overseer and his wife, tended their children, and cared for their horses. They raked leaves, husked corn, and worked in the kitchen garden, and in the winter they kept their owners warm by tending fires day and night. Little distinguished the labor of boys and girls at the youngest ages, but as they grew older they became more likely to engage in separate tasks. Girls usually cleaned homes and minded children, while boys tended horses and completed odd jobs around the yard (the work space located in back of the owner's home).[2]

Youngsters who cared for their owners' horses, watched their children, gathered their eggs, and manured their fields were in a position to inflict considerable damage on their owning family's property and, in the case of children who minded their owners' sons and daughters, their persons. One master found his buggy ruined when he left his horses in the care of a young boy while he visited a neighbor. A planter's baby died when the girl charged with tending him fed him laudanum to put him to sleep. A slaveholding mother observed that an "infant may, as likely as not, be dropped into the fire or out of the window."[3] With much at stake, owners heightened their use of punitive disciplinary measures for children who did not perform jobs adequately. They hesitated to frighten younger children by flaunting their power to punish, but they believed that youngsters in the middle years had the capacity to distinguish between right and wrong or at least to modify their behavior through fear of punishment. Experience often proved them right. Unable to determine which slave child had burned down his barn while playing with matches, a Virginia planter lined up all the children he could find and gave each one a whipping, which produced the desired result. Although the actual culprit avoided punishment by hiding in the corn field, she never again played with "fire sticks," according to her later testimony.[4]

The master's and mistress's interactions with slave children in their middle years continued to be paternalistic, but owners' ideas of appropriate paternalistic behavior shifted from that modeled on an indulgent or permissive parent to one reflecting a belief in the adage that to spare the rod was to spoil the child. As they undertook to teach slave children how to work, slaveholders were concerned not only with teaching the children skills, but also with instilling the attitudes necessary to carry out tasks with alacrity and an abject attitude. Their methods included corporal punishment and religious teachings, and they enlisted the aid of parents and other slaves to achieve their desired objective: a docile, hard-working, dependent slave.

Southern society—white and black—accepted corporal punishment as an appropriate means of disciplining children, and both slaveholders and slaves thought children should be attentive to spiritual matters. But slave parents employed corporal punishments and religious precepts to meet more expansive educational ends than did owners. They understood that their children needed to learn the skills necessary to perform the owner's labor, but they were determined that their children should learn more than how to be a slave in the field. After they grew to adulthood, children would need to know how to assume family roles, including those of husband or wife, mother or father. They also would be expected to play a part within the larger slave community, perhaps as healer or leader or exhorter. Whereas owners during children's middle years concentrated their energies on ensuring that they became satisfactory and satisfied slaves, parents focused on teaching their children to become people who were enslaved.

Children had their own ideas about how they wished to spend their days. Neither their owners nor their parents could control exactly what youngsters learned, no matter how hard they might try to impart particular lessons. Curious about the world around them, boys and girls wished to explore it in their own way, but they also feared the punishments that followed infractions of rules and dereliction of duties. They listened to the adults around them and drew their own conclusions about what it meant to be enslaved.

For much of the nineteenth-century adult population charged with training or socializing children, whatever the goal might be, whipping or other types of hitting passed for "education." Slaveholders held the legal right to chastise slave children and employed corporal punishment liberally upon those with whom they came in frequent contact. Mainly these slaves worked inside the big house or lived on smaller farms where owners encountered them in the course of a normal day. A former Virginia slave who learned to spin and weave from her "missy" recalled receiving "many a whippin' 'fore I could do it good." George Jackson's mistress used to supervise him as he pulled weeds from the garden in Virginia. "Sometimes I pulled a cabbage stead of weed," Jackson later recalled. At such times the mistress scolded and beat him, which made him cry. "She told me she had to learn me to be careful," he explained. Masters and mistresses who employed the whip and whatever other corporal punishments they deemed necessary never doubted the benefits of strict disciplinary measures or their right to administer them. Sara Davis Bethea, mistress of a rice plantation, assured the young slaves she punished that they had to learn to behave now or suffer worse treatment later. "I'm not mad," she explained, "but . . . you might have to suffer worse den dis if you don' learn better while you young."[5]

Slave children were whipped routinely by members of the owning class for not working, for disobeying arbitrary rules, for disrupting the plantation, for demonstrating insolence, and for destroying property. Former Alabama slave Dolph Parham remembered that even though he had what he considered a good relationship with his owner, "Master George" had to whip him on occasion to get him to perform his chores, which consisted of tending the cows and carrying water to the big house. One Alabama planter administered blows to an older boy for hitting his sister after she let a turkey escape from his trap. Henry Banks's Virginia master disciplined him for many infractions, sometimes beating the boy hard enough to draw blood. Most of Henry's transgressions involved work, but he was once beaten for looking angry. H. C. Bruce's master whipped the Virginia youth for lying.[6]

Mistresses, too, punished children in their middle years, especially those who worked in their homes. Punishable offenses included malingering, performing chores poorly, violating rules of racial etiquette, and appropriating items belonging to the owning family. Elizabeth Keckley's Virginia mistress verbally abused the young girl and had her whipped for dereliction of household duties. Delia Garlic's Virginia mistress deliberately burned her with a hot iron when the baby left in the young girl's charge hurt his hand. Both offenses were related to work, but another of Delia's mistresses knocked her out with a stick of wood for blackening her eyebrows with smut from the fireplace. The mistress, who blackened her eyebrows in this fashion, considered the girl guilty of mocking her betters. Jenny Procter's Alabama mistress punished her severely for taking a biscuit. In this case, the master chastised his wife, complaining that the time Jenny would lose from work while she recovered from her injuries would pay for several biscuits. Lucretia Heyward's South Carolina mistress whipped her hard enough to cut "my back w'en I don't do to suit her," according to the former slave.[7]

Punishment of children for even minor infractions could be severe, but most masters and mistresses refrained from using the harsher methods applied to adult hands. Owners often held a child's head between their knees and administered blows to the backside with a hand or paddle. Although this could hurt, the blows did not break the flesh as did the lash so often applied to the backs of older slaves. Some owners avoided hitting altogether and pulled children's ears to correct their behavior.[8] The milder disciplinary actions did not permanently disfigure children and therefore did not detract from the worth of a slave in the market. Corporal punishment often produced the desired short-term result, which encouraged its use.

Children punished repeatedly by owners tended to be those who worked or played near masters or mistresses. Slaveholders usually turned the responsibility for disciplining other children over to adult slaves, whom they charged with supervising the youngsters. Parents and other slaves had little compunction about relying on corporal punishment to correct children's behavior. They were especially quick to inflict penalties if a child's actions interfered with adult slaves' ability to complete their own work or if they were held accountable for the youngster's performance, situations that might focus their owners' wrath upon themselves. Solomon Jackson's grandmother, a plantation cook in Alabama, disciplined not only her own grandson but also other children who pilfered sugar, cheese, or crackers from the pantry. The children on one large rice plantation who loaded rice onto a schooner bound for market were kept moving by their slave supervisor, Abby Manigault, who threatened to switch any who fell behind. The youngsters must have believed her willing to follow through on the threat because they kept up the pace she set, even after they grew tired of carrying baskets and buckets of the grain from the rice house.[9] Beginners of all ages found cotton picking difficult, and children who picked cotton for the first time worked slowly and often left too much cotton on the plant. Adults grew frustrated with children who had difficulty carrying out their instructions and resorted to physical punishments in an effort to improve their performance. One former Alabama slave recalled that his mother taught him to pick cotton by hitting him with "a pole" when he failed to follow her directions. Only five years of age, Virginia slave Katie Blackwell helped train oxen to pull a plow by walking in front of the animals and turning in the right direction as the slave in charge—her Uncle Bob—called out commands. Little Katie bore the brunt of blame and a whipping when the animals refused to turn in the right direction.[10]

Because the disciplinary measures employed by slaves generally pleased owners, slaves retained the major responsibility for children's chastisement, and they defended their customary right to discipline children against encroachment. Although owners and slaves readily resorted to physical punishment of any children they supervised, men employed by owners to oversee plantation operations could not act with such impunity. Generally hired on the largest plantations, overseers usually confined their corporal correction of slaves to those able to work as adults. When overseers recruited young children to work in the fields during especially busy times, as occurred occasionally, slaves openly opposed their attempts to correct children. They knew that overseers exercised only as much power as their employers granted them, and they negotiated with owners as necessary to ensure that they—not an unrelated white man—served as their children's disciplinarians. When a newly hired overseer overstepped his authority by whipping the children on an Alabama cotton plantation, one of the mothers complained to her owners, apparently expecting that they would act to protect the children. They proved the mother's confidence had not been misplaced by promptly dismissing him.[11]

Overseers hesitated to discipline slave children for fear that angry parents would complain to owners or refuse to cooperate in the fields, and they acknowledged their limited authority in this area in the pages of agricultural journals. One overseer writing in the *Farmer and Planter* noted that adult slaves might use a switch to command obedience and work from children, but overseers did as well or better with "a mild word of encouragement or praise." Another advised against "fretting" and terrifying young slaves because it might render them less capable of working rather than improve their performance. If children "are working wrong show them how to work right; have patience and they will soon learn; or if they are too stupid put them at something else."[12] Not all overseers or owners heeded such advice, but most held to the view that the behavior of youngsters was best shaped by means other than corporal punishment; preferably they would leave discipline, if not to owners, then to parents or to other slaves.

Owners and parents inflicted punishment for different reasons. Slave-holders chastised children for their own convenience or benefit, while parents did so out of concern for the youngsters. By their middle years, sons and daughters understood this. Most children judged one as cruel, the other as harsh but caring. The distinction held true even for parents who punished severely. Fathers and mothers knew this and did not worry so much about cultivating a child's affection as they did about garnering his or her respect and obedience. In contrast, youngsters harbored fierce and last-ing resentment of owners, especially if they believed a punishment unfair. Frank Ziegler expressed bitterness toward his master more than eighty years later over a whipping he once received for falling asleep in the corn crib where he had been sent to husk corn for the horses. The former slave's childhood labors taxed his endurance and left him constantly exhausted.[13]

Although they accepted in principle the need for discipline, children usually tried to avoid whippings, no matter who administered them. When Nancy Williams's mother directed her daughter to pick up wood chips for the fire, the young girl refused. Anticipating punishment, Nancy flew to her master. Nancy did not explain the situation or appeal for his protection, but merely hung around him for a while. She may have suspected he would have sided with her mother. She also probably understood that such an ac-tion would only inflame her mother's anger. Nancy knew that her master's presence would intimidate her mother, and she had probably observed on previous occasions that her mother avoided her owner's intervention in her daughter's discipline. The young girl may not have realized why: by inter-jecting himself in the daughter's correction, the master would undermine the mother's authority over her daughter. As it was, Nancy succeeded in warding off the whipping, but only briefly. Her mother eventually caught her and, according to Nancy's later recollection, "beat de debil outa me."[14] Like Nancy's mother, other slave parents preferred to keep problems of dis-ciplining children to themselves, rather than risk the possibility that owners would take over the task.

At times, children appealed openly to either owners or parents for more favorable rulings regarding punishments proposed by the other. If masters or mistresses proved sympathetic, the children could at best expect re-prieves rather than repeals because parents could administer a whipping or scolding out of the owner's sight, as did Nancy's mother. Slave parents could not easily counter owners' efforts to punish children. Children had more success appealing for leniency when masters and mistresses disputed the need for correction. The two sometimes held conflicting attitudes toward behavior, which encouraged children to plead for mercy from one to the other. More often children sought or accepted the mistress's protection from the master's discipline. The Virginia slave girl Julia Williams ran to her mistress for protection when her master tried to whip her, for example.[15] Apparently at least a small number of children successfully mitigated punishments in this fashion.

Some children ran from one adult to another for protection, but others simply ran. Pauline Worth ran from her mistress when she tried to use a switch on the young girl. Pauline had not wanted to sweep the yard, which made her mistress mad. Former Alabama slave Daniel Taylor remembered taking off "to the woods" with his mother "tight in behind me with a hickory [switch]." Former slave Berry Smith recalled that he and another boy appropriated a horse belonging to Indians who had left Alabama, only to learn they would be whipped for the action. The two comrades hid out in the woods, hoping—in vain as it turned out—to remain long enough that their owner would forget about the incident or lose interest in administering the punishment.[16] Children who ran away to escape punishment were emulating adult slaves, who sometimes fled as a means of avoiding punishment for infractions of plantation rules.

The majority of children—like the majority of adults—never resorted to running away. Instead, they tried to do as they were told. Alabama slave Charity Grigsby avoided whippings meted out to other slave children by attending to her work "lak mistus showed me." Cooperating with owners protected children provided they performed competently, but a willingness to cooperate was not always sufficient to protect a slave child from an owner's wrath. The Virginia slave Elizabeth Keckley received a severe lashing her first day on the job as nursemaid to her owners' baby because she rocked the cradle so "industriously" in an effort to please the mistress that she pitched the baby onto the floor.[17]

Slaveholders considered themselves to be surrogate parents acting in the best interests of the youngsters. They felt justified in disciplining slave boys and girls, even severely, but they also continued to reward children with material goods, special privileges, and praise as they had when the children were younger, only now the rewards most often went for work well performed. One mistress improved her young house girl's demeanor—considered especially important for household slaves—with the promise of a new dress. During cotton harvests, special prizes went to the most productive hands, but all slaves, including children who picked small amounts of cotton alongside parents, received something for their efforts. Planters provided Christmas presents to children who were good; bad children received switches. "Dat was to teach education to be a good chile and try to wuk better," explained one of the recipients. Hattie Clayton, who enjoyed attending church in Alabama each Sunday, knew she could accompany the older hands only if she pleased her owner through the week. Some children received monetary prizes. In Virginia, Thomas S. Watson handed out cash after the wheat harvest to those slaves he considered deserving, including the children. George Coulton's Virginia master praised the youngster for taking good care of the stock, and also gave him fifteen or twenty dollars each Christmas as a reward for his dependability.[18]

Parents encouraged such behavior on the part of owners by teaching their children not only to work but also to mind their manners around owners, which helped them avoid trouble and reap the meager rewards slavery had to offer. The paternalistic attitude of owners was not the same thing as real benevolence, but children who learned to display the demeanor and behavior that slaveholders termed "manners" were more likely than other children to avoid punishment and to elicit favors from owners. Consequently, Mary Thompson learned as a young girl in Alabama to behave in ways that rewarded her master and mistress for treating her well. "If dey treated me right, I tried to do right," she said. Parents like Mary's taught their children that slavery obligated owners to care for slaves, even as it compelled slaves to do their owners' bidding. Of course, the idea that owners should comport themselves as good masters and mistresses represented an ideal that few if any slaveholders lived up to, but the principle allowed slaves at least to stake a claim to humane living and working conditions for themselves and their children. Slaves on St. Helena Island voiced in song the possible consequences for owners who did not uphold their end of the paternalistic bargain: "If you treat me good I'll stay 'till de Judgment day, But if you treat me bad, I'll sho' to run away."[19]

OWNERS recognized the important role that parents and other relatives played in teaching a child how to be a slave. Youngsters respected parents and extended kin, which encouraged them to imitate their habits. Slave children raised by and around slaves who pleased their masters and mistresses often grew up to do the same. Mistress Eliza G. Robarts's slave Hannah became a good servant, in Robarts's estimation, much like her Aunt Clarissa, who had raised her. Slave children whose parents did or did not obey owners often followed a similar path. Susan Snow described her mother as mean to everyone. The young girl grew up in Alabama just like her mother, fighting with everyone she knew, black and white, and earning more whippings than any other slave on the place. Former Virginia slave H. C. Bruce observed that children grew up emulating their parents, by and large. The slaves "whom the master trusted and seldom had occasion to even scold for neglect of duty" reared their children to accept the master's bidding. One Alabama overseer blamed all his management problems on one family. "All those children of Jennys are perfect *mules in disposition*," he wrote, charging them with stealing, arson, and the destruction of property by other means.[20]

Most parents, hoping their children would learn to avoid the harsh repercussions that followed defiance of authority, taught their sons and daughters the intricacies of plantation etiquette as they demonstrated job skills. Many of the boys and girls who as infants had been taken from their mother and placed under the supervision of a caretaker or left in the slave quarter alone while the mother worked were now returned to a parent's side as helper. "When I got most big enuff to work," former South Carolina slave Melvin Smith explained, my mistress "give me back to my ma." In Alabama, Billie Smith assisted his father in making wash tubs and wagon wheels, and Penny Thompson helped her mother cook by gathering eggs, toting water, "an de lak."[21] The custom pleased mothers and fathers, who preferred the arrangement whereby sons and daughters learned the pace and methods of work under their own jurisdiction rather than under the direction of owners, overseers, or even other slaves.

Appointing a parent as teacher preserved harmony on the estate and carried benefits for owners, who held parents responsible for their children's competence and comportment. Some owners went so far as to organize work around family labor, in which case parents were charged with ensuring that their children carried out any related tasks of which they were capable. This was often the case during wheat harvest, and on cotton plantations children frequently picked cotton or weeded grass near their mother or father. Jesse Williams ran behind his mother and father as they plowed in South Carolina to knock the dirt off the cotton plants.[22] Rice and tobacco planters, by contrast, were less likely to establish field units composed of parents and their youngest children. Even so, some youngsters worked with family members at chores outside the field.

Most planters recognized the benefits that accrued from allowing parents to oversee their children's labor, including no doubt the avoidance of protests that surely would have accompanied the discontinuance of the practice. However, others feared that parents who headed work gangs would establish a less demanding pace if their wives and children had to keep up. In addition, owners sometimes wanted children to receive training in skills that parents had not mastered. Under these circumstances, slaveholders would entrust the instruction of children to another slave whom they deemed dependable. Such a slave was Charity Anderson of Alabama, who taught many youngsters to weave, knit, wash, and iron for her owner's family. She had a long history as a loyal household servant, having begun her career of service as a young girl in her owner's dining room. Owners at times assigned women like Anderson to teach their own daughters how to cook and keep house; the daughters would need to know how to complete these chores in order to supervise slaves properly when they eventually established their own homes.[23]

If parents could not oversee children in the field, owners did not release able-bodied workers from meeting daily work quotas to assume the task but instead assigned youngsters to the care of someone whose work they considered less valuable and less demanding. Elderly workers, when available, often took youngsters in hand and assumed responsibility for their training. Pairing youngsters and older workers to perform chores solved two problems: when energetic children assisted older men and women with their work, the older workers' productivity increased and the youngsters gained a measure of supervision and training. Older slaves worked at a slower pace suitable for inexperienced youngsters, whereas the need to train and supervise children would have slowed so-called prime hands who worked at a faster pace. Because slave children were taught to respect elders, this arrangement worked well, especially if the older workers were grandparents or other relatives. In Alabama, Oliver Bell worked with his grandfather, who taught him to weed corn and cotton and to pull fodder. Skills learned from elderly slaves were not limited to agricultural work. Josephine Bristow's grandmother taught her to weave at a young age in South Carolina. Amos Gadsden, another slave from South Carolina, received training in the yard from "Old Tony." Thomas Goodwater helped his grandmother cook in their owner's Charleston home. This strategy pleased owners by ensuring that "there were no drones" on the plantation, in the words of a former Alabama slaveholder. It placated parents by placing children under the supervision of relatives or at least other slaves.[24]

Sometimes older children taught skills to boys and girls younger than themselves. In Virginia, teams of children who picked worms from tobacco plants often completed this chore on their own, with older children assuming responsibility for instructing younger ones on how to perform the task. Masters or overseers checked from time to time on the quality of the children's work, usually displaying little patience for those who left worms behind. One former slave retained into old age vivid memories of her failure at this task and the punishment for her negligence: "Old Masser . . . picked up a hand full of worms . . . an' stuffed 'em inter my mouth." This achieved the desired effect of having the girl, aged five or six at the time, exercise greater care in inspecting the tobacco plants. In Virginia, the practice of making children bite or eat any worms they left behind on tobacco plants was commonplace, and the children apparently favored biting worms over getting hit. When given a choice, Simon Stokes chose biting worms over receiving three lashes on his bare back. "Yo' could bite right smart quick, and dat wuz all dat dar wuz ter it; but dem lashes done last a pow'full long time," he explained.[25]

Children who learned trades or who trained to work in their owners' homes were more likely to receive job training under the tutelage of adults other than slaves. Annie Wallace's mistresses, dressmakers in Virginia, taught her to sew, weave, and knit so she could assist them in business. Sarah Brown learned to sew from her South Carolina mistress. Little Sallie Reynolds sat by her Alabama mistress "ready to fetch and carry" as her owner pleased. She also helped her mistress gather herbs from the garden.[26]

Overseers' wives also helped train boys and girls for household jobs. In Alabama, the overseer's wife taught the slave girl Irene "how to ac' in de Big House." Annie Stanton learned housekeeping skills—how to set the table, wash the dishes, clean, iron, spin, weave, and make candles—by working in her overseer's house in Alabama.[27] The practice allowed overseers and their families to benefit from a child's labor while the youngster acquired skills that enhanced his or her value to owners, either by expanding the services the slave might render to the owning family and its guests or by increasing the worth of the slave in the marketplace.

The number of children—girls especially—assigned to house service exceeded the number who would practice the occupation in adulthood. On large plantations, owners found it advantageous to train more children to work in their homes than they could possibly hope to use. They could identify easily the most capable and most trustworthy of the youngsters, keep these children at work in their homes, and relegate the rest to the field or other outdoor tasks. Training extra house servants also provided families with waiting maids and butlers for their sons and daughters, who would one day establish homes of their own. Slaveholders preferred house slaves who had been specially trained for the job. These individuals, they believed, developed a "house look," which was "not the acquisition of a day." House service brought slaves into intimate contact with owners and their guests, and girls and boys assigned the work had to master elaborate rituals of racial etiquette. Simply carrying out chores did not satisfy most owners, who insisted on adhering to mannerisms that emphasized the subordination of their slaves. Owners preferred house servants who in their estimation appeared neat, clean, mannerly, and devout.[28]

Houseboys and girls commonly slept and ate in the owner's house. For children who had grown up in the slave quarter, the introduction to housework involved moving from quarter cabin to big house, a change that had the potential to isolate the youngsters from the slave community and leave them dependent on owners for sustenance and knowledge. No doubt the move troubled children and parents, but any anxiety would have been mitigated by the knowledge that other slaves most likely would watch over them. Young house servants usually worked under the supervision of other slaves—frequently female relatives—and answered to them for misbehavior or incompetence in completing chores. In addition, parents insisted that their children visit them in the slave quarter. Emma Howard, sold at age six or seven from Virginia to Alabama in the company of her mother and some of her sisters, experienced her first separation from her mother after she went to work in the planter's Lowndes County home. She saw her mother twice each week when she went to the slave quarter to take a bath; her aunt and one of her sisters worked nearby in the kitchen. Emma's visits to her mother, however infrequent, and her working relationships with other slaves exposed her to the mores and news of the slave community. Former Alabama slave Chock Archie explained that he "was reared in my master's back yard" and "ate in his kitchen," but visited his mother's cabin where he heard "talk about what had happened to the slaves." John Glover of South Carolina worked "round de white folks house," but returned to the slave quarter each night to sleep.[29]

Wherever they worked, owners expected slave children in their middle years to acquire habits of obedience and industriousness. Not content to leave children's instruction solely in the hands of other slaves, owners looked for ways to ensure their appropriate behavior. Many considered religious instruction to be useful in this regard. South Carolina rice planter Robert F. W. Allston bragged that many of his slaves performed "their services for me as a religious duty." Religious education helped justify slavery in the minds of many slaveholders, who believed that Africans and their descendants benefited from the exposure to Christianity that had accompanied their enslavement.[30] Although owners hoped to benefit in practical ways from the religious training they provided to slave children, they presumably also hoped that their young charges would find salvation.

Religious education for children varied significantly from plantation to plantation, but it grew more common in the last two decades before the Civil War, beginning in coastal South Carolina and Georgia and spreading rapidly across the lower South. The change occurred as members of the southern clergy joined the growing ranks of southerners who found support for the South's peculiar institution in biblical passages. Gradually, evangelical ministers eliminated a fear held by southerners in the early days of the republic that slaves might find in Christianity a pathway to temporal freedom. By the mid-1840s, slaveholders no longer doubted the compatibility of Christianity and slavery. In fact, planters came to believe that religious instruction might prove a new means of social control and help stabilize slavery in the South. Many owners began establishing Sunday schools for children on the home plantation or allowing youngsters to attend church alongside adults.[31]

The instructors and content of lessons varied, but most focused more on the needs and convenience of owners than on those of the slave children. A wide variety of people taught children Bible lessons. In some places, clergymen conducted religious classes. Slaveholder James R. Sparkman brought the rector of the Episcopal church to his South Carolina plantation "for the catechetical instruction of all the smaller negroes." On other plantations, the overseer's wife assumed responsibility for "teaching children the catechism, including the ten commandments, the Lord's prayer, &c."[32] More commonly, the mistress or her daughter undertook this assignment, some with greater success and enthusiasm than others. Mary Jones, the wife of a Georgia minister, delighted "in the work of teaching the Negroes," which apparently included catechism lessons. Many other mistresses who held Sunday religious observances simply had the children sing hymns. Even the most conscientious instructors failed to administer consistently to the slaves' spiritual needs. Mary Jones did not reside year-round on any one of her husband's three estates, and the slaves had to adjust to her comings and goings. Although her husband was a minister, he filled in only occasionally during her absence. Even the Episcopal rector limited his visits to one each fortnight from October to June. Slave children usually attended services of short duration. Brief oral services "conducted in a sprightly and animated manner," interspersed with questions and the use of picture cards, fulfilled the "duties of Christian masters" toward children.[33]

All religious instruction by the owning class—whether directed toward children or adults—stressed the importance of obedience and respect for the southern social order. Aaron Ford as a young slave in South Carolina heard sermons admonishing slaves to obey owners and likening heaven to working in God's kitchen. Bob Young's South Carolina owners insisted on the value of his learning to serve others so he would know how to serve the Lord: "If you can't serve your earthly father, how [will you] serve your Heavenly Father?"[34] Owners hoped that slave parents would play a role in the educational process by attending services as observers, then reinforcing the Sunday school lessons throughout the week.

Slave parents generally encouraged their children to profess Christianity, or at least those aspects of the faith that accorded with their own understanding of the spiritual world. Christianity held as much advantage for slaves as it did for their owners. The public ceremony of baptism offered many parents an opportunity to proclaim their willingness to raise children according to Christian precepts. This put pressure on owners to respect slaves' parenting responsibilities and might have made some hesitate to sell children away from their families—particularly mothers—before they matured sufficiently to perform adult work. Of course religious denominations varied in their interpretations of who should or could be baptized; some churches permitted the baptism of catechized adults only, whereas others called for the baptism of children. Whether or not their children were baptized, parents took comfort in knowing that they had committed their sons and daughters to the care of God.[35] Thus, the parents' embrace of Christianity did not represent solely an attempt to gain earthly advantage but rather a genuine effort to find spiritual solace for sorrow and hope for the future.

Slave parents who raised their children as Christians took their responsibilities for teaching Christian doctrine seriously. Mundy Holmes's first memory in South Carolina was of his mother making him memorize the Lord's Prayer. Adele Frost, also of South Carolina, learned her catechism from her grandmother. The slave child Henry Brown lived in fear of hell, for his father, a preacher who occasionally spoke in the white church, made it sound real to the child.[36]

Whatever the denomination, slaveholders granted or withheld permission for church attendance, but owners who wished to govern their slaves' religious experiences found their efforts thwarted by the slaves' use of a variety of strategies to worship as they pleased. Parents recognized that biblical passages and Christian doctrine could be cited in ways favorable to slaves, and they often shared with their children interpretations of Bible passages or sermons that differed from those provided by owners. Some slaves even posited that the Bible consisted of two parts: one for whites and another for blacks. Youngsters absorbed this lesson by listening to their parents' explanations of scripture and comparing them with those of their owners. The situation at times proved frustrating to owners, who might end up arguing with slaves about mundane affairs through references to specific passages of scripture. When one slaveholder directed his slave to eat quickly, the bondsman quoted a Bible passage urging anyone engaged in a task to carry it out to the fullest extent possible. Later, when his owner asked this same slave to work harder in the field, he replied by quoting a Bible passage that warned against excessive concern with gaining riches. Slaveholders who counted on religious teachings to help control slaves felt so threatened by interpretations of the Bible that differed from their own that slaves often found it necessary to discuss religion and to pray in secret. Despite owners' efforts to control their slaves' religious observances, slaves learned about Christianity from one another, as well as from representatives of the owning class. [37]

The different teachings and expectations of slaves and slaveholders often placed youngsters in precarious situations. Slave parents insisted that children accept their explanations of the world in which they lived; slaveholders demanded no less. Neither slaveholders nor parents could force slave children to accept their interpretations of scripture, but both attempted to require children's attention to religious matters. Although children often looked forward to religious instruction, some did not. Young children could find it taxing to sit still and pay attention to abstract discussions. Charlie Grant and his companions on a plantation near Mars Bluff, South Carolina, kept quiet during Sunday services only after they were threatened with a whipping. When Charlie's mistress asked during one of the lessons who had made him, the young boy credited his father, not realizing that Miss Lizzie expected him to say God. A white preacher eventually baptized Charlie, but he appeared to learn the catechism only reluctantly.[38] Children like Charlie nevertheless looked forward to Sundays, because they enjoyed eating the cakes or biscuits that were offered after the mistress adjourned

Sunday lessons. They also appreciated the break in the work routine, which taxed the youngsters, in part because they worked for two sets of adults.

SLAVE parents—like most other nineteenth-century people—believed that boys and girls with the physical capacity to do so should work. They staked a claim to their services, and as a result, children found themselves pressed into working for much of the day. At the slave quarters, children performed chores for their families that were no less demanding and in many cases similar to those they carried out on behalf of owners. Children cleaned, cooked, washed clothes, and gathered wood, and they often watched younger siblings or the infants of friends and relatives. They fed chickens and gathered eggs, just as they did for their owners, and they helped garden, the youngest among them scaring birds away from the crops. Along the Atlantic coast, they beat rice for the family table with a mortar and pestle. Youngsters everywhere contributed to their family's diet by fishing and hunting or trapping rabbits and other small game. Children also helped parents complete work assigned by owners. At times they sat up late at night carding wool, cotton, or flax or spinning it into thread so that mothers could meet production quotas while attending to their families' needs.[39] Of course, this labor benefited children directly, unlike the work they completed for their owners.

Throughout the day, children were incorporated into the world the slaves made, as they learned skills valued in the slave quarter but not in the big house. When children helped a parent gather herbs for use in conjuring, their owners neither profited nor approved. Thus, much of a slave child's education and training occurred out of the sight of owners. In the slave cabin and quarter, youngsters participated in cultural patterns that encompassed every aspect of life, material and spiritual. As they grew, children learned to assume a wide range of responsibilities from trapping animals to tending children. Boys in the Haynes family learned from their fathers to carve wood, weave, and make baskets. Girls learned quickly to cook everyday fare by observing their mothers or grandmothers preparing meals in the fireplace, in contrast to girls who spent months or years training to cook in their owners' kitchens. Jobs performed on behalf of slaves did not involve the extensive and formal training associated with those completed on behalf of owners.[40]

Education in the slave quarter centered on patterns of living, rather than on job skills and outward demeanor. Whereas owners concentrated on training children to act in a manner that enhanced an owner's economic worth and social prestige, parents imparted to children ways of living that ensured their individual survival and that of the larger slave community. Some slave activities centered on subsistence, but others concerned less tangible matters. Slave children learned, primarily through observation and imitation but also through verbal instruction, how to hunt, fish, garden, eat, sleep, dance, court, marry, make music, pray, and play. Adult slaves modeled for children attitudes and assumptions about the material and spiritual world. Tom Morris, born in Virginia and relocated to Mississippi, formed ideas about ghosts and magic by listening to his mother's explanations for why noises occurred in the night and observing her reliance on a rabbit's foot worn around her neck to keep spirits away.[41] Not all slaves believed in conjuring, of course, but beliefs and practices related to conjuring survived from one generation to another. When parents provided children with amulets to avoid being hexed, they shared their own trust in and fears of conjuring.

Grandparents or other older adults often played an important role in communicating folkways to a new generation. "De ole folks learn us all a chile orter know," recalled a former Virginia slave whose education at the hands of her grandmother covered preventive health measures and medicinal cures, astronomy, proper methods of butchering, identification of plants and roots, and methods of ensuring good luck. Other information passed on to children by older members of the slave community included when to plant and how to "stop a screench owl from squenching," keep spirits away, read signs to foretell the future, prevent dogs from following a trail, ward off bad luck, and care for a baby.[42]

Even though not all slave children took adults' advice to heart, most children believed adults, particularly when they offered guidance on navigating the confusing and frightening world of the supernatural. Of course, not all directions were consistent. Some slaves taught children to keep a Bible in their cabins or to take other measures to keep spirits away; others told children not to fear them. Alabama slave Solomon Jackson acquired a variety of amulets to protect himself from ghosts, including a hog's tooth and a foot from a rabbit that had hopped over a grave. Stories that circulated in the quarter probably planted ideas of "ha'nts" in his head, some with human form but others more ethereal. He used this information to interpret events in his own life. Solomon's experience fetching water for his mistress from the spring at night rendered the stories credible, in his estimation. "A heap er times I got up to de big house frum de spring wid th' water—hit wouldn' be no more'n a cup full in de bucket," the former slave recalled. Solomon believed that the spirits siphoned the water from the bucket, but the liquid must have sloshed out as the frightened boy ran from the spring to the safety of the house.[43]

As children observed adults interact with one another, they learned how to resolve disputes to ensure order within the slave community. When valuables such as chickens disappeared on one South Carolina cotton plantation, the slave men held court, quizzing the likely suspects, using a Bible or sieve or graveyard dust to ferret out the truth. If the Bible or sieve turned in response to an answer from a man thought innocent, he explained why: he might tell how he passed by a chicken coop on the night of the theft. The graveyard dust worked differently. A slave swore his or her innocence and drank a mixture of the dust and water. Liars supposedly died and went to hell, but innocent people remained unharmed. The men handed out punishments they considered appropriate after they determined guilt.[44]

Parents and other adults taught slave children rules intended to avoid danger and ensure their health and safety. Former slave Fannie Berry expressly remembered her mother teaching her as a young girl not to seek shelter under a tree in a rainstorm if lightning occurred.[45] But slave children grew up in a particularly dangerous world in which owners or overseers might construe even small offenses, a word or a look, as challenging their authority and deserving of harsh punishment. Thus, lessons of survival went beyond the usual admonitions offered by parents everywhere not to play near the creek or tease dogs and included instructions on how to avoid trouble with owners and overseers. Guidance in this area began early and continued unrelentingly, as parents and other adults sought to inculcate behavior that would avert retaliations against children, their parents, or other slaves.

Parental admonitions frequently focused on preventing delinquent behavior that might result in whippings, sale, or other punishment. Martha Showvely's Virginia mother repeatedly told her to mind her own business and avoid meddling in other people's affairs. Lucinda Elder, also of Virginia, "learnt to mind" and to watch her manners. Joseph Sanford's father advised him "to be tractable, and get along with the white people in the best manner I could, and not be saucy." Elizabeth Keckley learned "to triumph over so many difficulties" by displaying a willingness to serve others.[46]

Not all slave children learned the same set of values because slaves did not all agree on what constituted acceptable responses to the conditions of slavery. Slaves who became Christians, for example, raised their children in expectation that they would do the same. Other parents emphasized other belief systems, including conjuring. At times, a father and mother provided contradictory advice. Joseph Sanford, who ended up a fugitive in Canada after fleeing his Virginia home in 1856, had received different advice from his two parents. His father had urged Joseph to cooperate with his owners, but his mother sent him to the big house to snatch salt for her bread. Joseph's fugitive status suggests that he listened more to his mother than to his father. Ben Horry must have learned he could ignore some plantation rules, because he helped his father prepare stolen rice for sale in the local black market.[47]

Despite efforts by slaves to solidify family and community ties through participation in a shared culture, a small number of children came to accept for themselves a role as a member—albeit inferior—of the owning family. This most often occurred among the estimated 5 percent of young slaves who lived in their owners' homes, apart from their mothers and fathers. Abbey Mishow grew up on a rice plantation in South Carolina. Her mother died soon after Abbey's birth, and her mistress raised the little girl. Abbey never experienced life in the slave quarter. She wore clothes that differed from those worn by the children of the plantation's field hands, and she accompanied the owning family on their summer sojourns away from the plantation. She hardly missed her mother at all, she maintained in old age, because her mistress raised her "just like a pet." A slave girl named Anna Humphrey complained of her mother's behavior to her Alabama owners, then accepted their offer to have her live in their home. Anna believed that her mother favored her older sister. Resentful, she rejected the idea that she had interests common to people living in the slave quarter, including her mother. Perhaps after she turned against her mother, other slaves spurned her, giving her little choice in the matter. The young girl became dependent on her white family and years later expressed satisfaction with her situation.[48] Her experience serves as a reminder that parents competed with owners to inculcate in children the values and behaviors they believed appropriate and that parents occasionally lost the contest, despite the advantage of shared intimacy with and love for their children.

Children reacted differently to similar conditions of enslavement, some identifying more with the owning class than others. Eliza Scantling, like Anna, grew up in her owner's home. Reflecting upon her early years, Scantling later said that her mistress had treated her more as a daughter than as a slave. Scantling looked after her mistress's child and came to believe that the youngster left in her care "would rather be wid me than wid her own mother!" Perhaps Scantling set out deliberately to divert the youngster's affections from the child's natural mother to herself, just as the mistress had taken the place of her own mother. The Eliza Scantlings of the South, who took loving care of their owners' children, reinforced the idea in owners' minds that slavery forged a genuinely affectionate bond between slave and slaveholder. But not all slave girls reacted as Eliza had. Many disliked caring for their owners' children. Genia Woodberry objected to the job expressly because she had to live in the big house, apart from her parents. At night Genia rocked the owner's children to sleep while singing them a lullaby. She missed her own mother at this time of day, but she could not show it because her owners objected to any display of her true emotions. Genia did not blame her unhappiness on the treatment she received from her mistress: "Dere ain' nobody ne'er been no better den Miss Susan was to me." Rather, her separation from her mother appears to have accounted for her melancholy.[49]

THROUGHOUT much of the day, slave children found themselves pressed by two sets of adults, slave and free, to meet two different sets of expectations. When they had time for play, children sought to express their own interests. Whereas adults wanted children to learn skills and attitudes necessary to the smooth functioning of the plantation or its slave community, children in their middle years preferred playing. Opportunities for play depended on the level of chores children had to perform. Some former slaves recalled a multitude of games, but others remembered only work. Katherine Eppes of Alabama engaged in "a mighty lot of playin'." One game, "Sail away Rauley," involved holding hands and spinning "in a ring, gittin' faster an' faster an' dem what fell down was outa de game." Former Virginia slave Ben Brown, on the other hand, said, "It wuz jus work, eat an sleep foh most of us, dere wuz no time foh play." Slaves often sang, told stories, or played after work, but Ben usually fell asleep without engaging in these activities. Exhaustion from heavy work responsibilities also prevented Frank Ziegler from playing. His chores left him too tired for anything but sleep.[50]

Although they varied in the amount of time they believed appropriately spent in play, slaveholders and parents generally found it desirable to accommodate the wishes of children for games and other pleasurable activities, but only after they completed their chores. Owners objected if they saw children playing during working hours, and assigned extra jobs to any youngsters found idle. This was particularly true during the busy season. Gus Askew, for example, had no time for play during cotton picking time in Alabama.[51] As they grew older and took on greater work responsibilities, children found their opportunities for recreation diminishing. Many played only in the evening or on special holidays.

In their middle years, black children continued to play with white companions, but they also enjoyed relationships with other slave children and parents. The presence of black playmates, whether large or small, reduced the reliance of slave children on the white family—young masters and misses in particular—for pleasurable activities that provided a respite from harsh lives. Ring games, popular with slaves, incorporated children of all ages. Adults liked to join the children, and many ring games, enjoyed in the evening or on holidays, attracted participants of more than one generation. Adult slaves grabbed opportunities for making life pleasurable for children, even striving to make work agreeable. Sabe Rutledge described breaking oxen to the plow as "fun for us boys."[52]

When they had time, adults entertained children with songs, stories, and riddles. Tales of slave tricksters, whether told to break up the monotony of chores or in the hours after parents put away their working implements, served to educate slaves about how to use guile to circumscribe the slave system, for they described how the weak and powerless, man or beast, might overcome the strong and powerful. Annie Reed's mother told the Alabama slave girl about how Brer Rabbit employed subterfuge in order to avoid work, consume butter belonging to others, and avoid punishment for his misdeeds. He grunted to make people think he was working, then lied about an emergency at home, which gave him an excuse to leave the work site long enough to consume the butter Sister Fox had churned for dinner. While the other animals debated how to punish the culprit, Brer Rabbit begged to be thrown into a fire, rather than in a brier patch. Intending to inflict the worst possible penalty, his associates "th'owed him in de brierpatch," only to watch the sly rabbit scoot up the hill laughing and saying, "Thank you . . . I was bred and born in uh brierpatch!" At times, the trickster stood for the master, in which case the tale illustrated how a slave might survive under a capricious slaveowner. Stories also informed children about the past. Henry Brown learned of his grandparents' enslavement in Africa, their passage across the Atlantic, and the slave pen on Sullivan's Island where they awaited sale through their recounting of the story.[53] The lessons embedded in the tales reinforced behaviors taught children in more overt ways.

Slaves of all ages savored tales as entertainment. Bigger boys and girls delighted in telling stories themselves, especially scary ones. Frightening younger children became part of the fun. Young slaves "would gather 'round and tell ha'nt tales" until they became too "scared to go home in the dark," recalled one former Alabama slave. The wooden screw that was used to press cotton into bales would turn in the wind, its creaking noise creating an eerie atmosphere: "We older children would run and make out we thought it was the spirits. We knowed better but the little children was afraid." The stories heard by a young Virginia boy concerning "hants and speerits an devils" scared him so that he "ran to bed an' covered mah head." Other former slaves also recalled ghosts and spirits as common themes of stories; the frightening specters of "Raw Head" and "Bloody Bones" still figured frequently in tales told by adults to make children mind, as they had in earlier years, only now they seemed less fearsome and more entertaining.[54]

Some types of play exposed children to danger or reflected their anxieties about the perils they confronted in life. Knives held an attraction for children; Louis Hughes cut off his brother's finger while the two played with one in Virginia. Alice Marshall recalled a ring game that required running with a knife: "One chile would git outside de circle an' slip a knife to someone in de circle. When dat person feel de knife in his hand, he tek out an' run an' de person on his right would chase him an' ketch him." Children on other plantations played a similar game without the knife. Alice's mother probably served as inspiration for the innovations added by Alice and her playmates. Each Sunday, the slave woman slipped into the owner's storehouse with a knife to cut off a piece of meat, which she served to her family. Alice knew of this, and the ring game probably allowed her and the other children an opportunity to act out their fears surrounding the theft of meat and its surreptitious consumption. Other games played by children reflected anxieties about other aspects of slave life. Children played "Hide the Switch" on some plantations, surely in reaction to the whippings they witnessed or heard about. Like children in other times and places, slave boys and girls acted out real-life events through games of make-believe in which they assumed the identities of adults around them.[55]

Both slaveholders and adult slaves tried to channel children's energies and desire for play in ways that enhanced their own interests. Mistresses often encouraged little girls to sew by having them fashion dolls or clothing for their dolls. One girl, who practiced sewing by making pants from scraps of leftover material for her "dolls" made of forked sticks, also practiced knitting for her mistress by using broom straws. Her mistress ultimately expected to benefit from the girl's improved sewing and knitting skills. In contrast, a slave's learning to swim did not benefit owners. Swimming, in fact, increased a slave's chance of escape in adulthood, because men and dogs found it difficult to track a slave who could traverse waterways. Some owners actively discouraged slaves from swimming, and others only tolerated it. The latter probably included owners who recognized the futility of attempting to prevent slaves from entering the creeks, rivers, and lakes found throughout the South. Slave parents presumably encouraged their children to learn how to swim, both to protect the child from drowning and because swimming represented a skill that slaves found useful in adulthood.[56] When they played, children gave little thought to who would ultimately benefit from their games but judged activities according to the pleasure they brought.

In their middle years, children assimilated the advice and admonitions of adults and discovered through punishments and rewards the bounds of behavior appropriate to particular situations. In doing so, they began to work out their own understanding of what it meant to be born in bondage. Their interactions with slaveholders and slaves taught them that they must learn to work and serve to their owners' satisfaction, but they also had to work in the quarter to satisfy parents. Life in the slave quarter was constrained by conditions of oppression, just as it was in the owners' fields and homes, but children found opportunities to express themselves in the quarter that expanded beyond the role of slave defined for them by their owners. Their families helped them learn what it meant to be a man or a woman, a parent or a child, a teacher or a playmate, as much as a slave. Children's engaging in play demonstrated that slavery had not robbed them of a desire for pleasure and that they maintained the will to make a world for themselves even as they shouldered the burdens of enslavement. Although slaveholders and slaves alike expected children to assume heavy responsibilities, occasionally they outwitted all the adults who attempted to manage them and helped to make the slave quarter a place of joy as well as sorrow.

5

❧

TO THE FIELD

As a young boy in Alabama, the slave Henry prepared and scattered manure; cleared brush left behind by tree trimmers; helped plant corn, cotton, and peas; and ran errands. Eight years later in 1854, the labors of the more mature Henry involved hauling manure; cutting trees; plowing; and digging holes for planting watermelons. Henry moved in the spring of that year from his master's home estate to one of his outlying plantations known as the "Bohannon place." He returned "home" each fall after that to help with butchering and once in 1856 to paint his owner's house, but otherwise Henry achieved the anonymity of a field hand, his individuality obscured in his owner's records—the only known source for learning about Henry's life—by the use of such phrases as "hoeing cotton with all hands at Bohannon place." Yard jobs formerly performed by Henry in his youth fell to other slaves. Adult men picked up some of the chores; younger boys performed the others. "Little John" ran errands and helped rake and spread manure, plant, and clear brush. In November of 1856, Henry began building a slave cabin on the outlying estate, one he conceivably hoped to occupy with a wife and children.[1]

Like Henry, other slave boys gradually assumed more demanding work for their owners as they grew to manhood. Girls also experienced the shift from less demanding yard or household chores to field work as they grew older. Julia Rush of St. Simons Island began service to her master and mistress as a playmate to one of their daughters. She later worked in the kitchen, and still later, she went to the field. She eventually learned to plow better than any man she knew.[2]

By the age of seven or eight, boys and girls could perform a variety of chores competently, and by age ten or twelve, most were capable of working alongside adults in the field. One former Alabama slave explained that youths were trained to "do anything dat come to han'." A former Virginia slave boasted of her capabilities at the age of ten: "I could do any kind o' house wuck an' spin an' weave ter boot." When she approached the same age, Minerva Meadows, who grew up in Alabama, already knew how to help in the fields, clear new ground, burn brush, tote water, serve in her owner's dining room, and perform other household chores.[3] Owners watched closely the physical development of children between the ages of eight and twelve, knowing that during these years the majority of boys and girls would gain the strength, endurance, dexterity, and knowledge necessary for completing difficult work. They demanded that children perform whatever chores they could and expected youths to cultivate the cash crop at the earliest possible time.

Slaves wanted to forestall their owners' design to place their sons and daughters in the field at young ages. Slave families engaged in a variety of economic activities intended to make their lives more bearable. They peddled rice, corn, honey, chickens, eggs, produce, and other petty items, both with and without their owners' approval. During her brief stay on her husband's Georgia plantations, Fanny Kemble Butler became aware that slaves supplemented their diets and also earned small sums of cash by trapping the fowls found in abundance on the island, by raising poultry, and by selling moss—collected from trees and used for stuffing mattresses, sofas, and other furnishings—to a storekeeper in the nearby town of Darien. Slave carpenters built boats, which they sold to neighboring planters, earning as much as sixty dollars for each. Butler's slaves also trapped animals and sold the furs. They earned cash by clearing paths and driveways, and some slaves "bartered away the cooper's wares, tubs, piggins, etc., made on the estate." Boys and girls helped with such activities, which provided slaves a small measure of independence from their owners and defined the slave family's interests as different from those of the owner. This explains why

Pierce Butler and his overseer—along with other slaveholders—attempted to minimize these activities. In 1839, Butler's slaves complained that they could not keep pigs or cows or travel to town easily, as in earlier days, suggesting that their owner had succeeded in reducing such events if not in stamping them out.[4]

As youths grew older and became more capable of completing complex tasks, their assistance was more valuable to parents as well as to owners. Older sons and daughters supplied much of the food that made its way to the slave family's table, watched younger siblings, manufactured cloth and clothing, and assisted with cleaning and laundering. Those youths who worked all day in their owners' fields or kitchens, however, had less time to assist their families. In addition, they suffered physically and were subjected to the discipline of overseers once they began working as adult hands. Children old enough to work regularly at cultivating the cash crop could not expect to escape the harsh whippings and other corporal punishments meted out to adults. As valuable workers, they could command high prices in the slave market, which further worried parents—and their children.

Children who did not go to the field were seldom scrutinized directly by owners during the day, a situation that created opportunities for them to contribute to their family's welfare through means that owners found objectionable. Many made substantial contributions to the family table through the appropriation of forbidden foods, despite efforts by owners to halt the practice. Children sent to work in the big house and ostensibly supervised by household slaves returned to the cabin with pockets full of salt or whatever else lay at hand. Henry Baker's Alabama mistress banned the construction of pockets in boys' breeches in an attempt to thwart theft, and masters arranged for fences to be built around fruit trees and even placed orchards at a distance from the slave quarters. Still, the appropriation of foodstuffs continued. Orchards were especially hard hit by young thieves, who sometimes raided peach, apple, and plum trees before the fruit even had a chance to ripen. Former slave Levi Pollard recalled eating many pears, despite his master's prohibition. "I climb de tree at night an eat 'em up dare," the adult Pollard later admitted. Carter Jackson estimated that he pilfered two or three chickens each week in his youth, deterred neither by whippings nor by scoldings from his master. Henry Johnson of Virginia concocted a successful scheme to lure one of his owner's turkeys to his cabin. After breaking its neck, he reported its death to his mistress, who asked him to dispose of the carcass, as he had supposed she would. "Dat night we cooked him, and didn't we eat somethin' good," Johnson later bragged. If chickens and turkeys proved too troublesome for youngsters to handle surreptitiously, eggs were not so difficult to conceal. Tom Morris occasionally slipped an egg to his mother, who cooked it without detection in the owner's kitchen. Through such subsistence activities, children helped to define the slave family as an economic unit and to decrease the family's dependence on owners for survival.[5] Slaves stood to gain by prolonging childhood for youths. Slaveholders wanted to shorten it as much as possible.

The question was not whether enslaved youths would end up working in their owners' fields. The overwhelming majority would do so. Only a small number of slaves working on large plantations where slaves specialized in different types of jobs would be assigned permanently to other work, in their owner's home perhaps or as skilled carpenters or seamstresses elsewhere on the plantation. Rather, the question was when youths would stop carrying out children's chores and begin the work of an adult hand.

As children grew capable of working in the crop, owners might have forced them into the field with a whip, but slaveholders understood this would bring protests from the adult work force and alienate the children. Instead, they devised ways of extracting more work from children as they grew older, so that the transition to adult labor occurred gradually as boys and girls became physically capable of performing more taxing duties and dependable enough to see them through to completion. Youngsters barely past infancy could gather wood chips for fires, but it took a bit more strength and agility to balance a pail on the head over any distance. Tending livestock required more responsibility on the part of a child than gathering wood or hauling water, and many older youths (mostly boys but also some girls) assumed this job one or two years before taking on field work. In a typical sequence, a slave boy around the age of seven or eight might first tend cows, next join the field hands as a water carrier between the ages of eight and ten, and finally begin wielding a hoe between the ages of ten and twelve. Levi Pollard experienced these changes, eventually learning to plow, first with one horse, then with two.[6]

Slaveholders were willing for children to assume adult work gradually, in part because older children made important economic contributions to plantations and farms without going to the field. Some churned butter for sale or for home consumption. Black babies or other slaves probably drank the remaining buttermilk, while owners consumed any butter that was not sold. Other youths helped ensure a crop's success by preparing and scattering manure and other fertilizers. A large number of former slaves interviewed by government agents in the 1930s recalled sweeping or raking the yard and animal barns as youngsters. Some of their sweepings would have made their way into a compost heap for later application to the soil. "A large supply of manures" was "indispensable for successful management," according to John Horry Dent, who cultivated cotton in Alabama. Another planter considered the maintenance of a compost heap so important that he "flogged the chamber maid for emptying the contents of her vessels elsewhere."[7]

The older a boy or girl grew, the more childhood became "filled with duties." Former slaveholders and slaves alike cataloged with regularity a host of children's chores that were both time-consuming and physically taxing to young bodies. "The young," according to one Alabama planter's son, "did nothing . . . except drive cows & calves to their different pastures and pick up and bring wood and chips for their mothers . . . [and] pick cotton in the fall with their mothers." He described this as the work of children no older than age seven.[8] By the time a child reached the age of eight or ten, he or she usually worked throughout the day for much of the year.

On some plantations, older children gained experience working in squads through their assignment to so-called "trash gangs," which operated on the largest plantations. Members of trash gangs performed less arduous work than other field hands and often labored at a slower pace, so they employed elderly workers, pregnant women, new mothers, disabled slaves, and field hands recovering from bouts of illness, in addition to children. Some large slaveholders organized separate children's gangs, which they generally left under the supervision of adult slaves. In summer, a children's gang might prepare and sow the turnip patch, pile and scatter manure, clean the slave quarters, and clear fence corners and ditches. An Alabama contributor to the *Cotton Planter and Soil* recommended employing children's gangs or trash gangs in making hay. Children's gangs could spread the cut hay on the field for curing "as well as the best hands," he thought.[9]

Children's work squads consisted of youngsters working in pairs or in larger groups under the direct supervision of adults or near-adults. On an Alabama plantation near Cahaba, gangs of boys watered trees, shelled corn, dug potatoes, picked peaches, gathered turkey manure, stacked wood, shucked corn for the hogs, and thinned corn by hand. One such gang spent a day in August 1845 "piling brush" and "cutting up limbs for firewood" with the older slave John. Later that month, working under Ned's supervision in an outlying field, the "boys knocked down weeds" all day and into the night. Boys on this plantation performed tasks of similar arduousness and complexity whether they worked with women or men. They assisted women in raking, digging ditches, clearing woods, pulling cotton stalks, and burning brush, and they helped men mark sheep, hoe potatoes, scatter manure and ashes, and shell corn. They worked with both men and women to build embankments and stack newly cut brush and wood.[10]

Children's work crews could include both boys and girls, but in Alabama they usually consisted of boys too young to work regularly in the cotton fields but old enough to carry out a substantial set of chores. One gang included boys from ages seven to ten who worked together "don' fust one thing den anudder." Boys may have worked in separate squads in Alabama and elsewhere, at least in part because girls were more likely to be employed in the big house. Generally, the older the children, the more likely it was that their work would be segregated by gender.[11]

The superiority of girls as cotton pickers may also explain their relative absence in children's work gangs. Curiously, the planter near Cahaba who noted the work of boys never commented on the assignments given to girls. They may have been among the children he listed as picking cotton in the fall of 1855 or fighting the prairie grasses that seemed to inundate the fields in the summer of 1856. Girls frequently went to work in the cotton field at an earlier age than boys, who spent more years working around the yard at odd jobs. Although men eclipsed women as cotton pickers in adulthood, girls proved better cotton pickers than boys until about age sixteen.[12]

Slaveholders held firm notions regarding the types of tasks for which boys and girls should be trained. Although they wanted men and women to be able to work at similar tasks in the field, they instructed boys and girls with the expectation that as men and women they would perform different types of chores during the slack season or when special needs arose. Notions about the appropriate sexual division of labor were ingrained in the minds of slaves as well as slaveholders. One South Carolina smallholder accepted that his family might have to go without milk when almost everyone in the household came down with the measles, leaving no female available to milk the cow. Cyrus, a slave man, had been prevailed upon to attempt the job; but to no one's surprise, he failed in carrying out the task. Inquiries directed at slaves during a sale in Richmond, Virginia, reflected the prospective purchasers' different expectations about the work of men and women: "'Are you a good cook? seamstress? dairymaid?'—this to the women, while the men would be questioned as to their line of work: 'Can you plow? Are you a blacksmith? Have you ever cared for horses?'"[13]

Despite this sexual division of labor, boys and girls often did similar chores and men and women were present at all stages of cultivation, whatever the crop. Amelia Walker did not think it inappropriate that her mother plowed in the field until after emancipation, when to her dismay she "learned" that men and women should not engage in the same type of work. "[I] thought women was 'sposed to work 'long wid men, I did," the former Virginia slave exclaimed. Yet, even though men and women both cleaned the ditches needed for rice cultivation, only men dug the ditches deeper when this became necessary. Men referred to scattering seeds as women's work. During butchering, men and women usually performed separate tasks. Men killed, scraped, cleaned, and sectioned the hogs, whereas women, with the help of some men, rendered lard and made sausages. Older boys more often than girls cared for horses, assisted the blacksmith, and worked in separate children's gangs. Children of both sexes frequently began field work as part of women's gangs, which commonly worked shorter hours, at an easier pace, or at less demanding tasks than men's gangs. On George Walker's Alabama plantation men each day hoed seventy rows, seventy yards long, while women completed only sixty rows. Boys could anticipate the end of labor in these women's gangs and the assumption of at least some of the duties associated with men.[14]

The assignment of tasks to be performed on behalf of owners reflected notions of gender held by the master, mistress, or overseer. Thus, Alabama master Willis P. Bocock considered only girls suited for helping with the laundry; mistress Jane Sexton looked for a girl to take on the job of seamstress. Masters and mistresses hesitated to assign children work deemed inappropriate for their sex even when it was convenient or necessary for them to do so. In fact, they occasionally went to great lengths to conceal such assignments from their neighbors. When the mistress of George Frazier, a waiting boy, insisted that he wear a bonnet outdoors, she may have hoped to preserve his fair complexion, but it is also likely that she thought neighbors would consider a girl more suitable for the role of a mistress's personal servant. Harriet Martineau, who visited the Alabama black belt in 1835, reported another case of cross-gender dressing: a mistress dressed a slave girl in boy's clothing because she thought that friends and acquaintances would consider a boy more suitable for the role of carriage attendant. These examples suggest that southerners held agreed-upon notions of appropriate work roles for male and female slaves, including children, even as some of them violated those standards.[15]

Slaves, too, had firm ideas about gender-appropriate behavior. Mothers and fathers, together with their children, must have decided which children would trap wild game or steal chickens (mostly boys) and which would help cook them for the table (mostly girls). Slaves took action to enforce the gendered division of labor when it was threatened. The slaves on the plantation where George Frazier lived beat him for complying with his mistress's order to wear a bonnet. Such childhood experiences helped slave youths define their future roles as men and women.

DESPITE such gendered notions of work, children of both sexes eventually cultivated crops, and most were introduced to agricultural routines a year or more before they became regular field hands. Each adult working squad was assigned a water carrier, whose presence reduced the need for breaks in the work routine and kept plantation operations running smoothly. Henry Baker "toted watuh tuh de plow han's" from the ages of seven to ten. During the busy season, children carried dinner to the field so that slaves could maintain a steady pace of work. At Black's Bluff in Alabama, Charlie Johnson, along with the plantation's other slave children, toted food to the hands in the field, including his mother, father, thirteen brothers and sisters, and other cotton pickers, who did not stop work but ate their corn pone as they moved up and down the cotton rows. Children assigned to this task learned the names of the various fields and the shortest routes to and from the work site, in preparation for the time when they would join the hands as full-time workers. If they filched part of the food on the way, as sometimes happened, owners knew that irate parents and other slaves would punish the children or report the incident to the overseer. Members of one youth gang in Alabama who "had eaten the food nearly all up" by the time they arrived in the field managed to get away unpunished—perhaps they disappeared before the hands became aware of the short rations—but each child received a whipping at the end of the day after the adults came in from the field.[16]

Youths made economic contributions through the completion of such jobs, but owners realized their largest profits when both boys and girls engaged in sustained field work. When children began to show signs that they could wield a hoe or handle a plow well enough to join the ranks of the field hands, owners offered a variety of inducements to children and their parents to tempt youngsters into the field. Willis P. Bocock, an Alabama planter, gave fathers a hen for each child put to cultivation. Another slaveholder who traveled throughout Alabama and Mississippi reported similar practices in both states: "Every hand or youth who works in the field has the privilege of raising chickens—they sell them and eggs, or eat them, as they please. They also raise corn and sell the same." In this way, children who began work in the field not only increased the family's food rations but also earned a small amount of cash.[17]

Hoping that hunger would propel some children into taking on adult labor, owners withheld full rations from slave children. Rules for plantation management published in *DeBow's Review* advised that "each person doing any work" should receive double the rations provided "each child at [the] negro-houses." These instructions for plantation managers recommended 1 pound of bacon and $\frac{1}{2}$ peck of corn meal each week for children between ages two and ten. Once children began working alongside adults, the suggested portion more than doubled to $2\frac{1}{2}$ pounds of bacon and $1\frac{1}{2}$ pecks of corn meal. Discussions of food allotments in the *Southern Cultivator* and other agricultural journals regularly distinguished between slaves "large enough to go to the fields to work" and those too small to do so. A widely circulated article by "Tattler" observed that owners commonly provided "each hand that labors, whether man, woman, or child," with equal rations. Thus, on many plantations, children—"water carriers and all"—received the same rations as more productive adults if they regularly contributed their labor to the field in any capacity. Those who did not could end up "half-famished."[18]

The need of growing bodies for more food pressured children into assuming adult work as early as possible, but when they yielded to their owners' wishes and went to the field, they did so to reap benefits for their families or to fill their hungry bellies—not to further their owners' interests. Parents who wanted to prolong their youngsters' childhood by withholding them from the field confronted this dilemma: they could spare a son or daughter from taxing labor only by denying nourishment to that child or to other family members who would need to stretch their own rations to satisfy the child's increasing appetite. Some parents managed to solve this quandary by finding additional sources of food for their families. In fact, the inadequacy of rations for growing children helps explain why so many slave families persisted in gardening, hunting, trapping, fishing, and stealing, even when owners seemingly provided adequate rations or when they had little time for these activities. Through their efforts to provide for their own subsistence, slave families might delay a child's initiation into adulthood. The more slaves engaged in economic activities of their own, the more independence they might gain. Few slaves managed to attain enough economic clout to keep sons or daughters out of the field for long, however. Most found it difficult to do so for only a short period.

Families able to secure food for older youths still might not have other material goods needed by sons and daughters. Clothing served as another incentive by owners to get children into the field. The youngest slaves on the plantation went about "scantily clad." A former Alabama slave stated that she and the other young children went "naked 'til we was big enough to work." All little boys and girls wore one-piece garments that were similarly, but not identically, constructed. Boys wore "shirt-tails" made of home-spun or purchased cloth, usually a plainly woven, coarse cotton fabric known as osnaburg. These fell from the shoulders to below the knees; they resembled the shirts worn by slave men and were so ubiquitous that former slaves sometimes used the term "shirt-tail boy" or "shirt-tail fellow" to de-note a child's age or stage of development. Little girls wore similarly styled garments—one-piece costumes seamed at the shoulders, which they re-ferred to as "shifts" or "shimmys" or "dresses." Shifts fell below the knee, as did shirt-tails. Many shifts were made of the same type of homespun or purchased cloth, though girl's clothing was more often patterned and color-ful. Some girls wore dresses cut from durable calicos or, in the summer, lightweight cotton fabrics such as checkered ginghams.[19]

Youngsters of both sexes often suffered through a spell of cold weather before their owners got around to clothing them for the winter, because planters provided clothes to working hands first, children afterward. Gen-erally, the more involved slaveowners became in the market economy, the more they relied on purchasing cloth or clothing for their slaves. In many cases, an owner's ability to purchase slave clothing depended on the har-vest and on market conditions for the crop. This meant that slaves could not count on receiving their winter cloth or allotment of clothes until late fall or early winter. Alabama overseer William Graham began distributing "warm clothing and shoes" to adults on the fifteenth of November, but he did not even purchase "a bolt of yard cloth for the children's clothing" until the following day. Still, the children did not receive their new clothes right away, for the fabric needed to be cut and sewn into garments, and he ran short of material and had to return to town for more. Even after waiting for and finally receiving their clothing, the children might not be adequately clothed to protect them from the weather. Alabama planter John Chappell in 1862 paid more than three times as much to clothe an adult hand as he did a child. Few owners distributed shoes to children who did not work in the field. Most youngsters had to make do with moccasins their fathers fashioned from animal hides, or even with rags they wrapped around their feet. Former slave Susan Calder dreaded doing errands barefooted in cold weather. "How you going to send me out wid no shoe, and it cold?" she once asked her mother. Susan's master, who overheard the child's lament, was moved to provide her with shoes, but most other children found their owners unsympathetic to their needs.[20]

The indifference of some owners to slave children's need for clothing was sufficiently embarrassing to apologists for the southern slave system that some individuals felt compelled to remind slaveholders publicly of their obligation to clothe children. One Virginia planter in the pages of the *Farmers' Register* insisted that "the youngest negro child on your farm should be clothed." Some states passed laws requiring owners to clothe their slaves adequately. South Carolina had such a law on the books as early as 1740, but others did not follow until the late antebellum period. Georgia enacted similar legislation in 1857. An Alabama law of 1852 required masters to clothe slaves properly, but owners violated this law with impunity. Because many slaveowners did not fulfill their obligations to clothe children, slave parents struggled to keep sons and daughters clean, warm, and dry.[21] Mothers on one Alabama plantation resorted to dressing children in old "gunny sacks wid holes cut for our head and arms," while they washed their child's only garment and waited for it to dry. For this reason, slave parents contemplating the approach of cold weather thought long and hard before deciding to resist their owners' efforts to place children in the field, especially if owners promised they could perform less demanding labor than regular field hands. Isaac, whose first field job in Alabama required him to carry water for the workers, received a shirt, two pairs of "pantaloons," and shoes when his owner distributed clothing that year. Children on this plantation who did not go to the field received "one frock apiece."[22]

Children who worked alongside adults in the field acquired blankets for themselves as well as clothes, which served as a further inducement for them to undertake field work. Mothers also received blankets for children who did not go to the field, but rarely enough for each child in the family to have one of his or her own. Presumably brothers and sisters shared blankets until they were old enough to work in the field and "earn" their own. Those planters who distributed blankets regularly to youngsters often gave them coverings inferior in quality to those provided to working hands. Slave women, frequently working in groups, pieced together scraps of material left over from other sewing projects to make quilts, which supplied extra bedding for the family. Charlie Grant, who spent his days in slavery in the cotton-producing region of South Carolina, explained why: "Dey had a lot of chillun to cover."[23]

Some of the money men earned through extra work went to purchase blankets, cloth for making them, or clothing to keep children warm. Ishrael Massie's father used the money he made growing "extra tobacco" in Virginia to purchase clothing for his family. York Wright, also of Virginia, peddled goods and worked for others for pay when he was not in his owner's field, gaining enough money to acquire substantial property that included tools, a horse and wagon, and provisions for his family. One man enslaved on a South Carolina cotton plantation covered his own feet with tree bark, rather than purchasing shoes for himself with the money he made by working Sundays. He preferred using his cash to buy articles of clothing for his family, who resided on another plantation. Owners complained, sometimes justifiably, that slaves purchased alcohol, tobacco, or even firearms with their money; however, most slaves spent their earnings on clothing, coffee, or other items wanted by spouses and children. James R. Sparkman, a rice planter, noted that most of the money slaves acquired went toward purchasing "comforts and presents to their families," such as food, clothing, cloth, mosquito nets, buckets, sieves, and pocket knives.[24]

Need eventually forced children into the field, but slave families found ways to exercise some discretion in deciding when youngsters began work there. A determined family might succeed in withholding a child from the field, at least for a short while. Perry Sid Jemison shared a double log cabin next to the Cahaba River in Alabama with his father, mother, two brothers, and two sisters. His grandparents, Snooky and Anthony Jemison, were an important presence in his life and also lived in the slave quarter. Through careful conservation and the pooling of their resources, the Jemison family delayed sending young Perry to the fields beyond the age when most children began regular field duties in the region. Jemison stated in his later years that he was "near grown" by the time he donned work clothes and began obtaining rations from the master as a member of the work force.[25]

Perry survived with only one garment, the one-piece shirt-tail worn by boys who had not begun regular field work. His mother laundered it once a week, and while it was drying, Perry probably wrapped himself in one of the "very respectable quilts" his mother fashioned from bits of cloth. At night, he slept on a "common hay mattress" and used the quilt as a bedcover. Because Perry's master withheld food allowances for any children not yet in the field, he shared rations allotted to his mother and grandmother, which his grandmother prepared for him. Perry also ate a variety of other foods, including raccoons, possums, rabbits, fish, and vegetables, which he and his relatives most likely supplied.

Exactly why Perry's family wished to keep him out of the field is not clearly stated in the sparse account he later gave of his life. Slaves worked hard on the plantation, from before daylight to after dark, sometimes seven days a week. Because adults worked such long hours, Perry may have done the greater share of the hunting, fishing, and gardening that provided much of his family's food. Perhaps Perry's parents wanted to protect him from the harsh work regimen in the field. As a young boy, Perry had been seriously injured while playing with his father's scythe, and his parents may have wished to spare the boy from further physical harm. Perry's mother considered the master rigid; her word choice suggests a dispute over plantation policies involving the boy's role on the plantation. The Jemison family undoubtedly had a number of reasons for wanting to keep Perry from the field, and their success in this endeavor—however brief—reflected their determination to control some aspects of their domestic life.

To overcome such resistance, owners often ameliorated the worst aspects of field work for children. Alabama planter James H. Ruffin excused the youths on his two estates from the field for several days when he thought it "too cold for the children to pick." He also arranged for some of the youngest children to start work later in the picking season than the older hands. Young Amy did not begin picking until August 30, 1841, although most hands began picking on the sixteenth of that month.[26] Children who began adult work joined the slaves who kept the slowest pace.

Most children viewed field labor as arduous and undesirable. Mary Thompson counted herself fortunate for having escaped field labor in Alabama by working in her owner's house. Nevertheless, many boys and girls looked forward to appeasing hunger, securing clothing and blankets to protect them from harsh sun and chilling frosts, and identifying with adult slaves, despite the strenuousness of field work. More than seventy years after the fact, former slave Ben Horry of South Carolina vividly recalled the excitement of first donning the pants, coat, and shoes associated with manhood. Ben's attitude was typical of older children whose families could not supply them with food and clothing. Older youths, forced to make a choice between working for their parents or working for their owners, sometimes calculated that they could do better for themselves by working in their owners' fields than around their parents' cabins. The difficulty of field labor soon dampened any enthusiasm, however. Stripped of his job tending calves and assigned to agricultural labor following an infraction of plantation rules, Alabama slave George Young deeply regretted having committed the transgression "when I foun' out how 'twas" in the field.[27]

Some of the children working in their owners' homes found it tempting to try their hand in the field, because life in the big house had its own set of drawbacks. House and yard workers performed less strenuous jobs than field laborers, but they interacted more with their owners, who supervised their activities around the clock. The willingness of some house servants to transfer to other work sites serves as a reminder that all children worked. Youths who made decisions about when to begin field work were not choosing between the alternatives of leisure and labor. Rather, they were calculating which set of chores offered the greatest benefit or cost them the least effort.

Most boys and girls began regular field work as soon as they were able "ter keep up er row." The timing differed, depending not only on the resources of the parents but also on the crop under cultivation. Children on cotton plantations took on field jobs around the age of ten, at least in the late antebellum period, although some girls may have gone to the field earlier to pick cotton. Henry Baker's experience was typical for boys in Alabama; his owner deemed him "big 'nuf tuh 'come a hoe han'" at age ten. When Jean M. Chapron hired a slave family to help pick his cotton in 1840, he expressed confidence that the oldest son, age twelve or thirteen, would prove useful in the field "& very likely . . . the second child." Having hired the family sight unseen, however, he could only hope that the younger children might prove capable of field work.[28]

Youths often reached the age of twelve, or even their mid-teens, before adults trusted them to hoe around tender tobacco shoots. They went to the fields to pick worms from the plants at much younger ages, however. Former slave Nancy Williams was typical in that she began working around tobacco as a regular field hand at about age twelve, but she checked the plants for worms at the age of five or six.[29] Although worming occurred in the field, it was viewed as children's work. Seasonal and requiring little skill, worming did not earn young laborers the extra rations or privileges that went along with the assumption of adult work. Other procedures associated with cultivating tobacco required a degree of dexterity that young children did not possess; therefore, most young children in tobacco regions first inspected plants for worms, graduated to more difficult jobs in the big house and yard, and finally tackled the more skilled tasks associated with tobacco cultivation.

Children generally assumed field duties in rice cultivation later than they

did with cotton and sometimes even tobacco. Robert M. Allan, in an effort
to sell a group of slaves to a rice planter, offered assurances that "the eldest
of the children at 12 . . . will very soon be able 'to take to the field,' and even
now, will be serviceable in picking cotton." Youths frequently reached their
mid- to late teens before joining adults in the rice fields. Most rice planters
expected their hands to work by the task, which they defined as the amount
of work a slave in his or her prime could complete in a day. They assigned
old, young, and impaired slaves less demanding tasks than those completed
by other hands, and these workers became known as three-quarter hands,
half hands, or even quarter hands. But these designations rarely applied to
children younger than fourteen or fifteen, and often quarter hands avoided
work in the rice fields. "I did not know it was *usual* to put quarter-hands in
the field," mistress Susan Cumming complained when she saw Lucy's
name on her overseer's roster of field workers. Nevertheless, some pubescent slaves went to the field because they had attained the necessary
strength and stamina and because owners had succeeded in overcoming
their slaves' objections to changing customary practices. Charles Manigault's use of teenagers in his fields probably reflects the uneven pace at
which individual children grew. In 1849, he rated two fourteen-year-olds
and one twelve-year-old as half hands, but seven youths in this age group
avoided working in rice altogether. Children of ages fifteen and sixteen were
counted as half, three-quarter, or in one case, a prime hand, reflecting their
different abilities. The inability and unwillingness of slaves to work in the
cash crop until their mid- or even late teens helps explain why rice planters
complained of having so many "idle" slaves living at their expense. At Rose
Hill, Nathaniel Heyward's South Carolina rice plantation, only 42 percent
of the slaves worked in the field. One planter from the Colletin District of
South Carolina lamented that "in order to have 25 full hands one must be
at the cost of 50 negroes."[30]

Many slave children throughout the South found their earliest introduction to agricultural labor as human scarecrows, sent to the fields to keep
birds from demolishing grain crops intended for market or for home consumption. Henry Murray of Alabama joined another slave in blowing horns
and ringing bells to keep birds out of the rice, rye, and wheat.[31] Children
also pulled weeds from among corn stalks and, in the prairie lands of the
Alabama black belt, battled the grass that unceasingly pushed its way
through the soil. Along the coast, children thrashed rice and loaded ships
bound for market with the grain. Boys and girls also helped harvest Virginia's wheat. Men with scythes and cradles went ahead to cut, and women

followed to rake and bind the grain. The youngsters stacked the sheaves or helped rake and bind if the woman's pace fell behind that of the man.

All of this was children's work and did not bring youngsters the benefits associated with adult labor. On plantations and farms devoted exclusively to grain, many youths waited until their mid- to late teens to don the work shirts, pants or skirts, kerchiefs or hats that symbolized a working hand because the more difficult aspects of wheat harvests greatly taxed the slaves' health. Planters had to pay extra attention to their slaves' diets during harvest, furnishing them with special foods and drinks believed to maintain strength and stamina. A "harvest drink," consisting perhaps of water, vinegar, molasses, and ginger, was "carried to the field daily in a cart and moved about after the hands," who drank it periodically in place of water. Children kept busy in the wheat fields by furnishing older hands with cups of the brew, but they avoided the most strenuous tasks associated with the wheat harvest until they were nearly grown.[32]

Whatever the crop, strength and dexterity counted for more than age in determining when youngsters began field work. Boys and girls of small stature or with disabilities might avoid field work altogether, or at least delay assumption of it. On the other hand, children whose physical development occurred prematurely began field work early. Eliza Scantling began plowing on her owner's rice plantation while still a girl, because she was large for her age. Silas Jackson of Virginia, in an interview conducted many years later, recalled: "I was a large boy for my age, when I was nine years of age my task began." At ten, Walter Calloway already "was makin' a reg'lar han' 'hin' de plow" in Alabama. In Virginia, West Turner, who "was big an' strong for [his] age," began working in the field at age seven or eight. Unable to reach the handles of a plow, West learned "to stick my head under de cross bar an' wrap my arms roun' de sides whilst another boy led de mule." West's work burden did not end when he left the field for the day. Each night, his owner expected all the slaves to pick seeds from the amount of cotton that would fill one of their shoes. West had to work longer than other boys and girls because his shoes were larger than theirs. He found this so upsetting that he wrapped his feet in rags each night, hoping to stunt their growth. West's experience was not unusual. When children worked in the fields, they also joined the older slaves in completing other chores carried out at night or during the off-season. Martha King began working in the weaving room as well as in the cotton field at age ten.[33]

The age at which children began regular field work depended not only on the parents' resources, the type of crop grown, and the child's physical development, but also on the owner's perceived labor needs. A shortage of labor that threatened financial ruin could upset normal routines and send a young child to the field, as owners desperately tried to turn the situation around. Left short-handed in the field by the deaths of two of his best hands and the disappearance of five others into the woods, Alabama planter Jean M. Chapron instructed his overseer to put "all the little Folks that we have that can Pick" in the field, rather than jeopardize the crop. At the other extreme, an abundant crop combined with high prices also enticed planters and overseers to press very young children into field labor. Two or more children could work together to perform tasks that would prove too difficult for one. George White of Virginia described the method he and his brothers devised to break up ground: "Two would get in front of de plow . . . an' pull while de others would get behind to hold de plow." Jim Allen's owner paired him with a girl in Alabama "to mek one han'" capable of "carryin' one row." The situation in which overseers taxed youngsters beyond their physical endurance worried the editor of a popular agricultural journal, who reminded overseers that they should take into account "inequalities" when assigning tasks, including those expressed by differences in age.[34]

The need for labor in the cotton-producing South affected the timing of slave children's introduction to adult work not only in newly settled regions but also in the older sections of the South. When cotton prices ran high and labor grew scarce in Alabama and other parts of the lower South, the search for new workers extended beyond nearby quarters into Virginia and the rest of the upper South, where stagnant or declining markets for tobacco or wheat created a surplus of labor. Many youths from Virginia, South Carolina, Georgia, and other older seaboard states encountered their first sustained field work as a result of increased cotton cultivation in Alabama and other faraway places. Some began work in the field after they were sold as cotton hands, but others took on new jobs at home. Planters who sold or sent workers to the expanding "Cotton Kingdom" found it necessary to carry out farming operations with fewer workers at home. Under such circumstances, younger slaves might be recruited to take the place of departed workers. Following the transfer of fifteen hands in 1835 and 1836 from his estate in King George County, Virginia, to the Alabama black belt, one planter added a new category to his meticulously kept inventory of slave occupations: "Boys at work." They consisted of John, a nine-year-old carpenter; Jerry and Edward, nine-year-old crop hands; George, a seven-year-old crop hand; and John William, an eight-year-old "at the mill." In

previous inventories, children under ten had been listed separately from the
other slaves, without occupations.[35]

MOST slave youths ended up working in the field, but other jobs were
available to selected slaves. Owners with sizeable slaveholdings required
some slaves to perform personal or household services for the owning family and its guests, many of which called for physical maturity or elaborate
training. These jobs were often filled by youths who began work in the big
house at a young age and remained there while they grew older. As they
proved themselves capable, they took on more challenging tasks until eventually they became quite adept at cooking, waiting on family members, or
performing other specialized jobs. As a young girl in Alabama, Nicey Pugh
cleaned in the big house and helped her grandmother feed the other slaves.
When she grew older, she assumed responsibility for washing the "milk
things" and with help from another girl drove the cows from the pasture.
Nicey drew water from the well for the cistern under the dairy, gathered
eggs, and picked peaches. She also picked burrs out of the wool, washed
and spread it on the grass to dry, carded wool and cotton, and spun both
into thread. Over time, Nicey's chores became more complex and so extensive that she worked into the night to complete them.[36]

Housework performed by older girls such as Nicey could be taxing, even
dangerous. Doing the laundry required heavy lifting, for example, and exposed workers to hot water, harsh soaps, and bleaches. Consequently, only
"the largest girls" and women engaged in it.[37] Generally, a child's transition
into more difficult house jobs did not create the same tension between
slaves and slaveholders as did the introduction to field labor. For one thing,
the children and their parents were accustomed already to the rhythm and
nature of the work. In addition, owners found it difficult if not dangerous to
keep children in a household occupation if they preferred outside work.
Disgruntled slaves often performed poorly, deliberately or unintentionally.
Property damage could result, as well as harm to the owning family. This
situation gave a few slave youths some discretion in the types of jobs they
performed, although only on large plantations and only when they wished
to leave the house for the field.

Wealthier planters (particularly those along the rice coast) arranged for a
small number of slave children—those deemed especially trustworthy and
talented—to receive extensive instruction for specialized occupations by ap-
prenticing them or sending them to schools in urban centers such as

Charleston. This training often began about the time the youth otherwise would have begun field work. Occupations for boys requiring elaborate training included that of "gentleman's servant." Robert Allston sent four boys to Charleston for lessons on the violin. Girls attended schools that taught them how to sew fancy clothes, prepare superfine pastries, or dress the mistress's hair. Training for jobs that brought children into contact with owners or their guests could take years to complete, and it could begin before the child reached his or her teenage years. Many valets began their careers of service as young houseboys who brushed flies from the dinner table, then took on additional responsibilities as they grew older.[38]

The cost of elaborate training meant that only older youths or adults who were drawn to an occupation and likely to stick with it were trained for the position. Men and women who taught valuable skills to slave children belonging to others expected compensation for their services, especially if they operated a business establishment or a school. When family members or neighbors taught skills to slave children, disputes could arise about whether the trainers deserved fees for their services or whether they should pay wages for the work the children performed during the period of instruction. The planter Edward Carrington Cabell took slave children from his family's estate in Virginia to his home in Florida, where he put them to work. When his parents tried to charge him for the use of the children, he insisted that the training they received represented a fair exchange for their labor. "They have been greatly improved by my wife" who taught them housekeeping skills, he argued.[39] Even if no fee was paid, the owner who arranged for the child's education lost the labor that would have been available otherwise. Consequently, owners did not make decisions lightly about which slaves were to receive elaborate instruction.

Owners had the final say as to which children learned what skills, but overseers, parents, and children attempted to influence the decision, sometimes successfully. When his South Carolina overseer tried to force Jacob Stroyer to undertake work in the field, the slave boy appealed to his mistress, who agreed to let him train as a carpenter rather than as a field hand. She justified the decision with her belief that Jacob would work harder in a job he liked. Nonetheless, the overseer succeeded in putting the youth in the field during the mistress's absence from the plantation.[40] Owners considered the advice of overseers because they understood the needs of the crop. They took the wishes of parents and other adult slaves into consideration because they relied upon them to cooperate in the workplace and to train the youngsters. Of course, they also depended on children to cooperate with slave instructors and to carry out the occupation satisfactorily once they learned the trade.

Children interested in mastering particular skills made better pupils than those who were forced to engage in an unwanted occupation, as Jacob's mistress understood, and on occasion a child's interests and talents became the deciding factor in whether he or she gained certain competencies. Children even taught themselves independently skills they wished to know. One mother admonished her son for attempting to learn how to repair clocks by taking apart a broken one that had been discarded by his owners: "Your marster aint said you can made a clock 'tick-tock,' and you can't do it." The young boy apparently paid no attention, for he learned clock repair well enough to support himself following emancipation. On the other hand, some children could not or would not master certain skills, and they were better left to perform other jobs. Alabama mistress Jane Sexton complained of her inability to teach the slave girl Milley how to sew: "She seems to have no idea whatever of using the needle . . . She will never make a seamstress in my opinion." Instead of continuing Milley's instruction, Sexton sought another girl more inclined toward the occupation. "If you have one you think can be taught, I will take it," she assured the slaveholder who had convinced her to give Milley a try at sewing. Potential purchasers preferred to take slaves for a trial period prior to entering into a final purchase agreement to make sure of the slave's ability to perform special skills.[41]

Only a small number of jobs performed by slaves required reading or writing. Lafeyette Price learned to read in Alabama, "so I could ten' t' business," but his experience was unusual. Slaveholders tended to believe that literacy left slaves ill-suited for work in the fields, and many worried that slaves would use skills of reading and writing to learn of freedom or, even worse, to counterfeit documents that would enable them to escape slavery. Consequently, they severely restricted the number of slaves with access to written materials, with the result that only about 10 percent of slaves ever learned to read. One Virginia slaveholder tried to ensure that Marshall Mack, the boy he dispatched to deliver mail in the neighborhood, never even looked at the addresses on the letters he delivered. The youth carried the letters in a sack, and someone from each household on the route would search through its contents to determine whether any letters were intended for the family.[42]

Slave parents, like owners, did not agree on the need for literacy. Those who could read did not necessarily teach their children. Eliza Evans never learned to read or write despite having a mother and father who could do so. Generally, parents concentrated their energies on improving their children's living conditions or decreasing the time youths spent on their owners' work, rather than on teaching them to read and write. Former Virginia slave Bacchus White observed that reading and writing was "no more use . . . dan de fifth wheel to a wagon." Those slaves who encouraged their children to read and write tended to live on plantations or farms where masters or mistresses did not oppose or even encouraged slave literacy. Alabama slave Dellie Lewis, whose owners routinely allowed house servants to learn to read, listened to her grandchildren read from the "blue-back speller," correcting them as needed. She could not read herself, but she memorized well and could question the children when something they read did not sound right. Encouraged by a father who taught him his letters and a mother who promised him a gold dollar if he learned to read and write, Benjamin Holmes in South Carolina became literate largely on his own by asking other people to teach him "a word or two at a time." Benjamin's lessons occurred in plain view of members of the owning class at the tailor's shop where he worked. Evidently they did not object to his study, for they helped him interpret "all the signs and all the names on the doors."[43]

Except for the small number of slave children in specialized occupations requiring a degree of literacy, opportunities to learn to read declined as children grew older. Many—perhaps most—children in their middle years learned to recite the alphabet and to recognize individual letters, even a few words of one or two syllables. Usually they learned from one of the white children they waited upon, although sometimes black boys and girls shared lessons learned from white children with friends in the quarter, which increased the number of literate slave children beyond that intended by the original instructors. Laws governing the education of slaves were never enforced effectively in the courts and did not apply to children who "played school."[44]

White children who enjoyed sharing their lessons with black playmates saw no reason to keep their activities secret. When they assumed the role of instructor, they imitated the educational methods used by their own teachers. Most of them used as a primer Noah Webster's *Elementary Spelling Book*, popularly known as the "blue-back" speller. This text began with the alphabet, then moved on to syllables and consonant combinations. The author's incorporation of moral and religious precepts into the lessons helped allay owners' worries about allowing slave children to study from the volume.[45]

Most owners who were aware that their children were teaching slave boys and girls the alphabet, even teaching them to read, did nothing to stop the practice. One Virginia planter learned of the practice when he found his son "whipping a little slave boy his own age" and asked for an explanation. "Well, that's what the teacher did to me today 'cause I didn't know my lesson. An he doesn't know it no better'n I do," the youngster replied. The slave boy H. C. Bruce learned to read from the young master, his constant companion, who taught him lessons every day after school. When his Virginia master discovered Bruce's ability, he merely corrected the youth's spelling, even though another member of the owning family (the young master's aunt) vehemently opposed the lessons. Many slaveholders were not concerned about these lessons in part because in this type of play the white children assumed a position superior to that of their black playmates. Moreover, slave children never obtained the same educational opportunities as their white counterparts. Although some slave children attended school alongside the young master or miss, they did not have the teacher's attention, since their presence reflected their status as maids and valets rather than pupils. "I'm educated, but I aint educated in de books," explained a former slave who attended classes in Alabama: "Didn't nobody teach us." Owners expected slaves to "read and write dem cotton rows," by which George Rullerford of Alabama meant that slaves had to concentrate on mastering agricultural tasks.[46]

Slaveholders held conflicting opinions on the need to deny literacy to slaves, and individuals disagreed about the issue even within the same family. This created or constricted opportunities for slave children to learn reading, depending on who held the upper hand. A minority of white southerners considered it a Christian duty to teach slaves to read. Virginia planter Charles Bruce bought primers for the slave children on his plantation and established a Sunday school, where the children not only heard Bible stories and prayed but also studied how to write the letters of the alphabet. The alphabet lessons ended when the old mistress who disapproved of the lessons—possibly Bruce's mother-in-law—bribed each child with cake to give up his or her "New York Primmer." Former slave Levi Pollard, one of the children who yielded to temptation, later reported the incident.[47]

The situation on the Bruce plantation was unusual in that mistresses encouraged slaves to read more often than masters did. Although the southern states restricted or prohibited slave literacy, they did not hold mistresses accountable if they were found to be educating slaves. Fanny Kemble Butler felt no compunction about teaching her waiting boy, Aleck, to read. Because the law deemed wives subordinate members of their husband's household, Fanny probably reasoned that her husband, Pierce, would stand between her and any penalty. Nevertheless, Fanny limited Aleck's instruction to memorizing the letters of the alphabet. By learning these, she hoped he might pick up reading on his own or with the help of other slaves. Only a small number of either masters or mistresses made more concerted efforts to educate their slaves.[48]

As youngsters matured, their work responsibilities absorbed increasing amounts of their time and interfered with their studies. They also grew increasingly aware of the prohibitions against literacy and the punishments some literate slaves suffered. They could be whipped for even looking into a book. The widespread reports of grisly punishments inflicted on slaves who learned to read and write clearly conveyed the wish of white southerners to stamp out slave literacy. Slaves who could read "kep' dat up deir sleeve, dey played dumb lack dey couldn't read a bit tell a'ter surrender," according to former slave Sarah Fitzpatrick. Mary Thompson never learned to read and write as a slave in Alabama for fear that white people would cut off her fingers in retaliation, a fear shared by other slaves. Charley Mitchell recalled that "white folks" in Virginia planned to cut the fingers off an individual who practiced writing his "initials on the barn door with charcoal." A number of former slaves reported whippings by owners for simply holding or looking into a book. No one knew how many punishments of this sort actually occurred, but slave youths and their parents heard about and feared these cruel punishments and acted accordingly.[49]

Most slave youths expressed little desire to learn to read, even when punishment seemed unlikely. Some youngsters found it difficult or undesirable to devote time to lessons. Lucindia Washington in Alabama hid her books "to keep f'um havin' to study." Another Alabama slave, Sarah Fitzpatrick, turned down a chance to learn because she thought it would be "too much trouble." Even those who tried to learn sometimes failed, in part because they had unrealistic expectations. Amy Penny wanted to learn to read so badly that she slept with her books under her head. "But I couldn't learn," the former Virginia slave reported. She attended only four lessons before she abandoned her attempt.[50]

Despite the dangers and difficulties of study, a minority of youths risked punishment to gain a knowledge of reading. Julia Frazier spent her days in Alabama cleaning house, churning, sewing, and cooking. She looked forward to cleaning the library, where she could look at the books as she worked, especially one history book that included pictures of kings, queens, and American Indians. She "used to fly to dat book and hold it lookin' at de pictures whilst I dusted wid de other hand." Her mistress tried to keep her from opening the pages, but Julia's desire for knowledge proved greater than her fear of any whippings her mistress might administer. She exercised caution by avoiding the books when she suspected the mistress might come around to check on her.[51] The practice taught Julia more than history or literacy: she learned that she could do as she pleased, as long as she avoided detection—a lesson that served slaves well in adulthood. Julia acted on her own, demonstrating that at least some slave youths, as they matured, made their own decisions about important matters without consulting owners or parents.

By the time slave children reached adolescence, not many had attained literacy. Most slaves who gained more than a rudimentary understanding of the alphabet did so not as young children but as older youths and adults. Instead, slave children were well trained in the practical arts and ready to enter the adult world of work. When they did so, slave youths gained for themselves better food and clothing, but at the same time the family lost some of its ability to serve as a buffer between the child and his or her owner. Families remained influential, but children who "earned" some of the privileges of adulthood wanted more freedom to choose their own paths. Few chose to defy authority by becoming literate, but the fact that some did probably worried parents. The challenge for slave parents as their children approached adolescence was to rein in their son's or daughter's rebelliousness to ensure that acts of defiance did not go far enough to bring down the wrath of owners upon the youth, the parents, or the larger slave community.

Adolescence held special perils for young slaves. As they took up the hoe and the plow and donned the clothing of adults, teenagers entered a world characterized by hard work, but also by the threat of sale and, for girls, sexual exploitation. Young slave girls entering puberty attracted attention from masters, their sons, and other white men in the neighborhood, and slaves able to perform diverse chores appealed to a wide range of buyers and could easily be sold at high prices if the need for cash or credit arose.

Children of slaves were subject to two authorities: the slave family, backed by the larger slave community, and the owner. Each struggled to establish control over the youngsters.

Pregnancy and childbirth posed a dilemma for the slaveholder. Excusing an expectant or new mother from her duties in the field could jeopardize the crop, but it would help to ensure the nurture and survival of her children.

Even the site of slave family life—the cabin—was subject to the owner's prerogative. Unable to marry legally, couples hoped that owners would recognize their unions and allow them to build housing of their own. Often the slaveholder granted permission only after the woman gave birth to one or more children.

On many (particularly small) plantations, infants accompanied adults to the field. Having an older child tend the baby minimized disruptions to the work routine.

Planters with large slaveholdings often preferred to establish day nurseries. Here, infants in South Carolina rest in rice fanner baskets, watched by older children.

Slave children witnessed droves (called coffles) of slaves headed for new homes, which kindled anxieties about possible separation from parents. Although young children were seldom sold, they knew the likelihood of sale increased as they became older.

On Sundays, slaves frequently presented sons and daughters to their owners for inspection. The ritual at the "big house" forced parents to acknowledge external control over both themselves and their children.

Slave children participated in rituals that encouraged owners to act paternally. They presented flowers or other small gifts in the hope that members of the owning family would reciprocate with kindness or favors.

Play often brought black and white youngsters together, but opportunities for interaction diminished as black children grew older. Increasing work responsibilities left them little time for fun.

Slave children performed chores that benefited their families as well as owners. Sweeping the yard around the cabin was work that commonly fell to young girls and boys.

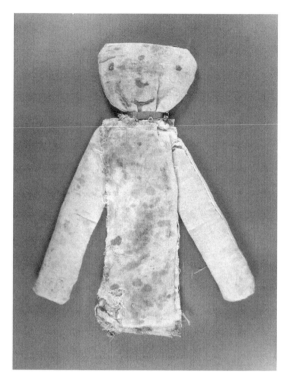

Owners expected children to learn work skills as soon as they were capable. Mistresses sometimes encouraged young girls to master sewing skills by having them make dolls or clothing for dolls.

Many youths gained their first exposure to field work by carrying water to the work hands. Children who served as water carriers helped ensure that no time was wasted and simultaneously learned how to behave in the field.

Initiation into field work rendered slave children vulnerable to sale. State laws prohibiting the sale of children did not apply to those old enough to be field hands.

The threat of sale was constant. Distraught slave mothers often appealed to the paternalistic impulses of owners in an effort to prevent the sale of their children.

Slaves worried about the possibility of sexual abuse as girls approached adolescence. Family members tried to protect them, but this often proved difficult, especially when a master perpetrated the abuse.

Even though the sale of slaves rendered family lives unstable, adolescents craved close relationships. Dances played an important role in courtship as slave youths sought to carve out lives of their own.

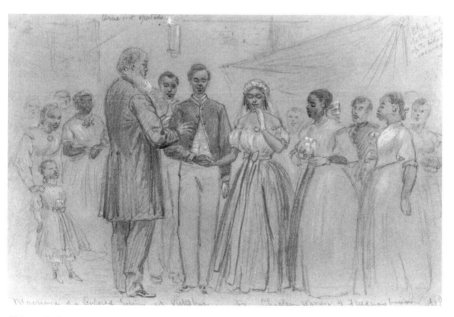

Although slaves could not marry under law, men and women joined together in marriages recognized by the slave community. Following the Civil War, many former slaves participated in ceremonies that recognized relationships of long standing.

The memories of former slaves interviewed in the 1930s by agents of the Works Progress Administration (WPA) are a crucial source for understanding the experience of growing up in bondage. Long after emancipation, Laura Clark of Alabama and Ben Horry of South Carolina recalled details of a childhood enslaved.

6

RISK OF SALE
AND SEPARATION

O n s o m e n i g h t s , former Virginia slave Ishrael Massie recalled, the house servants would visit the slave quarters. Their long faces told the story: "Marsa an' Missus been talkin' 'bout money." This meant they would sell slaves when the next slave trader came around. At times the servants knew the names of the slaves to be sold: "Den sech prayin', honey. Dem what ain't named would pray to God ole Marsa ain't gonna sell dem, an' dem what been named would pray dey get a good Marsa." Massie's sister Sadie was one of those sold. Her purchaser took her to Southampton, too far for her to remain in touch with her family. Jennie Patterson also was sold in Virginia. Long after the event she recalled few details of the transaction at the courthouse, except that she "was scared to death," because she did not know how she would fare.[1] Competence at work rendered slave youths susceptible to sale. Death, sickness, poor market conditions, drought, floods, or other disasters that threatened the crop or brought about an unexpected need for cash made all slaves vulnerable, but adolescents and young adults were particularly likely to be sold because they had both the competence and the physical stamina that planters desired in working hands. As slaves on the verge of adulthood mastered work skills, tensions heightened on plantations and farms.

Slaves and owners viewed the stage of development from the early to mid-teens quite differently. Slaves considered adolescence a time of sorrow because the likelihood grew as children approached their mid-teens that owners would break the bonds that held families together, wrenching teenagers from their families of origin after they became proficient at adult tasks. Indeed, sales of slaves in the interregional slave trade peaked between the ages of fifteen and twenty-five, and vulnerability to sale began to increase for youths as early as age eight and certainly by the age of ten, when they could work competently with the cotton crop. Owners, in contrast, viewed the maturation of enslaved children as a very positive event. Slaveholders knew that as children reached their teenage years, they would soon prove valuable as "prime hands," as first-rate workers were called, whether they worked at home or were sold at premium prices.

Flush times encouraged the purchase and relocation of slaves. Economic opportunities fueled by the growing textile industries in New England and Europe encouraged slaveholders and would-be slaveholders to move westward into states such as Alabama, newly opened to settlement in the antebellum years. The fertile soil of the southwestern United States promised high yields and profits for planters with enough land and labor to plant and harvest the cotton processed in the mills. Men and women who relocated to frontier areas to grow staple crops often brought bondsmen and women with them, but they also relied on purchasing slaves after they had cleared land and accumulated the capital necessary to commence or increase cotton cultivation. This situation put adolescent, and even prepubescent, slaves at risk for separation from their families. Many were forced to travel to new homes, where they were put to work planting and harvesting the staple crop. Sugar production, limited in the antebellum United States to southern Louisiana, required additional slaves, many of whom were brought to the region from older areas of settlement through slave markets in New Orleans. The transfer of slaves from more established areas of the country to the developing cotton and sugar regions constituted a demographic revolution. Youths old enough to work competently in the cotton fields sold readily, particularly during years when high prices for the crop tempted planters, eager to grow more cotton, to compete for slaves in the open market.

The risk of separation from families through sale was relatively low for very young children, but it increased when children neared the age when they could begin adult work. Between 1820 and 1860, about 10 percent of adolescent slaves living in the upper South were sold in the interregional slave trade. A similar percentage of slaves were sold in their twenties. As slaves moved into their thirties, their chance of sale diminished substantially, but by then many of them had borne children who were or soon would be at risk for sale. Youths living in regions that imported slaves, rather than exported them, were at less risk for sale than their more northern counterparts. Even so, sales did occur in the new states of the lower South, and the possibility existed that a region might undergo a transition and began exporting slaves, as occurred in central Alabama. Consequently, slaves throughout the South worried about being sold.[2]

Purchasers expected to recoup the cost of slaves quickly by putting them immediately to remunerative work. Generally, slaves purchased from a different area of the country had to become accustomed to their new environment, master unfamiliar work routines, and establish new social relationships within a brief period. This discouraged the purchase of young children or slaves who were old and frail. Instead, planters sought teenagers and young adults, slaves whose physical condition qualified them as prime hands and who might be expected to labor for many years to come. Young men and women coming of age could be expected to choose spouses and rear children after being uprooted from their families of origin, which added to their attractiveness as a financial investment. All slaveholders gained from the situation, those who bought laborers as well as those who sold them. Middlemen who facilitated the traffic in slaves also realized a profit by extracting a fee for arranging the sales.

Robert Byrd Beverley was one of many planters who purchased prepubescent and adolescent children without their parents. Lured from Virginia to Alabama by the promise of profits in cotton, Beverley sold land in the former state and used the proceeds to purchase "boys, 10 or 12 years old or 15," whom he relocated from Virginia to his new cotton plantation. Beverley's boys probably worked in the field, as did most slaves, but planters at times purchased older children or adolescents to work in their homes so they could place as many adults as possible in the crop. If youths acted as house servants, then able-bodied adults would not have to be diverted from field to house work. Virginia planter Ben Tinsley acquired nine-year-old Martha Showvely to make beds, clean, fill water pitchers, perform other odd jobs, and help with the cooking. Fannie Brown was sold at a young age from Virginia to Texas, where she spun and wove cloth and cooked for her new owners.[3]

Generally, sales of girls peaked at somewhat younger ages than boys.

Girls matured sooner than boys, making them effective workers in the field at earlier ages, and preteen and teenage girls were prized as house servants. Slaveholders who purchased an adolescent girl could expect to benefit from the births of children throughout her fertile years. Consequently, the majority of girls sold were between the ages of thirteen and nineteen or twenty. The majority of slaveholders preferred boys in their late teens through early twenties, although some boys were sold at younger ages as well.[4]

Both slave youths living in areas of the country with high rates of slave sales or migrations and those living in areas that imported slaves experienced movements of slaves as dislocations, even if they avoided sale themselves. Some youths from slave-exporting areas of the country went west or south alone; others accompanied parents, extended kin, or friends. Still others remained at home, watching as parents, other relatives, and friends left for unknown places and remaining at risk themselves for future sale or relocation. All suffered great anguish as a result, because important relationships were severed and no one could be certain of remaining untouched by the trade. For those youths whose families were affected by the long-distance slave trade or by owners' migrations, separations generally had the same degree of finality as death. Slave youths could end up living so far from family members that they neither saw nor heard of them again. Over time, relocated slaves might begin to establish family ties in the new environment by marrying or attaching themselves through informal adoptions to unrelated slaves; however, slave-importing areas could undergo a transition and begin exporting slaves. When the cycle of separation began anew, slaves experienced yet more distress as newly formed family ties were sundered. Slaves also went through a cycle of family construction, destruction, and reconstruction when slaveholdings were dispersed as owners' children came of age and set up new households or when owners died, necessitating the settling of estates and the dispersal of slaves to heirs.[5]

Youths who avoided permanent separations from their families remained subject to short-term dislocations as long as they could perform jobs that adults wanted done. Overseers and owners orchestrated movements of slaves from one plantation to another to complete tasks more efficiently; most of these hands worked only for short periods—as little as part of a day. Such short-term assistance often was lent gratis from one planter to another, but when slaves stayed for the duration of planting or harvesting or longer, the slaves' owners expected payment for their labor. At times, exchanges of working hands sent older youths to neighboring plantations for a year or more. On other occasions, older youths were left at home to tend younger brothers and sisters and to keep the family economy functioning until parents returned from neighboring estates. Virginia planter Benjamin Franklin Nalle pleaded with his mother in August of 1860 to lend him a boy: "I lack a boy or two & if you can send George over immediately, you will oblige me very much." Former Virginia slave Nancy Williams was hired by a "po' white man" to help his wife mind the baby, wash dishes, and help cook dinner. Randall Flagg worked as a water boy for contractors building a grist mill in the neighborhood. One Virginia merchant, who served as a middleman between slaveowners and individuals who wished to hire temporarily the labor of slaves, kept up an active business marketing "NEGROES, of both sexes, between the ages of 10 and 30 years." Georgia planter Alexander Telfair instructed his overseer to see that one of Elsey's older daughters cared for Elsey's younger children and fed her chickens whenever the mother, a midwife, attended black and white births in the neighborhood. Labor exchanges occurred in all parts of the South.[6]

The older the child, the more likely owners were to discount family ties in deciding whom to keep and whom to sell or rent out to others. Statutory prohibitions occasionally prevented the permanent separation of young children from their mothers, but older children remained vulnerable because no state legislatures banned the sale of children capable of field work. Laws restricting the sale of younger children generally affected only the interstate slave trade and had no effect on local exchanges or migrations. Moreover, officials seldom enforced the statutes, even when legislative acts expressly prohibited the sale of slaves across state lines. Consequently, slave youths worried whenever they heard owners discussing a need for cash for fear they would hear: "John, Mary, James, I want you to get ready and go to the courthouse with me this morning."[7]

In the short term, the sale of slave youths—particularly of preteens and early teens—fluctuated depending on trends in cotton prices. Traders of prepubescent children and young adolescents found buyers only when cotton prices remained high. If conditions were favorable, boys and girls as young as eight sold well. Cotton prices generally rose in the antebellum period, providing ever-new opportunities for selling young children, but fluctuations in cotton values ensured that the market for children under twelve or fifteen remained volatile. Serious financial crises, such as the panic that occurred in 1837, and periods of prosperity, as occurred in the 1850s, could depress or improve the market for all slaves, but less extreme economic oscillations could retard or abet the sales of children. Ben Davis, an itinerant who normally plied his trade around Perry County, Alabama, wrote his Virginia supplier in late November 1848 that because of low prices slaves of "fine size" continue to sell well, but "the demand for small Negroes is not so fair." The situation turned around quickly. Two weeks later, Davis advised his slave purveyor to send him any slaves he had on hand, including boys and girls. If the demand was "brisk," girls as young as ten and boys as young as twelve could be sold as "plough hands," and buyers might be found for even younger children.[8]

THE PRICES paid for slave children depended on their ability to perform agricultural or household chores, not their age. Planters expected each slave they purchased "to excel in something"—that is, to have been trained to work. Consequently, speculators who purchased children solely to profit from their resale sometimes taught them work skills before putting them up for auction. Generally, the training involved jobs outside the field. According to one informant, girls learned to "do different things such as: weave, cook, sew, and maid service."[9] Few slaves worked in the field every day, year-round. Most—on some plantations and farms, all—household slaves were assigned to the field during periods of peak labor demand, and slaves accustomed to work in the fields performed other types of jobs during slack seasons when crops did not demand their attention. Many cotton, tobacco, and grain producers planned for this contingency by purchasing or training house servants who could work in the field periodically and by acquiring field hands who could perform a variety of other chores. Rice planters with large slaveholdings preferred to maintain sharper distinctions between house and field servants than did other planters, but even rice planters expected slaves to work in a variety of occupations.[10] Knowledge of a slave's work skills helped would-be purchasers make decisions about whether to purchase a slave and how much to pay.

Price lists and other records pertaining to sales of slave children frequently classified youths by their physical development, as evidenced by their height or weight. Purchasers relied on such external measurements to gauge whether the child had the strength, dexterity, physical stamina, and good health necessary for completing plantation chores. At times, sellers assigned arbitrarily to a child an age that reflected the youth's physical maturation rather than his or her chronological age. This caused considerable confusion among many slaves as to their exact date of birth. Anna Maria Coffee, traded eleven times in South Carolina and Virginia before she reached her twenties, never knew her true age. In later life, the former slave explained that sellers "made my age jus' what dey wanted it."[11]

Charlotte Thornton's experience selling slaves to an Alabama planter illustrates the principle that physical attributes determined the prices paid for youthful slaves. Payments received by this Virginia piedmont planter for individual boys and girls reflected the perceived physical strengths and weaknesses of each. Columbus, age twelve or thirteen and "well grown," sold for less than Kezia, his seven-year-old sister, because he had once broken his right arm and it had been "badly set." Columbus's younger brother Tom, age eleven, sold for more than his younger sister and considerably more than the older but injured Columbus. John, thirteen years old and apparently unrelated to the other boys, sold for less than Tom: he was "healthy but not well grown for his age." The Alabamian who purchased these four children also bought the unrelated slave girl Milly, described as "healthy and strong, well formed." Her "homely face," also noted, apparently detracted from her value, for her purchaser was able to negotiate her price down to $550 from $650.[12]

For girls, the physical attributes that determined a slave's market value included notions of beauty held by the owning class. Girls reached puberty at about the same time as their physical capacity for work increased sufficiently to make them efficient and effective laborers. Accordingly, they confronted double jeopardy: they were at risk not only for sale but also for sexual exploitation. Some unprincipled men even purchased young female slaves expressly for sexual gratification. Eighteen-year-old Rosena Lipscombe's new owner expected her to act as his concubine after he purchased her in Virginia and carried her "down south." Virginian Tom Greene purchased a slave woman named Betty specifically because "he was a bachluh . . . an' he need a 'oman," according to a former slave who lived on an adjoining property. More frequently, masters, masters' sons, and other men who visited or lived in the neighborhood felt themselves entitled to the sexual favors of any female slaves they encountered, pubescent and adolescent girls included. Neither the law nor aggrieved mistresses, who disapproved of sexual relationships between white men and black women, could prevent the practice.[13] Not all white men forced themselves upon enslaved women, but enough did to make a girl's adolescent years a constant source of concern for girls, their parents, and the larger slave community.

Slave girls who were deemed pretty according to slaveholder standards could be sold as prostitutes, or "fancies" in the vernacular of the day. Fredericka Bremer, a Swedish visitor on a tour of the United States, observed "fancy women for fancy purchasers" on display at a Richmond jail. R. M. Owings offered to purchase from his Charleston supplier "all likely and handsome fancy girls" that could be had "at reasonable prices." "Fancies" were generally of lighter skin and sold at higher prices than other slave women. In the Richmond market in 1859, prices paid for fancy women exceeded those paid for prime female field hands by 30 percent or more. An attractive slave woman sold for $1,500 in Columbia, South Carolina, according to Bremer. Relatively few slaves were ever sold as "fancies," but a knowledge of the trade added to the distress of slave girls and their parents as female children approached puberty.[14]

Although would-be purchasers took an interest in the physical attributes of slave women, a desire for economic gain fueled the majority of slave sales. Planters worried about maintaining the best possible balance between the acres of cultivated land at their disposal and the number of hands available to work this land. A surplus of labor kept some slaves idle, at least part of the time; a surplus of land represented a lost opportunity for profit. But slaveholders sold and relocated slaves to settle estates and pay debts as well. Many children were purchased as part of a larger group—perhaps the entire population of a plantation, or one heir's portion of the slave population. These groups generally included slaves of different ages, some of whom were related, which eased some of the worry about the fate of children placed on the market. Youngsters sold "in the round" had a chance of remaining with at least some family members and friends. When they contemplated the purchase of a group, planters took into account how many children there were, what proportion of the group they constituted, and what percentage of the children were physically mature or nearly so. The presence of children, particularly those nearing puberty, helped ensure future prosperity, provided they were accompanied by a sufficient number of fully working adult hands. No one wanted to purchase "too many small negroes," but having too few youths was equally undesirable.[15]

Being purchased together did not guarantee that family members would stay together, however—especially if the sale involved a speculator. Families sold to individuals usually went to live with their new owners, but those purchased by speculators who bought and resold slaves for profit could end up scattered. Even slaves belonging to a planter migrating from one region to another might not stay with family members if the slaveholder deemed a sale necessary or desirable. Former slave Tom Morris began the journey south from Virginia with both of his parents. Tom's father and mother had lived on separate plantations in Virginia, but his mother's

owner, who planned to relocate to Mississippi, purchased the husband ostensibly to keep the family together. This must have been a ploy intended to
obtain Tom's father for a favorable price or to secure the cooperation of
mother and child, because all three family members did not end up in
Mississippi. His new owner sold Tom's father before the traveling party
reached its destination. Former Virginia slave Susan Keys remembered at
age eleven or twelve walking in a drove of slaves, called a coffle, all the way
from the District of Columbia to Mississippi, where she was sold to new
owners. Some of her companions never made it to Mississippi because they
were sold along the way.[16]

PARENTS who never saw their children again experienced a deep and lasting grief. Those who lost a child through sale occasionally compared their
emotional pain to the sorrow associated with a child's death. Aunt Crissy,
the mother of seven children, lost two of her older daughters to the slave
trade. When her second youngest, Hendley, died of illness, she "sorrered
much," but found a measure of comfort in her religious faith: "Praise gawd,
praise gawd, my little chile is gone to Jesus." Turning to her master, she expressed her continuing torment over the sale of her daughters: Hendley's
"one chile of mine you never gonna sell." Time assuaged neither the heart-
ache nor the anger associated with her earlier loss.[17]

The disappearance of children represented more than an emotional loss.
Sons and daughters made substantial contributions to the slave family's
economy, as previously demonstrated. Moreover, the family, backed by the
larger slave community, stood as a buffer between the slaveholder and the
young slave; members of either or both might act to assuage the child's
physical and emotional sufferings under the slave system. Youths torn from
families and communities of origin faced an uncertain future, and slave parents were loath to let them go without a struggle or without at least ensuring their ability to cope in new surroundings.

Whereas slaveholders acted to separate families, parents reacted to keep
family relationships intact. This, in turn, prompted owners to enact coun-
ter-measures, and parents to follow several strategies to achieve their purpose. First, parents tried to prolong childhood; adult slaves who came up
with ways to keep their children from engaging in field work knew that as
long as children avoided adult work they might be shielded from fully experiencing the shock of slavery, including separation from family. Whatever
success they experienced was transitory, however, because owners would

not tolerate the loss of field labor for long. Accordingly, parents also taught sons and daughters how to behave if threatened with separation. At one extreme, parents contested sale or other types of relocation that took children away from loved ones. At the other, they advised children to make the best of whatever situations awaited them. Most took more than one approach, acting to prevent the severing of family relationships while simultaneously teaching a child how to get along in new surroundings. For their part, slave youths reflected the range of behaviors exhibited by members of their parents' generation. Some challenged the conditions of oppression, while others adopted an attitude intended to placate owners and ward off trouble.

As occurred with other contested conditions of enslavement, slaves whose families were torn apart might refuse to cooperate in completing their owners' work. Fathers were especially likely to bargain with their labor to preserve family relationships. They ran away, and then sent word through other slaves of their willingness to return if an owner called off a pending sale. One Virginia man, sold apart from his wife and children, hid in the woods for twelve months until another planter agreed to purchase him and reunite him with his family. Another father, upon learning he had been sold, threatened to commit suicide rather than to leave his family in Georgia, which convinced his buyer to renege on the planned purchase. Still another, who had successfully escaped bondage in Virginia, took the unusual step of volunteering for reenslavement in order to remain with his young son. The father had escaped from slavery by hiding out in the vicinity of his owner's plantation, and the boy's mother had nurtured the youth until she died and his owner sold the boy to a Texas planter. Realizing the boy would have no one to care for him in Texas, the father followed him there, and then came forward and identified himself. The boy's new owner, who benefited from the situation, accepted the father's offer to be reenslaved in Texas and did not return the man to his legal owner.[18]

If fathers were more inclined to withdraw or threaten to withdraw from the work site in an attempt to keep their families intact, mothers were more likely to pin their hopes on owners' responding sympathetically to an outpouring of grief. No hard-and-fast rule describes the individual responses of parents to separation from their children: some mothers ran away, and fathers practiced passive as well as overt forms of resistance to keep their families together. Nevertheless, mothers were more likely to call upon owners to act on paternalistic impulses. Bettie Tolbert of Alabama recalled mothers who would plead: "Don't sell my child, have mercy on me, Lord Jesus." Impassioned protests by parents at the point of sale occasionally elicited the desired reaction from slaveholders. One mother put up such a fit following the sale of her children to slave traders that her Virginia master agreed to let her accompany her daughters to their new home. No doubt her owner worried that she would prove of limited use if left behind, impaired by her grief. He also may have worried that the continued public display of despair by the mother would reveal his identity as a cold and calculating slave trader, rather than as a father figure concerned for the welfare of his slaves. Planter John White Nash of Virginia was apparently trying to unite a family when he offered to hire "Cary, Cate and her three children." He noted that he undertook to do only because "my man Thom is so importunate upon the subject."[19] Nash must have realized he could gain better cooperation in the work place if Thom's family came to live with him. His actions had the added advantage of marking him as a humanitarian, in his own mind and in the view of others who did not question the legitimacy of slavery.

Protests at the point of sale tended to be vociferous, and the possibility of vehement protests against the separation of a family probably deterred some owners from selling children away from their families, especially since separating families increased dissatisfaction among slaves and made them less docile and dependable. Consequently, most young children affected by the slave trade were sold along with at least one parent, almost always the mother. When planter Press Keys of Alabama purchased a woman in Florida, her four children were included. "He buy'd us foe tergetthah," one of the children later explained, "so dat Mammy would be bettah satterfahd."[20] The situation worked better for mothers and for younger children: when sales occurred, fathers were much less likely to remain with their children than were mothers, and teenagers were far more likely to be sold than were younger boys and girls.

Owners were receptive to the pleas of mothers on behalf of young children in part because keeping mothers and children together held other advantages for owners besides decreasing slave dissatisfaction. A mother's care increased the likelihood that youngsters would survive to adulthood and work in the house or fields, because mothers provided much of the nurturing that children needed in order to survive. By keeping young children with parents and concentrating sales on older youths and young adults, slaveholders could promote themselves as kind-hearted—and prosperous as well.

The act of separating families by sale marked a planter as a poor master and manager. When financial difficulties forced Thomas B. Chaplin, a St.

Helena Island planter, to sell "about ten prime Negroes," he agonized over the "very unpleasant extremity." He considered nothing "more mortifying and grieving" than "to select out some . . . to be sold . . . to separate families, mothers & daughters, brothers & sisters." Chaplin worried that his neighbors would laugh "and say it serves you right, you lived beyond your means." Other owners spoke of sundering family ties in similar terms and attempted to sell family members together when circumstances forced them to reduce their labor forces. It was not unknown for slaveholders, worried about the censure of their neighbors, to hide sales from them.[21] Slaves encouraged and benefited from such worries among owners.

Slaves, desperate to maintain families intact yet with few resources to prevent separations, occasionally employed tactics that included threats of violence or other harm to owners. Unwilling to relocate to Alabama at the insistence of their owner, slaves in North Carolina "took the desperate resolution" of concocting a potion of poison that claimed the lives of two of their owner's daughters. The Baton Rouge *Republic* carried news of this "Shocking Occurrence." Stories of retaliation, including physical confrontation and conjuring, reminded slaveholders to exercise caution in separating slave families. All planters understood the threat to physical safety that violence posed, but they were divided about the ability of slaves to harm through the invocation of a spell, as were the slaves themselves. At least some members of the owning class worried about the supernatural power attributed to certain slaves, and some slaves employed hexes to affect the behavior of owners whose actions they could not otherwise control. Slaves in Amelia County, Virginia, believed they had prevented their relocation to Alabama by employing a conjurer to work his magic power upon their master.[22] It is difficult to know how successful these maneuvers actually were. The large number of slaves traded in the antebellum years suggests that such strategies were generally ineffectual, yet even more slaves might have been relocated if slaves had never employed such strategies.

Slave parents through their behavior acknowledged the existence of large-scale family dissolution throughout the South. Even as they resisted separation from their children, parents taught them how to cope if parents were no longer around to care for them. Family stories served to prepare youngsters for what might lie ahead. Parents, grandparents, and other older relatives reminisced about their lives and the lives of ancestors, hoping that treasured memories might remain with children even when parents could not. Many of the narratives provided models for enduring the hardships associated with bondage, including family separation. Eliza Evans, a slave in

Alabama, learned the story of her grandmother's capture in Africa, passage across the Atlantic, and sale in America. Her grandmother subsequently ingratiated herself with her owners to such an extent that "they gave her a grand wedding when she was married" and never sold any of her children or grandchildren. Evans came to admire her grandmother's achievement in getting along with her owners, but her family's teachings were not limited to stories of how to accommodate slaveholders. As a girl, Evans often stood guard for the adults when runaway slaves slipped into the slave quarter to get something to eat and to pray with compatriots.[23]

Stories could be sung as well as spoken to prepare children for the emotional trauma of separation. Emma Howard learned as a young child in Virginia to sing this verse:

> Mammy, is Ol' Massa gwine sell us tomorrow?
> Yes, my chile.
> Whah he goin sell us?
> Way down South in Georgia.

Those parents who ignored the subject of sale or other types of separations risked their children's learning of or experiencing the situation unexpectedly. Parents did not wish to worry young children unnecessarily, but they wanted all children armed with knowledge that would help them cope with the distress of sudden family partings. Sometimes they delayed discussions too long, and youngsters learned inadvertently of slave sales from older children or by overhearing the conversations of adults. In either case, children were frightened and saddened. The song little Emma learned, she later recalled, "always made me cry."[24]

Because parents could not exercise sufficient power to ensure that their children would remain with their families, anxiety ran high in the slave quarter about how the youths might behave when parents were not around to guide them. Parents usually counseled children of all ages to mind their manners around adults. After he migrated with his owner to the West, Elizabeth Keckley's father kept up a regular correspondence with his wife and child, who remained in Virginia. Nearly every letter contained this advice for his daughter: "Tell my darling little Lizzie to be a good girl." When Louis Hughes's master took him from his family in Virginia, Louis's mother begged her son to "be a good boy . . . and always behave yourself properly." At such traumatic moments, other relatives joined parents in cautioning children to behave. Laura Clark's grandmother urged her to pray and advised her to obey all adults she encountered at her new home, so that "everyone will like you." Little Laura was only six or seven years old when she was taken from her family in North Carolina by slave traders and sold in Alabama. She "remembered what my grandma say, and whatever they told me to put my hand to, I did, and I was obedient." Laura's grandmother specifically instructed the young girl to "mind both black and white" at her new home. If Laura heeded this advice, she would avoid trouble with the white folks but also with slaves—and Laura later credited this advice with aiding her survival. The mother of Louis Hughes told the boy to "be polite to every one," not just owners.[25] Such advice reflected parents' hope that unrelated slaves would step in and care for children in the absence of relatives, as well as the wish for children to avoid the ire of owners.

Children had to be polite to everyone, but they had to put their trust in other slaves rather than owners. A common practice whereby children referred to older, unrelated slaves using kinship terms, such as "aunt" and "uncle," reinforced the idea that slaves, rather than owners, would care for children separated from their parents. The language of kinship served to instruct the child in the hierarchy of the slave community and emphasized the child's dependence on and need to obey older slaves. A requirement instituted by some slaveholders that children refer to them in familial terms probably represented their understanding of this use of the language of kinship by the slave population. Owners who adopted the practice must have hoped to insert themselves into the list of people whom young slaves learned to treat with respect and obedience. Hester Hunter, who lived on a rice plantation, was taught to call her mistress "my white mammy." Growing up in Arkansas, Belle Williams learned to call her mistress "Mother Hulsie." Long after slavery ended, George Fleming used the word "daddy" to describe his master.[26]

Parents used given names, as well as kinship titles, to emphasize that individual children belonged to the larger slave community. They were less concerned that children have unique names than that they have names that associated them with other slaves. Parents called children by the names of grandparents, aunts, uncles, dead siblings, other family members, and unrelated slaves, as if to remind everyone that all slaves had a stake in caring for the children. Generally, it was not difficult to find adult slaves willing to accept responsibility for caring for children when parents were unavailable. When the slave woman known as Crecie died in childbirth on the Gowrie rice plantation, the child's grandmother raised the infant for four years and then the boy's great-aunt took over. The elderly slave Molly raised her grandchildren and great-grandchildren on the Butler estate. "Fictive kin" also played a role as the need arose.[27]

Owners objected to the close-knit ties that developed among slaves as reflected in these naming practices. They believed that the slave's most important relationship was with his or her owners. When slaves shared the same name, owners added descriptive terms—"Cook Renty or Old Lucy, or Little Dick"—in an effort to emphasize the individuality of slaves, rather than their commonality with one another. Slaveholders might go so far as to insist on naming the children themselves, choosing at times fanciful names drawn from classical mythology or the Bible. Other owners chose diminutives of names held by members of the owning class. One owner named a slave boy after his boat.[28]

To assert their authority, slaveholders occasionally changed the names of their slaves, particularly those whom they purchased or brought into their homes to wait upon family members and guests. One slave youth had his name changed when he became valet to his master, a promotion from his former position as waiting boy. The name change occurred for the convenience of the owner, whose daughter's name sounded similar to that of the slave. The master wanted to ensure that the right person appeared whenever he called for his valet. After Virginia planter Thomas S. Watson purchased two girls in 1843, his mother changed the name of the youngest from Louisa, listed on the deed of sale, to Amelia, which became shortened to Mealy. The girl preferred the name Juliet. Both mother and son no doubt recognized that by changing the girl's name, they exercised their legal right to supersede a previous claim to the child by her parents, who probably named her Juliet, and her former owners, who most likely called her Louisa. Some slaves went by two names, one approved by the owner and another "basket name" known only to other slaves.[29]

The strategies that parents employed to counter owners' attempts at separating children psychologically from their families probably had some effect, though outcomes could be unpredictable and inconsistent. Slave naming patterns often reflected a desire on the part of adult slaves to avoid family separations, if only symbolically, a fact that Juliet apparently understood. Yet the small number of very young children parted from their parents would have had difficulty even remembering their families of origin. Neither Vicey nor Harry McElmore recalled anything of their families because speculators had purchased them in Virginia and Kentucky and peddled them in Alabama at a young age. Isaac Johnson was too young to understand what was happening when a man from Montgomery purchased him from North Carolina. His two sisters cried as he left home for the last time, but Isaac did not share in their distress because he "wanted to ride in the surrey" that would carry him to his new home. Only later did he understand the significance of the event.[30] In such cases, the common slave practices of naming children for relatives and maintaining family surnames failed to serve the intended purpose of signifying family relationships, at least from the perspective of the children. Purchasers of children rarely had any interest in preserving memories of severed relationships by explaining the situation to children when they grew older and capable of understanding the situation. The older the child was when separated from parents, the more likely he or she was to attach significance to a name.

Slave parents controlled neither their children's responses to enslavement nor their owners' responses to tactics intended to preserve families. Instead of surrendering to their slaves' pleas or threats, most owners simply tried to minimize parents' objections. They punished severely those who carried on when the time came to part from their children and argued that slaves did not suffer from family separations. Some went so far as to insist that children were better off without their parents because slaves were indifferent or careless toward their children. Yet, when it came to the act of separating families, the behavior of slaveholders did not reflect this assertion. Owners who sold slave youths often made sure to carry out the transaction when parents were not around to raise a storm of protest. Planters at times acted with such stealth that family members had no time even to say goodbye, let alone orchestrate a protest. One planter simply pulled up to a woman's work station and ordered her into his buggy, explaining "I boughtcha dis mawnin." Other planters practiced various forms of deception for the same purpose. In Scottsville, Virginia, Louis Hughes's owner told the boy's family that he was taking the eleven-year-old slave to Richmond to work on a canal boat operating between that city and Scottsville. Louis and his mother were told that they would see each other periodically when the boat returned home. Instead, the owner turned Louis over to a slave trader, who eventually sold the youth to Mississippi.[31]

Owners who planned to part children from their parents confronted protests by the youths, just as they did from their parents. Generally, sons and daughters used the same methods employed by their parents. A slave girl named Nancy Williams yelled "loud's I could" when her master offered her services for hire, then ran home shortly after she arrived at her new residence. She never returned to her would-be employer, probably by the mutual consent of all concerned. The infant she had been hired to watch nearly choked to death when she left him alone to eat toast. Her ineptitude had jeopardized the safety of the infant, and the subsequent harsh punishment meted out for her inexperience displeased her owner, who—like other slaveholders—objected to the mistreatment of his property by people who hired temporarily the services of his slaves. Louise Jones also ran away, charging that the Virginia woman who hired her "was de meanes' white 'oman in de world." Like Nancy and other youths who ran from new masters or mistresses, Louise headed toward home and family.[32]

Trying to prevent their sale, some slave youths "fout an' kick lak crazy folks" when placed on the auction block, and they occasionally succeeded in playing on an owner's sympathy or discomfort to avoid separation from their families. Thomas Johns of Alabama was one of many slaves pledged from birth to one of his owner's children. Thomas grew up under his mother's care, but when he became old enough to begin adult work in earnest—at about age ten or twelve—his owner, who had migrated to Texas, returned to claim his property. Thomas, who had received gifts from his master in anticipation of his making the trip, at first cooperated with the planned move, but he had a change of heart when the time for parting from his mother drew near. Mustering as much charm as he could, Thomas asked his master to understand: "I ain't goin' with you to Texas and leave de only mother I got. I jus' cain' do dat." Thomas's words persuaded the master, who allowed the boy to remain where he was.[33] The master may have felt genuine sympathy for the boy, although he probably worried as well about the possibility that Thomas, homesick for his mother, would prove of little use in Texas. At any rate, by leaving Thomas with his mother, the Texan benefited his own parents and added to the worth of the family estate.

Thomas was fortunate. The majority of slave youths promised to others—whether sold or given away—had no assurances that they would ever again see parents or other loved ones. This was true even of children who were rented temporarily to neighboring planters. Although some of these children returned home after their term of service expired, others did not, either because they continued to work for the men and women who hired them or because they learned skills that made them attractive to purchasers.

The sorrow that children felt over permanent separation from their parents lasted a lifetime and heightened appreciation of family ties among youngsters who rightly feared the consequence of losing the love and protection of parents and other relatives. Mariah Bell, many years after the incident, wept at the memory of her mother crying and waving to her as they parted. Her granddaughters shared her anguish as she told the story: "We all used to sit around her and we would all be crying with her when she told that so many, many times."[34] Although slave family ties were often truncated and tenuous, they nevertheless represented a critical source of support—a barrier between slave youths and slaveholders that absorbed some of the harshness of slavery. When the ties were severed, children were pushed toward early adulthood. They were forced not only to shoulder a heavy burden of toil but also to suffer considerable emotional distress.

Slave youths without parents around to protect them could find themselves at high risk for sale in the market or forced to fulfill adult roles in the slave quarter. The slave trade created parentless children, but so did the high rates of mortality among the slave population. A small number of young people were alone because their parents had escaped servitude. Whatever the cause, youths alone might have no one to cook or care for their clothes—particularly boys, who seldom performed these chores for themselves—and owners had few compunctions about selling them when parents were not around to protest. Ella Belle Ramsey at age ten found herself left to cope with a younger brother and sister after her mother ran away from her Virginia home. Adding to her misfortune, both her master and the sheriff believed she knew about her mother's escape and attempted to force her to reveal the details. In her later years, Ramsey explained all she knew: "One night I woke up an' reach out an' my mother wasn't dere. I got up an' look for her an' couldn't find her." Ramsey's owner sold her shortly afterward, and she never heard from any of her family again. Ramsey's mother left no explanation for her disappearance, which was unusual. Men ran away more often than women. When mothers abandoned children to escape slavery, the most common justification was unrelenting cruel treatment, including sexual abuse, by owners or in some cases by other slaves.[35]

Racial stereotypes of the day encouraged sexual abuse of slave youths parted from parents by allowing white exploiters to blame the black victims for their predicament. Many white southerners considered black women inherently promiscuous because of their supposedly insatiable sexual urges. When asked to recall slavery years after its demise, former Alabama slaveholder M. T. Judge alleged that "young slave girls, as young as 13 or 14 years" commonly solicited "the caresses of men," both "of their own race" but also of "sons of their masters, overseers or any other White men in the neighborhood." Mistresses, too, tried to deny the reality of black women's sexual molestation. Mary Chesnut of South Carolina, who tended to be more honest about slavery than most mistresses, observed that even though "the mulattoes one sees in every family exactly resemble the white children" and every mistress can name "the father of all the mulatto children in everybody's household," those "in her own she seems to think drop from the clouds, or pretends so to think." Chesnut's mother-in-law apparently was one of those who refused to acknowledge the nature of black women's sexual exploitation, because she advised her daughter-in-law not to send female servants on errands that took them into the street, for fear they would, in the older woman's words, be "tempted, led astray," rather than attacked or raped.[36]

Sexual abuse of slave women occurred routinely on many plantations and was not limited to girls separated from their families. But the sale of slaves that broke up families and communities increased the vulnerability of slave girls to sexual exploitation because they lacked family and friends to threaten retaliation for mistreatment. Girls who had been sold, unknown within their new community, could find themselves subject to sexual abuse by other slaves, as well as by members of the owning class. The same held true for girls left in their original communities, if family and friends were no longer around to protect them.

Mothers tried to prepare their daughters as they approached puberty for what might await them. They wanted to forewarn daughters of the potential for sexual exploitation so they could take protective measures, but at the same time, they hoped to prolong childhood for their daughters. Girls who knew a lot about human sexuality hardly qualified as children in the minds of their white owners, a fact which caused some parents to wait too long to address the issue. As a result, girls might reach the age of maturity with no clear understanding of the human reproductive cycle. A few even went to their marriage beds without knowing what to expect. Minnie Folkes, who was only fourteen when she married in Virginia, believed that marriage entailed no more than cooking, cleaning, washing, and ironing for a husband. For three months, she and her spouse abstained from sex, because her mother had warned her previously not to engage in the act. At her young husband's urging, the couple visited Minnie's mother to clarify the situation. Only then did Minnie agree to carry out "my duty as a wife."[37]

Folkes's experience suggests that adults somehow managed to keep sexual activities hidden from view, despite the crowded conditions associated with slave cabins and quarters, and to treat the subject as taboo so that children knew not to raise the topic in conversation. To protect children from learning too much, parents sent them out to play or to fetch water from the spring; youngsters who hung around when they were not wanted risked having their legs switched with a nettle brush. One mother apparently kept her son from investigating love-making by telling him the noises he heard in the night—"knockin' and knockin' kinder easy, and [a voice that] sed 'Mary' kinder low"—came from ghosts.[38]

Slave children's lack of knowledge about sexuality might seem peculiar, given that young children were not shy about their bodies. The skimpy clothing worn by boys and girls alike, as well as the attendance of children at the grooming and dressing of whites, ensured that children had ample opportunities to satisfy their curiosity about the human body. Life on southern plantations and farms exposed children to at least the rudiments of reproduction, for slave children witnessed the arrival of newborn animals, including chicks, puppies, lambs, calves, and kids. Yet accurate explanations of where babies came from were unavailable. Fanciful stories about storks and other imaginary means of human reproduction often substituted for discussions of human sexuality and served to deflect questions by young children about their parentage—or more specifically about the identity of fathers, some of whom preferred to remain anonymous.[39]

Despite the secretiveness surrounding sexual matters, young people eagerly sought to create intimate relationships with one another when they reached their mid- to late teens. For them, as for other youths, the attentions of a special boy or girl brought joy and excitement. Because their lives were otherwise more notable for neglect, impoverishment, hard labor, and distress, everyone wanted someone to cherish. In addition, youths who were working as adults and subject to slavery's worst features considered themselves entitled to the privileges of adulthood, including love and its sexual expression.

For young people separated from their families of origin, early marriage offered an emotional and material haven. Marriage could provide assistance in carrying out the tasks of daily living, as well as love and intimacy. For young women, marriage provided a measure of protection from sexual abuse, both from members of the owning class and from other slaves. Lizzie Hobbs, long after her father left with his owner for the West, was raped by a white man following her departure from her mother's home in Virginia to work as a housegirl in North Carolina. Carolyn Holland, sold twice as a youth, felt vulnerable to sexual exploitation and married at a young age in Alabama because her seventeen-year-old husband promised her protection from the sexual attentions of another slave man. Of course, slave husbands could not always protect their wives from sexual abuse by others, especially by men of the owning class; but their presence deterred some advances.[40]

The formation of new families offered a means of assuaging the loss of family relationships as a result of sale, death, or other circumstances. New family ties established through marital alliances extended beyond spouses to include other kin, who could serve as a buffer against the adversities of slavery. The frequent disruption of slave unions through sale and migration prompted one slave to call slave marriages "a farce."[41] Nonetheless, slave youths, even those whose families had been torn apart, recreated family ties. At a younger age, parentless children might have sought out parental figures—"fictive kin"—among the slaves they encountered in their new surroundings or even among members of their owning families. But by their mid-teens, slave youths more often sought solace for past losses among their peers.

Despite the pain associated with previous partings, the overwhelming majority of young adults chose to marry (or remarry if parted from spouses) and have children, whether they went to new homes or stayed behind. "Some uv de time dey'ud sell uh man wife 'way en den he hadder ge' annuder wife," former slave Louisa Collier of South Carolina explained. The desire to create or recreate families occurred even among slaves who did not grow up in family units. Ary and Wilsie Varner met as children in Alabama after each had been sold from their respective families. Too young to remember parents or other relatives, they "grew up together" and married as soon as "they were old enough." Their shared sense of loss and yearning for family must have attracted them to each other and motivated the two to marry.[42]

Patterns of migration and slave sales threw young men and women from different regions together, and their common experiences drew them to one another. Many future husbands and wives met as newcomers on plantations and farms far from the places they called home. Amy Chapman's parents, who had not known each other in their native Virginia, met and married upon their sale to Alabama. A native of the Alabama black belt, Benjamin Holland met his wife after his forced removal to Texas. She, too, had been forcibly transferred to that state from her home in central Virginia. This mixing of slaves from different places facilitated marriage, because slaves tended to avoid endogamous unions. When slave youths moved to new areas of the South, the likelihood increased that they would encounter unrelated slaves whom they could wed. Owners recognized this and kept purchasing slaves to keep "de slaves from marrying in dere famblies."[43]

Thus, the patterns of relocating and trading slaves that developed in the South both separated established families and aided in the creation of new ones. Without the intermingling of slaves brought about by the slave trade and the relocation of owners, some slave youths would have encountered difficulties in finding marriage partners. The isolation and small size of some slaveholdings, the low density of the slave population in some places, the skewed age structure and sex ratio typical of many slaveholdings, and the presence of large numbers of kin in one location sharply limited opportunities for slaves to marry. The opening of new areas of the South to settlement by slaveholders and the influx of slaves—men and women in equal numbers—into these regions increased the chances that all slaves of marriageable age would find suitable partners.[44]

Although the mobility of slaves helped resolve the problem of limited opportunity for marriage, it also created grief and anxiety among the people forcibly taken from one area of the South to another. The forced movement of slaves not only shattered existing family ties but also obscured family origins and thus created anxieties about a potential spouse's family lineage, knowledge considered important in slave culture. These anxieties manifested themselves in stories about marriages between close family members—typically a mother and a son—who, separated by the slave trade, later met and wed without recognizing each other. As the reports demonstrate, slaves felt their losses keenly and did not, as some slaveholders suggested, move in and out of family relationships without experiencing emotional turmoil. But slaves did marry in large numbers and at young ages. Courtship and marriage represented important stages of a slave's life.[45]

7

YOUNG LOVE AND MARRIAGE

When Ethel Jane, a woman on the next plantation, caught the eye of Walton, the Virginia youth requested a pass from his master to go and see her. A pass constituted written proof to patrollers and other free people that an owner had given the slave who carried it permission to travel for a specific purpose. Walton's master granted the entreaty, and Ethel Jane appeared willing to have the slave youth visit. But Ethel Jane's owner decided that Walton "was too small" to come calling on his slave. This brought the budding romance to an end.[1]

Like the owners of Ethel Jane and Walton, other slaveholders expected to decide the timing of courtship and coupling among their slaves and to constrain their slaves' choice of partner. Slaveholders who sought to control slave courting practices simultaneously encouraged sexual relationships within the slave quarter because this resulted in the formation of new families whose children expanded their holdings and because it accorded with their notions of proper management of slaves. Fostering family life among slaves helped to avert criticism of the southern slave system and of slave-

holders. Planters who gave consideration to their slaves' desire for families
set themselves apart from less caring plantation owners throughout the
Americas who denied their slaves the benefits of this most fundamental of
human institutions. Southern courts treated slaves as incapable of entering
into civil contracts, including marriage. Yet no state law expressly forbade
slaves from entering into unions they considered permanent, and nothing
prevented individual planters from permitting slave couples to participate
in marriage rites of their own or their owners' choosing.[2]

Even the most benevolent of slaveholders, however, were far from willing
to grant slaves independence in family matters or to guarantee that slave
couples could remain together. Because slave marriages often occurred off
the home place, they entangled owners in alliances with neighbors, whose
actions would affect a couple's ability to maintain the relationship. Even
when courtship occurred exclusively on the home place, rivalries among
suitors might disrupt the peace on the plantation, necessitating—in the
owner's mind—interference in the private lives of slaves. To ensure that
courtship proceeded smoothly and to their own liking and to assert their
authority in the matter, slaveholders claimed for themselves the role of surrogate parents who oversaw courtship and arranged marriages in the best
interests of everyone, owners and slaves alike. Walton's efforts at courting
were spurned not by Ethel Jane but by her master.

Slave youths were unwilling to grant owners the right to dictate the
terms of courtship or marriage, at least not without attempting first to forge
their own fate in these matters. Those who worked as adults generally considered themselves mature enough to make their own choices about whom
and when to court and marry. Although their choices were circumscribed
by their owners' power to grant or withhold passes for visiting and other
privileges that helped or hindered slaves in defining themselves as couples,
this did not stop slaves like Walton from attempting to woo women who
seemed unattainable. Ethel Jane's master and his son both maintained a
sexual interest in her, which could account for why the slaveholder turned
away Walton's overtures. Yet Walton pursued the young woman, and Ethel
Jane apparently encouraged him. She probably hoped that he would help
fend off unwanted sexual advances from her owners. Most likely Walton
worked as a man on his home estate and thought himself entitled to a man's
privileges, including female companionship of his own choosing.

Slave parents also sought to have a say in whom their sons and daughters
courted and when they married. Life in the quarter was difficult at best;
family helped slaves survive the deprivations and overcome the dehuman-

ization of enslavement. New family alliances had to be crafted carefully to make sure they enhanced, rather than curtailed, fragile routines of survival. Of course, not all slave youths had parents able to negotiate on their behalf. As a result of the slave trade, high mortality rates among slaves, and patterns of planter migration, many slave youths had no parents nearby to concern themselves with overtures from would-be suitors. In these cases, members of the larger slave community might step in to see that the interests of the slaves were not totally subordinated to those of owners.

Adult concern with slave courtship began as soon as boys and girls started to take a romantic interest in one another, which commenced around the time they grew old enough to work as adults and to be at risk for sale. Slave youths began performing work as prime hands in their midteens and married by their late teens or early twenties, and this period came to constitute a separate stage of a slave's life. At this time, young people shouldered heavy work burdens and suffered emotional anxiety as they awaited possible separation from their families, but they also enjoyed the companionship of other boys and girls of similar ages who shared comparable conditions of servitude. Owners, hoping to use to their advantage the attraction that adolescents had for one another, accommodated their desire for social activities by scheduling dances, candy pulls, and games, which they thought made slave youths more content, encouraged coupling and the birth of children, served as an incentive to improve productivity, and provided planters with a means of controlling behavior. Entertainments could be scheduled as a reward for work well done or withdrawn as a punishment for misbehavior. Alabama slave Hattie Clayton enjoyed dances on Saturday nights, for example, but only if her mistress found work in the field performed to her satisfaction the week before.[3] Dances were particularly popular among slave youths; consequently, the promise of a dance at the end of the week motivated young slaves such as Hattie to do their owners' bidding.

Slaves did not leave the question of whether or when to hold dances entirely to their owners' discretion. They initiated many dances by seizing on any special event as cause for celebration, and they risked punishment by holding them anyway when owners disapproved. When Pierce Butler arrived on his Georgia plantation for the first time with his wife and children, his slaves insisted that he let them stage a ball to mark the importance of the event. The knowledge that slave youths violated their orders by holding clandestine frolics encouraged slaveholders to schedule dances regularly and to grant permission for their slaves to frequent those sponsored by nearby planters. Joseph Maxwell allowed his slaves to use his barn for dances each Saturday night, which attracted his neighbors' slaves as well. Former slave Fannie Berry said that about a hundred slaves attended dances held at a neighbor's plantation in Virginia. Most owners preferred that their slaves participate in such supervised social events rather than deceive their owners as to their whereabouts.[4]

One advantage of scheduling dances was that slaveholders had some control over the invited guests. Owners worried about their slaves' choice of companionship. Clinton Clay of Virginia was particularly concerned to keep poor whites from attending dances and mixing with his slaves, although some managed "to steal in" despite his efforts. An Alabama planter staged parties—complete with food and a new dress—for any slave girl of courting age who expressed a desire for one, but he limited her choice of guests to those slaves of whom he approved. By planning and supervising social events such as dances, slaveholders might keep slave youths from seeking the attentions of someone they disliked.[5]

Social events could be manipulated to encourage relationships between boys and girls of whom owners approved, as well as to prevent particular relationships from blossoming. Slaveholders liked to promote romances between their slaves and those belonging to a relative, in part because the alliances blurred the distinctions between the owner's family and the slave family by seeming to incorporate slaves into the former. If a marriage resulted from the courtship, any children born to the couple would remain in the family, an added advantage. Another benefit of encouraging slave youths to mix with boys and girls belonging to relatives was that owners could obtain reliable reports on the character and activities of sweethearts. Slaves found such matches attractive because they offered increased opportunities for visiting spouses and children during events that brought the white family together. Slave men who married under such circumstances easily obtained permission to visit their families, sometimes for weeks at a time during slack periods of labor. Generally, men and women who found partners among slaves belonging to their owners' extended kin forged ties that proved more durable than those of slaves who married outside the family. Even when slaveholders relocated to new areas of the South, they rarely severed entirely their familial relationships back home. Through family correspondence, slaves who belonged to two branches of the same owning family might learn the fate of loved ones from whom they had been separated. Many planter families who migrated westward were followed by extended kin, increasing the chance that separated family members would one day join relatives in the new location.[6]

Slave youths, for their part, enjoyed the dances and other amusements offered by slaveholders, but the activities they organized on their own were more to their liking. At dances planned by owners, slaves had to be on their guard, knowing that their behavior would be scrutinized. In contrast, dances held in secret could become rowdy and involve couples in activities other than dancing. Former slave Sara Colquitt confessed that she and other slaves in attendance at one such dance "sho' did more'n dance." For this reason, dances organized without owner approval had to be held at some distance from slaveholders' homes to prevent their detection. On the Virginia plantation where Nancy Williams lived, young couples regularly slipped off in pairs to clandestine dances in the woods. Older youths traveled considerable distances to attend similar festivities elsewhere. One former slave recalled that he and his friends thought nothing of walking twelve miles to a dance.[7]

Dances as rituals of courtship offered models for consolidating gender identities, as boys and girls approaching adulthood conformed to expectations about male and female roles. The rituals could be competitive. At the dances Nancy Williams attended, boys flattered the girls they wished to impress and competed with one another by betting cash on which girl could out-dance the others. The girls, in turn, tried to impress boys with their dresses and other adornments, as well as their dancing abilities. Nancy recalled "dancin' wid a glass o' water on my head an' three boys a-bettin' on me." Her dancing attire consisted of a wreath bedecked with ribbons for her head, a yellow dress, and matching shoes dyed with paint intended for the barn. She used money she earned from quilting to purchase some of her finery, and probably also some small sums given to her from time to time by her master. Evidently, she spent whatever cash she accumulated on herself, without turning it over to her parents. Nancy knitted some items of apparel, including her stockings. By her own admission, Nancy dressed more elaborately than the other girls on her plantation, but most girls of courting age also attended to their appearance. To create fancy outfits, they sometimes starched their petticoats using hominy water, making them "so stiff that every time you stopped they would pop real loud." Other girls made hoops out of grapevines to make their skirts stand out in the fashion of the ladies of the owning class. "Gals always tried to fix up fo' partyin', even ef dey ain't got nothin' but a piece of ribbon to tie in dey hair," former Virginia slave Fannie Berry recalled.[8]

Girls considered stylish clothing important for courting. Owners understood this and frequently purchased items of clothing for women as incentives for hard work. Female slaves could look forward to acquiring items of clothing routinely following the harvest, when work was most demanding. Alabama planter John M. Chapron purchased calico and shawls for his female slaves during the cotton-picking season. One former slave attributed the lack of parties in the slave quarter where she grew up to a lack of appropriate clothing. "We wouldn't a had no cloes fo' goin' aroun'," she explained.[9]

So important were fancy clothes and other adornments to girls of courting age that they went to great lengths to obtain them. Virginia slave Mary Wyatt risked punishment by "borrowing" a dress from her mistress to wear to a dance, sneaking it out of the house under her petticoat. The master showed up at the dance but—much to Mary's relief—did not recognize or question her attire, which indicates that he commonly saw young female slaves wearing finery on special occasions. One Alabama mistress allowed her housegirls to wear her jewelry to church from time to time. All they had to do was ask for it and refrain from taking other items without permission. By liberally granting permission to use such fancy items, this mistress hoped to prevent theft or unauthorized borrowing by girls of courting age. Owners included beads, earrings, and other personal ornaments among their gifts to teenage girls and women. When slave girls could not obtain such items from other sources, they fashioned beads of dried berries and tucked rose or honeysuckle petals in their bosoms to enhance their attractiveness.[10]

Whereas girls tended to use fancy clothing or jewelry to attract boys, boys were more apt to "borrow" a means of transportation for visiting or to master a musical instrument to impress girls. Young men went about at night on horseback or mule so frequently that slaveowners felt the need to keep stock locked up at night to ensure that the animals were rested for the next day's work. Boys played fiddles, tambourines, banjos, and sets of bones to set the rhythm for dance steps. Older boys, who took pride in their musical accomplishments, serenaded girls at their homes in between dances, whenever they got the chance. Boys who were too young to attend the dances as participants practiced instruments in hopes of attending the events as musicians. As a youngster, Ned Chaney yearned to "git big enough ter knock bones" at dances.[11]

Boys also provided the alcohol that figured in some of the entertainments. The alcohol may have been stolen for the occasion or purchased with the small sums of money older boys accumulated by performing extra chores for owners or neighboring planters; by doing favors for their owners' guests; or by selling goods which they grew, handcrafted, or stole. Slave couples in Bedford County, Virginia, met surreptitiously to dance, listen to love songs, and drink wine. Dave Lowry recalled dancing to a love song whose lyrics encouraged drinking as part of the dance routine. At the refrain, "Rule over, rule under, give me a glass of drink wine, Don't want no more snow water," couples stopped dancing to sip a cup of wine.[12]

Competition by young men for the attention of girls occasionally extended beyond the dance floor to involve physical confrontations. In South Carolina, Griffen and Essex, from different plantations, fought for first place in the affections of a slave girl named Cindy. They disrupted the peace so often that their masters forced Cindy to end the competition by agreeing to take one or the other as her husband. In a similar incident, young men living on separate plantations, with supporters from their respective communities, challenged each other. The feud between Renty and Scipio ended when the object of their rivalry chose Renty for her husband. The woman's master heard about the disturbance but took no action, probably because the incident was resolved to his satisfaction. Renty lived on the same plantation as the young slave woman. By rejecting Scipio's attentions, she ensured that neither he nor his friends would return to stir up trouble in the quarter. Such conflicts between rival suitors helped convince some planters to discourage their slaves from courting men and women who belonged to other owners. Jealousies and flirtations roiled relations in the slave quarter as it was, and owners did not wish to extend them beyond the plantation's boundary if they could help it.[13]

Owners found it difficult to control relationships across property boundaries, however, in part because hands routinely visited from neighboring estates to help with extra work during harvest and other busy times of year. Slave youths took advantage of such events to socialize. Corn shucking usually involved slaves from nearby plantations, and the owner whose corn was shucked provided food and occasionally alcohol to make the event festive, despite the extra work required from each hand. Corn shucking—more commonly cause for revelry in the tobacco and cotton-producing regions of the South than in rice country—frequently evolved into dances that could last all night. Adele Frost enjoyed one in South Carolina that went until the early morning hours.[14]

Adults found it difficult to suppress the interest of boys and girls in one another—on or off the home place—when everyday work routines brought them together. Almost any event, from quilting parties to working in the fields, could serve as an occasion for flirting. Sometimes flirtatious behavior interfered with work. Boys attending quilting parties would try to grab a newly finished quilt and throw it over one of the girls. If a boy succeeded, he "was entitled to a hug and a kiss." Most adults tolerated such behavior; however, George Taylor disrupted field work so frequently by flirting with the girls that he had to be reassigned from picking cotton, which involved both sexes, to plowing, which occupied primarily men.[15]

Masters and mistresses expected to be kept abreast of romantic developments involving their slaves. Master John Chaplin of South Carolina, in a move typical of other slaveholders, insisted that slaves inform him when they began to court. Other owners interrogated young couples about their activities when they were out of sight, and they seldom hesitated to share their own views about what constituted appropriate behavior between sweethearts. Sarah Fitzpatrick's owners went so far as to ask her what she and her beau talked about when they were together. The former Alabama slave reported that her "Mistus use'ta look at my dress an' tell me when hit wuz right . . . Sometime she make me go back an' put on nother one, tell us what to wear, tell us to go back an' com' our heads." The ability of Sarah's mistress to interject herself in her slave's courtship stemmed in part from Sarah's position as a house servant. Girls who worked and lived at some distance from their owners' homes enjoyed greater independence in deciding how to dress or fix their hair for a walk with their beaus.[16]

Masters and mistresses were especially likely to scrutinize a favored house servant's love life because they feared the possible loss of services if a trained houseboy or girl married a field hand and moved to the slave quarter. Some discouraged house servants from courting and marrying at all, although they found it difficult to deny requests for permission to marry after a romance blossomed. Mistress Mary S. Mallard objected to her house slave Tenah's proposed marriage to Niger, but she soon relented and helped stage an elaborate celebration for the couple.[17] Although owners maintained the authority to forbid courtship, house servants could retaliate by performing their duties less diligently, and their access to the big house provided opportunities for destroying especially prized property or even harming members of the owning family.

When youths belonged to different owners, masters and mistresses involved themselves in slave courtship by writing letters and passes. If a boy wanted to court a girl, he could ask his master to write her a letter. Girls rarely if ever initiated the process, for it was considered the boy's prerogative to inaugurate the courtship, at least so far as the public display of the romance was concerned. The young woman's mistress would read the letter to her slave and respond after consulting the girl. Masters and mistresses corresponded on behalf of their slaves even if the slaves could read and write, because custom and, in some places, legal prohibitions against slave literacy required boys and girls to keep their learning a secret. By becoming involved in letter-writing romances, owners kept themselves informed of developments in a courtship and were in a position to intervene or offer advice if they thought it necessary. Even when owners were not involved in such letter-writing campaigns, they asserted a right to grant or withhold permission for young men to visit sweethearts living off the home place.

The system of requiring slaves to have passes when off the plantation or farm, common throughout the South, stemmed in part from the desire of owners to control visiting between courting couples. Thus, slaves under the age of physical maturity might "go play and diden need no pass," but those old enough to court and form sexual liaisons needed permission to visit.[18] Passes could be issued if a slaveholder wished to encourage a particular relationship or withheld if he or she wanted to discourage its development. Patrollers—men who looked for slaves off the plantation without a pass— did their best to control courtship according to the wishes of owners who approved or denied passes as they pleased.

Parents, like owners, tried to regulate the romantic attractions of slave youths. When their sons and daughters attended adult-sanctioned parties or dances at night, parents and other adult slaves usually served as chaperones or at least let the young people know when to come home by using field calls (also called hollers or shouts). Older slaves might escort boys and girls home following a night of partying. As children grew older and bolder, parents found it more challenging to regulate visiting, especially when it occurred off the home estate. Although girls journeyed off the home place for other reasons, boys usually visited girls in courtship, instead of the other way around. If an owner granted a slave boy's request to visit a special girl on another plantation and issued him a pass, parents found it difficult to overrule the slaveholder's decision in the matter.[19] Parents of girls found it a bit easier to control their visitors, but even they were hard-pressed to keep their daughters away from boys if the couple had gained their owners' consent for the courtship.

When young people living on separate holdings were determined to see each other, efforts by owners and parents alike to keep a couple apart often proved inadequate. Considerable visiting occurred off the plantation as boys and girls courted "on the sly." By age fifteen, George Coulton was already experienced at avoiding Virginia patrollers; he considered it "a great sport" to outrun them. Boys stole through meadows and back woods to visit "pretty gals," but girls could initiate the visits by letting it be known that they wanted the boys to come. Girls and boys living on separate estates who wanted to meet surreptitiously devised ways of communicating to make known their plans for group activities and to arrange for couples to meet. Some boys blew horns, but drums also sufficed. Field calls beckoned slaves to clandestine meetings, often held after dark. Coded messages signaled the desire for a meeting at a particular place and time, or warned visitors to return home right away. When masters in one area of Alabama attempted to curtail social visiting between adjoining plantations, the visits continued despite punishments. In fact, some owners found that punishment only prompted slaves to run away.[20]

Slaves in central Virginia, where small slaveholdings predominated, courted off the plantation more often, but slaves in central Alabama and along the coasts of South Carolina and Georgia were not immune to the charms of those who lived off the home place. Errands of all types brought slave youths into contact with neighboring slaves and widened their choices of sweethearts. Nathan Beauchamp met his future wife, Mimi, when each went to Eufaula, Alabama, he to bring back supplies for the plantation and she to sell baskets. They got to know each other by sharing a ride in the wagon Nathan drove on this and subsequent occasions. Reuben Fitzpatrick accompanied his master, a magistrate, on his rounds in Alabama, sometimes staying away overnight. Reuben enjoyed his travels, which required him to sleep in different slave quarters where he doubtless enjoyed meeting girls his own age.[21]

Housegirls generally found it more difficult to meet admirers than girls who worked in the field. Not only did their owners supervise them more closely, but they also had fewer opportunities to talk and walk with boys. Mildred Graves of Virginia regretted working in her owner's home because it curtailed opportunities for engaging in the amusements enjoyed by young folks during their courting years. When a field hand she barely knew asked her to marry him, she said yes right away "'cause I was tired livin' in de house where dey wasn't no fun." Sallie Stevenson jumped at the chance to marry in South Carolina at age thirteen. As a housegirl, she had rarely been out from under the watchful eye of her mistress, even sleeping in her mistress's bedchamber at night. After marrying she remained a servant in the big house, but she slept in a separate room with her own family. To enable them to interact with boys of a similar age, owners sometimes dispatched girls whom they did not wish to keep as a permanent part of the domestic staff from the house (where they worked mainly with women) to the field (where they encountered both sexes). Nancy Williams said she worked in her owner's home as a girl, but "when I got growd up an' start dis cou'tin dey took me ouder de house an' put me in de fiel to wuck."[22]

Owners worried if a slave woman did not show an early interest in courting. For slaveholders who intervened in courtship, the question was not whether slaves would marry, but which slaves, when, and under what circumstances. Slaveholders wanted to increase their labor forces by encouraging young slaves to have children, which would augment their financial assets. Especially in the upper South, planters counted on slave sales to supplement their earnings from farming tobacco and wheat. They readily acknowledged the link between a profitable estate and slave childbirths. Writing in the pages of the *Cotton Planter and Soil,* one planter admitted that "no inconsiderable part of a farmer's profits . . . [are] in the little negroes he succeeds in raising." An estimate of the profits to be realized from a Virginia property worked by four men and four women stated frankly that the largest profits from the plantation would be realized from the future increase of the slave labor force, "for no person can doubt but that four young men and four women . . . would double and triple themselves in value in twenty years." The author of these words boasted of his profit from the increase of his slaves in the past: "I placed a negro man and woman on a small plantation . . . which negros cost me about $800 in 1818 . . . and they have now [thirteen years later] nine children worth between 3 and 4000 Dollars."[23]

In buying slaves, planters often tried to make sure that each hand had an opportunity to marry. "My number of hands is thirty," remarked an Alabama planter in the pages of an agricultural journal. "I have them as near equally divided as possible of males and females. I do this in order that each man may have his own wife on the premises." One fifteen-year-old slave youth, at the direction of his Alabama master, chose a wife from a passing coffle of slaves. Some traders sold slaves in pairs—man and woman —to ensure the possibility of reproduction. Purchases of potential marriage partners occurred most often in places where labor needs left planters short-handed. Under these circumstances, the acquisition of a new slave represented an opportunity for economic gain through increased production of the staple crop and increased reproduction of the slave force.[24]

Most slave youths needed little encouragement to develop a romantic interest in the opposite sex. Both slave and slaveholding communities placed their hopes for the future on the reproduction of the slave population through the births of slave children; the earlier women entered into sexual relationships, the longer they had to bear children. Thus, early coupling suited the purposes of both slaves and owners, and slaves of both sexes began courting by their mid-teens. On those occasions when a girl proved slow to favor someone special, owners interfered.

Efforts by slaveholders to foster childbearing ranged from subtle persuasion to outright force. Some owners compelled slaves to enter into marriages or other types of sexual relations through physical coercion. One former slave attested to the practice thus: "White folks would make you take dat man whe' if you want him or no." That situation was uncommon, however. The extensive effort that would have been required to force sexual partners upon slaves and ensure that the couple stayed together deterred all but the most ardent of would-be breeders from attempting to force coupling. Nevertheless, the knowledge that forced pairings occurred occasionally worried slaves and pushed them into early marriages of their own making, rather than marriages arranged by their owners.[25]

Although most efforts by owners to encourage coupling were not overtly coercive, people believed the contrary. Travelers to the South reported the practice of deliberately breeding slaves for sale as fact, and slaves considered the practice widespread. Many slaves believed that owners bred slaves, whether for sale or for their own use, much as they did stock. Former slave Mandy McCullough understood that her master raised children for sale in Alabama. Joseph Holmes thought all Virginia masters "raised niggers tuh sell." Explanations for how breeding occurred differed from slave to slave. Viney Baker believed her father to be a "stock nigger," by which she apparently meant a physically superior man kept by his owner specifically to impregnate women. Alice Wright, born in Alabama during the late antebellum period, reported that owners put "medicine in the water (cisterns) to make young slaves have more children." The fact that owners prized "good breeding" women, preferring to purchase rather than to sell them, reinforced such notions, as did the presence of sizeable numbers of children who did not know their fathers. Viney Baker had moved from her native Virginia to North Carolina when very young. Her subsequent separation from her mother, also at a young age, left her with no one to explain her lineage.[26]

When stories of forced breeding circulated in the South, slave girls worried about the fate that awaited them. Many preferred early marriage to remaining vulnerable to an owner's attempts to coerce marriage. Nevertheless, a large number of female slaves resisted the impulse to marry at the first opportunity. For slave women, menarche occurred around age fifteen, but most women did not bear children until they reached their late teens or early twenties; one study found the average age at which slave women had their first child to be 20.6 years. The fact that they did not bear children three or four years earlier, as soon as they became physically capable, suggests that they succeeded in maintaining some control over when and whom they married.[27]

Occasionally, owners tried to manipulate slaves' sexual relationships to produce preferred physical traits. Former slave Henry H. Buttler thought that owners wanted to approve marriages in Virginia mainly in order to breed slaves for desirable physical characteristics. Thomas Johns maintained that owners paired large men and women in the area of Alabama where he grew up, even if they were married to other people. The former slave cited the case of "a big woman" married to a "little man," whose owner made him leave "so's dere would be big children, which dey could sell well." Jim Allen, also of Alabama, reported that his master paired "a good nigger man an' a good nigger woman," directing them to marry and produce children, so as to avoid purchasing slaves in the market. Carrie Davis recalled that an exchange of men and women between plantations occurred in Alabama whenever her master "wanted to mix his stock of slaves wid a strong stock an 'nother plantation." Such efforts by owners to coerce or pressure slaves into marrying affected both young men and women; however, women were far more frequently the victims of forced sex.[28]

Although slaves no doubt admired men and women of exceptional strength or carriage, other qualities determined the desirability of spouses, as evidenced by the need for owners to manipulate or even strong-arm large or muscular slaves to couple with one another. One Missouri woman, pressured by her owner to remarry following her forced separation from her husband, chose as her new spouse a man too sickly to father children or to work at heavy agricultural tasks, hardly the outcome her owner intended. Her decision indicates that her motivation for marrying differed from that propelling her owner to push for her remarriage. For slaves, marriages created alliances that were important in maintaining patterns of life within the slave quarter and helpful for enduring bondage. Slaveholders hoped to produce obedient, industrious workers through slave pairings, which contradicted the notion that owners acted with parental concern for their slaves. When slave youths chose small or weak partners, they not only created networks of supportive kin but directly challenged their owners' attempts at manipulating slave marriages for their own ends. However erroneous their beliefs about the deliberate breeding of slaves may have been, Mandy

McCullough, Joseph Holmes, Viney Baker, and Alice Wright understood clearly that owner interference in intimate matters was not benign.[29] Even though most owners did not force particular partners upon their slaves, they did care about the physical attributes of slave spouses. Some devised tests of physical endurance for deciding when and whom slaves could marry. Charlie Van Dyke of Alabama maintained that his master would not allow "a man to marry unless he could split a hundred rails a day." More often, the ability to engage in regular field work indicated a slave's eligibility for marriage. Former South Carolina slave Toby Brown said that "half hands" could marry, a term employed commonly on the rice-growing coast to describe youths in their middle to late teens who had the capacity to undertake adult work in the field. The practice of linking the ability to work with eligibility for marriage prevented marriages between slaves who had not matured physically, but it also prevented physically impaired slaves from marrying. Disabled slaves might marry if their impairments were the result of accidental injury rather than heredity, however.[30]

Boys and girls who matured early and began performing adult labor at an especially early age often accepted a definition of adulthood tied to physical development and tried to use it to their advantage. They cited their physical attributes to claim the privileges afforded adults, including opportunities for marriage. George Earle, for one, took a wife at age fourteen because he "was as big as any grown man and nobody could tell any difference." Most slaves and slaveholders apparently considered fourteen too young for marriage; a more suitable age for such a commitment was thought to be the late teens. But George—whose sale to new owners presented the opportunity—lied about his age. He justified the falsehood on the ground that his ability to perform the work of a man entitled him to a wife.[31]

Because owners preferred that their slaves be content with their husbands or wives, they concentrated their efforts to ensure impregnation only when it became apparent that a slave's fertile years were passing her by. The younger the woman, the more likely her owner was to allow her to turn down overtures from a suitor; however, older women might find themselves pressured into accepting a proposal, especially if the prospective groom found the match attractive. Masters might even assign husbands to women who by a certain age had not entered into marriages of their own choosing; occasionally they approved a marriage between a man who wanted to marry and a woman who refused the match. In most of these cases, owners left the problem of bringing the recalcitrant "wives" into line to their "husbands."[32]

Incidents of forced marriage may explain why some owners established rules forbidding husbands and wives to fight.

Because slaveholders knew that boys and girls developed an interest in one another of their own accord, most employed only subtle measures to bring particular slaves together. Owners took notice when slaves took a fancy to each other, because they could easily pressure couples into marriage by exploiting an existing attraction. Former Virginia slave Georgina Gibbs recalled that if her master saw couples spending time together "he would marry them." Resistance on the part of the slaves was minimal under such circumstances. All "young girls must marry," observed one northern woman witnessing the end of slavery in South Carolina, "but, usually, mild means are effectual." Everyone understood the consequence of delayed marriage—forced pairing or sale.[33]

Slave women had little choice but to become sexually active at an early age. Women who bore children generally enjoyed greater stability in their place of residence and in their family relationships, at least until their children grew old enough to command high prices in the slave market. A woman who did not become a mother while young risked being sold because "she didn't bear children like dey wanted her to." It did not matter whether the women had husbands or not. By parting childless couples, slaveholders revealed their lack of scruples concerning the sanctity of slave unions, although some of the owners who sold these women probably congratulated themselves for respecting the slave family by avoiding the sale of mothers. Many previously childless women became pregnant after their sale. Some may have avoided sexual intercourse previously because they could not find husbands to their liking or because they did not like the partners to whom they had been assigned. Others loved their first husbands and grieved at the parting.[34]

Slaveowners offered rewards for women to bear children, even as they punished those who did not. Slaves responded to incentives because they had their own reasons for wanting to marry and raise children. A cabin, complete with furnishings, represented one benefit of establishing a family with an owner's approval. Newly constructed cabins afforded privacy for young couples, most of whom knew only the crowded conditions of their parents' homes. Household furnishings included beds and bedclothes, implements for cooking and eating, and tables and chairs. Householders also usually obtained small patches of land for growing food or, in some cases, crops for cash. An Alabama planter who allowed slaves to grow corn in what he called the "negroes' field" allotted extra land to slave families. A

Virginia planter permitted all slaves to raise poultry; those with families could raise hogs. Still another Virginia master gave each slave family land for raising poultry and vegetables, together with an annual cash payment of $10.00 if they grew their own food. Mothers sometimes received special items of apparel and worked shorter hours in the field than other hands so they could cook, clean, do laundry, and attend to their babies. Although every couple did not obtain all these benefits, most slaves improved their living conditions through marriage and parenting.[35]

Slaves did not marry and have children solely to reap material rewards, but children helped ensure the family's access to the material goods required for survival. The rewards and privileges extended to parents, coupled with the ability of children to contribute to a family's welfare through such activities as gathering food and fuel, substantially improved the living conditions of most slaves. Indeed, single slaves rarely lived alone because they would have experienced a significant decrease in their standard of living. Slaveholders recognized this and assigned single slaves to live with established families, instead of living in barracks as occurred in other times and places in the Americas. Single slaves provided families with an extra pair of hands for growing food and carrying out other subsistence activities.[36]

SLAVE COUPLES could reap rewards only if they gained an owner's approval for marrying. The process of obtaining permission for marriage was similar to that for courting. The ability of slaveowners to withhold permission for passes or for separate cabins and other material goods strengthened the importance of securing the owners' consent rather than the parents'. In traditional agricultural societies, parents held the land and other resources that couples needed to begin married life. In the antebellum South, slave youths had to negotiate with owners for many of these items. The prospective bridegroom initiated the request to marry by approaching his owner. If the owner approved of the match and the woman belonged to another slaveholder, he or she wrote to the woman's owner. The woman's owner would reply, usually after consulting with the prospective bride and inquiring about the character of the intended groom. Owners carefully considered the prospective bridegroom's character and other attributes because a husband's visits to his wife brought him in contact not only with her but also with other slaves living on the estate. The Jones family, headed by a Presbyterian minister, preferred that their slaves marry members of a church, for example.[37]

Slaveholders rejected some, perhaps even the majority, of requests to marry, particularly those from field hands, who tended to be less familiar to them than house servants. Owners often said no outright, or they agreed in principle to the marriage without taking steps to ensure that it actually occurred. Julia Woodberry never married, although she "was engaged by letter" to a man in her native South Carolina. Her owners kept such close watch on her activities that she "never didn' slip de hay," either, by which she meant that she and her fiancé never engaged in sexual relations. Slaves, for their part, learned not to accept the first answer they received from owners. When Niger asked to marry Tenah, her mistress at first denied his request to marry the house servant, but the couple obtained her blessing a short time later.[38]

Slaves found it easier to negotiate marriages with owners if both slaves belonged to the same person; but many prospective brides and grooms belonged to different owners, especially in the upper South. Farmers with small slaveholdings generally did not object to their women finding husbands off the home place because the women would bear children, which would add to the owner's wealth, and because owners of limited means could not afford to purchase potential marriage partners. Owners with large slaveholdings consented less readily to a slave woman's choosing a husband from off the home plantation, reasoning that on larger holdings women could find husbands at home. Charles Manigault refused permission for any of the women on his South Carolina plantation to take husbands from a different estate, for example. Another planter expressed this view in the pages of a widely circulated agricultural journal: "On small farms where there are very few negroes, it may be proper to allow them to visit to a limited extent, but on large plantations there can be no want of society, and consequently no excuse for visiting except among themselves." Slaves who objected to finding a spouse on the home place should remain single, the author continued. Masters whose slaveholdings had an imbalance in the sex ratio should purchase suitable partners for their slaves, for they would be better off paying "an extra price for such an one as his would be willing to marry, than to have one man owning the husband and another the wife."[39]

Owners hoped to avoid the distress associated with dissolving families. The slaveholders' concept of what it meant to be a "good master" or "good mistress" required that they help married couples remain together; the act of selling husbands and wives did not accord with the benevolent image that slaveholders liked to convey. However, owners got around the problem of wanting to appear respectful of slave family relationships yet wishing to benefit from the sale of slaves by convincing themselves that relationships between young slave couples lacked importance. They applied the term "marriage" only to those unions of which they approved. Plantation record books, in which owners sometimes made notations of family groups, displayed a pattern whereby slaves were sorted into categories of "married" and "unmarried," depending on whether owners approved of the match. Because slaves sanctioned some unions of which owners disapproved, the lists made it seem as though some young men and women engaged in prenuptial intercourse with regularity. The slaveholders' distinctions between "married" and "unmarried" slaves were no doubt in part a reaction to critics of slavery in the North who complained about the interregional slave trade's disruption of slave family life. Slave couples regarded as "unmarried" might be separated without compunction and without tarnishing a planter's paternalist image. Thus, the "problem" of separating spouses could be reduced if slaves married only those suitors approved by owners.[40]

Owners were more likely to recognize marriages between slaves who lived on the same estate. Planters who claimed both husband and wife could keep the spouses together if they relocated to new areas of the South. If they needed cash or credit, they could choose to sell an unmarried slave or a couple, or at least someone other than the spouse of a favored slave or one whom they often encountered. A master whose slaves had mates on neighboring plantations could find his independence compromised as he argued with a neighbor about the fate of a married couple after he made plans to emigrate west or to sell slaves. Although state law gave owners the authority to move or sell slaves as they wished, custom required that slaveholders at least appear to consider ways of keeping slave families intact. The only exceptions involved slaves sold because of serious infractions of plantation rules or extenuating financial circumstances.

While some owners tried to maintain control of their estates by preventing slaves from marrying off the plantation or farm, others hoped to achieve the same end by purchasing an intended bride or groom. Harris Mosley's owners purchased his wife from an adjoining Alabama plantation after the couple decided to marry. This strategy had the desired effect of pleasing the slaves and ensuring their ties to the plantation. By occasionally uniting couples through purchase, slaveholders fanned hope among other couples living on separate estates that one day they too might be united. Most slaves who married off the home place continued to maintain separate residences, however, and children born to such unions were considered the property of the mother's owner.[41]

A genuine desire to please young people in love motivated some slave-holders who purchased husbands and wives. Owners who procured spouses from other estates benefited by keeping the children under the care of both parents. This helped to ensure the children's survival and the growth of the slaveholder's work force. Not all offers to purchase husbands or wives represented serious attempts to unite couples, however. Owners who had no intention of purchasing a particular husband or wife some-times made a token offer at a very low price. They felt the need to display at least a semblance of consideration for their slaves' desire to live with spouses, as a means of maintaining the fiction that slaveowners acted in the best interests of their slaves. They also feared retaliation from slaves, who might run away, work at a slower pace, or engage in other behavior in-tended to hurt the owner's economic interests. Failure to exert any effort to purchase a bride or groom signaled an owner's unwillingness or inability to respect the union, and it imparted the message that slaves could expect no favors from their owners if they continued the relationship.

A major advantage of purchasing a slave's spouse was the curtailment of visiting between plantations. Owners' reluctance to approve marriages off the home place stemmed in part from a recognition that clandestine visiting between spouses, which occurred regularly, challenged patriarchal author-ity. In the view of the owning class, surreptitious visits to wives in the night challenged the slaveholder's dominion over slaves and threatened public safety. But owners found it difficult to enforce rules aimed at keeping slaves on their home estates. Measures taken by two masters and local patrollers could not prevent Lewis Singleton from slipping away from his Alabama plantation to visit the woman he loved. Powerless to keep the couple apart, Singleton's master relented and "traded two hosses an' some money" to purchase the young woman, thereby ending Singleton's night travels and not inconsequentially his ongoing defiance of plantation rules. The master's desire to keep Singleton from visiting his sweetheart probably stemmed in part from his wish to make sure the slave appeared in the field adequately rested for work each morning, instead of fatigued from roving at night. The young woman's master apparently had tried unsuccessfully to insist that she choose a husband from among his own slaves. Slaveholders who curtailed the mobility of their own slaves to regulate courting resented owners who permitted theirs to roam about as they pleased.[42]

The practice of buying spouses appealed mostly to larger planters such as those found in Alabama and along the rice coast, during periods when high prices for agricultural products made expansion of the labor force attractive or when favorite house servants wanted to marry slaves belonging to other planters. Neighboring planters were reluctant to part with a valuable hand during economic booms, however, and they often proved unwilling to sell favorite servants, particularly if they considered them well-trained or loyal members of the household. Hetty and Dick's respective owners agreed in advance that the couple should live together after their marriage, which meant that one of the owners had to sell one of the pair to the other. Dick displeased his owners by stating a preference to live with his wife. They hated to lose a well-trained butler, but they also resented his willingness to sever the personal relationship he had formed with them. Dick's decision, which he apparently made with no regret, exposed as fantasy the widespread belief among slaveholders that a slave's most important relationship was the one he or she maintained with an owner. Many slaves were not so fortunate as Dick, whose owners went ahead with the sale despite their hurt feelings.[43]

The tactic of purchasing slave spouses held little attraction for a slaveowner with limited means or with a labor force already too large. Only the wealthiest planters or those with the ambition and means to expand agricultural operations could take advantage of the strategy. Consequently, planters along the rice coast and in cotton country bought spouses more often than Virginia's tobacco and wheat planters. But smallholders throughout the South lacked the means to buy new slaves. When hard times forced a South Carolina minister to sell his farm and remove west with his family, he never contemplated purchasing his slave Betty's husband, who lived on a nearby farm; he had barely enough cash to purchase a small piece of land and the provisions necessary to see his family through the first year of frontier living.[44]

Smallholders of necessity relied heavily on neighbors to supply spouses for their slaves. Some, as interested in the growth of the labor force as in the cultivation of a crop, preferred to own female over male hands. Nancy Washington belonged to a smallholder in South Carolina who chose to limit his holdings to females. She married at age sixteen to a man belonging to a rich planter in the neighborhood. His owners were unhappy about the situation, but they raised no outright objection. Washington explained later that "dey hab good manners." Her words indicate that wealthy planters felt pressured to accept alliances between their slave men and bondswomen belonging to poorer neighbors. To have done otherwise would have violated the rules (or "manners" in Washington's words) of the paternalistic ethos that characterized the South.[45]

Wealthy slaveowners thus helped to support the South's slaveholding re-gime by supplying mates for a smallholder's female slaves and making it possible for a farmer with only one or two slaves to expand his or her labor force. For their part, smallholders took care not to presume upon their neighbors' generosity. They did not want to upset their rich and more pow-erful neighbors by granting their slaves carte blanche to court whomever they pleased, and they withheld approval for their own slaves to marry off the home place until they had secured the neighbor's cooperation. Even in Virginia, where the custom of "abroad" marriages predominated, slavehold-ers could not assume their slaves would be welcome to court a woman liv-ing on another man's estate. A neighbor might spurn a slave man's over-tures toward his bondswoman for many reasons, ranging from the would-be husband's small stature to the owner's wish to reserve the woman for his own sexual pleasure. Letters written by owners to secure permission for their slaves to court and marry partners living on separate holdings spelled out an agreement between owners as much as slaves. Smallholders who owned female slaves awaited word from wealthy neighbors as to whether they might enter into an alliance, cemented by the web of kinship that would tie together the lives of their bonded men and women.[46]

Slaveholders occasionally went to great lengths to ensure that a slave did not marry a particular man or woman to avoid entangling themselves with a particular slaveholder whom they disliked. When a slave formed a relation-ship with another slave, the owner wanted assurances that any family ties thus established would not jeopardize his ability to act independently. Lewis W. Paine, a free resident of Georgia in the 1840s, noted that when two slaves who wanted to marry had separate owners, the marriage could not take place if the owning "families are at variance" with each other. Owners feared that a hostile planter might use slaves to spy on or disrupt plantation operations. When Virginia slave George Johnson asked to marry a woman from a nearby farm, his master sent Johnson to Alabama to live with one of his sons. Only when the woman died two years later did his master allow him to return to Virginia. Yet despite such complications, marriages of slaves living on separate holdings occurred frequently.[47]

YOUNG slave couples seeking to marry sought not only the permission of owners for marriage but also that of parents. Even though slaveholders maintained the authority to approve or disapprove marriages by controlling many of the resources slaves needed to begin married life, slave parents found ways to influence their children's marital choices. On most slave-holdings, members of a slave family, and sometimes the larger slave community, found it necessary to pool resources and cooperate to ensure that everyone maintained an adequate diet and secured shelter from the elements. Children, needing this community support, were reluctant to alienate parents by marrying against their wishes. Thus, the precariousness of everyday life enhanced the ability of parents to participate in decisions about their children's marriages.

The resources that parents had to share—albeit meager—could help young couples avoid total dependence on their owners. Many slaveholders allocated land for slaves to garden or to graze animals. Although some owners parceled out this land to individual families, others left decisions about its use to the slaves. When slaves decided who had access to land or to the products of communal gardening and pasturing, they could grant or withhold resources important for young couples. Parents often had seeds or plant cuttings to share with their children, as well as household implements and hand-crafted tools. Cabin construction usually fell to men. Although a young husband might build a cabin himself after securing permission from an owner, he almost always counted on help from other slaves. If he lived on a separate estate from his wife and children, he found it especially hard to construct a home without the cooperation of the slaves on his wife's plantation. Thus, fathers and mothers, and also unrelated slaves, found ways of influencing the marital choices of slave youths, just as owners did. Unrelated slaves could justify their interference on the ground that they would need to interact with any new spouse in their midst, who of necessity would be entrusted with the slave quarter's secrets.[48] Also, many young couples had no parents present to assist them in establishing a new household.

Parents found it difficult, but not impossible, to reject a son's or daughter's choice of spouse if an owner approved of the match. When Virginia slave Philip Coleman "took a great fancy to" a young woman whom he hoped to marry, his master, who wanted to encourage the relationship, felt it necessary to make "overtures to the young woman's mother." She "put up so strong objection" to a proposed wedding that it was called off, despite the wishes of her daughter, the proposed bridegroom, and the master. Maria Bracey of South Carolina never married the man she loved because her father objected to the union.[49] In deciding whether to approve a marriage, owners considered the likely reaction of parents whose cooperation they valued in the house and field.

In the long term, parents and other adult slaves recognized that their children's welfare and that of the slave community hinged on the ability of slave youths to assume adult roles, including those of spouse and parent. The insecurity of slave life worked both ways. Just as young couples needed the support of family and community, so did the slave community require the cooperation and contributions of the younger generation to sustain patterns of living in the slave quarter. When young couples requested permission to marry, older slaves usually acquiesced, confining their interference to manipulating the choice of marriage partner and the timing of the wedding. To do otherwise might force young couples to elicit the support of their owners, which would have undermined solidarity in the quarter.

Still, the poverty of slave families meant that many parents were reluctant to grant permission for sons and daughters to establish separate households because they would give up the economic help of their children. When a daughter continued to live with her family of origin following a marriage, her parents benefited from the contribution of food and other assistance to the household from her husband. Although they might live on a different estate, slave men through their contributions to the welfare of wives and children established a claim to the roles of husband and father despite their absence during much of the week. Some husbands furnished their families with considerable property. Absalom Ransom of Virginia kept chickens, bacon, a hog, a blanket, and "a large counterpaine" at the home of his wife, who lived two miles away on another estate. Men hunted and fished, and some appropriated large animals, such as hogs, sheep, and even cows, for clandestine butchering. Slave men chopped and hauled wood for heating and cooking, which consumed considerable time. Former slave Nancy Settles, of Edgefield, South Carolina, recalled that her father, who lived on another plantation, visited the cabin regularly and performed chores while he was there. On Saturday evenings he would "chop wood out uv de wood lot and pile up plenty fur Ma till he come agin." On Wednesday evenings, he would come after hunting, bringing possum and coon for the table.[50]

The ability of men to provide material goods for their families encouraged parents to approve early marriage for their daughters. The parents of the intended bride would assess the man's willingness and ability to provide for a new family. Sons probably encountered greater difficulty in obtaining parental consent for marriages, because at least some of their labor went to help support their new family instead of their family of origin.

These economic circumstances help to explain why parents sometimes forbade marriages that owners approved. The efforts of slave men on behalf of
their families did not go unnoticed by their owners either, since some of the
man's labor would indirectly benefit his wife's owner rather than his own.
While owners with female slaves might have been willing to approve almost
any matches with men who lived "abroad," many hesitated to do so because they also owned men themselves, and stood to lose the labor of these
young men if they took brides on neighboring estates. This may explain, in
part, why slave men tended to marry at older ages than slave women. Slave
men generally were sold at slightly older ages than women, which meant
that many of those relocated through sale were older than their female
counterparts when they arrived in areas where they could establish relatively stable households. Another reason is that slave boys matured physically at a somewhat later age than slave girls.[51]

ONCE OWNERS and slaves agreed that a marriage could take place, the
parties involved had to decide what, if any, ceremony would mark the occasion. Slaves considered weddings important events. They wanted a public
ceremony, complete with vows and a special supper. Wedding ceremonies
held special appeal to slaves because they gave recognition to marriages
that had no legal standing. Owners objected to them for the same reason.
At the beginning of the antebellum period, slaveowners arranged weddings
only for a small number of favorite slaves, because financial and religious
considerations made them unwilling to assent to any public ritual that implied the couple would not be sold separately or remarry after being parted
from a spouse. Ministers expected any couples they united to pledge their
faithfulness until death. Owners who allowed slaves to marry were thus obligated by moral and religious principles to help the couple live up to their
vows. Consequently, few slaves married under the auspices of a church. By
the 1840s, however, the situation had changed. Churches had split into
northern and southern factions, and southern clergy were eager to prove
they could minister to the slaveholding regime without challenging the institution of slavery.[52]

   In the late antebellum years, an increasing number of ministers concluded that they could participate in ceremonies which they knew might
someday be dissolved through the actions of owners. As ministers grew
more flexible in their attitudes toward slave marriages, owners became more
willing to grant slaves a religious ceremony. At the behest of owners, clergy-

men altered the traditional marriage rite to imply that owners might part couples joined in matrimony. One minister married a couple with the words "until death or distance do you part." Another, who performed a marriage service for a slave couple in the dining room of the Henry Tutwiler home in Alabama, made it clear that Tutwiler's authority superseded any he had from God to perform the service. "By virtue of the authority given me by Mr. Tutwiler," the preacher told the couple at the start of the ritual, "I will perform the ceremony which will unite you two as man and wife."[53] Slaves thus found it easier to gain access to religious ceremonies when slaveholders and ministers conspired to divest the rite of its meaning.

These shifting attitudes toward slave marriages did not meet with the approval of all church officials or even all slaveholders. Holland Nimmons M'Tyeire criticized the trend toward slave marriages divested of traditional meaning in an essay that Alabama Baptists thought prizeworthy. The published version of the composition, *Duties of Christian Masters,* promoted marriage ceremonies for slaves, complete with a "marriage supper," but it recommended that owners skip the ceremony entirely rather than make a mockery of it by altering the words of the marriage service to change its meaning. Any "impediments should be looked into" before the ceremony, "and if any grave ones exist, they should work a prohibition," M'Tyeire warned; "the master, as he fears God, is bound to respect this rite." After 1840, other denominations joined the Alabama Baptists in admonishing slaveholders to respect the marriage vows of their slaves. "Every Christian master should so regulate the sale or disposal of a married slave, as not to infringe the Divine injunction forbidding the separation of husband and wife," advised a committee of South Carolina Episcopalians. Such warnings notwithstanding, the trend was in the opposite direction. Increasing numbers of slaves "married" in ceremonies that held little meaning in the minds of the owners who organized them. In fact, the number of slave weddings conducted by individual ministers at times exceeded the number of marriages they performed for their white congregants. Slaves never constituted more than 7.9 percent of Episcopal church membership in Alabama from 1848 to 1860, but they never accounted for less than 14.5 percent of the weddings. At one point, the proportion of slave weddings among Alabama Episcopalians rose to one-third of the total.[54]

As the number of slave weddings increased, so did the number of complaints by church synods and conferences that married slaves were not adhering to their sacred vows. For the most part, church governing bodies blamed masters for separating couples through sale, rather than clergy for uniting couples under circumstances that all but ensured wedding vows would be broken. Nevertheless, church officials refrained from enforcing injunctions against slave family separations, although some individual churches did discipline slave members for adultery and other infractions of rules related to marriage. In 1854, the Charleston Presbytery recommended to no avail that church courts and ministers enforce "on *Masters* themselves, the obligation to adhere more rigidly to the Saviour's command, and refrain from separating their married servants, except in cases of criminal offence."[55]

Despite the changing attitudes of ministers, some slaveholders remained skeptical about the wisdom of calling in a minister to perform a slave wedding—perhaps out of religious conviction, or the difficulty of persuading local clergy to cooperate in altering the service to the owner's liking. Even in the late antebellum years, many slaveholders preferred to officiate themselves at the wedding to make sure no misunderstandings occurred over the precise meaning of the ceremony. Most weddings conducted by owners pointedly omitted the phrase "until death do us part." Slaves understood perfectly the meaning of the omission, but one Virginia master went further by expounding during the ceremony upon his ability to part the couple. This owner, during the wedding of Joshua and Beck, expressed his intention to sell the wife if she did not improve her behavior. "I never wish to part man & wife," he said, but if such action becomes necessary, Joshua should understand the conditions under which he marries Beck. If she should be sold, Joshua "must not then say I have taken his wife from him." Other slaveholders, who approved the increasing numbers of slave marriages in the late antebellum years, made every effort to impress upon slave couples their power to dissolve marriages if the partners did not adhere to a rigid set of standards for behavior on and off the field. Thus, owners manipulated marriage ceremonies to control their slaves.[56]

After they resolved their doubts that marriage ceremonies would hinder their ability to sell slaves, owners were free to devise elaborate weddings and receptions, limited only by their finances. Favorite slaves sometimes enjoyed great feasts, along with ceremonies that mimicked those of the owning class in all respects but one: the inclusion of language admonishing no one to separate the couple. Affluent slaveholders turned slave weddings into elaborate events designed to enhance their reputations as wealthy and beneficent members of the owning class. Details of the actual ceremonies often fell to the women of the white household. Mistresses more often favored house servants with elaborate weddings, but festive dinners and dances also marked the marriages of field hands. Whether simple or elaborate, most ceremonies occurred on Sundays or at night and at less busy times of the year, such as during the Christmas holidays or following harvest or planting.[57]

Slaves, who benefited from the festivities by receiving better food, extra clothing, and opportunities for visiting, liked elaborate weddings. They were often granted time off from field or house duties to attend both the marriage service and any reception that followed. Both bride and groom gained extra attention from relatives and friends among the slave community and from their owners, any of whom might provide gifts of food and special clothing. As the ceremony approached, attention centered on the couple. Levi Pollard summoned up the spirit of cooperation and excitement that pervaded the quarter community at such special moments. The bride would be dressed in white with a pretty veil, which she obtained either from the "white folks" or from another slave who had saved hers from a previous ceremony. The bride's "best girl friends would be her maids," who attended her before and through the ceremony. The maids were "dressed fit ter kill." The groom dressed in "Sunday clothes," most likely checked pants and a plain colored coat—hand-me-downs from the master. The groomsmen "wore de best dey had. Dey duty wuz ter look af'er him 'til he got hanked up." Fannie Berry, who married as a slave in her Virginia mistress's parlor, recalled her marriage ceremony performed by "Elder Williams": "The house wuz full of colored people. Miss Sue Jones and Miss Molley Clark (white) waited on me. Dey took de lamps and we walked up to de preacher. One waiter joined my han' an' one my husband's han'." After the ceremony, her owners gave her a reception in the dining room. "We had everything to eat you could call for," she said, and "no white folks to set down an' eat 'fo' yo'." Dancing added to the slaves' enjoyment of the occasion. Other celebrations—many more modest than those described here—occurred on plantations and farms throughout the South.[58]

Slaves appreciated opportunities for socializing and celebrating with fancy dress and food, but they also recognized that owners who willingly invested resources in a wedding—even if limited to the donation of chickens for a simple supper—respected the sanctity of the union more often than those who did nothing. Slaves especially welcomed participation by white preachers, in the hope that their presence would give pause to owners who might be tempted at a later date to separate the couple through sale, even when the ceremony omitted language to this effect. Although the willingness of owners to respect the sanctity of slave marriages waned as the Cotton Kingdom expanded and the slave trade remained active, slaves clung to the hope that their owners would abide by the customs of an earlier era when they made some attempt to keep together couples united in the few marriage rites they arranged.

When slaveholders refused permission for marriage ceremonies or corrupted the meaning of a Christian wedding, slaves took it upon themselves to ensure that couples pledged their love publicly and according to their own understanding of God's command. Sometimes owners approved a marriage, then left decisions about the details of the ceremony to slaves. Under all these circumstances, slaves engaged in rituals to their liking. One Virginia master told a couple they could ask "Ant Lucky to go 'haid an' marry you." This she did by rounding up other slaves who formed a ring around the couple as she read from the Bible.[59]

Slave couples relied on other slaves to participate in these rituals, which invested marriages with meaning derived from their own religious and cultural assumptions. Black preachers—usually slaves who could read and sometimes write—performed some, but not all, of the ceremonies in the quarter. All slaves who officiated at services unattended by owners emphasized that marriages lasted forever, even though they knew circumstances could force the separation of the couple. "What God hath joined together let not man put asunder," one slave preacher thundered.[60] His words—echoed in many other ceremonies organized by slaves—sounded in direct defiance of owners, who insisted that Christianity did not require them to respect slave marriages by keeping couples together.

The plantation's slave community played an important role in weddings that went beyond a presence at the ritual. Older slaves counseled youths as to the wisdom of a particular match. Carolina Johnson and Mose Harris, slaves in Virginia, consulted an older slave woman about whether they should marry. In an effort to impress upon the young couple the seriousness of their commitment, the elderly woman asked them "to think 'bout it hard fo' two days." When two days passed without a change of mind on the part of either bride or groom, she arranged for the ceremony, which consisted of calling all the slaves together at the end of the day to pray for the couple. The participating slaves ceremoniously assured the couple that God sanctified the marriage even if the owner did not. The larger slave community's involvement in weddings could extend to revelry that lasted into the night. Stepping or jumping over a broomstick laid in the doorway of the house the couple planned to occupy was part of the fun on many plantations. Husbands who did not land first or jump highest or meet whatever other criteria the slaves agreed upon were teased that their wives would prove more a master than a helpmate. One former slave described charivaris as a part of wedding rituals in Virginia: "At night dey would git a crowd together, get cups made of tin cans, cow horns an' anything to make a noise." After bedtime, the slaves congregated "'bout de house of de newly weds an' make a racket, 'till dey was invited in an' fed, maybe dey would dance awhile."[61]

When the end of the Civil War created opportunities for couples to marry legally, some former slaves did not take advantage of it. Among them were those who insisted they were "already married in the eyes of God" and did not need additional rituals "to secure a state of matrimony." Nevertheless, large numbers of former slaves availed themselves of the opportunity to marry following the war, even though government policy granted legal status to "customary marriages" among former slaves and rendered this step unnecessary. Mildred Graves and her husband, who married when enslaved simply by jumping over a broom in Virginia, later reaffirmed their commitment to each other by paying for "a real sho' nuff weddin' wid a preacher."[62] In deciding whether to reaffirm marriage vows following emancipation, former slaves considered the nature of the wedding rituals they had engaged in during slavery.

During their enslavement, most couples complied with the mores of the slave community, which recognized the majority of sexual unions as marriages even if owners did not. Former Virginia slave Charles Grandy went so far as to describe the loving relationships that had developed between men and women under slavery as "a lot mo' bindin'" than those he observed in the 1930s, when a government agent interviewed him about his life. Speaking of his relationship with Lucilla Smith, Thomas H. Jones echoed the sentiments of many slaves who established families on their own without help from owners, churches, or legal institutions: "We *called* it and *we considered* it a *true marriage*." Slaveholders, who claimed the right to regulate intimate relationships among slaves, insisted that only they could legitimate a marriage. They withheld their permission for marriage when it suited their needs, and then counted as evidence of the slaves' immorality any sexual relationships that developed among slaves without their consent. Yet the relationships slaves established without their owners' approval offer evidence that slaves were unwilling to cede to slaveholders the right to define kinship ties. Though often impermanent and fragile, the family ties of slaves were too important to be left to an owner's discretion.[63]

EPILOGUE

Elizabeth Keckley's life was extraordinary by any standard. Known in childhood as Lizzie Hobbs, she was born in bondage about 1824. Ten years before the Civil War brought about a general emancipation of slaves, she managed to purchase her freedom and that of her son George with $1,200 in borrowed funds, repaid from money she later earned by sewing. Shortly after the outbreak of war, she went to work as a seamstress in the Lincoln White House and became a confidante of Mary Todd Lincoln. Keckley witnessed firsthand a wide range of historical figures and events associated with the nation's greatest crisis, which she recorded in a memoir published in 1868. Most of Keckley's writing focuses on her four years in the White House, but *Behind the Scenes* also relates autobiographical details of her thirty years of enslavement, including the events of her childhood that she later said "influenced the moulding of my character."[1]

Growing up, Keckley learned she could not put her trust in the paternalistic impulses of owners, which were tempered by a desire for profits and, in some cases, for sexual pleasures. While she was a young girl, Lizzie's father—who lived on a different estate from his wife and daughter—accompanied his master to the West as part of a wave of migration intended to enhance the welfare of white planters. At age fourteen, now a trained house servant, Lizzie was separated from her mother when her owners lent her to their oldest son, a change that necessitated her removal from Virginia to North Carolina. The absence of family and friends left her vulnerable to abuse, and the reality of oppression resounds in her memoir. "I— I— became a mother," she wrote, a cryptic reference to having been raped by a white man.[2]

Although they tolerated such treatment of slaves, slaveholders cited the ideals of paternalism to justify continuation of the South's peculiar institution. They considered their relationships with slaves of the utmost importance and insisted that slaves were like subordinate members of their families. They demanded the slaves' labor and obedience, and in return promised them sustenance, kindly treatment, and personal security, provided this proved economically feasible and the slaves exhibited satisfaction with their inferior status. Not all slaveholders lived up to the bargain, nor did all slaves. But owners were confident of their right to direct the lives of slaves, including the behavior of parents and children. Slaveholders called their invasions into the private lives of slaves benevolence, but parents viewed them in more complex terms. On one hand, their children sometimes benefited from an owner's paternalistic interference; on the other, interventions were often coercive, undermining relationships within the slave family and threatening solidarity within the slave quarter.

The existence of large numbers of slave children on antebellum slaveholdings encouraged owners to assume paternalistic attitudes and behaviors toward their slaves, as did increasing criticisms of slavery throughout the Atlantic world and changing attitudes about the importance of child rearing. In addition, the closing of the international slave trade and the spread of slavery into an expanding United States splintered families and fostered among slaveholders the idea that they should assume some degree of responsibility for slave children. Many acted *in loco parentis,* even if they did not carry out child-rearing tasks themselves but designated other slaves to perform them. Owners argued that the children fared better under their jurisdiction than under the care of parents, but slaveholders clearly expected to benefit themselves from their attentions to youngsters: slaves raised from childhood would love them more, exhibit greater loyalty, and labor harder in the field than any purchased in the market. The maturation of the children would serve to replenish owners' work forces as older slaves died or became too frail to labor. Moreover, adult slaves would be more tractable when they became parents, since their children were dependent upon owners for food, clothing, shelter, supervision, and security. In these circumstances, parents were less likely to rile owners by refusing to work in the customary manner. Of course, the situation worked both ways, in that planters were hesitant to provoke parents by mistreating slave children for fear that parents would refuse to carry out the owners' work in the usual way.

Slave parents pushed slaveholders to act paternalistically because manifestations of paternalism helped children survive and a people persist. Indeed, they did more than accept a paternalistic bargain; they pressed planters to enter into one. But they understood the predicament in which they were placed: when they encouraged owners to ensure their children's health and safety, they relinquished what they viewed as their parental prerogatives. Slave parents always proceeded cautiously in encouraging owners to attend to their children. Unable to throw off the yoke of slavery, slaves made an outward commitment to paternalism, although dedication to the ideal was constrained by the knowledge that it undermined their authority over their children.

Slaves were reluctant to relinquish their sons and daughters to the slaveholder's care because they wanted to shield children from slavery's worst features and to offer an interpretation of the social order that differed from that provided by owners. Slaveholders wanted children to believe in the tenets of paternalism and to derive their identities from membership in the owner's family, but parents wanted youngsters to model their behavior on that of other slaves and to learn about life at their parents' knees, or from other relatives. When circumstances prevented parents or other kin from guiding their children to adulthood, they wanted unrelated slaves to assume the responsibility—not slaveholders. "Fictive kin"—slaves who stepped in to help carry out the tasks and rituals of daily life in the absence of relatives—were made necessary by owners, who treated slaves as interchangeable commodities when they bought, sold, or relocated them according to their own economic interests, but they helped hold paternalism in check. By emphasizing family as a flexible institution—able to absorb displaced children as well as youngsters of mixed race—slaves detracted from the slaveholder's ability to teach children that the interests of slaves and slaveholders were joined.

Slavery was a relationship between people, the terms of which had to be negotiated and renegotiated to reflect child development. Owners were in a hurry for slave children to grow up and watched carefully for signs that they had matured enough to learn basic skills, assume work burdens, and reproduce the labor force. Parents countered by attempting to prolong childhood while looking for ways to ensure children's physical and psychological survival. As a result, childhood under slavery was peculiar. Unable to bargain on their own behalf, infants suffered whatever care slaves and slaveholders cobbled together, as the two came to terms over how to keep mothers at productive and reproductive labor. But as they grew, children increasingly took it upon themselves to negotiate with owners over living and working conditions, using tactics ranging from artful deception and duplicity to outright defiance, in imitation of their parents. By early childhood, slave boys and girls had learned it was possible to manipulate all the adults around them; by adolescence, they struggled to have some say in their own fate, especially when it came to courtship and marriage. Although they were constrained by bondage and poverty, slave youths wanted to make of life what they could. By the time they arrived at the brink of adulthood, they stood ready to use whatever openings they might find in the slaveholder's need for labor or desire for outside approval to negotiate the terms under which they lived and worked.

In retrospect, Elizabeth Keckley appears to have embodied many of the qualities that slaveholders valued in their slaves. She worked diligently and developed, in her own words, "a pleasing nature" by altering her behavior to suit slaveholders. Her outward demeanor was obedient, even docile. Yet she did not accept slavery as a legitimate means of ordering society, nor did she surrender psychologically to the institution. Both her actions and her comportment reflected her wish to endure, if not outlast, servitude. She resisted rape and judged this and other instances of physical and emotional abuse routinely heaped upon slaves as reprehensible. But she also rejected slavery in a milder form. When she purchased freedom for herself and her child, she was living under conditions that were not deemed especially harsh by the standards of the day. Nevertheless, she—along with other slaves—renounced the idea that slavery could ever be made acceptable to the enslaved people. The celebrated abolitionist Frederick Douglass, who risked capture and its harsh consequences rather than endure slavery in Maryland, explained the desire of slaves for freedom as "human nature." He once observed: "Give [the slave] a *bad* master, and he aspires to a *good* master; give him a good master, and he wishes to become his *own* master." When freedom came to slaves as a result of the Civil War or through other means, they celebrated, to the consternation of slaveholders.

Following her emancipation, Keckley wrote that slavery was a wrong "inflicted upon me; a cruel custom deprived me of my liberty . . . I would not have been human had I not rebelled."[3]

As did Keckley, the majority of slaves learned while growing up to demonstrate compliance with their owner's directives through outward appearance and work habits without internalizing the owner's understanding of class and race. As young children, they knew that slaveholders got dainties while slaves got crusts. When they grew older, they worried about the cruelties that passed for discipline on southern plantations, but they did not succumb psychologically to the terrors of enslavement. As young adults, the majority of slaves married and raised sons and daughters of their own, an action that expressed faith in the future and attested to the humanity of a people born in bondage.

Although few slaves gained freedom through self-purchase as Keckley did, the majority of slaves born in the antebellum years did not spend their entire lives in servitude. Nearly four million people gained freedom at the time of the Civil War. They had endured conditions of oppression virtually unfathomable to citizens of the modern United States. In the 1930s, decades after emancipation, many former slaves spoke about their experiences to government agents involved in preserving the memories of slavery as part of the Federal Writers' Project of the Works Progress Administration. For the most part, their recollections reflected their age of understanding when slavery collapsed. Some people spoke of early childhood, when owners sought to instill in them a sense of love and loyalty toward masters and mistresses; others recalled a harsher version of slavery associated with the age at which children began to work and to pay dearly for the mistakes of youthful inexperience. Still others revealed the sorrows associated with coming of age: sale and sexual exploitation. Their memories were not all negative: former slaves also recalled the joys of growing up, the excitement of scary stories told in the dark or of romantic trysts after hours. Together their stories speak of fortitude, resilience, and a people's determination to persist.

The contest that engaged slaves and slaveholders for the control of bonded children was not one between equals, which makes the slaves' accomplishment all the more remarkable. Not only did individual slaves survive, but an African-American people as well. The experience of rearing children in bondage helped unite them, as did the ordeal of growing up enslaved. When they first entered their owners' fields as full-time workers, when they married, began families, or assumed other adult responsibilities, slaves carried with them the experiences of childhood. Within families supported by a larger community, children learned what it meant to be a slave but also what it meant to be a man or a woman, a husband or a wife, a parent or a child, which is how they endured.

ABBREVIATIONS

NOTES

ACKNOWLEDGMENTS

INDEX

ABBREVIATIONS

ABSP   Records of Ante-Bellum Southern Plantations from the Revolution through the Civil War, ed. Kenneth M. Stampp, University Publications of America

ADAH   Alabama Department of Archives and History, Montgomery

NQS   H. C. Nixon Questionnaire on Slavery, Alabama Department of Archives and History, Montgomery

S1   Series 1 of George P. Rawick, ed., *The American Slave: A Composite Autobiography,* 41 vols. (Westport, Conn.: Greenwood Press, 1972–1979)

S2   Series 2 of George P. Rawick, ed., *The American Slave: A Composite Autobiography,* 41 vols. (Westport, Conn.: Greenwood Press, 1972–1979)

SS1   Supplement, Series 1 of George P. Rawick, ed., *The American Slave: A Composite Autobiography,* 41 vols. (Westport, Conn.: Greenwood Press, 1972–1979)

SS2   Supplement, Series 2 of George P. Rawick, ed., *The American Slave: A Composite Autobiography,* 41 vols. (Westport, Conn.: Greenwood Press, 1972–1979)

SHC   Southern Historical Collection, Wilson Library, University of North Carolina, Chapel Hill

UVAL   University of Virginia Library, Charlottesville

VHS   Virginia Historical Society, Richmond

VSLA   Virginia State Library and Archives, Richmond

NOTES

Introduction

1. On Hunter, see Charles L. Perdue, Jr., Thomas E. Barden, and Robert K. Phillips, eds., *Weevils in the Wheat: Interviews with Virginia Ex-Slaves* (Charlottesville: University Press of Virginia, 1979), pp. 149–151.

2. Willie Lee Rose, *Slavery and Freedom,* ed. William W. Freehling (New York: Oxford University Press, 1982), pp. 37–38.

3. Perdue, Barden, and Phillips, eds., *Weevils in the Wheat,* pp. 205–211; Robert William Fogel, *Without Consent or Contract: The Rise and Fall of American Slavery* (New York: W. W. Norton, 1989), p. 128.

4. Ira Berlin, *Many Thousands Gone: The First Two Centuries of Slavery in North America* (Cambridge, Mass.: Harvard University Press, 1998), pp. 126–127, 149, 423 n. 13.

5. United States Bureau of the Census, *Historical Statistics of the United States, Colonial Times to 1970,* Part 1 (Washington, D.C.: United States Bureau of the Census, 1975), pp. 17–18. These figures closely resemble those of present-day nonindustrial nations. See United Nation's Children's Fund, *The State of the World's Children, 1991* (New York: Oxford University Press, 1991), pp. 102–103, 110–111. Nearly 43 percent of United States slaves were under age fourteen in 1820 at the start of the antebellum period, and 45 percent were younger than fifteen in

1860 on the eve of the Civil War. In comparison, at the height of the post–World War II "Baby Boom," 31 percent of the U.S. population was under age fourteen. By 1990, that percentage had fallen to 23 percent. United States Bureau of the Census, *Statistical Abstract of the United States: 1990* (Washington, D.C.: U.S. Bureau of the Census, 1990), p. 18. The U.S. population figures are striking standing alone, but they appear even more so when placed within the context of the demographic phenomenon that brought millions of Africans to the Americas. By conservative estimates, 10 million African slaves were brought by traders to the Americas between the years 1450 and 1850, but fewer than 450,000 made their way to areas that now form part of the United States. See Philip D. Curtin, *The Atlantic Slave Trade: A Census* (Madison: University of Wisconsin Press, 1969), pp. 88–89, 92. Curtin never presented his data as definitive, and other scholars have refined his figures, but his basic premise stills stands. See Paul E. Lovejoy, "The Volume of the Atlantic Slave Trade: A Synthesis," *Journal of African History* 23 (1982), pp. 473–501; Joseph E. Inkori and Stanley L. Engerman, "Introduction: Gainers and Losers in the Atlantic Slave Trade," in *The Atlantic Slave Trade,* ed. Joseph E. Inkori and Stanley L. Engerman (Durham, N.C.: Duke University Press, 1992), pp. 5–6; David Eltis and David Richardson, "The 'Numbers Game' and Routes to Slavery," *Slavery & Abolition* 18 (April 1997), p. 2. The number of children born to enslaved mothers exceeded the number of slaves who died in British colonies other than in mainland North America, but only shortly before emancipation, with the result that the phenomenon never had the impact there as in the United States. See Philip D. Curtin, *The Rise and Fall of the Plantation Complex: Essays in Atlantic History* (New York: Cambridge University Press, 1990), pp. 173–174.

6. The question of whether slaves fared best in the United States or in other parts of the Americas has engaged scholars since the appearance more than fifty years ago of Frank Tannenbaum's seminal study *Slave and Citizen: The Negro in the Americas* (New York: Vintage, 1946). On criteria for comparing slave societies, see Eugene D. Genovese, "The Treatment of Slaves in Different Countries," in *In Red and Black: Marxian Explorations in Southern and Afro-American History* (New York: Pantheon, 1971), Chap. 7. On the status of comparative slavery studies today, see George M. Frederickson, "From Exceptionalism to Variability: Recent Developments in Cross-National Comparative History," *Journal of American History* 82 (Sept. 1995), pp. 593–598.

7. George P. Rawick, ed., *The American Slave: A Composite Autobiography,* SS2, Vol. 5, pp. 1485–1486, and SS1, Vol. 12, pp. 190–192.

8. U. B. Phillips, *American Negro Slavery* (New York: D. Appleton, 1918); *The Negro Family: The Case for National Action* (Washington, D.C.: U.S. Government Printing Office, 1965).

9. Stanley M. Elkins, *Slavery: A Problem in American Institutional and Intellectual Life* (Chicago: University of Chicago Press, 1959), p. 131; John W. Blassingame, *The Slave Community: Plantation Life in the Antebellum South* (New

York: Oxford University Press, 1972); Eugene D. Genovese, *Roll, Jordan, Roll: The World the Slaves Made* (New York: Pantheon, 1974); George P. Rawick, *From Sundown to Sunup: The Making of the Black Community* (Westport, Conn.: Greenwood Press, 1972); Herbert G. Gutman, *The Black Family in Slavery and Freedom, 1750-1925* (New York: Pantheon, 1976); Charles Joyner, *Down by the Riverside: A South Carolina Slave Community* (Urbana: University of Illinois Press, 1984).

10. Kenneth M. Stampp, *The Peculiar Institution: Slavery in the Ante-Bellum South* (New York: Vintage, 1956), 340-343. Gutman's *The Black Family in Slavery and Freedom* rejected the idea that modern social problems associated with the black family were rooted in slavery.

11. Genovese, *Roll, Jordan, Roll*, pp. 3-7, 91, 587-598.

12. Ibid., pp. 502-519.

13. James Oakes, *The Ruling Race: A History of American Slaveholders* (New York: Knopf, 1982).

14. E. Franklin Frazier helped frame the debate when he termed the family "matrifocal" in *The Negro Family in the United States* (Chicago: University of Chicago Press, 1939). Deborah Gray White uses the phrase "community of women" to describe women's response to enslavement in *Ar'n't I a Woman?: Female Slaves in the Plantation South* (New York: W. W. Norton, 1985); Brenda E. Stevenson uses the term "matrifocal" in *Life in Black and White: Family and Community in the Slave South* (New York: Oxford University Press, 1996). On the characterization of the slave family as matrifocal or matriarchal, see Claire Robertson, "Africa into the Americas? Slavery and Women, the Family, and the Gender Division of Labor," in *More than Chattel: Black Women and Slavery in the Americas,* ed. David Barry Gaspar and Darlene Clark Hine (Bloomington: Indiana University Press, 1996), pp. 9-20.

15. Thomas L. Webber, *Deep Like the Rivers: Education in the Slave Quarter Community, 1831-1865* (New York: Norton, 1978); Wilma King, *Stolen Childhood: Slave Youth in Nineteenth-Century America* (Bloomington: Indiana University Press, 1995), p. xxi.

16. Rawick, ed., SS2, Vol. 4, Pt. 3, p. 1330. Former slaves who lived into the 1930s and whose interviews have been published needed to establish their ages to qualify for government assistance under New Deal programs and deeply regretted their inability to do so. On notching sticks, see H. C. Bruce, *The New Man: Twenty-Nine Years a Slave, Twenty-Nine Years a Free Man* (Miami: Mnemosyne, 1969), pp. 11-13.

17. Archibald Alexander Little to Dr. Andres Glassess Grinnan, 27 March 1850, Grinnan Family Papers, VHS; Robert W. Withers Papers, Vol. 2, 1823-1853, SHC; quote in Henry Bibb, "Narrative of the Life and Adventures of Henry Bibb, An American Slave," in *Puttin' on Ole Massa,* ed. Gilbert Osofsky (New York: Harper and Row, 1969), p. 114.

18. "Laura Clark: Children in Every Graveyard," in Virginia Pound Brown and

Laurella Owens, *Toting the Lead Row: Ruby Pickens Tartt, Alabama Folklorist* (University: University of Alabama Press, 1981), p. 123; Rawick, ed., SS2, Vol. 3, Pt. 2, p. 639; SS1, Vol. 5, p. 284; and S1, Vol. 6, pp. 103, 329.

19. The WPA interviews have been published as George P. Rawick, ed., *The American Slave: A Composite Autobiography,* 41 vols. (Westport, Conn.: Greenwood, 1972–1979), cited in this work by series number and volume. Some of the interviews have been collected into separate volumes, as indicated in the notes. Responses to the Nixon questionnaire remain unpublished and are located at the Alabama Department of Archives and History in Montgomery. On the scholarly debate about the accuracy of slave narratives, see Charles T. Davis and Henry Louis Gates, Jr., *The Slave Narrative* (New York: Oxford University Press, 1985).

20. On the changing piedmont economy, see Lynda J. Morgan, *Emancipation in Virginia's Tobacco Belt, 1850–1870* (Athens: University of Georgia Press, 1992); John Thomas Schlotterbeck, "Plantation and Farm: Economic Change in Orange and Greene Counties, Virginia, 1716–1860" (Ph.D. diss., Johns Hopkins University, 1980); Cynthia A. Kierner, "Women's Piety within Patriarchy: The Religious Life of Martha Hancock Wheat of Bedford County," *Virginia Magazine of History and Biography* 100 (Jan. 1992), p. 84.

21. William Dusinberre, *Them Dark Days: Slavery in the American Rice Swamps* (New York: Oxford University Press, 1996), pp. 414–415. On the Georgia rice counties, see Julia Floyd Smith, *Slavery and Rice Culture in Low Country Georgia, 1750–1860* (Knoxville: University of Tennessee Press, 1985), especially Chapter 2 and Appendix A. Joyner describes the plantations of All Saints Parish, Georgetown District, South Carolina, in *Down by the Riverside,* Chapter 1.

22. On Alabama black-belt estates, see James F. Woodruff, "Some Characteristics of the Alabama Slave Population of 1850," *Geographical Review* 52 (July 1862), pp. 379–388; Oakes, *The Ruling Race,* p. 249; James B. Sellers, *Slavery in Alabama,* 2d ed. (University: University of Alabama Press, 1964), Chapter 2.

23. Population figures have been rounded to the nearest 10,000 and are drawn from United States Census Office, *Census for 1820* (Washington, D.C: Gales & Seaton, 1821); U.S. Bureau of the Census, *Population of the United States in 1860* (Washington, D.C.: Government Printing Office, 1864). The Alabama black-belt is defined as the counties that in 1860 lay within the geographic division known by that name: Autauga, Dallas, Greene, Lowndes, Macon, Marengo, Montgomery, Perry, Pickens, Russell, and Sumter. The Virginia piedmont includes the counties of Albemarle, Amelia, Amherst, Appomattox, Bedford, Brunswick, Buckingham, Campbell, Charlotte, Culpeper, Cumberland, Dinwiddie, Fauquier, Franklin, Fluvanna, Greene, Goochland, Halifax, Henry, Loudoun, Louisa, Lunenburg, Madison, Mecklenburg, Nelson, Nottoway, Orange, Patrick, Pittsylvania, Prince Edward, Powhatan, and Rappahannock. The rice coast, or low country, is defined as the South Carolina counties of Beaufort, Charleston, Colleton, Georgetown, and Horry along with the Georgia counties of Bryan, Camden, Chatham, Glynn, Lib-

erty, and McIntosh. For demographic and economic characteristics of these areas and the rest of the South, see Sam Bowers Hilliard, *Atlas of Antebellum Southern Agriculture* (Baton Rouge: Louisiana State University Press, 1984). Because all of the areas studied were predominantly rural, my research focuses on the experiences of children reared on plantations and farms to the exclusion of the city.

24. In 1820, 44 percent of slaves in the Alabama black belt and 45 percent in Virginia's piedmont were younger than age fourteen. The population of South Carolina and Georgia low country never had as many children as did central Alabama or central Virginia. Children under age fourteen made up 32 percent of the population in 1820.

1. Birth of a Slave

1. Steven M. Stowe, "Obstetrics and the Work of Doctoring in the Mid-Nineteenth Century American South," *Bulletin of the History of Medicine* 64 (Winter 1990), p. 554; George P. Rawick, ed., *The American Slave: A Composite Autobiography,* SS1, Vol. 3, Pt. 1, pp. 204–205, and S1, Vol. 2, Pt. 2, p. 35.

2. Entry for 5 Aug. 1845, Plantation Diary, Vol. 2, Sturdivant Collection (microfilm, SHC); entry for 10 July 1858, David Gavin Diary, SHC; Rawick, ed., S1, Vol. 7, p. 24.

3. W. W. Hazard, "On the General Management of a Plantation," *Southern Agriculturalist* 4 (July 1831), in *Advice among Masters: The Ideal in Slave Management in the Old South,* ed. James O. Breeden (Westport, Conn.: Greenwood Press, 1980), p. 257.

4. A. R. Bagshaw to Charles Manigault, 14 Aug. 1844, in *Life and Labor on Argyle Island: Letters and Documents of a Savannah River Rice Plantation, 1833–1867,* ed. James M. Clifton (Savannah: Beehive, 1978), p. 15. Also Stephen F. Clark to Louis Manigault, 6 Aug. 1853, and Louis Manigault to Charles Manigault, 10 March 1854, ibid., pp. 158 and 181, respectively; Gabriel L. Ellis to Robert F. W. Allston, 20 June 1838, in *The South Carolina Rice Plantation as Revealed in the Papers of Robert F. W. Allston,* ed. J. H. Easterby (Chicago: University of Chicago Press, 1945), p. 252.

5. Letter of Stancil Barwick to Col. J. B. Lamar, 15 July 1855, in Ulrich B. Phillips, ed., *Plantation and Frontier, 1649–1863,* Vol. 1 (New York: Burt Franklin, 1910), pp. 312–313. Also K. Washington Skinner to Charles Manigault, 6 June 1852, in *Life and Labor on Argyle Island,* p. 99; entry for 22 July, "Report for Chicora Wood Plantation, July 18–24, 1858," in *The South Carolina Rice Plantation,* p. 262.

6. Robert William Fogel, *Without Consent or Contract: The Rise and Fall of American Slavery* (New York: W. W. Norton, 1989), pp. 127–128; Richard Steckel, "Slave Mortality: Analysis of Evidence from Plantation Records," in *Without Consent or Contract: The Rise and Fall of American Slavery, Conditions of Slave Life and the Transition to Freedom: Technical Papers,* Vol. 2, ed. Robert William Fogel

and Stanley L. Engerman (New York: W. W. Norton, 1992), pp. 407, 410; William Dusinberre, *Them Dark Days: Slavery in the American Rice Swamps* (New York: Oxford University Press, 1996), pp. 410–416 and n. 82, pp. 536–538; Ira Berlin and Philip D. Morgan, eds., *Cultivation and Culture: Labor and the Shaping of Slave Life in the Americas* (Charlottesville: University Press of Virginia, 1993), p. 21.

7. Frances Anne Kemble, *Journal of a Residence on a Georgian Plantation in 1838–1839* (New York: Alfred A. Knopf, 1961), pp. 114, 154, 170, 210. Also Mary Jones to Mary S. Mallard, 21 Oct. 1858, in *The Children of Pride: A True Story of Georgia and the Civil War*, ed. Robert Manson Myers (New Haven: Yale University Press, 1972), p. 454; Dusinberre, *Them Dark Days*, p. 253.

8. Kemble, *Journal of a Residence on a Georgian Plantation*, p. 154.

9. Rawick, ed., S1, Vol. 3, Pt. 4, p. 201; Charles Manigault to James Haynes, 1 March 1847, in *Life and Labor on Argyle Island*, p. 49; Kemble, *Journal of a Residence on a Georgian Plantation*, p. 295.

10. Kemble, *Journal of a Residence on a Georgian Plantation*, pp. 76–77, 235–236; Todd L. Savitt, *Medicine and Slavery: The Diseases and Health Care of Blacks in Virginia* (Urbana: University of Illinois Press, 1978), p. 115; Brenda E. Stevenson, *Life in Black and White: Family and Community in the Slave South* (New York: Oxford University Press, 1996), p. 193.

11. Charles L. Perdue, Jr., Thomas E. Barden, and Robert K. Phillips, eds., *Weevils in the Wheat: Interviews with Virginia Ex-Slaves* (Charlottesville: University Press of Virginia, 1976), p. 160.

12. Eugene D. Genovese, *Roll, Jordan, Roll: The World the Slaves Made* (New York: Vintage, 1974), pp. 144–147. Also Drew Gilpin Faust, *James Henry Hammond and the Old South: A Design for Mastery* (Baton Rouge: Louisiana State University Press, 1982), especially Chapter 10.

13. "Rules of the Plantation," *Southern Cultivator* 7 (June 1849), in *Advice among Masters*, p. 168; A Southern Planter, *Plantation and Farm Instruction, Regulation, Record, Inventory and Account Book*, (Richmond, Va.: J. W. Randolph, 1852), p. 5, in Philip St. George Cocke Papers, Cocke Family Papers, VHS. Also T. E. Blunt, "Rules for the Government of Overseers," *Southern Cultivator* 5 (April 1847), p. 61.

14. Kemble, *Journal of a Residence on a Georgian Plantation*, p. 274; Perdue, Barden, and Phillips, eds., *Weevils in the Wheat*, p. 160; entries for 1 and 7 May 1845, Plantation Diary, Vol. 2, Sturdivant Collection, Sturdivant Museum, Selma, Ala. (microfilm, SHC); Plantation Record of James H. Ruffin, Ruffin, Roulhac, and Hamilton Family Papers, SHC; John Campbell, "Work, Pregnancy, and Infant Mortality among Southern Slaves," *Journal of Interdisciplinary History* 14 (Spring 1984), p. 801; Mrs. A. M. French, *Slavery in South Carolina and the Ex-Slaves; or, The Port Royal Mission* (New York: Negro Universities Press, 1969), pp. 95–96; Barbara Bush, *Slave Women in Caribbean Society, 1650–1832* (Bloomington: Indiana University Press, 1990), pp. 28–30, 44.

15. Kemble, *Journal of a Residence on a Georgian Plantation*, pp. 276–277, 170, also p. 210; Robynne Rogers Healey, "Meanings of Motherhood: Maternal Experiences and Perceptions on Low Country South Carolina Plantations," presented to the Berkshire Conference on the History of Women, Chapel Hill, North Carolina, June 7, 1996, p. 20, made available by the author; Deborah Gray White, *Ar'n't I a Woman?: Female Slaves in the Plantation South* (New York: W. W. Norton, 1985), pp. 79–84.

16. Helen Varney, *Varney's Midwifery*, 3rd ed. (Sudbury, Mass.: Jones and Bartlett, 1997), p. 234.

17. Memorandum Book for Birdfield Plantation, 1850–1857, pp. 29–30, 66, James Ritchie Sparkman Papers, ABSP, Series A, Part 2: Miscellaneous Collections.

18. On antebellum medical knowledge of pregnancy and gestation periods, see Sally G. McMillen, *Motherhood in the Old South: Pregnancy, Childbirth, and Infant Rearing* (Baton Rouge: Louisiana State University Press, 1990), pp. 28–31. Quote in A. Curtis, *Lectures on Midwifery and the Forms of Disease Peculiar to Women and Children, Delivered to the Members of the Botanico-Medical College of Ohio* (Columbus, Ohio: Jonathan Phillips, 1841), p. 43.

19. Stowe, "Obstetrics and the Work of Doctoring in the Mid-Nineteenth Century American South," pp. 545, 652. Quote in Savitt, *Medicine and Slavery*, p. 168.

20. On planters who practiced medicine, see McMillen, *Motherhood in the Old South*, p. 68; James Oakes, *The Ruling Race: A History of American Slaveholders* (New York: Vintage, 1982), pp. 61–63; Georgia Bryan Conrad, *Reminiscences of a Southern Woman* (Hampton, Va.: Hampton Institute Press, n.d.), p. 11; Mary Jones to Charles C. Jones, Jr., 7 May 1861, in *The Children of Pride*, p. 674; Sally G. McMillen, "Antebellum Southern Fathers and the Health Care of Children," *Journal of Southern History* 60 (Aug. 1994), pp. 526–530.

21. Charlotte Ann Allston to Robert F. W. Allston, 19 April 1820, in *The South Carolina Rice Plantation*, p. 54; *Gunn's Domestic Medicine: A Facsimile of the First Edition* (Knoxville: University of Tennessee Press, 1986), pp. 305–338; Sally G. McMillen, "Antebellum Southern Fathers and the Health Care of Children," *Journal of Southern History* 60 (Aug. 1994), p. 527; "Contract between Charles Manigault and His Overseer, S. F. Clark, for the Year 1853, Chatham County, Georgia," in *Life and Labor on Argyle Island*, p. 136; Robert Byrd Beverley to Robert Beverley, 7 Jan. 1848 and 23 July 1841, Beverley Family Papers, VHS; Rawick, ed., S2, Vol. 8, p. 237.

22. Tattler, "Management of Negroes," *Southern Planter* 11 (Feb. 1851), p. 40; entries for 6 Dec. 1858 and 1 Jan. 1859, "Market Book," Mrs. W. G. Jones Papers, ADAH; *DeBow's* as cited in *The Southern Plantation Overseer, As Revealed in His Letters*, ed. John Spencer Bassett (New York: Negro Universities Press, 1968), p. 29; Robert Byrd Beverley to Robert Beverley, 7 Jan. 1848 and 23 July 1841, Beverley Family Papers, VHS.

23. James Williams, *Narrative of James Williams, an American Slave* (Boston: Isaac Knapp, 1838), pp. 61–65, 75; Perdue, Barden, and Phillips, eds., *Weevils in the Wheat*, p. 190; Rawick, ed., S1, Vol. 6, p. 91, and Vol. 2, Pt. 2, p. 234. On the authenticity of the narrative by Williams, see Charles H. Nichols, *Many Thousand Gone: The Ex-Slaves' Account of Their Bondage and Their Freedom* (Bloomington: Indiana University Press, 1963), p. xi.

24. *Gunn's Domestic Medicine*, p. 309; William P. Dewees, M.D., *Treatise on the Physical and Medical Treatment of Children* (Philadelphia: H. C. Carey and I. Lea, 1826), pp. 22–23; Catherine M. Scholten, *Childbearing in American Society, 1650–1850* (New York: New York University Press, 1985), p. 20; Curtis, *Lectures on Midwifery*, p. 85.

25. Rawick, ed., S2, Vol. 8, Pt. 1, p. 238, and SS1, Vol. 3, Pt. 1, p. 204; Dewees, *Treatise on the Physical and Medical Treatment of Children*, pp. 26–32. On the consequences of poor nutrition during pregnancy for slave women and infants, see Kenneth F. Kiple and Virginia H. Kiple, "Slave Child Mortality: Some Nutritional Answers to a Perennial Puzzle," *Journal of Social History* 10 (March 1977), pp. 284–309; "Sarah Fitzpatrick," in *Slave Testimony: Two Centuries of Letters, Speeches, Interviews, and Autobiographies* (Baton Rouge: Louisiana State University Press, 1977), p. 652; Perdue, Barden, and Phillips, eds., *Weevils in the Wheat*, pp. 78, 201–202, 245. Also Roderick A. McDonald, "Independent Economic Production by Slaves on Antebellum Louisiana Sugar Plantations," in *Cultivation and Culture*, pp. 290–291.

26. White, *Ar'n't I a Woman?*, p. 100.

27. Response of James M. Davison, NQS; Dewees, *Treatise on the Physical and Medical Treatment of Children*, pp. 26–32; Rawick, ed., SS1, Vol. 3, Pt. 1, p. 205.

28. On cultural transmissions among Europeans and Africans, see Lawrence W. Levine, *Black Culture and Black Consciousness: Afro-American Folk Thought from Slavery to Freedom* (New York: Oxford University Press, 1977), Chapters 1–3, especially pp. 3–5, 24; Charles Joyner, *Down by the Riverside: A South Carolina Slave Community* (Urbana: University of Illinois Press, 1984), especially pp. xx–xxi; Sterling Stuckey, *Slave Culture: Nationalist Theory and the Foundations of Black America* (New York: Oxford University Press, 1987).

29. Perdue, Barden, and Phillips, eds., *Weevils in the Wheat*, p. 207; "Carrie Dykes, Midwife," in Virginia Pounds Brown and Laurella Owens, *Toting the Lead Row: Ruby Pickens Tartt, Alabama Folklorist* (University: University of Alabama Press, 1981), p. 67. Also H. C. Bruce, *The New Man: Twenty-Nine Years a Slave, Twenty-Nine Years a Free Man* (Miami: Mnemosyne, 1969), p. 13.

30. Stowe, "Obstetrics and the Work of Doctoring in the Mid-Nineteenth Century American South," pp. 542–543; McMillen, *Motherhood in the Old South*, pp. 96–100; Michael Tadman, *Speculators and Slaves: Masters, Traders, and Slaves in the Old South* (Madison: University of Wisconsin Press, 1989), p. 128; Healey, "Meanings of Motherhood," pp. 10–11.

31. *DeBow's* cited in *The Southern Plantation Overseer*, p. 29; entry for 4 Sept. 1856, David Gavin Diary, Vol. 1, SHC.

32. See list of fees paid to slaves hired to perform specific services for the years 1857, 1859, 1860 in David Gavin Diary, SHC.

33. Entries for 10 July 1858 and 29 Nov. 1859, David Gavin Diary, SHC; also 7 Oct. 1833, John Berkley Grimball Diary, Vol. 1, SHC. On the resistance of white women to attendance at birth by male doctors, see McMillen, *Motherhood in the Old South*, pp. 68, 98-99; Scholten, *Childbearing in American Society*, p. 41; Sylvia D. Hoffert, *Private Matters: American Attitudes toward Childbearing and Infant Nurture in the Urban North, 1800-1860* (Urbana: University of Illinois Press, 1989), pp. 71-77.

34. J. Y. Bassett, "Report on Topography, Climate, and Diseases of the Parish of Madison Co., Ala.," in *Southern Medical Reports* 1 (1849), p. 264, also p. 276; response of James M. Davidson, NQS; Stowe, "Obstetrics and the Work of Doctoring in the Mid-Nineteenth Century American South," p. 562; Rawick, ed., SS1, Vol. 11, pp. 175-176; entry for 27 Dec. 1856, James M. Torbert Diary, ADAH; "Index for 1856" (p. 158) and "Index for 1858" (p. 207). (Page numbers refer to typed copy of diary.) Also, entries for 22 June 1850 and 30 May 1857, Jones Family Business Accounts, VSLA. Quote in John I. Garner to James K. Polk, 7 June 1840, in *The Southern Plantation Overseer*, pp. 141; William L. McCaa, "Observations on the Manner of Living and Diseases of the Slaves on the Wateree River" (Ph.D. diss., University of Pennsylvania, 1823), p. 12. Bush concludes in *Slave Women in Caribbean Society, 1650-1838* that slaves largely maintained control over childbirth there (p. 166).

35. Robert Byrd Beverley to Robert Beverley, 23 July 1841, Beverley Family Papers, VHS; entry for 5 Dec. 1858, "Market Book," Mrs. W. G. Jones Papers, ADAH; entries for 28 July 1851, 21 and 23 July 1860, Diary and Account Book, 1850-1853 (Vol. 1), Philip Henry Pitts Papers, SHC; Rawick, ed., S1, Vol. 4, Pt. 2, p. 18; "Account Book, 1819-1875," John Peter Mettauer Papers, VHS, pp. 14, 179; J. Marion Sims, *The Story of My Life* (New York: D. Appleton, 1884), Chapter 14.

36. Quoted in Stowe, "Obstetrics and the Work of Doctoring in the Mid-Nineteenth Century American South," p. 549. See also Healey, "Meanings of Motherhood," p. 22.

37. Joseph I. Waring, *A History of Medicine in South Carolina, 1620-1825* (Columbia: South Carolina Medical Association, 1964), p. 380; Stowe, "Obstetrics and the Work of Doctoring in the Mid-Nineteenth Century American South," p. 545.

38. French, *Slavery in South Carolina*, pp. 96-97; Stowe, "Obstetrics and the Work of Doctoring in the Mid-Nineteenth Century American South," p. 548.

39. Carrie Dykes reported midwifery practices in Sumter County, Alabama, to folklorist Ruby Tartt more than half a century following the Civil War. Since the midwife learned these practices at a young age from a former slave woman, it is reasonable to assume that they describe practices in the late antebellum period.

"Carrie Dykes, Midwife," in *Toting the Lead Row,* pp. 67–69; Rawick, ed., SS1, Vol. 3, Pt. 1, p. 95 and Vol. 11, p. 148; Kemble, *Journal of a Residence on a Georgian Plantation,* p. 364.

40. Savitt, *Medicine and Slavery,* pp. 120–122; Rawick, ed., SS1, Vol. 3, Pt. 1, p. 205.

41. "Carrie Dykes, Midwife," in *Toting the Lead Row,* p. 68; unnamed son of a Perry County planter, NQS; Karin Calvert, *Children in the House: The Material Culture of Early Childhood, 1600–1900* (Boston: Northeastern University Press, 1992), pp. 62–63; Dewees, *Treatise on the Physical and Medical Treatment of Children,* p. 72; William Capers, Sr., to Charles Manigault, 11 July 1860, in *Life and Labor on Argyle Island,* p. 302; McMillen, "'No Uncommon Disease,'" pp. 291–314; Kemble, *Journal of a Residence on a Georgian Plantation,* pp. 143, 235, 268, 301, 76.

42. Rawick, ed., SS1, Vol. 11, pp. 85–86; Georgia Writers' Project, *Drums and Shadows: Survival Studies among the Georgia Coastal Negroes* (Athens: University of Georgia Press, 1986), p. 69. On the importance of folk beliefs for slaves, see Levine, *Black Culture and Black Consciousness,* pp. 55–80. On how black midwives in twentieth-century Alabama combined practical help with spiritual guidance, see Linda Janet Holmes, "African American Midwives in the South," in *The American Way of Birth,* ed. Pamela S. Eakins (Philadelphia: Temple University Press, 1986).

43. Rawick, ed., S1, Vol. 3, Pt. 3, p. 273; Mary Jones to Joseph Jones, 13 May 1858, in *The Children of Pride,* p. 415. Medical experts advised two weeks of bed rest for their white clients, according to McMillen, *Motherhood in the Old South,* p. 65. In the North, women of the elite class usually remained in bed one or two weeks following childbirth, Hoffert notes in *Private Matters,* p. 117. Slaves in the West Indies left the navel cord undisturbed for nine days. During the first nine days of a baby's life, African and African-Caribbean parents sometimes "ritually neglected" their children (did not name them, for example), for fear that an infant might prove to be a "wandering ghost" whose existence on earth would prove short-lived. See Bush, *Slave Women in Caribbean Society, 1650–1832,* pp. 144–146. My study has not uncovered evidence of similar practices for the U. S. South.

44. Perdue, Barden, and Phillips, eds., *Weevils in the Wheat,* pp. 248–249; "Carrie Dykes, Midwife," in *Toting the Lead Row,* pp. 68–69. On the active participation of midwives in the births of African-American children into the 1940s, see Sharon A. Robinson, "A Historical Development of Midwifery in the Black Community: 1600–1940," *Journal of Nurse-Midwifery* 29 (July/Aug. 1984), p. 247.

45. Kemble, *Journal of a Residence on a Georgian Plantation,* p. 70; Duncan Clinch Heyward, *Seed from Madagascar* (Chapel Hill: University of North Carolina Press, 1937), p. 103.

46. Rawick, ed., SS1, Vol. 7, Pt. 2, pp. 369–374.

47. Alexander Telfair, "Rules and directions for my Thorn Island Plantation by

which my overseers are to govern themselves in the management of it," 11 June 1832, in Phillips, *Plantation and Frontier,* pp. 127–128.

48. Ray Mathis, *John Horry Dent: South Carolina Aristocrat on the Alabama Frontier* (University: University of Alabama Press, 1979), p. 85; Rawick, ed., SS1, Vol. 1, p. 360; also S1, Vol. 2, Pt. 1, pp. 132, 138.

49. John H. Morgan, M.D., "An Essay on the Causes of the Production of Abortion among Our Negro Population," *Nashville Journal of Medicine and Surgery* (1860), pp. 117–118; Rev. C. C. Jones to Mrs. Charles C. Jones, Jr., 10 Nov. 1859; Charles C. Jones, Jr., to Rev. C. C. Jones, 11 Nov. 1859; Mary Jones to Rev. C. C. Jones, 25 Nov. 1859; Charles C. Jones, Jr., to Rev. C. C. Jones, 12 Dec. 1859, in *The Children of Pride,* pp. 532–533, 534, 542, 545–546; Martia Graham Goodson, "Medical-Botanical Contributions of African Slave Women to American Medicine," in *Black Women in United States History,* Vol. 2, ed. Darlene Clark Hine (New York: Carlson, 1990), p. 117.

50. McMillen, "'No Uncommon Disease,'" pp. 301, 309, 311, 313; Rawick, ed., S2, Vol. 2, Pt. 1, p. 132.

51. Kemble, *Journal of a Residence on a Georgian Plantation,* pp. 98–99.

52. Dewees, *Treatise on the Physical and Medical Treatment of Children,* pp. 66–67, 75; Kemble, *Journal of a Residence on a Georgian Plantation,* p. 99; Calvert, *Children in the House,* pp. 20–21; Scholten, *Childbearing in America,* p. 62.

53. Dewees, *Treatise on the Physical and Medical Treatment of Children,* pp. 63–65, 81, 100–111; Louis Manigault to Charles Manigault, 26 Dec. 1854, in *Life and Labor on Argyle Island,* p. 190; Kemble, *Journal of a Residence on a Georgian Plantation,* p. 88.

54. Rawick, ed., S2, Vol. 8, pp. 241–242.

55. Rev. C. C. Jones to Mr.——, 26 Aug. 1861; John Johnson and A. G. Redd to Rev. C. C. Jones, 24 Sept. 1861; Rev. C. C. Jones to John Johnson and A. G. Redd, 16 Oct. 1861; John Johnson to Rev. C. C. Jones, 18 Nov. 1861; and Rev. C. C. Jones to John Johnson, 25 Dec. 1861, in *The Children of Pride,* pp. 741–742, 752–754, 773–776, 799–800, 828. Perdue, Barden, and Phillips, eds., *Weevils in the Wheat,* p. 301, also pp. 15, 91, 202; Thelma Jennings, "'Us Colored Women Had to Go through a Plenty': Sexual Exploitation of African-American Slave Women," *Journal of Women's History* 1 (Winter 1990), pp. 45–74.

56. Rawick, ed., S2, Vol. 9, Pt. 3, p. 92.

57. Perdue, Barden, and Phillips, eds., *Weevils in the Wheat,* pp. 108, 293; Rawick, ed., S1, Vol. 2, Pt. 2, p. 14.

58. Annie L. Burton, "Memories of Childhood's Slavery Days," in *Six Women's Slave Narratives,* ed. Henry Louis Gates, Jr. (New York: Oxford University Press, 1988), pp. 7–8.

59. "Martha Jackson: Yellow Gals Got Sent North" and "Amy Chapman's Funeral," both in *Toting the Lead Row,* pp. 143, 80. Rawick, ed., SS2, Vol. 10, Pt. 9, p. 4003 and Vol. 4, Pt. 5, p. 1826; "Notice" of sale, *Halcyon* [Greene County, Ala.],

20 Dec. 1823. James B. Cade, "Out of the Mouths of Ex-Slaves," *Journal of Negro History* 20 (July 1935), pp. 307–308. James Hugo Johnston, *Race Relations in Virginia and Miscegenation in the South, 1776–1860* (Amherst: University of Massachusetts Press, 1970), pp. 237–250; Thomas E. Buckley, ed., "'Placed in the Power of Violence': The Divorce Petition of Evelina Gregory Roane, 1824," *Virginia Magazine of History and Biography* 100 (Jan. 1992), pp. 29–78, especially pp. 42–43, 51.

60. Perdue, Barden, and Phillips, eds., *Weevils in the Wheat*, p. 207.

61. Kemble, *Journal of a Residence on a Georgian Plantation*, pp. 249, 276.

62. Heyward, *Seed from Madagascar*, p. 115; James M. Torbert Diary, ADAH, passim, quote from p. 241. (Page number refers to typed copy.)

2. New Mothers and Fathers

1. Entries for 15 April and 24 Nov. 1835; 19 Feb. 1837; John G. Traylor Diary, ADAH. Also response of James M. Davison, NQS.

2. Herbert G. Gutman, *The Black Family in Slavery and Freedom, 1750–1925* (New York: Vintage, 1976).

3. William Howard Russell, *My Diary North and South* (New York: Harper, 1954), p. 77; "Agreement by Robert F. W. Allston to Purchase Hogs from the Slaves, 1859," in *The South Carolina Rice Plantation as Revealed in the Papers of Robert F. W. Allston*, ed. J. H. Easterby (Chicago: University of Chicago Press, 1945), p. 350; "Ben Graham," in *Slave Testimony: Two Centuries of Letters, Speeches, Interviews, and Autobiographies*, ed. John W. Blassingame (Baton Rouge: Louisiana State University Press, 1977), p. 636. On African influence in the configurations of slave households, see Brenda E. Stevenson, *Life in Black and White: Family and Community in the Slave South* (New York: Oxford University Press, 1996), pp. xii, 222–223.

4. A Southern Planter, *Plantation and Farm Instruction, Regulation, Record, Inventory and Account Book* (Richmond, Va.: J. W. Randolph, 1852), p. 6, in Philip St. George Cocke Papers, VHS. Entries dated 1825, 1827, and undated; Fry Account Book; Virginia Papers Collected by Hillis Fry McLemore; UVAL. Also Charles L. Perdue, Jr., Thomas E. Barden, and Robert K. Phillips, eds., *Weevils in the Wheat: Interviews with Virginia Ex-Slaves* (Charlottesville: University Press of Virginia, 1976), p. 230.

5. Louis Manigault to Charles Manigault, 25 and 27 Feb. 1854, in *Life and Labor on Argyle Island: Letters and Documents of a Savannah River Rice Plantation, 1833–1867*, ed. James M. Clifton (Savannah, Ga.: Beehive, 1978), pp. 171, 173; Young Planter, "Summer Work," *Cotton Planter and Soil* 1 (Oct. 1857), p. 310; entries for 24 Nov. 1835; 19 and 23 Dec. 1837; 18, 19, and 24 Jan. and 15 April 1838; 14 and 19 Jan. 1839; 4, 5, and 7 Jan. 1843; John G. Traylor Diary.

6. Kate E. R. Pickard, *The Kidnapped and the Ransomed: The Narrative of Peter and Vina Still after Forty Years of Slavery* (Philadelphia: Jewish Publication So-

ciety of America, 1970), p. 118; George P. Rawick, ed., *The American Slave: A Composite Autobiography*, SS2, Vol. 1, p. 6; entries for 28 July 1845; 29 Sept. and 17, 20–22 Nov. 1856, Sturdivant Collection (microfilm, SHC); John Michael Vlach, *Back of the Big House: The Architecture of Plantation Slavery* (Chapel Hill: University of North Carolina Press, 1993), especially Chapters 2 and 11.

7. Small Farmer, "Management of Negroes," *Debow's Review* 11 (Oct. 1851), in *Advice among Masters: The Ideal in Slave Management in the Old South*, ed. James Breeden (Westport, Conn.: Greenwood Press, 1980), p. 123, also St. George Cocke, "Plantation Management.—Police," *Debow's Review* 14 (Feb. 1853), ibid., p. 127; Rawick, ed., S1, Vol. 1, p. 425, Vol. 2, Pt. 1, p. 246, and Vol. 6, Pt. 1, p. 9; "Henry Baker," in *Slave Testimony*, p. 669; Vlach, *Back of the Big House*, pp. 166–167.

8. Georgia Writers' Project, *Drums and Shadows: Survival Studies among the Georgia Coastal Negroes* (Athens: University of Georgia Press, 1940), pp. 26, 162; Rawick, ed., S2, Vol. 2, Pt. 2, p. 328; Mrs. A. M. French, *Slavery in South Carolina and the Ex-Slaves; or, The Port Royal Mission* (New York: Negro Universities Press, 1969), p. 160.

9. Stephen Crawford, "The Slave Family: A View from the Slave Narratives," in *Strategic Factors in Nineteenth Century American Economic History*, ed. Claudia Goldin and Hugh Rockoff (Chicago: University of Chicago Press, 1992), p. 347.

10. The work of slave men and women is detailed in Rawick, ed., *The American Slave*, 41 vols., cited in this book by series number and volume; in H. C. Nixon's survey, cited as NQS; and in many other sources, for example, French, *Slavery in South Carolina and the Ex-Slaves*, p. 155. Gutman, *The Black Family in Slavery and Freedom*, pp. 13, 155; Deborah Gray White, *Ar'n't I a Woman? Female Slaves in the Plantation South* (New York: W. W. Norton, 1985), p. 158–160; Jacqueline Jones, *Labor of Love, Labor of Sorrow: Black Women, Work, and the Family, from Slavery to the Present* (New York: Vintage, 1985), pp. 12–13; Robert William Fogel and Stanley L. Engerman, *Time on the Cross: The Economics of American Negro Slavery* (New York: W. W. Norton, 1974), pp. 141–142; John W. Blassingame, *The Slave Community: Plantation Life in the Antebellum South*, rev. ed. (New York: Oxford University Press, 1979), p. 178.

11. Rawick, ed., SS1, Vol. 1, pp. 99–101; M. W. Philips, M.D., "Plantation Economy," *Southern Cultivator* 4 (Aug. 1846), p. 127; A Planter, "Notions on the Management of Negroes, &c," *Farmers' Register* 4 (Dec. 1836 and Jan. 1837), in *Advice among Masters*, p. 282; Robert William Fogel, *Without Consent or Contract: The Rise and Fall of American Slavery* (New York: W. W. Norton, 1989), pp. 77–79.

12. Entry for 24 Sept. 1861, *Mary Chesnut's Civil War*, ed. C. Vann Woodward (New Haven: Yale University Press, 1981), p. 202; Georgia Bryan Conrad, *Reminiscences of a Southern Woman* (Hampton, Va.: Hampton Institute, n.d.), p. 11; Frances Anne Kemble, *Journal of a Residence on a Georgian Plantation in 1838–1839* (New York: Alfred A. Knopf, 1961), pp. 143, 194; "Inclosure" in letter from Sparkman to Benjamin Allston, 10 March 1858, in *The South Carolina Rice Plantation*,

p. 347; William P. Dewees, M.D., *Treatise on the Physical and Medical Treatment of Children* (Philadelphia: H. C. Carey and I. Lea, 1826), p. 70. Also William Capers, Sr., to Charles Manigault, 11 July 1860, in *Life and Labor on Argyle Island*, p. 302; entry for expenses for 1860, David Gavin Diary, SHC; entry for 5 July 1834, John Berkeley Grimball Diary, Vol. 2 of typed transcript, SHC.

13. William Capers, Sr., to Charles Manigault, 11 July 1860, in *Life and Labor on Argyle Island*, p. 302.

14. Kemble, *Journal of a Residence on a Georgian Plantation*, pp. 169, 180, 208; entry for 16 Jan. 1862, *Mary Chesnut's Civil War*, p. 282.

15. Kemble, *Journal of a Residence on a Georgian Plantation*, pp. 185, 199.

16. Rawick, ed., SS1, Vol. 1, p. 426.

17. Plantation Record of James H. Ruffin; Ruffin, Roulhac, and Hamilton Family Papers, SHC. Catherine M. Scholten, *Childbearing in American Society, 1650–1850* (New York: New York University Press, 1985), p. 27. A Southern Planter, *Plantation and Farm Instruction, Regulation, Record, Inventory and Account Book*, pp. 5, 29. Rawick, ed., SS1, Vol. 2, Pt. 2, p. 12; John Campbell, "Work, Pregnancy, and Infant Mortality among Southern Slaves," *Journal of Interdisciplinary History* 14 (Spring 1984), p. 807; "Inclosure" with letter of James R. Sparkman to Benjamin Allston, 10 March 1858, in *The South Carolina Rice Plantation*, p. 346; Sally G. McMillen, *Motherhood in the Old South: Pregnancy, Childbirth, and Infant Rearing* (Baton Rouge: Louisiana State University Press, 1990), p. 94.

18. Response of O. T. McCann, NQS. Medical literature often drew a distinction betwen "civilized" women and others who were supposedly savage. See W. Beach, *An Improved System of Midwifery Adapted to the Reformed Practice of Medicine* (New York: Charles Scribner, 1853), p. 97; Horton Howard, *A Treatise on Midwifery, and the Diseases of Women and Children* (Cincinnati: J. Kost, 1852), p. 110.

19. Kemble, *Journal of a Residence on a Georgian Plantation*, pp. 245, 293, 315. Also pp. 214, 222–223, 229.

20. J. S. Buckingham, *The Slave States of America*, vol. 2 (New York: Negro Universities Press, 1968), p. 193.

21. Plantation Book of Mary Foreman Lewis, Vol. 1: 1857–74, in Lewis Plantation Records, SHC.

22. Robert Byrd Beverley to Robert Beverley, 23 July 1841, Beverley Family Papers, VHS.

23. Jesse T. Cooper to Charles Manigault, 24 Aug. 1849, in *Life and Labor on Argyle Island*, p. 72; "Rules for the Government and Management of —— Plantation to Be Observed by the Overseer," in James Spencer Bassett, *The Southern Plantation Overseer as Revealed in His Letters* (New York: Negro Universities Press, 1968), p. 29.

24. John S. Haywood to George W. Haywood, n.d. Sept. 1835, in Ernest Haywood Papers, SHC; Plantation Diary, Vols. 2 and 3, Sturdivant Collection (microfilm, SHC). Only one notation of a slave birth appeared in this planter's records

for the years 1854 through 1856, although births were regularly recorded in the period 1844 through 1846. Also Robynne Rogers Healey, "Meanings of Motherhood," n. 24, p. 31, paper presented to the Berkshire Conference on the History of Women, Chapel Hill, North Carolina, 7 June 1996, made available by the author.

25. William B. Beverley to Robert Beverley, 4 July 1834 and 13 Sept. 1834; Robert Byrd Beverley to Robert Beverley, 20 Aug. 1835 and 10 May 1836, in Beverley Family Papers, VHS.

26. Rawick, ed., SS2, Vol. 9, Pt. 8, p. 3541 and Vol. 4, Pt. 1, p. 205.

27. "Management of Cotton Estates," *DeBow's Review* 26 (May 1859), in *Advice among Masters*, p. 287; R. W. N. N., "Negro Cabins," *Southern Planter* 16 (March 1856), p. 121.

28. Response of O. T. McCann, NQS; Charles Ball, *Fifty Years in Chains; or, The Life of An American Slave* (Indianapolis: Asher, 18[37]), p. 122.

29. Rawick, ed., SS1, Vol. 1, p. 99; also Vol. 11, p. 124, and S2, Vol. 11, p. 130. "Oliver Bell: That Tree Was My Nurse," in Virginia Pounds Brown and Laurella Owens, *Toting the Lead Row: Ruby Pickens Tartt, Alabama Folklorist* (University: University of Alabama Press, 1981), p. 135. Ball, *Fifty Years in Chains*, p. 122.

30. Rawick, ed., SS1, Vol. 1, p. 426.

31. Entries for 6 and 29 Dec. 1858, "Market Book," Mrs. W. G. Jones Papers, ADAH; entries for 13, 14, 15, 22, and 23 May 1846, Plantation Diary, Vol. 2, Sturdivant Collection.

32. Emphasis added. Towns, "Management of Negroes," *Southern Cultivator* 9 (June 1851), p. 88; Agreement with Overseer, Willis P. Bocock Papers, SHC. Also, Mississippi Planter, "Plantation Management," *Southern Cultivator* 17 (June 1859), p. 169.

33. "Rules of the Plantation," *Southern Cultivator* 7 (June 1849), in *Advice among Masters*, p. 168; T. E. Blunt, "Rules for the Government of Overseers," *Southern Cultivator* 5 (April 1847), p. 62; "Rules for the Government and Management of —— Plantation to Be Observed by the Overseer," in Bassett, ed., *The Southern Plantation Overseer*, p. 28. Also Duncan Clinch Heyward, *Seed from Madagascar* (Chapel Hill: University of North Carolina Press, 1937), p. 177.

34. A Mississippi Planter, "Management of Negroes upon Southern Estates," *DeBow's Review* 10 (June 1851); "The Duties of an Overseer," *Farmer and Planter* 8 (June 1857) and "Management of Cotton Estates," *DeBow's Review* 26 (May 1859), quoted in *Advice among Masters*, pp. 283, 205, 287. Also Mississippi Planter, "Plantation Management," p. 169.

35. "Health of Young Negroes," *DeBow's Review* 20 (June 1856), in *Advice among Masters*, p. 284-285.

36. Rawick, ed., SS2, Vol. 9, p. 3541, also Vol. 5, p. 1523; H. C. Bruce, *The New Man: Twenty-Nine Years a Slave, Twenty-Nine Years a Free Man* (Miami: Mnemosyne, 1969), p. 14; D. E. Huger Smith, *A Charlestonian's Recollections, 1846-1913*

(Charleston: Carolina Art Association, 1950), p. 27. Smith's memoir can also be found in Herbert Ravenel Sass, ed., *A Carolina Rice Plantation of the Fifties* (New York: William Morrow, 1936), pp. 59–97.

37. "The Slave's Story," in *Slave Testimony*, entry for 8 May 1835, Diary, George Augustus Beverly Walker.

38. Rawick, ed., SS1, Vol. 7, Pt. 2, p. 371; Perdue, Barden, and Phillips, eds., *Weevils in the Wheat*, pp. 226–227; Rawick, ed., SS1, Vol. 1, p. 256; Karin Calvert, *Children in the House: The Material Culture of Early Childhood, 1600–1900* (Boston: Northeastern University Press, 1992), pp. 125–126.

39. *From Fugitive Slave to Free Man: The Autobiographies of William Wells Brown* (New York: Mentor, 1993), p. 47.

40. Rawick, ed., S1, Vol. 6, p. 198. Also Towns, "Management of Negroes," p. 8; Calvert, *Children in the House*, pp. 72–77.

41. Rawick, ed., S2, Vol. 11, Pt. 7, p. 42, SS1, Vol. 11, p. 144, and S2, Vol. 8, Pt. 2, p. 241; Perdue, Barden, and Phillips, eds., *Weevils in the Wheat*, p. 309; Mary Jones to Joseph Jones, 13 May 1858, in *The Children of Pride: A True Story of Georgia and the Civil War*, ed. Robert Manson Myers (New Haven: Yale University Press, 1972), p. 415; Rawick, ed., S1, Vol. 6, p. 98. On white women breastfeeding black babies, see McMillen, *Motherhood in the Old South*, pp. 129–130.

42. A Southern Planter, *Plantation and Farm Instruction, Regulation, Record, Inventory and Account Book*, p. 5; Sally G. McMillen, "Antebellum Southern Fathers and the Health Care of Children," *Journal of Southern History* 60 (Aug. 1994), p. 517.

43. Robert Byrd Beverley to William Bradshaw Beverley, 20 June 1839, and Robert Byrd Beverley to Robert Beverley, 23 July 1841, Beverley Family Papers, VHS; B. M. Pearson to Samuel Pickens, 13 June 1842, Pickens Family Papers, ADAH; "Sarah Fitzpatrick," in *Slave Testimony*, p. 641; McMillen, *Motherhood in the Old South*, p. 118, also Table IV, Appendix One; Rawick, ed., SS1, Vol. 1, p. 32.

44. Rawick, ed., SS2, Vol. 9, p. 3602, also SS2, Vol. 6, Pt. 5, p. 2077; Benjamin Drew, *A North-Side View of Slavery. The Refugee: Or the Narratives of Fugitive Slaves in Canada* (New York: Johnson Reprint, 1968), p. 71.

45. "The Duties of an Overseer," *Farmer and Planter* 8 (June 1857) and "Rules of the Plantation," *Southern Cultivator* 7 (June 1849), both in *Advice among Masters*, pp. 205, 168; Rawick, ed., SS1, Vol. 1, p. 449; Virginia Clay-Clopton, *A Belle of the Fifties: Memoirs of Mrs. Clay, of Alabama*, ed. Ada Sterling (New York: Da Capo Press, 1969), p. 7; Fogel and Engerman, *Time on the Cross*, pp. 136–137. Southern physicians recommended weaning children between the ages of six and twelve months, although many planter women chose to breastfeed longer. See McMillen, *Motherhood in the Old South*, pp. 120–121. Physicians in the urban North recommended gradual weaning beginning between the ages of nine and twelve months, but mothers did not abide by any "hard-and-fast rules." See Sylvia D. Hoffert's *Private Matters: American Attitudes toward Childbearing and Infant*

Nurture in the Urban North, 1800–1860 (Urbana: University of Illinois Press, 1989), pp. 155–156.

46. Perdue, Barden, and Phillips, eds., *Weevils in the Wheat*, p. 323.

47. Tattler, "Management of Negroes," *Southern Planter* 11 (Feb. 1851), p. 41. Also Rawick, ed., S2, Vol. 11, p. 306.

48. A Southern Planter, *Plantation and Farm Instruction, Regulation, Record, Inventory and Account Book*, p. 6. Herbert S. Klein and Stanley L. Engerman suggest that slave women in the United States breastfed their children for a period of about one year, in contrast to slave women in the British West Indies, who breastfed for two years. Their evidence is longer intervals between births among the latter, which they argue stemmed from longer periods of breastfeeding that delayed conception. As Klein and Engerman acknowledge, the link between breastfeeding and contraceptive protection is far from clear, and the matter is complicated in the United States because slave infants received supplemental foods from a very young age, particularly during seasons of heavy work. If slave women continued to breastfeed their infants at night for periods well beyond a year, their experiences would have paralleled those of British West Indies slave women more closely than the study by Klein and Engerman suggests. See Klein and Engerman, "Fertility Differentials between Slaves in the United States and the British West Indies: A Note on Lactation Practices and Their Possible Implications," *William & Mary Quarterly* 35 (April 1978), especially pp. 358, 368–371, n. 35.

49. Few older slaves lived in central Alabama in 1820, compared to the South as a whole. Men and women age forty-five and older constituted slightly less than 6 percent of Alabama's black-belt slave population, but nearly 10 percent of the slaves found in all the southern states. The number of older slaves increased in the following decades, and by 1860, the percentage of slaves age fifty and older in Greene and other black-belt counties had risen to nearly 7 percent. The slave population in Virginia aged slightly over time, because in 1860 nearly 10 percent were age 50 or older. The situation differed along the rice coast where older slaves constituted an even larger proportion of the slave population than in Virginia, and the proportion of older slaves there remained high throughout the antebellum years. Eleven percent of slaves were age 50 or older in 1860. Population figures compiled from United States Census Office, *Census for 1820* (Washington, D.C.: Gales and Seaton, 1821) and U.S. Bureau of the Census, *Population of the United States in 1860* (Washington, D.C.: Government Printing Office, 1864).

50. Plantation Book of Mary Foreman Lewis, Vol. 1, Lewis Plantation Records, SHC; Rawick, ed., S1, Vol. 6, p. 398, and SS1, Vol. 1, p. 71; Edward Carrington Cabell, "Memorandum in regard to Hire of house servants," n.d., Cabell Family Papers, VHS. On slave women using female complaints to their advantage, see White, *Ar'n't I a Woman?*, pp. 79–84.

51. "On the Management of Slaves," *Southern Agriculturist* 6 (June 1833), in *Advice among Masters*, p. 51; Rawick, ed., SS1, Vol. 1, pp. 449, 452; Smith, *A*

Charlestonian's Recollections, 1846–1913, p. 15. Also response of P. F. Mitchell, NQS.

52. Rawick, ed., SS1, Vol. 1, p. 449; also "Provisions for Field Hands," *Southern Cultivator* 8 (May 1850), in *Advice among Masters,* p. 97; Calvert, *Children in the House,* pp. 66–67.

53. Rawick, ed., S1, Vol. 6, p. 90; Smith, *A Charlestonian's Recollections, 1846–1913,* pp. 15, 26.

54. Perdue, Barden, and Phillips, eds., *Weevils in the Wheat,* pp. 323; Rawick, ed., SS1, Vol. 1, p. 28; A Mississippi Planter, "Management of Negroes upon Southern Estates," *DeBow's Review* 10 (June 1851) and R. W. Gibbes, "Southern Slave Life," *DeBow's Review* 24 (April 1858), both in *Advice among Masters,* pp. 283 and 207–208.

55. Perdue, Barden, and Phillips, eds., *Weevils in the Wheat,* p. 185; "Ank Bishop: Gabriel Blow Soft! Gabriel Blow Loud!" in *Toting the Lead Row,* pp. 126–127.

56. Calculations from Plantation Book of Mary Foreman Lewis, Vol. 1: 1857–1874, Lewis Plantation Records, SHC.

57. Evidence from seven Alabama black-belt counties suggests that the work routines associated with cotton cultivation contributed to infant neglect and consequent infant mortality at certain times of year. Marilyn Davis Hahn, comp., *Alabama Mortality Schedule, 1850* (Easley, S.C.: n.p., 1983), pp. 61–70, 80–91, 122–127, 141–149, 183–197, 203–207, 230–236. The counties analyzed were Dallas, Greene, Lowndes, Marengo, Montgomery, Perry, and Sumter. For evidence from Georgia, see John Campbell, "Work, Pregnancy, and Infant Mortality among Southern Slaves," pp. 800, 809.

58. Cheryll Ann Cody, "Cycles of Work and of Childbearing: Seasonality in Women's Lives on Low Country Plantations," in *More than Chattel,* pp. 68, 72.

3. Young Children in the Quarter

1. Emphasis added. Entries for 15 July and 30 Aug. 1855, James M. Torbert Diary (typed copy), ADAH; Charles L. Perdue, Jr., Thomas E. Barden, and Robert K. Phillips, eds., *Weevils in the Wheat: Interviews with Virginia Ex-Slaves* (Charlottesville: University Press of Virginia, 1976), p. 323.

2. Robert William Fogel, *Without Consent or Contract: The Rise and Fall of American Slavery* (New York: W. W. Norton, 1989), pp. 127–128, 142–147; Richard H. Steckel, "Slave Mortality: Analysis of Evidence from Plantation Records," in *Without Consent or Contract: The Rise and Fall of American Slavery, Conditions of Slave Life and the Transition to Freedom: Technical Papers,* vol. 2, ed. Robert William Fogel and Stanley L. Engerman (New York: W. W. Norton, 1992), pp. 407, 409–410; Jeffrey R. Young, "Ideology and Death on a Savannah River Rice Plantation, 1833–1867: Paternalism amidst 'a Good Supply of Disease and Pain,'" *Journal*

of Southern History 59 (Nov. 1993), p. 680; William Dusinberre, *Them Dark Days: Slavery in the American Rice Swamps* (New York: Oxford University Press, 1996), pp. 80, 411–414, 416; Sally G. McMillen, *Southern Women: Black and White in the Old South* (Arlington Heights, Ill.: Harlan Davidson, 1992), p. 68; Richard H. Steckel, "A Dreadful Childhood: The Excess Mortality of American Slaves," *Social Science History* 10 (Winter 1986), p. 428.

3. John A. Calhoun, E. E. DuBose, and Virgil Bobo, "Report of Barbour County Agricultural Society," *Southern Cultivator* 4 (Aug. 1846), p. 114; also "The Cotton Power, and American Power," *American Cotton Planter* 2 (Nov. 1858), p. 331. George P. Rawick, ed., *The American Slave: A Composite Autobiography*, S1, Vol. 2, Pt. 2, pp. 11–12.

4. Rawick, ed., S1, Vol. 2, Pt. 1, p. 20.

5. Catherine M. Scholten, *Childbearing in American Society: 1650–1850* (New York: New York University Press, 1985), p. 71.

6. Tables 3, 4, and 5 in Peter Kolchin, *American Slavery, 1819–1877* (New York: Hill and Wang, 1993), pp. 242–244, also p. 101.

7. Anne Newport Royall, *Letters from Alabama, 1817–1822* (University: University of Alabama Press, 1969), p. 140; Rawick, ed., SS1, Vol. 3, Pt. 1, p. 10.

8. Rawick, ed., S1, Vol. 6, p. 197 and SS1, Vol. 1, pp. 245, 284, 426, and S1, Vol. 3, Pt. 3, p. 243; also S1, Vol. 2, Pt. 1, p. 143; Memoir, St. George Tucker Coalter Bryan, Grinnan Family Papers, VHS; Virginia Clay-Clopton, *A Belle of the Fifties: Memoirs of Mrs. Clay, of Alabama* (New York: Da Capo, 1969), p. 4. On Raw Head and Bloody Bones stories in the North, see Lydia Child, *The American Frugal Housewife,* 12th ed. (Boston: Applewood for Old Sturbridge Village, n.d.), p. 101.

9. Entries for 18 Oct. 1855 and 4 Jan. 1856, David Gavin Diary, SHC; entry for 11 Jan. 1859, Diary, John Edwin Fripp Papers, SHC; Rawick, ed., S2, Vol. 11, Pt. 7, pp. 164–165; Kate E. R. Pickard, *The Kidnapped and the Ransomed: The Narrative of Peter and Vina Still after Forty Years of Slavery* (Philadelphia: Jewish Publication Society of America, 1970), p. 165.

10. Rawick, ed., S1, Vol. 2, Pt. 2, p. 338.

11. Ibid., S1, Vol. 3, Pt. 3, pp. 10, 27, also S1, Vol. 2, Pt. 1, p. 101; Charles Joyner, *Down by the Riverside: A South Carolina Slave Community* (Urbana: University of Illinois Press, 1984), pp. 92–93.

12. Rawick, ed., S1, Vol. 6, pp. 426, 87, S2, Vol. 11, Pt. 7, p. 42, and SS1, Vol. 1, p. 449 and Vol. 12, p. 197; J. S. Haywood to George W. Haywood, 31 May 1835, Ernest Haywood Papers, SHC; O. T. McCann, NQS; "Henry Baker," in *Slave Testimony: Two Centuries of Letters, Speeches, Interviews, and Autobiographies,* ed. John W. Blassingame (Baton Rouge: Louisiana State University Press, 1977), p. 669. Todd L. Savitt notes the infrequent use of privies throughout the South. See *Medicine and Slavery: The Diseases and Health Care of Blacks in Antebellum Virginia* (Urbana: University of Illinois Press, 1978), p. 59; Perdue, Barden, and Phillips, eds., *Weevils in the Wheat,* p. 188.

13. Small Farmer, "Management of Negroes," *DeBow's Review* 11 (Oct. 1851), in *Advice among Masters: The Ideal in Slave Management in the Old South*, ed. James O. Breeden (Westport, Conn.: Greenwood, 1980), p. 68; responses of James M. Davison and Mrs. Y. B. Stewart, NQS; Charles L. Perdue, Jr., Thomas E. Barden, and Robert K. Phillips, eds., *Weevils in the Wheat: Interviews with Virginia Ex-Slaves* (Charlottesville: University of Virginia Press, 1979), p. 32; Rawick, ed., S1, Vol. 6, p. 295 and Vol. 2, Pt. 1, p. 158, and S2, Vol. 11, Pt. 7, p. 170.

14. Slave List dated 7 Dec. 1845 in *Life and Labor on Argyle Island: Letters and Documents of a Savannah River Rice Plantation, 1833–1867*, ed. James M. Clifton (Savannah, Ga.: Beehive, 1978), p. 32; entries for 19 Oct. 1832, 14 Oct. 1833, and 25 Oct. 1834, John Berkley Grimball Diary, SHC; Rawick, ed., S2, Vol. 11, p. 306, and S1, Vol. 6, p. 197 and Vol. 2, Pt. 2, p. 70; Holland Nimmons M'Tyeire, *Duties of Christian Masters* (Nashville, Tenn.: Southern Methodist Publishing House, 1859), p. 52.

15. Untitled memoir of Marie Gordon (Pryor) Rice, VHS; Rawick, ed., S1, Vol. 2, Pt. 2, p. 228.

16. Dusinberre, *Them Dark Days*, pp. 253–254.

17. Plantation Journal entry for 7 April 1845, James Haynes to Charles Manigault, 1 June 1846; Charles Manigault to Jesse T. Cooper, 10 Jan. 1848; Stephen F. Clark to Louis Manigault, 14 June 1853; Plantation Journal entry for 10 Dec. 1855, in *Life and Labor on Argyle Island*, pp. 22, 35, 62, 157; entry for 22 Sept. 1834, John Berkley Grimball Diary, SHC; Jacob Stroyer, "My Life in the South," in *Five Slave Narratives: A Compendium* (New York: Arno Press, 1968), p. 8.

18. Stroyer, "My Life in the South," pp. 8–9.

19. Ibid., pp. 9–11.

20. Slave Lists dated 30 April 1856 and 30 April 1857, in *Life and Labor on Argyle Island*, pp. 221, 249; Tattler, "Management of Negroes," *Southern Planter* 11 (Feb. 1851), pp. 39–40; H. C. Bruce, *The New Man: Twenty-Nine Years a Slave, Twenty-Nine Years a Free Man* (Miami: Mnemosyne, 1969), p. 14; Benjamin Allston, "Notes on the Management of a Southern Rice Estate," *DeBow's Review* 24 (April 1858), in *Advice among Masters*, ed. Breeden, p. 287; Rawick, ed., S1, Vol. 2, Pt. 1, p. 119; A Southern Planter, *Plantation and Farm Instruction, Regulation, Record, Inventory and Account Book*, p. 5 (Richmond, Va.: J. W. Randolph, 1852), in Philip St. George Cocke Papers, VHS; response of Mrs. R. M. Gune, NQS; Rusticus, "Plantation Management and Practice," *Cotton Planter and Soil* 1 (Dec. 1857), p. 375; D. E. Huger Smith, *A Charlestonian's Recollections, 1846–1913* (Charleston: Carolina Art Association, 1950), p. 15.

21. A Planter, "Notions on the Management of Negroes, &c.," *Farmers' Register* 4 (Dec. 1836 and Jan. 1837), in *Advice among Masters*, p. 282; Rawick, ed., S1, Vol. 3, Pt. 3, p. 27.

22. Rawick, ed., S1, Vol. 6, p. 343; John R. Turner, M.D., "Plantation Hygiene," *Southern Cultivator* 15 (May and June 1857), in *Advice among Masters*, p. 286.

23. Rawick, ed., S1, Vol. 3, Pt. 4, pp. 8–9, 222, and Vol. 6, pp. 63–64, 294–296.

24. Ibid., SS1, Vol. 3, Pt. 1, p. 168 and Vol. 1, p. 361; "Houses of Negroes—Habits of Living, &c," *Southern Cultivator* 8 (May 1850), in *Advice among Masters,* p. 168; also Rawick, ed., S1, Vol. 2, Pt. 1, p. 99.

25. Rawick, ed., S2, Vol. 17, p. 135 and Vol. 16, Pt. 12, p. 45, S1, Vol. 6, p. 20 and Vol. 7, p. 136, SS1, Vol. 11, pp. 168, 178, and SS2, Vol. 4, Pt. 3, pp. 1115, 1286; Stephen Crawford, "The Slave Family: A View from the Slave Narratives," *Strategic Factors in Nineteenth Century American Economic History,* ed. Claudia Goldin and Hugh Rockoff (Chicago: University of Chicago Press, 1992), p. 339; Perdue, Barden, and Phillips, eds., *Weevils in the Wheat,* p. 26.

26. Tattler, "Management of Negroes," p. 39; Nathan Bass, "Essay on the Treatment and Management of Slaves," Southern Central Agricultural Society of Georgia, *Transactions, 1846–1851,* John R. Turner, M.D., "Plantation Hygiene," *Southern Cultivator* 15 (May and June 1857), and R. King, Jr., "On the Management of the Butler Estate, and the Cultivation of Sugar Cane," *Southern Agriculturist* 1 (Dec. 1828), in *Advice among Masters,* pp. 12, 197, 92.

27. Rawick, ed., SS1, Vol. 7, Pt. 2, p. 423; Douglass, *Narrative of the Life of Frederick Douglass: An American Slave* (New York: Signet, 1968); Brown, *Narrative of William W. Brown,* 2d ed., in *From Fugitive Slave to Free Man: The Autobiographies of William Wells Brown* (New York: Mentor, 1993); Stowe, *Uncle Tom's Cabin or, Life among the Lowly* (New York: Penguin, 1981), pp. 623–624.

28. Alabama Code of 1852, Sections 2056–2057, reprinted in John V. Denson, *Slavery Laws in Alabama,* 3d ser. (Auburn: Alabama Polytechnic Institute Historical Studies, 1908), pp. 34–35. On the percentage of children sold separately from parents, see Michael Tadman, *Speculators and Slaves: Masters, Traders, and Slaves in the Old South* (Madison: University of Wisconsin Press, 1989), p. 171; Stephen Crawford, "The Slave Family," p. 341.

29. Judith Kelleher Schafer, *Slavery, the Civil Law, and the Supreme Court of Louisiana* (Baton Rouge: Louisiana State University Press, 1994), pp. 165–166.

30. On Alabama, see Tadman, *Speculators and Slaves,* pp. 84–86. Also Acts of 1831–1832, reproduced in Denson, *Slavery Laws in Alabama,* pp. 46–52, and Thomas Perkins Abernethy, *The Formative Period in Alabama, 1815–1828* (University: University of Alabama, 1965), pp. 167–169. On Georgia, see Tadman, *Speculators and Slaves,* pp. 90–93. On Virginia, see June Purcell Guild, *Black Laws of Virginia: A Summary of the Legislative Acts of Virginia Concerning Negroes from Earliest Times to the Present* (New York: Negro Universities Press, 1969), p. 86.

31. Perdue, Barden, and Phillips, eds., *Weevils in the Wheat,* pp. 319, 71, 16.

32. Rawick, ed., S1, Vol. 2, Pt. 2, pp. 140, 144, 177, 280; Perdue, Barden, and Phillips, eds., *Weevils in the Wheat,* pp. 33, 79, 123, 323; Bruce, *The New Man,* pp. 47–48; J. S. Buckingham, *The Slave States of America,* vol. 2 (New York: Negro Universities Press, 1968), p. 553; Octavia V. Albert, *House of Bondage, or Charlotte Brooks and Other Slaves* (New York: Oxford University Press, 1988), p. 21.

33. "Bettie Tolbert: Lost to the Refugee Wagons" and "Adelle Lemon: My Grandmother Fancied Her Butler," in Virginia Pounds Brown and Laurella Owens, *Toting the Lead Row: Ruby Pickens Tartt, Alabama Folklorist* (University: University of Alabama Press, 1981), pp. 138, 139; Rawick, ed., SS1, Vol. 1, p. 450 and S2, Vol. 11, Pt. 7, p. 96; "Rosa Barnwell," in *Slave Testimony,* p. 698; Ulrich B. Phillips, ed., *Plantation and Frontier Documents, 1649–1863,* vol. 2 (New York: Burt Franklin, 1969), pp. 75–81; Randolph B. Campbell, *An Empire for Slavery: The Peculiar Institution in Texas, 1821–1865* (Baton Rouge: Louisiana State University Press, 1989), p. 102; Schafer, *Slavery, the Civil Law, and the Supreme Court of Louisiana,* pp. 90–95.

34. Rawick, ed., S1, Vol. 3, Pt. 3, pp. 94, 275, Vol. 6, p. 212, and SS1, Vol. 1, pp. 1, 158, 456; entry for 13 Sept. 1856, David Gavin Diary; Dusinberre, *Them Dark Days,* p. 209; Perdue, Barden, and Phillips, eds., *Weevils in the Wheat,* p. 55, also p. 343; Smith, *A Charlestonian's Recollections,* p. 43; Rawick, ed., SS2, Vol. 8, Pt. 7, p. 214; "Timothy Smith," in *Slave Testimony,* p. 740.

35. Rawick, ed., S1, Vol. 6, p. 321; Charles Manigault to Louis Manigault, 21 Feb. 1856, in *Life and Labor on Argyle Island,* p. 209.

36. W. W. Gilmer, "Management of Servants," *Southern Planter* 12 (April 1852), p. 106; also Charles S. Johnson, *Shadow of the Plantation* (Chicago: University of Chicago Press, 1966), p. 38.

37. Russell, *My Diary North and South* (New York: Harper, 1954), p. 71; Rawick, ed., S2, Vol. 10, Pt. 5, p. 43.

38. Rawick, ed., SS2, Vol. 9, Pt. 8, p. 3473, and S2, Vol. 11, p. 207; also S1, Vol. 6, p. 34.

39. Ibid., SS1, Vol. 1, p. 448; "Laura Clark: Children in Every Graveyard," in *Toting the Lead Row,* p. 123.

40. J. G. Clinkscales, *On the Old Plantation: Reminiscences of His Childhood* (New York: Negro Universities Press, 1969), pp. 55–56, 100; Duncan Clinch Heyward, *Seed from Madagascar* (Chapel Hill: University of North Carolina Press, 1937), p. 191; also Lewis Paine, *Six Years in a Georgia Prison* (New York: n.p., 1851), p. 122; Daniel Blake Smith, *Inside the Great House: Planter Family Life in Eighteenth-Century Chesapeake Society* (Charlottesville: University Press of Virginia, 1980), pp. 83, 286–287.

41. Rawick, ed., SS2, Vol. 4, Pt. 4, p. 1330; Smith, *A Charlestonian's Recollections,* p. 44; Perdue, Barden, and Phillips, eds., *Weevils in the Wheat,* p. 109.

42. Rawick, ed., SS1, Vol. 1, p. 283, also S1, Vol. 2, Pt. 2, p. 310. On attitudes toward children, see Karin Calvert, *Children in the House: The Material Culture of Early Childhood, 1600–1900* (Boston: Northeastern University Press, 1992), p. 106.

43. Stroyer, "My Life in the South," pp. 12–13; also Rawick, ed., S1, Vol. 2, Pt. 1, p. 101, and S2, Vol. 13, Pt. 3, p. 207; quote in Dusinberre, *Them Dark Days,* p. 209.

44. Perdue, Barden, and Phillips, eds., *Weevils in the Wheat,* pp. 78, 80, 303.

45. Heyward, *Seed from Madagascar,* p. 177; entry for 5 March 1862, *Mary*

Chesnut's Civil War, ed. C. Vann Woodward (New Haven: Yale University Press, 1981), p. 297; quote in Dusinberre, *Them Dark Days,* pp. 320–321, 369.

46. Rawick, ed., S2, Vol. 11, p. 339.

47. Ibid., S1, Vol. 3, Pt. 3, p. 9.

48. Dusinberre, *Them Dark Days,* p. 323.

49. Rawick, ed., S1, Vol. 2, Pt. 2, pp. 71, 92.

50. Ibid., S1, Vol. 3, Pt. 3, pp. 214, 240, and Vol. 2, Pt. 2, p. 91; "David Holmes," in *Slave Testimony,* p. 297.

51. Rawick, ed., S1, Vol. 2, Pt. 2, pp. 92, 109.

52. Bruce, *The New Man,* p. 41; Perdue, Barden, and Phillips, eds., *Weevils in the Wheat,* p. 104.

53. Rawick, ed., S1, Vol. 2, Pt. 1, pp. 102–103, and Vol. 6, p. 20; entry for 8 May 1864, *Mary Chesnut's Civil War,* pp. 606–607; Stroyer, "My Life in the South," pp. 17, 20, 22, 30–32.

54. Rawick, ed., S1, Vol. 7, pp. 95–96; also S1, Vol. 2, Pt. 2, p. 197.

55. Ibid., S1, Vol. 3, Pt. 4, pp. 245–246; also Amelia Wallace Vernon, *African Americans at Mars Bluff, South Carolina* (Baton Rouge: Louisiana State University Press, 1993), p. 164.

56. Perdue, Barden, and Phillips, eds., *Weevils in the Wheat,* p. 15; also Rawick, ed., SS1, Vol. 3, Pt. 1, p. 23; Clinkscales, *On the Old Plantation,* p. 38.

57. Rawick, ed., SS2, Vol. 9, Pt. 8, p. 3875.

58. Ibid., S1, Vol. 2, Pt. 1, p. 293, Pt. 2, p. 285, and S2, Vol. 11, p. 316; Stroyer, "My Life in the South," p. 21; "Bettie Tolbert: Lost to the Refugee Wagons," in *Toting the Lead Row,* p. 138; Perdue, Barden, and Phillips, eds., *Weevils in the Wheat,* p. 245.

59. Gladys-Marie Fry, *Night Riders in Black Folk History* (Athens: University of Georgia Press, 1991, 1975), p. 58; Rawick, ed., S2, Vol. 11, Pt. 7, p. 163.

60. Rawick, ed., SS1, Vol. 10, Pt. 5, pp. 2007–2008; Perdue, Barden, and Phillips, eds., *Weevils in the Wheat,* p. 98. Also Rawick, ed., S1, Vol. 7, pp. 95–96.

61. Rawick, ed., SS2, Vol. 4, Pt. 3, p. 17, and SS1, Vol. 1, p. 112; Stroyer, "My Life in the South," p. 21. Also Rawick, ed., S1, Vol. 6, p. 343.

62. Rawick, ed., S1, Vol. 3, Pt. 4, p. 172.

63. Annie L. Burton, "Memories of Childhood's Slavery Days," in *Six Women's Slave Narratives,* ed. Henry Gates, Jr. (New York: Oxford University Press, 1988), p. 37; "Sarah Fitzpatrick," in *Slave Testimony,* pp. 647–648; Smith, *A Charlestonian's Recollections,* p. 43.

64. Rawick, ed., SS1, Vol. 5, pp. 210–211; Eugene D. Genovese, *Roll, Jordan, Roll: The World the Slaves Made* (New York: Vintage, 1974), pp. 462–463. Also Anthony S. Parent, Jr., and Susan Brown Wallace, "Childhood and Sexual Identity under Slavery," in *American Sexual Politics: Sex, Gender, and Race since the Civil War,* ed. John C. Fout and Maura Shaw Tantillo (Chicago: University of Chicago Press, 1993), pp. 24–25.

65. Rawick, ed., S1, Vol. 7, p. 12.

66. Perdue, Barden, and Phillips, eds., *Weevils in the Wheat*, p. 33.

67. Rawick, ed., SS1, Vol. 1, p. 159. Also Willie Lee Rose, "Childhood in Bondage," *Slavery and Freedom*, ed. William W. Freehling (New York: Oxford University Press, 1982), p. 37.

68. "Oliver Bell: That Tree Was My Nurse," in *Toting the Lead Row*, p. 135; Perdue, Barden, and Phillips, eds., *Weevils in the Wheat*, p. 327 (for an older girl who tried to protect her mother, see p. 285); Rawick, ed., S2, Vol. 8, Pt. 1, p. 282.

69. "Amy Chapman: The Masters Good but Overseers Mean," in *Toting the Lead Row*, p. 129.

70. Rawick, ed., S1, Vol. 3, Pt. 4, pp. 59, 117, and Vol. 6, p. 13; S2, Vol. 4, Pt. 1, p. 154.

71. Fogel, *Without Consent or Contract*, p. 128.

4. Education in the Middle Years

1. Charles L. Perdue, Thomas E. Barden, and Robert K. Phillips, eds., *Weevils in the Wheat: Interviews with Virginia Ex-Slaves* (Charlottesville: University Press of Virginia, 1976), p. 325; George P. Rawick, ed., *The American Slave: A Composite Autobiography*, S1, Vol. 6, p. 331.

2. "Ank Bishop: Gabriel Blow Soft! Gabriel Blow Loud!" in Virginia Pounds Brown and Laurella Owens, *Toting the Lead Row: Ruby Pickens Tartt, Alabama Folklorist* (University: University of Alabama Press, 1981), pp. 126–128; "Rules for the Government and Management of ——— Plantation to Be Observed by the Overseer," as published in *DeBow's Review* and as a separate pamphlet, in John Spencer Bassett, ed., *The Southern Plantation Overseer, As Revealed in His Letters* (New York: Negro Universities Press, 1968), p. 24; "Index for 1861," James M. Torbert Diary, ADAH; Rawick, ed., SS1, Vol. 3, Pt. 1, p. 169, and S1, Vol. 2, Pt. 1, p. 247; William Dusinberre, *Them Dark Days: Slavery in the American Rice Swamps* (New York: Oxford University Press, 1996), pp. 188–189; Frances Anne Kemble, *Journal of a Residence on a Georgian Plantation in 1838–1839* (New York: Alfred A. Knopf, 1961), p. 202. On working for overseers, see "An Overseer's Contract," 1822, in *The South Carolina Rice Planter as Revealed in the Papers of Robert F. W. Allston*, ed. J. H. Easterby (Chicago: University of Chicago Press, 1945), p. 245; entry for 7 Dec. 1832, John Berkley Grimball Diary, SHC; "Overseer Contract," in *Life and Labor on Argyle Island: Letters and Documents of a Savannah River Rice Plantation, 1833–1867*, ed. James M. Clifton (Savannah, Ga.: Beehive, 1978), p. 136.

3. Entry for 6 Oct. 1855, Plantation Diary, Sturdivant Collection (microfilm, SHC); response of P. F. Mitchell, NQS; Harriet Martineau, *Retrospect of Western Travel*, vol. 1 (New York: Haskell House, 1969), p. 221.

4. Perdue, Barden, and Phillips, eds., *Weevils in the Wheat*, p. 48.

5. Rawick, ed., S2, Vol. 4, Pt. 1, p. 154 and Vol. 16, Pt. 4, p. 46; S1, Vol. 2, Pt. 2, p. 343.

6. Ibid., SS1, Vol. 1, pp. 289, 301; Benjamin Drew, *A North-Side View of Slavery. The Refugee: Or the Narratives of Fugitive Slaves in Canada* (New York: Johnson Reprint, 1968), p. 73; H. C. Bruce, *The New Man: Twenty-Nine Years a Slave, Twenty-Nine Years a Free Man* (Miami: Mnemosyne, 1969), pp. 28–30.

7. Elizabeth Keckley, *Behind the Scenes: or, Thirty Years as a Slave, and Four Years in the White House* (New York: Oxford University Press, 1988), pp. 20–21; Rawick, ed., S1, Vol. 6, p. 130, Vol. 5, Pt. 3, p. 210, and Vol. 2, Pt. 2, p. 279.

8. Perdue, Barden, and Phillips, eds., *Weevils in the Wheat*, p. 162; Rawick, ed., SS1, Vol. 1, p. 32; Small Farmer, "Management of Negroes," *DeBow's Review* 11 (Oct. 1851), in *Advice among Masters: The Ideal in Slave Management in the Old South*, ed. James O. Breeden (Westport, Conn.: Greenwood, 1980), p. 84.

9. Rawick, ed., SS1, Vol. 1, pp. 214–215; Duncan Clinch Heyward, *Seed from Madagascar* (Chapel Hill: University of North Carolina Press, 1937), p. 105.

10. Perdue, Barden, and Phillips, eds., *Weevils in the Wheat*, p. 161.

11. Rawick, ed., S1, Vol. 3, Pt. 3, p. 243, and SS2, Vol. 6, Pt. 5, p. 1963.

12. S. D. Wragg, "Overseeing," *Farmer and Planter* 5 (June and Sept. 1854), in *Advice among Masters*, p. 284; "Overseers (Part 2)," *Southern Planter* 16 (May 1856), p. 148.

13. Perdue, Barden, and Phillips, eds., *Weevils in the Wheat*, p. 249; Rawick, ed., SS1, Vol. 1, p. 465.

14. Rawick, ed., S2, Vol. 16, Pt. 4, p. 103, also S1, Vol. 6, p. 7; Perdue, Barden, and Phillips, eds., *Weevils in the Wheat*, p. 317.

15. Rawick, ed., S1, Vol. 7, p. 134, also S2, Vol. 8, Pt. 2, p. 63.

16. Ibid., S1, Vol. 3, Pt. 4, p. 260, Vol. 6, p. 368, and Vol. 7, p. 128.

17. Ibid., S1, Vol. 6, p. 172; Keckley, *Behind the Scenes*, pp. 20–21.

18. Mary Jones to Mary Sharpe Jones, 10 Sept. 1855, in *Children of Pride: A True Story of Georgia and the Civil War*, ed. Robert Manson Myers (New Haven: Yale University Press, 1972), p. 153; entries for 21 and 29 Nov. 1835, Diary of George Augustus Beverly Walker, ADAH; entry dated July 1851, Memoranda Book of Thomas S. Watson for 1851, and entry for 22 July 1854, Memoranda Book of Thomas S. Watson for 1853–1855; Watson Family Papers; ABSP, Series E, Part 1; Rawick, ed., SS2, Vol. 8, p. 3176, SS1, Vol. 1, p. 96 and Vol. 3, Pt. 1, pp. 169, 171.

19. Rawick, ed., SS2, Vol. 9, Pt. 8, p. 3861 and S1, Vol. 3, Pt. 3, pp. 274–275.

20. Eliza G. Robarts to Rev. and Mrs. C. C. Jones, 20 May 1861, in *The Children of Pride*, p. 679; Rawick, ed., SS1, Vol. 10, Pt. 5, p. 2004; Bruce, *The New Man*, pp. 39–40; Robert Byrd Beverley to Robert Beverley, 7 Jan. 1841, Beverley Family Papers, VHS.

21. Rawick, ed., S1, Vol. 13, Pt. 3, p. 288, SS1, Vol. 10, Pt. 5, p. 1989, and SS2, Vol. 9, Pt. 8, p. 3871.

22. Brenda E. Stevenson, *Life in Black and White: Family and Community in the Slave South* (New York: Oxford University Press, 1996), p. 192; Perdue, Barden, and Phillips, eds., *Weevils in the Wheat*, p. 26; Rawick, ed., S1, Vol. 3, Pt. 4, p. 202.

23. Ray Mathis, *John Horry Dent: South Carolina Aristocrat on the Alabama Frontier* (University: University of Alabama Press, 1979), p. 75. Rawick, ed., S1, Vol. 6, pp. 12-13; response of M. T. Judge, Sr., NQS.

24. John Witherspoon DuBose, "Recollections of the Plantation," Part 2, *Alabama Historical Quarterly* (Summer 1930), p. 115; Rawick, ed., S1, Vol. 2, Pt. 1, p. 100 and Pt. 2, pp. 92, 166; "Oliver Bell: That Tree Was My Nurse," in *Toting the Lead Row*, p. 134; response of M. T. Judge, Sr., NQS.

25. Perdue, Barden, and Phillips, eds., *Weevils in the Wheat*, pp. 322, 281.

26. Ibid., p. 293, also p. 227; Rawick, ed., S1, Vol. 2, Pt. 1, p. 140 and Vol. 6, p. 327.

27. Rawick, ed., S1, Vol. 6, pp. 321, 353.

28. Elizabeth Fox-Genovese, *Within the Plantation Household: Black and White Women of the Old South* (Chapel Hill: University of North Carolina Press, 1988), p. 153; Robert F. W. Allston to Benjamin Allston, 25 May 1855, in *The South Carolina Rice Plantation*, p. 123; Charles C. Jones, Jr., to Rev. and Mrs. C. C. Jones, 30 June 1858, and Mary Jones to Charles C. Jones, Jr., 7 July 1858, in *The Children of Pride: A True Story of Georgia and the Civil War*, pp. 427-428; Rawick, ed., S1, Vol. 2, Pt. 1, p. 131 and Pt. 2, p. 92.

29. Rawick, ed., SS1, Vol. 1, pp. 155, 157-158, and S1, Vol. 6, p. 211; James B. Cade, "Out of the Mouths of Ex-Slaves," *Journal of Negro History* 20 (July 1935), p. 311; Rawick, ed., S1, Vol. 2, Pt. 2, p. 139.

30. Allston quoted in Dusinberre, *Them Dark Days*, p. 308. See also Mary Jones to Charles C. Jones, Jr., 28 Sept. 1860, in *The Children of Pride*, p. 611. On Christianity in Africa, see John Thornton, *Africa and Africans in the Making of the Atlantic World, 1400-1680* (New York: Cambridge University Press, 1992), Chapter 9.

31. Blake Touchstone, "Planters and Slave Religion in the Deep South," in *Masters and Slaves in the House of the Lord: Race and Religion in the American South, 1740-1870*, ed. John B. Boles (Lexington: University Press of Kentucky, 1988), pp. 99-100, 104-106, 125; Albert J. Raboteau, *Slave Religion: The "Invisible Institution" in the Antebellum South* (New York: Oxford University Press, 1978), pp. 149, 157-161; D. E. Huger Smith, *A Charlestonian's Recollections, 1846-1913* (Charleston: Carolina Art Association, 1950), p. 30; Anne Sinkler Fishburne, *Belvidere: A Plantation Memory* (Columbia: University of South Carolina Press, 1950), p. 63.

32. Response of O. T. McCann, NQS; "Inclosure," James R. Sparkman to Benjamin Allston, 10 March 1858, in *The South Carolina Rice Plantation*, p. 349; A Southern Planter, *Plantation and Farm Instruction, Regulation, Record, Inven-*

tory and Account Book (Richmond: J. W. Randolph, 1852), p. 5, in Philip St. George Cocke Papers, VHS; Rawick, ed., S1, Vol. 3, Pt. 4, p. 129.

33. Mary Jones to Mary Sharpe Jones, 29 Jan. 1855, in *The Children of Pride,* p. 132; also Rev. C. C. Jones to Mary Sharpe Jones, 10 Jan. 1856, p. 183; Rev. C. C. Jones to Mary Jones, 18 Nov. 1859, p. 536; Rev. C. C. Jones to Mary Jones, 22 Nov. 1859, p. 539; Rev. C. C. Jones to Mary Jones, 26 Nov. 1859, p. 543. Entry for 8 Dec. 1861, in Mary Chesnut, *Mary Chesnut's Civil War,* ed. C. Vann Woodward (New Haven: Yale University Press, 1981), p. 260; "Inclosure," James R. Sparkman to Benjamin Allston, 10 March 1858, in *The South Carolina Rice Plantation,* p. 349; also entry for 3 April, Diary, John Edwin Fripp Papers, SHC. Holland Nimmons M'Tyeire, *Duties of Christian Masters* (Nashville, Tenn.: Southern Methodist Publishing House, 1859), pp. 189–192.

34. Mrs. A. M. French, *Slavery in South Carolina and the Ex-Slaves; or, The Port Royal Mission* (New York: Negro Universities Press, 1969), pp. 126–127, 259; Rawick, ed., S1, Vol. 2, Pt. 2, p. 78, also p. 184, and Vol. 3, Pt. 4, p. 273; Touchstone, "Planters and Slave Religion in the Deep South," p. 121.

35. On the incorporation of Christianity into African and African-American understanding of the spiritual world, see Thornton, *Africa and Africans in the Making of the Atlantic World, 1400–1680,* Chapter 9. On the importance of baptism to Methodist slave women during an earlier period, see Cynthia Lynn Lyerly, "Religion, Gender, and Identity: Black Methodist Women in a Slave Society, 1770–1810," in *Discovering the Women in Slavery,* ed. Patricia Morton (Athens: University of Georgia Press, 1996), pp. 216–217.

36. Rawick, ed., SS1, Vol. 11, p. 192, S1, Vol. 2, Pt. 2, p. 89 and Pt. 1, pp. 125–126.

37. Lewis W. Paine, *Six Years in a Georgia Prison* (New York: n.p., 1851), p. 150; Rawick, ed., S1, Vol. 2, Pt. 1, p. 197; Raboteau, *Slave Religion,* p. 177.

38. Rawick, ed., SS1, Vol. 11, pp. 170–171.

39. Ibid., S1, Vol. 2, Pt. 1, pp. 309–310, Vol. 3, Pt. 3, p. 10 and Pt. 4, pp. 67–68; Frances Anne Kemble, *Journal of a Residence on a Georgian Plantation in 1838–1839* (New York: Alfred A. Knopf, 1961), p. 312.

40. Georgia Writers' Project, *Drums and Shadows: Survival Studies among the Georgia Coastal Negroes* (Athens: University of Georgia Press, 1986), p. 8; Rawick, ed., S1, Vol. 6, p. 113 and Vol. 2, Pt. 2, p. 309.

41. Rawick, ed., SS1, Vol. 9, Pt. 4, p. 1588 and Vol. 12, p. 200.

42. Perdue, Barden, and Phillips, eds., *Weevils in the Wheat,* pp. 246–250.

43. Rawick, ed., S2, Vol. 16, Pt. 12, p. 98, and SS1, Vol. 1, p. 216.

44. Jacob Stroyer, "My Life in the South," *Five Slave Narratives: A Compendium* (New York: Arno Press and The New York Times, 1968), pp. 57–59. On divination (including judicial ordeals to determine guilt or innocence) among slave societies of the Atlantic world, see Thornton, *Africa and Africans,* p. 240–246.

45. Perdue, Barden, and Phillips, eds., *Weevils in the Wheat,* p. 32.

46. Ibid., p. 265; Rawick, ed., SS2, Vol. 4, Pt. 3, p. 1285; Drew, *A North-Side View of Slavery*, pp. 358–359; Keckley, *Behind the Scenes*, p. 19.

47. Drew, *A North-Side View of Slavery*, pp. 358–359; Rawick, ed., S1, Vol. 2, Pt. 2, pp. 299–300.

48. Stephen Crawford, "The Slave Family: A View from the Slave Narratives," in *Strategic Factors in Nineteenth Century American Economic History*, ed. Claudia Goldin and Hugh Rockoff (Chicago: University of Chicago Press, 1992), p. 339; Rawick, ed., S1, Vol. 3, pp. 197–198 and SS2, Vol. 5, Pt. 4, p. 1826–1831.

49. Rawick, ed., S1, Vol. 3, Pt. 4, pp. 80, 200. On the image of the black mammy, see Deborah Gray White, *Ar'n't I a Woman? Female Slaves in the Plantation South* (New York: Norton, 1987), pp. 46–61.

50. Rawick, ed., S1, Vol. 6, p. 120, S2, Vol. 16, Pt. 8, p. 12, and SS1, Vol. 1, p. 467.

51. Perdue, Barden, and Phillips, eds., *Weevils in the Wheat*, p. 292; Rawick, ed., S1, Vol. 6, p. 15.

52. Perdue, Barden, and Phillips, eds., *Weevils in the Wheat*, p. 203; Rawick, ed., SS2, Vol. 4, Pt. 3, p. 1115, and S1, Vol. 3, Pt. 4, p. 67.

53. On the use of didactic stories by slaves to socialize children, see Lawrence W. Levine, *Black Culture and Black Consciousness: Afro-American Folk Thought from Slavery to Freedom* (New York: Oxford University Press, 1977), especially pp. 90–133. Rawick, ed., SS1, Vol. 1, pp. 310–312 and S1, Vol. 2, Pt. 1, pp. 122–123.

54. Rawick, ed., SS2, Vol. 8, Pt. 7, p. 211, S2, Vol. 16, Pt. 12, p. 12, S1, Vol. 6, p. 280, and SS1, Vol. 12, p. 193.

55. Perdue, Barden, and Phillips, eds., *Weevils in the Wheat*, pp. 201–202, 81; Louis Hughes, *Thirty Years a Slave: From Bondage to Freedom: The Institution of Slavery as Seen on the Plantation and in the Home of the Planter* (New York: Negro Universities Press, 1969), p. 202; Rawick, ed., S2, Vol. 10, Pt. 5, p. 321.

56. Perdue, Barden, and Phillips, eds., *Weevils in the Wheat*, p. 295; Rawick, ed., SS1, Vol. 11, p. 195, and S1, Vol. 7, p. 13.

5. To the Field

1. Henry's experience reconstructed from work records (Plantation Diary, Vols. 2 and 3, Sturdivant Collection) for years 1844 to 1846 and for 1854 to 1860 held by the Sturdivant Museum, Selma, Alabama, for slaveholdings in Dallas County, as well as some possibly located in Bibb County (microfilm, SHC).

2. George P. Rawick, ed., *The American Slave: A Composite Autobiography*, S2, Vol. 13, Pt. 3, p. 229.

3. Rawick, ed., S1, Vol. 7, p. 77, S2, Vol. 15, Pt. 2, p. 284, and SS1, Vol. 1, p. 258.

4. Ibid., SS1, Vol. 1, p. 301, and S2, Vol. 13, Pt. 3, p. 289; "Plantation Life in the South," *Southern Cultivator* 18 (June 1860), p. 183; Charles Ball, *Fifty Years in*

Chains; or, The Life of an American Slave (Indianapolis: Asher, 18[37]), pp. 128-129, 195; D. E. Huger Smith, *A Charlestonian's Recollections, 1846-1913* (Charleston: Carolina Art Association, 1950), p. 29; Charles L. Perdue, Jr., Thomas E. Barden, and Robert K. Phillips, eds., *Weevils in the Wheat: Interviews with Virginia Ex-Slaves* (Charlottesville: University Press of Virginia, 1976), p. 210; entries for 11 June 1861 and 25 Feb. 1862, John Joel Chappell Diary, ADAH; K. Washington Skinner to Charles Manigault, 13 Oct. 1852, in *Life and Labor on Argyle Island: Letters and Documents of a Savannah River Rice Plantation, 1833-1867*, ed. James M. Clifton (Savannah: Beehive, 1978), p. 123; Frances Anne Kemble, *Journal of a Residence on a Georgian Plantation in 1838-1839* (New York: Alfred A. Knopf, 1961), pp. 58, 62, 73, 83-84, 90, 146, 217, 313, 323, 317-318.

    5. "Henry Baker," in *Slave Testimony: Two Centuries of Letters, Speeches, Interviews, and Autobiographies*, ed. John W. Blassingame (Baton Rouge: Louisiana State University Press, 1977), p. 657; Perdue, Barden, and Phillips, eds., *Weevils in the Wheat*, p. 227; Rawick, ed., SS2, Vol. 5, Pt. 4, p. 1885, S2, Vol. 11, pp. 208-209, and SS1, Vol. 9, Pt. 4, p. 1582.

    6. Perdue, Barden, and Phillips, eds., *Weevils in the Wheat*, p. 228.

    7. Rawick, ed., SS1, Vol. 1, pp. 157, 155, 313; A Southern Planter, *Plantation and Farm Instruction, Regulation, Record, Inventory and Account Book* (Richmond: J. W. Randolph, 1852), p. 7, in Philip St. George Cocke Papers, VHS; Ray Mathis, *John Horry Dent: South Carolina Aristocrat on the Alabama Frontier* (University: University of Alabama Press, 1979), p. 54; Planter, "A Practical Plantation Manual," *American Cotton Planter* 8 (July 1857), p. 231.

    8. Chatahoochee, "Agricultural Policy and Practice," *Cotton Planter and Soil* 1 (Oct. 1857), p. 313; Rawick, ed., SS1, Vol. 3, Pt. 1, pp. 243, 245, and S2, Vol. 17, p. 65; response of unnamed son of a Perry County planter, NQS.

    9. Entries for 7 and 9 Feb., 1 March, 28 Oct. 1845 and 23 and 24 Feb., 14 March 1855, Plantation Diary, Vols. 2 and 3, Sturdivant Collection; entry for 22 Aug. 1855, Robert Christian Diary, ADAH; entry for 23 Dec. 1836, George Augustus Beverly Walker Diary, ADAH; Rawick, ed., S1, Vol. 6, p. 313; S. D. Wragg, "Overseeing," *Farmer and Planter* 5 (June and Sept. 1854), in *Advice among Masters: The Ideal in Slave Management in the Old South*, ed. James O. Breeden (Westport, Conn.: Greenwood, 1980), p. 284; Louis Manigault to Charles Manigault, 19 and 23 April 1853, in *Life and Labor on Argyle Island*, pp. 155-156; Young Planter, "The Plantation: Summer Work," *Cotton Planter and Soil* 1 (Oct. 1857), p. 310; A——, "On the Management of Negroes," *Cotton Planter and Soil* 2 (Jan. 1858), p. 20.

    10. Based on an analysis of work records for the years May-April 1845/46 and May-April 1855/56, Plantation Diary, Vols. 2 and 3, Sturdivant Collection.

    11. "Henry Baker," in *Slave Testimony*, p. 657.

    12. Entries for Oct. and Nov. 1855 and July 1856, Plantation Diary, Vol. 3, Sturdivant Collection; Jacob Metzer, "Rational Management, Modern Business Practices, and Economies of Scale in the Ante-Bellum Southern Plantations," *Ex-*

plorations in Economic History 12 (April 1975), pp. 136–137; Perdue, Barden, and Phillips, eds., *Weevils in the Wheat,* p. 281.

13. *The Old Pine Farm: or, The Southern Side. Comprising Loose Sketches from the Experience of a Southern Country Minister, S.C.* (Nashville, Tenn.: Southwestern Publishing House, 1859), pp. 93–96; Louis Hughes, *Thirty Years a Slave: From Bondage to Freedom* (New York: Negro Universities Press, 1969), pp. 7–8.

14. Perdue, Barden, and Phillips, eds., *Weevils in the Wheat,* p. 292; Duncan Clinch Heyward, *Seed from Madagascar* (Chapel Hill: University of North Carolina Press, 1937), pp. 30–31; Rawick, ed., SS2, Vol. 1, pp. 10–11, and Vol. 8, Pt. 7, p. 3197; entry for 8 May 1845, Diary, George Augustus Beverly Walker Papers, ADAH; also response of Mrs. Y. B. Stewart, NQS.

15. Agreement with Overseer, Willis P. Bocock Papers, SHC; Rawick, ed., S2, Vol. 8, Pt. 2, p. 214; Harriet Martineau, *Retrospect of Western Travel,* vol. 1 (New York: Haskell House), pp. 222–223.

16. "Henry Baker," in *Slave Testimony,* p. 657; "Ank Bishop: Gabriel Blow Soft! Gabriel Blow Loud!" and "Charlie Johnson: Reckon You Might Say I's Just Faithful," in Virginia Pound Brown and Laurella Owens, *Toting the Lead Row: Ruby Pickens Tartt, Alabama Folklorist* (University: University of Alabama Press, 1981), pp. 126, 130; response of O. T. Mann, NQS; Perdue, Barden, and Phillips, eds., *Weevils in the Wheat,* p. 154; Heyward, *Seed from Madagascar,* pp. 176–177; Annie L. Burton, "Memories of Childhood's Slavery Days," in *Six Women's Slave Narratives,* ed. Henry Louis Gates, Jr. (New York: Oxford University Press, 1988), p. 4.

17. Agreement with Overseer, Willis P. Bocock Papers, SHC; "Plantation Life in the South," *Southern Cultivator* 18 (June 1860), p. 183.

18. St. George Cocke, "Plantation Management—Police," *DeBow's Review* 14 (Feb. 1853), Robert Collins, "Essay on the Treatment and Management of Slaves," *Southern Cultivator* 12 (July 1854), and A Small Farmer, "Management of Negroes," *DeBow's Review* 11 (Oct. 1851), all three in *Advice among Masters,* pp. 103, 20; Tattler, "Management of Negroes," *The Southern Planter* 11 (Feb. 1851); Kemble, *Journal of a Residence on a Georgian Plantation,* p. 301. Also "Inclosure," James R. Sparkman to Benjamin Allston, 10 March 1858, in *The South Carolina Rice Plantation as Revealed in the Papers of Robert F. W. Allston,* ed. J. H. Easterby (Chicago: University of Chicago Press, 1945), p. 346.

19. William Howard Russell, *My Diary North and South* (New York: Harper, 1954), p. 71; Perdue, Barden, and Phillips, eds., *Weevils in the Wheat,* p. 30; Rawick, ed., S1, Vol. 5, Pt. 3, p. 211. Also SS1, Vol. 1, p. 357, and S1, Vol. 6, p. 343 and Vol. 7, p. 94.

20. Entry for 19 Aug. 1852, James M. Torbert Diary, ADAH; entries for 15 Nov., 5 and 8 Dec. 1858, "Wm Grahams Journal of Mr Mrs B. S. Gilmers Plantation Comemcing on Thursday the 3rd November 1858—and ending on the 31st December 1858," Mrs. W. G. Jones Papers, ADAH; K. Washington Skinner to Charles Manigault, 29 Oct. 1852, in *Life and Labor on Argyle Island,* p. 124; "Inclosure,"

The South Carolina Rice Plantation, p. 347; Advertisement, *Winyaw Intelligencer* [Georgetown, South Carolina], 1 Jan. 1825, in *Plantation and Frontier Documents,* vol. 2, ed. Ulrich B. Phillips (New York: Burt Franklin, 1969), p. 47; entries for 21, 23, and 25 Oct. 1861, John Joel Chappell Diary; Rawick, ed., S1, Vol. 2, Pt. 2, pp. 228–229.

21. H., "Remarks on Overseers, and the Proper Treatment of Slaves," *Farmers' Register* 5 (Sept. 1837), in *Advice among Masters,* p. 141. Also John S. Wilson, M.D., "The Peculiarities & Diseases of Negroes," *American Cotton Planter and Soil of the South* n.s., 4 (Feb., March, April, May, Aug., Sept., Nov., and Dec. 1860) and A. P. Merrill, M.D., "Plantation Hygiene," *Southern Agriculturalist* 1 (Sept. 1853), both in *Advice among Masters,* pp. 287–288, 185; Benjamin Drew, *A North-Side View of Slavery. The Refugee: Or the Narratives of Fugitive Slaves in Canada* (New York: Johnson Reprint, 1968), p. 105; Thomas D. Morris, *Southern Slavery and the Law, 1619–1860* (Chapel Hill: University of North Carolina Press, 1996), pp. 195–196; response of P. F. Mitchell, NQS.

22. Rawick, ed., SS1, Vol. 12, p. 193; Plantation Record of James J. Ruffin (especially entry for Jan. 1842), Ruffin, Roulhac, and Hamilton Family Papers, SHC; also A Southern Planter, *Plantation and Farm Instruction, Regulation, Record, Inventory and Account Book,* p. 6.

23. See work and clothing distribution records in Plantation Record of James H. Ruffin, Ruffin, Roulhac, and Hamilton Family Papers, SHC; Ball, *Fifty Years in Chains,* p. 202; "Inclosure," *The South Carolina Rice Plantation,* p. 347; Rawick, ed., S1, Vol. 2, Pt. 2, p. 175.

24. Perdue, Barden, and Phillips, eds., *Weevils in the Wheat,* p. 210; Lynda J. Morgan, *Emancipation in Virginia's Tobacco Belt, 1850–1870* (Athens: University of Georgia Press, 1992), p. 45; Ball, *Fifty Years in Chains,* p. 78. See also Planting Account for 1830, Diary of A. J. Lawton, Alexander R. Lawton Papers, SHC. Rawick, ed., SS2, Vol. 5, Pt. 4, p. 1525, and SS1, Vol. 1, p. 427; "Inclosure," James R. Sparkman to Benjamin Allston, 10 March 1858, in *The South Carolina Rice Plantation,* p. 350; Philip D. Morgan, "Work and Culture: The Task System and the World of Lowcountry Blacks, 1700–1800," *William & Mary Quarterly,* 3d ser. 39 (1982), pp. 563–599, and "The Ownership of Property by Slaves in the Mid-Nineteenth-Century Low Country," *Journal of Southern History* 49 (Aug. 1983), pp. 399–420.

25. Rawick, ed., S2, Vol. 16, Pt. 12, pp. 50–53.

26. See entries for 1841, Plantation Record of James H. Ruffin, Ruffin, Roulhac, and Hamilton Family Papers, SHC.

27. Rawick, ed., SS2, Vol. 9, Pt. 8, p. 3860; S1, Vol. 2, Pt. 2, p. 310, and Vol. 6, p. 434. For another view, see Eugene D. Genovese, *Roll, Jordan, Roll: The World the Slaves Made* (New York: Vintage, 1974), p. 505.

28. Rawick, ed., SS1, Vol. 1, pp. 95, 492, also S1, Vol. 7, p. 170; "Henry Baker," in *Slave Testimony,* p. 657; Chapron to James Martin, 22 July 1840, in Jean Marie

Chapron, Letterbook, ADAH; John Witherspoon DuBose, "Recollections of the Plantation," Part 2 (Summer 1930), p. 115; entry for 16 Sept. 1836, Diary, George Augustus Beverly Walker.

29. Rawick, ed., SS1, Vol. 3, Pt. 1, p. 169, and SS2, Vol. 4, Pt. 3, p. 1287; Perdue, Barden, and Phillips, eds., *Weevils in the Wheat,* pp. 316, 322.

30. Robert M. Allan to Robert F. W. Allston, 6 Jan. 1837, *The South Carolina Rice Plantation,* pp. 66–67; Susan M. Cumming to Rev. C. C. Jones, 22 March 1856 (emphasis in original), in *The Children of Pride: A True Story of Georgia and the Civil War,* ed. Robert Manson Myers (New Haven: Yale University Press, 1972), p. 199; Slave List, *Life and Labor on Argyle Island,* pp. 64–68; Heyward, *Seed from Madagascar,* pp. 84; entry for 2 June 1832, John Berkley Grimball Diary, SHC; "List of Negroes Belonging to Elizafield Plantation," in Albert Virgil House, ed., *Planter Management and Capitalism in Ante-Bellum Georgia: The Journal of Hugh Fraser Grant, Ricegrower* (New York: Columbia University Press, 1954), pp. 252–254.

31. Rawick, ed., SS1, Vol. 9, Pt. 4, p. 1615.

32. Ibid., SS2, Vol. 1, p. 375; Perdue, Barden, and Phillips, eds., *Weevils in the Wheat,* pp. 102, 105, 292, 26. On harvest drinks and foods, see "Harvest Drink, Diet and Medicine" by Blair Burwell with accompanying comments by the editor, *Southern Planter* 16 (June 1856), pp. 183–184.

33. Gabriel E. Manigault to Louis Manigault, 11 Dec. 1860, in *Life and Labor on Argyle Island,* p. 311; Rawick, ed., S1, Vol. 3, Pt. 4, p. 78, Vol. 6, p. 51, Vol. 7, p. 170, S2, Vol. 16, Pt. 8, p. 29, and SS2, Vol. 5, Pt. 4, p. 1330; Perdue, Barden, and Phillips, eds., *Weevils in the Wheat,* p. 288.

34. Chapron to James Martin, 22 July 1840, in Jean Marie Chapron, Letterbook, ADAH. Also Franklin, "Overseers," *Southern Cultivator* 2 (10 July 1844), p. 107; William H. Cook, "Overseers and Plantation Management," *Cotton Planter and Soil* 2 (April 1858), p. 112; Perdue, Barden, and Phillips, eds., *Weevils in the Wheat,* p. 309; Rawick, ed., S1, Vol. 7, p. 2; A Burke Planter, Letter to the Editor, *Southern Cultivator* 2 (26 June 1844), p. 97.

35. Agricultural Journal, B. Tayloe, United States Agricultural Library, Beltsville, Md.

36. Rawick, ed., SS1, Vol. 1, pp. 297–299.

37. Agreement with Overseer, Willis P. Bocock Papers, SHC.

38. "Benjamin Holmes," in *Slave Testimony,* p. 618; Robert F. W. Allston to Benjamin Allston, 25 May 1855, in *The South Carolina Rice Plantation,* p. 123; William Dusinberre, *Them Dark Days: Slavery in the American Rice Swamps* (New York: Oxford University Press, 1996), p. 329; Rawick, ed., S1, Vol. 2, Pt. 2, p. 279; entry for 13 May 1835, Diary, John Berkley Grimball, SHC; Smith, *A Charlestonian's Recollections,* pp. 59, 65; Heyward, *Seed from Madagascar,* p. 198.

39. Edward Carrington Cabell, "Memorandum in regard to Hire of house servants," to H. C. Cabell, n.d., in Cabell Family Papers, VHS.

40. Jacob Stroyer, "My Life in the South," *Five Slave Narratives: A Compendium* (New York: Arno Press and The New York Times, 1968), pp. 30–32.

41. Rawick, ed., SS1, Vol. 1, p. 212; letter to Col. S. Pickens from Jane Sexton, 18 Aug. 1845, Samuel Pickens Letters, Pickens Family Papers, ADAH; Michael Tadman, *Speculators and Slaves: Masters, Traders, and Slaves in the Old South* (Madison: University of Wisconsin Press, 1989), pp. 102–103.

42. Rawick, ed., SS2, Vol. 8, Pt. 7, p. 3171, and S1, Vol. 7, p. 213; also Perdue, Barden, and Phillips, eds., *Weevils in the Wheat*, p. 196; Janet Duitsman Cornelius, *"When I Can Read My Title Clear": Literacy, Slavery, and Religion in the Antebellum South* (Columbia: University of South Carolina Press, 1991), pp. 7–10. For different estimates, see Theresa A. Singleton, "The Archaeology of Slave Life," in *Before Freedom Came: African-American Life in the Antebellum South*, ed. Edward D. C. Campbell, Jr., with Kym S. Rice (Richmond and Charlottesville: Museum of the Confederacy and University Press of Virginia, 1991), p. 171; Barbara Finkelstein, "Reading, Writing, and Acquisition of Identity in the United States: 1790–1860," in *Regulated Children/Liberated Children: Education in Psychohistorical Perspective*, ed. Barbara Finkelstein (New York: Psychohistory Press, 1979), p. 138, n. 50.

43. Rawick, ed., S1, Vol. 2, Pt. 1, pp. 124–125 and Vol. 7, p. 94, SS1, Vol. 1, p. 243, and SS2, Vol. 5, Pt. 4, p. 1524; Perdue, Barden, and Phillips, eds., *Weevils in the Wheat*, p. 305; "Benjamin Holmes," in *Slave Testimony*, p. 618.

44. Rawick, ed., SS1, Vol. 7, Pt. 2, p. 372, Vol. 8, Pt. 3, p. 1061, Vol. 12, p. 199, and S1, Vol. 2, Pt. 2, p. 95; response of J. R. Emerson, NQS; Perdue, Barden, and Phillips, eds., *Weevils in the Wheat*, p. 330. Virginia, South and North Carolina, and Georgia banned the teaching of slaves to read beginning in the 1830s and lasting through 1865. Alabama in 1832 enacted fines for anyone attempting to teach a slave to read or write, but the state's legal code did not include this provision in 1852. Virginia's law exempted slaveholders who wanted to educate their own, individual slaves to read. Laws passed in other states either expired before the end of the antebellum period or exempted slaveholders who taught their own slaves, or both. Evidence does not indicate many prosecutions for violations of these laws. Cornelius, *"When I Can Read My Title Clear,"* pp. 32–34.

45. Cornelius, *"When I Can Read My Title Clear,"* pp. 68–71.

46. Perdue, Barden, and Phillips, eds., *Weevils in the Wheat*, p. 301; Rawick, ed., SS1, Vol. 1, pp. 70, 358, and Vol. 10, Pt. 5, p. 2006; H. C. Bruce, *The New Man: Twenty-Nine Years a Slave, Twenty-Nine Years a Free Man* (Miami: Mnemosyne, 1969), pp. 25–26; untitled memoir, Marie Gordon (Pryor) Rice, VHS.

47. Perdue, Barden, and Phillips, eds., *Weevils in the Wheat*, pp. 229–230.

48. Rawick, ed., S1, Vol. 2, Pt. 1, p. 223; Kemble, *Journal of a Residence on a Georgian Plantation*, pp. 271, 300, 314.

49. Rawick, ed., SS1, Vol. 1, pp. 255, 426, SS2, Vol. 9, Pt. 8, p. 3861, and S1, Vol. 5, Part 3, p. 110; "Sarah Fitzpatrick," in *Slave Testimony*, p. 643; also Cornelius, *"When I Can Read My Title Clear,"* pp. 66–67.

50. Rawick, ed., S1, Vol. 6, p. 410, and S2, Vol. 15, Pt. 2, p. 160; "Sarah Fitzpatrick," in *Slave Testimony*, p. 643.

51. Perdue, Barden, and Phillips, eds., *Weevils in the Wheat*, pp. 97–98.

6. Risk of Sale and Separation

1. Charles L. Perdue, Jr., Thomas E. Barden, and Robert K. Phillips, eds., *Weevils in the Wheat: Interviews with Virginia Ex-Slaves* (Charlottesville: University Press of Virginia, 1976), pp. 211, 219.

2. Michael Tadman, *Speculators and Slaves: Masters, Traders, and Slaves in the Old South* (Madison: University of Wisconsin Press, 1989), pp. 45, 141–142, 171, 177.

3. Robert Byrd Beverley to Robert Beverley, 9 Jan. 1833, Beverley Family Papers, VHS; Perdue, Barden, and Phillips, eds., *Weevils in the Wheat*, pp. 264–265; Rawick, ed., SS2, Vol. 4, p. 154.

4. Tadman, *Speculators and Slaves*, pp. 25, 129, 142–143; also Frederic Bancroft, *Slave-Trading in the Old South* (Baltimore: J. R. Furst, 1931); Stephen Crawford, "The Slave Family: A View from the Slave Narratives," in *Strategic Factors in Nineteenth Century American Economic History*, ed. Claudia Goldin and Hugh Rockoff (Chicago: University of Chicago Press, 1992), p. 341.

5. Tadman, *Speculators and Slaves*, pp. 175–176; James Oakes, *The Ruling Race: A History of American Slaveholders* (New York: Vintage, 1982), p. 77; Herbert G. Gutman, *The Black Family in Slavery and Freedom, 1750–1925* (New York: Vintage, 1976), pp. 129–138.

6. Benjamin Franklin Nalle to Ann (Botts) Nalle, 15 Aug. 1860, Nalle Family Papers, VHS; Perdue, Barden, and Phillips, eds., *Weevils in the Wheat*, p. 318; George P. Rawick, ed., *The American Slave: A Composite Autobiography*, SS1, Vol. 3, Pt. 1, p. 243; Lynda J. Morgan, *Emancipation in Virginia's Tobacco Belt, 1850–1870* (Athens: University of Georgia Press, 1992), p. 59. "Rules and directions for my Thorn Island Plantation," 11 June 1832, in Ulrich B. Phillips, ed., *Plantation and Frontier, 1649–1863*, Vol. 1 (New York: Burt Franklin, 1910), p. 127. Also entries for 25 and 30 June, 4 and 5 July 1855; Thomas S. Watson Diary, 1841–1855, Watson Family Papers, ABSP, Series E, Part 1, Selections from the UVAL. John G. Traylor Diary, passim, ADAH; entry for 20 Sept. 1834, John Berkley Grimball Diary, SHC; Sarah L. Fountain to Hannah L. Coker, 10 Feb. 1836, in Fletcher M. Green, *The Lides Go South . . . and West; the Record of a Planter Migration in 1835* (Columbia: University of South Carolina Press, 1952), p. 15; Rawick, ed., SS1, Vol. 4, Pt. 2, p. 612; Morgan, *Emancipation in Virginia's Tobacco Belt*, Chapter 3; Brenda E. Stevenson, *Life in Black and White: Family and Community in the Slave South* (New York: Oxford University Press, 1996), pp. 184–186; Edna Greene Medford, "'There was so many degrees in slavery . . .': Unfree Labor in an Antebellum Mixed Farming Community," *Slavery & Abolition* 14 (Aug. 1993), pp. 39–

41; Joel Spigener to William K. Oliver, 17 Feb. 1834, in Harvey H. Jackson, Jr., and Harvey H. Jackson, III, eds., "Notes and Documents: Moving to Alabama: The Joel Spigener–William K. Oliver Letters, 1833–1834," *The Alabama Review* 48 (Jan. 1995), p. 34; Loren Schweninger, "The Underside of Slavery: The Internal Economy, Self-Hire, and Quasi-Freedom in Virginia," *Slavery & Abolition* 12 (Sept. 1991), pp. 1–22.

7. Thomas D. Pitts to Mrs. David H. Pitts, 10 Jan. 1832, Pitts Family Papers, ADAH; Perdue, Barden, and Phillips, eds., *Weevils in the Wheat*, p. 166; Tadman, *Speculators and Slaves*, pp. 83–93. On laws restricting slave sales, see Chapter 4.

8. Tadman, *Speculators and Slaves*, pp. 65–68, 105–106, 108, 115, 117, 129–132; Ulrich B. Phillips, *American Negro Slavery* (Baton Rouge: Louisiana State University Press, 1966), p. 245. Benjamin Davis to Dear Sir, 23 Nov. 1848, Benjamin Davis to Dear Sir, 7 Dec. 1848, Benjamin Davis to Joseph Dickinson, 23 Nov. 1848, and Dickinson, Hill & Co. to Joseph Dickinson, 20 Dec. 1858, Joseph Dickinson Papers, ABSP, Series F, Part 1, Selections from the Duke University Library. Rawick, ed., S1, Vol. 6: *Alabama and Indiana*, p. 1. Also Edmund L. Drago, ed., *"Broke by the War": Letters of a Slave Trader* (Columbia: University of South Carolina Press, 1969), pp. 123–126.

9. Response of M. T. Judge, NQS; Rawick, ed., SS2, Vol. 7, Pt. 6, p. 2591, and SS1, Vol. 7, Pt. 2, p. 423.

10. Entries for 8 March 1816, 16 Jan. 1817, undated 1818, and undated 1819, Plantation Journal of A. J. Lawton, SHC; Charles Ball, *Fifty Years in Chains; or, The Life of an American Slave* (Indianapolis: Asher, 18[37]), p. 55; Duncan Clinch Heyward, *Seed from Madagascar* (Chapel Hill: University of North Carolina Press, 1937), pp. 74, 187; Rawick, ed., S2, Vol. 11, Pt. 7, p. 229, and S1, Vol. 3, Pt. 4, p. 79; *The Old Pine Farm: or, The Southern Side. Comprising Loose Sketches from the Experience of a Southern Country Minister, S.C.* (Nashville, Tenn.: Southwestern Publishing House, 1859), p. 39.

11. John Brown, *Slave Life in Georgia: A Narrative of the Life, Sufferings and Escape of John Brown, a Fugitive Slave* (Savannah: Beehive, 1991), p. 16; Rawick, ed., SS1, Vol. 5, p. 284; Tadman, *Speculators and Slaves*, p. 50.

12. Valuation of the slaves of Mrs. Charlotte Thornton in Virginia and Alabama, "sold conditionally to Mr. A. Glopell of Alabama.—May 1838," Fitzhugh and Marye Law Office Papers, UVAL. Also undated valuation list [probably for 1855], Robert Christian Diary, ADAH.

13. Perdue, Barden, and Phillips, eds., *Weevils in the Wheat*, pp. 86, 250; Peter W. Bardaglio, *Reconstructing the Household: Families, Sex, and the Law in the Nineteenth-Century South* (Chapel Hill: University of North Carolina Press, 1995), pp. 55, 66–68.

14. Deborah Gray White, *Ar'n't I a Woman?: Female Slaves in the Plantation South* (New York: W. W. Norton, 1985), p. 37; Tadman, *Speculators and Slaves*, p. 126. On the sexual abuse of women, see Thelma Jennings, "'Us Colored Women

Had to Go Through a Plenty': Sexual Exploitation of African-American Slave Women," *Journal of Women's History* 1 (Winter 1990), pp. 45–74; Nell Painter, "Soul Murder and Slavery: Toward a Fully Loaded Cost Accounting," in *U.S. History as Women's History: New Feminist Essays,* ed. Linda K. Kerber, Alice Kessler-Harris, and Kathryn Kish Sklar (Chapel Hill: University of North Carolina Press, 1995), pp. 125–146.

    15. Entry for 7 Jan. 1837, Diary, George Augustus Beverly Walker, ADAH.

    16. Rawick, ed., SS1, Vol. 9, Pt. 4, p. 1579 and Vol. 8, Pt. 3, p. 1280, also p. 1327. See also Rev. C. C. Jones to Charles C. Jones, Jr., 26 March 1857, in *The Children of Pride: A True Story of Georgia and the Civil War,* ed. Robert Manson Myers (New Haven: Yale University Press, 1972), p. 309.

    17. Perdue, Barden, and Phillips, eds., *Weevils in the Wheat,* p. 183.

    18. Ibid., p. 42; Frances Anne Kemble, *Journal of a Residence on a Georgian Plantation in 1838–1839* (New York: Alfred A. Knopf, 1961), p. 138; also Randolph B. Campbell, *An Empire for Slavery: The Peculiar Institution in Texas, 1821–1865* (Baton Rouge: Louisiana State University Press, 1989), p. 167; Rawick, ed., S1, Vol. 4, Pt. 2, pp. 177–178.

    19. "Bettie Tolbert: Lost to the Refugee Wagons," in Virginia Pound Brown and Laurella Owens, eds., *Toting the Lead Row: Ruby Pickens Tartt, Alabama Folklorist* (University: University of Alabama Press, 1981), p. 139; Rawick, ed., S1, Vol. 5, Pt. 3, p. 80; John White Nash to Samuel Hatcher, 18 Dec. 1825, Nash Family Papers.

    20. Rawick, ed., SS1, Vol. 1, p. 177.

    21. Theodore Rosengarten, *Tombee: Portrait of a Cotton Planter with the Journal of Thomas B. Chaplin* (New York: William Morrow, 1986), p. 347; Rev. C. C. Jones to Charles C. Jones, Jr., 17 Jan. 1856, in *The Children of Pride,* pp. 184. Also Mary Jones to Charles C. Jones, Jr., 31 Jan. 1856; Rev. C. C. Jones to Mary Jones, 23 Oct. 1856; Charles C. Jones, Jr., to Rev. and Mrs. C. C. Jones, 26 Dec. 1859; Eliza G. Robarts to Rev. and Mrs. C. C. Jones, 20 May 1861, pp. 185, 255, 551, 679.

    22. 23 July 1822, in *Plantation and Frontier Documents,* vol. 2, pp. 120–121; "Martha Jackson: Yellow Gals Got Sent North," in *Toting the Lead Row,* pp. 144–145; H. C. Bruce, *The New Man: Twenty-Nine Years a Slave, Twenty-Nine Years a Free Man* (Miami: Mnemosyne, 1969), pp. 55–56.

    23. Rawick, ed., S1, Vol. 7, pp. 92–93.

    24. Ibid., SS1, Vol. 1, p. 155.

    25. Elizabeth Keckley, *Behind the Scenes: or, Thirty Years as a Slave, and Four Years in the White House* (New York: Oxford University Press, 1988), p. 25; Louis Hughes, *Thirty Years a Slave: From Bondage to Freedom* (New York: Negro Universities Press, 1969), p. 6; "Laura Clark: Children in Every Graveyard," in *Toting the Lead Row,* pp. 123, 125.

    26. William Howard Russell, *My Diary North and South* (New York: Harper, 1954), pp. 76–77; Rawick, ed., S1, Vol. 2, Pt. 2, p. 340, SS2, Vol. 1, Pt. 8, p. 292, and SS1, Vol. 11, p. 129. On the language of kinship, see Herbert G. Gutman, *The Black*

Family in Slavery and Freedom, 1750–1925 (New York: Pantheon, 1976), pp. 45, 93–97, 186, 188–190, 216–227; Olivia Harris, "Households and Their Boundaries," *History Workshop Journal* 18 (Spring 1982), pp. 143–152.

27. Mary Jones to Charles C. Jones, Jr., 10 July 1856, in *The Children of Pride,* p. 227; Robynne Rogers Healey, "Meanings of Motherhood: Maternal Experiences and Perceptions on Low Country South Carolina Plantations," presented to the Berkshire Conference on the History of Women, Chapel Hill, N.C., 7 June 1996, and made available by the author, p. 6; Rawick, S1, Vol. 2, Pt. 1, p. 112; William Dusinberre, *Them Dark Days: Slavery in the American Rice Swamps* (New York: Oxford University Press, 1996), pp. 120, 261; Gutman, *The Black Family in Slavery and Freedom,* pp. 220–226.

28. D. E. Huger Smith, *A Charlestonian's Recollections, 1846–1913* (Charleston: Carolina Art Association, 1950), p. 28; Heyward, *Seed from Madagascar,* p. 97. Also Kemble, *Journal of a Residence on a Georgian Plantation,* p. 245; Charles Manigault to Louis Manigault, 28 Nov. 1856, and "Plantation Journal," May 1861 and May 1862, in *Life and Labor on Argyle Island: Letters and Documents of a Savannah River Rice Plantation, 1833–1867,* ed. James M. Clifton (Savannah: Beehive, 1978), pp. 235, 322.

29. Rawick, ed., S1, Vol. 3, Pt. 3, p. 215, also Vol. 2, Pt. 1, p. 122; Deed for the sale of Sally Ann and Louisa, 13 Nov. 1843, Thomas S. Watson Diary, 1841–1855, ABSP, Series E, Part 1, Selections from the UVAL; Gutman, *The Black Family in Slavery and Freedom,* p. 576, n. 5.

30. Rawick, ed., SS1, Vol. 1, p. 448, also p. 425; Philip Henry Pitts Papers, SHC; Rawick, ed., S2, Vol. 8, Pt. 2, p. 131, also deed dated 10 Aug. 1818, Nash Family Papers, VHS.

31. Lewis W. Paine, *Six Years in a Georgia Prison* (New York, 1851), p. 173; Ray Mathis, *John Horry Dent: South Carolina Aristocrat on the Alabama Frontier* (University: University of Alabama Press, 1979), p. 185; response of P. F. Mitchell, NQS. Rawick, ed., S1, Vol. 2, Pt. 2, p. 231; Perdue, Barden, and Phillips, eds., *Weevils in the Wheat,* p. 319; Hughes, *Thirty Years a Slave,* pp. 5–7, 10–13.

32. Perdue, Barden, and Phillips, eds., *Weevils in the Wheat,* pp. 318, 186.

33. Ibid., p. 79, also p. 42; Rawick, ed., SS2, Vol. 6, Pt. 5, pp. 1954–1955.

34. Rawick, ed., S2, Vol. 8, p. 237.

35. Levi Coffin, *Reminiscences of Levi Coffin* (New York: Arno and The New York Times, 1968), passim; also Rawick, ed., SS2, Vol. 8, Pt. 7, pp. 3228–3229, and S1, Vol. 7, pp. 13–14; White, *Ar'n't I a Woman?,* pp. 70–74.

36. Response of M. T. Judge, NQS; entry for 18 March 1861, *Mary Chesnut's Civil War,* ed. C. Vann Woodward (New Haven: Yale University Press, 1981), pp. 29, 31; White, *Ar'n't I a Woman?,* pp. 38–41.

37. Perdue, Barden, and Phillips, eds., *Weevils in the Wheat,* pp. 95–96.

38. Rawick, ed., S2, Vol. 8, Pt. 2, p. 2, and SS1, Vol. 9, Pt. 4, p. 1588; Anthony S. Parent, Jr., and Susan Brown Wallace, "Childhood and Sexual Identity under Slav-

ery," in *American Sexual Politics: Sex, Gender, and Race since the Civil War,* ed. John C. Fout and Maura Shaw Tantillo (Chicago: University of Chicago Press, 1993), pp. 24–26.

39. Rawick, ed., SS1, Vol. 5, pp. 210–211; also Eugene D. Genovese, *Roll, Jordan, Roll: The World the Slaves Made* (New York: Vintage, 1974), pp. 462–463.

40. Rawick, ed., S1, Vol. 7, pp. 12–15, Vol. 6, pp. 186–187, and Vol. 2, Pt. 2, pp. 167, 304–306; Keckley, *Behind the Scenes,* p. 39.

41. Rawick, ed., S1, Vol. 4, Pt. 1, p. 180.

42. Ibid., S1, Vol. 2, Pt. 1, p. 219, and SS1, Vol. 1, p. 425. Also Kate E. R. Pickard, *The Kidnapped and the Ransomed: The Narrative of Peter and Vina Still after Forty Years of Slavery* (Philadelphia: Jewish Publication Society of America, 1970), p. 109. On remarriage, see Eugene D. Genovese, "American Slaves and Their History," in his *In Red and Black: Marxian Explorations in Southern and Afro-American History* (New York: Pantheon, 1972), p. 112.

43. "Amy Chapman: The Masters Good but Overseers Mean," in *Toting the Lead Row,* p. 128; Rawick, ed., SS2, Vol. 5, Pt. 4, p. 1758, also S2, Vol. 8, Pt. 1, pp. 33, 131; Gutman, *The Black Family in Slavery and Freedom,* pp. 87–93; Perdue, Barden, and Phillips, eds., *Weevils in the Wheat,* p. 105.

44. Charles Joyner, "The World of the Plantation Slaves," in *Before Freedom Came: African-American Life in the Antebellum South,* ed. Edward D. C. Campbell, Jr., with Kym S. Rice (Richmond and Charlottesville: Museum of the Confederacy and University Press of Virginia, 1991), p. 59. Also Donald M. Sweig, "Northern Virginia Slavery: A Statistical and Demographic Investigation" (Ph.D. diss., College of William and Mary, 1982); Brenda E. Stevenson, "'All My Cherished Ones': Marriage and Family in Antebellum Virginia" (Ph.D. diss., Yale University, 1990), especially pp. 398–408; Brenda E. Stevenson, *Life in Black and White: Family and Community in the Slave South* (New York: Oxford University Press, 1996), Chapter 7; Tadman, *Speculators and Slaves,* pp. 22–25.

45. Perdue, Barden, and Phillips, eds., *Weevils in the Wheat,* pp. 89, 105; Rawick, ed., S1, Vol. 2, Pt. 1, pp. 124–125.

7. Young Love and Marriage

1. Charles L. Perdue, Jr., Thomas E. Barden, and Robert K. Phillips, eds., *Weevils in the Wheat: Interviews with Virginia Ex-Slaves* (Charlottesville: University Press of Virginia, 1976), p. 300.

2. On the legal status of slave marriages, see Margaret A. Burnham, "An Impossible Marriage: Slave Law and Family Law," *Law and Inequality* 5 (July 1987), pp. 187–225. My study employs the term "marriage" when referring to relationships that slaves called marriages. Historians have been inconsistent in their classification of slave unions as marriages. Reynolds Farley flatly denies the existence of marriages among slaves in *Growth of the Black Population: A Study of Demographic*

Trends (Chicago: Markham, 1970), p. 21; Kenneth M. Stampp recognizes only those unions approved by owners as marriages in *The Peculiar Institution: Slavery in the Ante-Bellum South* (New York: Vintage, 1956), p. 341. Robert William Fogel correctly attributes discrepancies in the characterization of slave unions to the historians' greater or lesser reliance on slave sources; see *Without Consent or Contract: The Rise and Fall of American Slavery* (New York: W. W. Norton, 1989), pp. 183–184.

3. James Trussell and Richard Steckel, "The Age of Slaves at Menarche and Their First Birth," *The Journal of Interdisciplinary History* 8 (Winter 1978), p. 477–505; George P. Rawick, ed., *The American Slave: A Composite Autobiography*, SS1, Vol. 1, p. 96.

4. Frances Anne Kemble, *Journal of a Residence on a Georgian Plantation in 1838–1839* (New York: Alfred A. Knopf, 1961), p. 117; Rawick, ed., S1, Vol. 7, p. 129, and S2, Vol. 13, Pt. 3, p. 206; Perdue, Barden, and Phillips, eds., *Weevils in the Wheat*, p. 49.

5. Perdue, Barden, and Phillips, eds., *Weevils in the Wheat*, p. 326; Rawick, ed., SS2, Vol. 9, Pt. 8, pp. 3873.

6. Perdue, Barden, and Phillips, eds., *Weevils in the Wheat*, p. 229; Robynne Rogers Healey, "Meanings of Motherhood: Maternal Experiences and Perceptions on Low Country South Carolina Plantations," paper presented to the Berkshire Conference on the History of Women, Chapel Hill, N.C., 7 June 1996, pp. 5 and 32, n. 28; made available by the author. On the westward movement of planter families, see Fletcher M. Green, *The Lides Go South . . . and West; the Record of a Planter Migration in 1835* (Columbia: University of South Carolina Press, 1952); Jane Turner Censer, "Southwestern Migration among North Carolina Planter Families: 'The Disposition to Emigrate,'" *Journal of Southern History* 57 (Aug. 1991), pp. 407–426. For a different view, see Joan E. Cashin, *A Family Venture: Men and Women on the Southern Frontier* (New York: Oxford University Press, 1991).

7. Rawick, ed., S2, Vol. 13, Pt. 3, p. 206, SS2, Vol. 9, Pt. 8, pp. 3873, S1, Vol. 2, Pt. 2, p. 169 and Vol. 6, p. 89; Perdue, Barden, and Phillips, eds., *Weevils in the Wheat*, pp. 316.

8. Perdue, Barden, and Phillips, eds., *Weevils in the Wheat*, pp. 294, 316–317, 49; Rawick, ed., S2, Vol. 2, Pt. 1, p. 58; responses of unnamed son of a Perry County planter and H. M. Buck, NQS.

9. John M. Chapron to James Martin, 25 May, 9 Aug., 20 Sept. 1839 and 22 July 1840, Letterbook, Jean Marie Chapron Papers, ADAH; Rawick, ed., SS1, Vol. 1, p. 151.

10. Perdue, Barden, and Phillips, eds., *Weevils in the Wheat*, p. 333; "Sarah Fitzpatrick," in *Slave Testimony: Two Centuries of Letters, Speeches, Interviews, and Autobiographies*, ed. John W. Blassingame (Baton Rouge: Louisiana State University Press, 1977), p. 652; Mary S. Mallard to Mary Jones, 29 May 1860, in *The Children of Pride: A True Story of Georgia and the Civil War*, ed. Robert Manson

Myers (New Haven: Yale University Press, 1972), p. 583; Jeffrey R. Young, "Ideology and Death on a Savannah River Rice Plantation, 1833–1867: Paternalism amidst 'a Good Supply of Disease and Pain,'" *Journal of Southern History* 59 (Nov. 1993), p. 704; Rawick, ed., S1, Vol. 2, Pt. 2, p. 52.

11. Young Planter, "The Plantation: Summer Work," *Cotton Planter and Soil* 1 (Oct. 1857), p. 310; Perdue, Barden, and Phillips, eds., *Weevils in the Wheat*, p. 316; Rawick, ed., S1, Vol. 2, Pt. 2, p. 300, SS1, Vol. 7, Pt. 2, p. 374.

12. Perdue, Barden, and Phillips, eds., *Weevils in the Wheat*, p. 1, also p. 82.

13. J. G. Clinkscales, *On the Old Plantation: Reminiscences of His Childhood* (New York: Negro Universities Press, 1969), pp. 12–14, 16, 20; D. E. Huger Smith, *A Charlestonian's Recollections, 1846–1913* (Charleston: Carolina Art Association, 1950), pp. 49–52.

14. Rawick, ed., S1, Vol. 2, Pt. 1, pp. 124, 89; Roger D. Abrahams, *Singing the Master: The Emergence of African American Culture in the Plantation South* (New York: Penguin, 1992), p. 4.

15. Rawick, ed., SS1, Vol. 1, p. 245, and S1, Vol. 6, p. 370.

16. Ibid., S1, Vol. 3, Pt. 3, p. 201; "Sarah Fitzpatrick," *Slave Testimony*, p. 643.

17. Mary S. Mallard to Mary Jones, 20 Jan. 1861, Mary Jones to Ruth B. Jones, 22 Jan. 1861, and Mary S. Mallard to Mary Jones, 25 Jan. 1861, in Myers, *The Children of Pride*, pp. 643–644, 646.

18. Rawick, ed., SS1, Vol. 12, p. 193.

19. Ibid., SS2, Vol. 9, Pt. 8, pp. 3873–3874, and S2, Vol. 13, Pt. 3, p. 231; "Sarah Fitzpatrick," *Slave Testimony*, p. 644; Georgia Writers' Project, *Drums and Shadows: Survival Studies among the Georgia Coastal Negroes* (Athens: University of Georgia Press, 1986), p. 140.

20. Rawick, ed., S1, Vol. 3, Pt. 4, p. 243, S2, Vol. 16, Pt. 8, p. 33, and SS1, Vol. 4, Pt. 3, p. 203; Perdue, Barden, and Phillips, eds., *Weevils in the Wheat*, p. 198; *Toting the Lead Row: Ruby Pickens Tartt, Alabama Folklorist*, ed. Virginia Pound Brown and Laurella Owens (University: University of Alabama Press, 1981), p. 148, n. 24; A Southern Planter, *Plantation and Farm Instruction, Regulation, Record, Inventory and Account Book*, in Philip St. George Cocke Papers, VHS, p. 10.

21. Rawick, ed., S1, Vol. 6, pp. 26, 122.

22. Perdue, Barden, and Phillips, eds., *Weevils in the Wheat*, pp. 122, 316; Rawick, ed., S1, Vol. 3, Pt. 4, p. 126.

23. Rusticus, "Plantation Management and Practice," *Cotton Planter and Soil* 1 (Dec. 1857), p. 375; "Judge Daniels Estimate of the value of James River Low Ground and Slave labor——(unique)," in Cocke Family Papers, UVAL.

24. "Management of Slaves," *DeBow's Review* 13 (Aug. 1852), in *Advice among Masters: The Ideal in Slave Management in the Old South*, ed. James O. Breeden (Westport, Conn.: Greenwood, 1980), p. 242; Rawick, ed., S2, Vol. 11, Pt. 7, p. 245, and SS2, Vol. 6, Pt. 5, p. 2081.

25. Rawick, ed., S1, Vol. 2, Pt. 2, p. 23; White, *Ar'n't I a Woman?*, p. 103. On de-

liberate breeding of slaves, see Thelma Jennings, "'Us Colored Women Had to Go through a Plenty': Sexual Exploitation of African-American Slave Women," *Journal of Women's History* 1 (Winter 1990), pp. 48-52; Richard Sutch, "The Breeding of Slaves for Sale and the Westward Expansion of Slavery, 1850-1860," in *Race and Slavery in the Western Hemisphere: Quantitative Studies*, ed. Stanley L. Engerman and Eugene D. Genovese (Princeton, N.J.: Princeton University Press, 1975), pp. 173-210; Brenda Stevenson, "Distress and Discord in Virginia Slave Families, 1830-1860," in *In Joy and In Sorrow: Women, Family, and Marriage in the Victorian South*, ed. Carol Bleser (New York: Oxford University Press, 1991), p. 119; Chapter 4 of Frederic Bancroft, *Slave-Trading in the Old South* (New York: Frederick Unger, [1959]), especially pp. 67-73.

26. J. S. Buckingham, *The Slave States of America*, vol. 2 (New York: Negro Universities Press, 1968), p. 43; Rawick, ed., S1, Vol. 6, p. 90, SS2, Vol. 1, p. 7, S2, Vol. 14, Pt. 1, p. 71 and Vol. 11, pp. 128-129.

27. Trussell and Steckel, "The Age of Slaves at Menarche and Their First Birth," p. 477-505.

28. Rawick, ed., SS1, Vol. 4, Pt. 2, p. 203, S1, Vol. 7, p. 4 and Vol. 6, p. 107. On sexual exploitation, see Chapter 6.

29. Ibid., S2, Vol. 11, p. 129-130.

30. Ibid., S1, Vol. 6, p. 399 and Vol. 2, Pt. 1, p. 124; Perdue, Barden, and Phillips, eds., *Weevils in the Wheat*, p. 327.

31. Rawick, ed., SS2, Vol. 4, Pt. 3, p. 1244.

32. Perdue, Barden, and Phillips, eds., *Weevils in the Wheat*, pp. 161, 265; Deborah Gray White, "Female Slaves in the Plantation South," in *Before Freedom Came: African American Life in the Antebellum South*, ed. Edward D. C. Campbell, Jr., and Kym S. Rice (Richmond and Charlottesville: Museum of the Confederacy and University Press of Virginia, 1991), p. 105; Catherine Clinton, "Reconstructing Freedwomen," in *Divided Houses: Gender and the Civil War*, ed. Catherine Clinton and Nina Silber (New York: Oxford University Press, 1992), pp. 308-309.

33. Perdue, Barden, and Phillips, eds., *Weevils in the Wheat*, p. 105; also Kate E. R. Pickard, *The Kidnapped and the Ransomed: The Narrative of Peter and Vina Still after Forty Years of Slavery* (Philadelphia: The Jewish Publication Society of America, 1970), p. 153; A. M. French (Mrs.), *Slavery in South Carolina and the Ex-Slaves; or, The Port Royal Mission* (New York: Negro Universities Press, 1969), p. 93.

34. John Brown, *Slave Life in Georgia: A Narrative of the Life, Sufferings, and Escape of John Brown, a Fugitive Slave* (Savannah: Beehive, 1991), p. 18; Rawick, ed., S2, Vol. 11, pp. 303-304.

35. Rawick, ed., SS1, Vol. 1, p. 425; entries dated 1825, 1827, and undated, Fry Account Book, Virginia Papers Collected by Hillis Fry McLemore, UVAL; A Southern Planter, *Plantation and Farm Instruction, Regulation, Record, Inventory*

and Account Book, p. 6; Francis Boykin, "Management of Negroes," *Southern Field and Fireside* 1 (30 June 1860), and Francis Boykin, "Virginia Husbandry: Observations Made Thereon by the Editor of the American Farmer on an Excursion in that State during the Last Summer," *American Farmer* 2 (16 March 1821), both in *Advice among Masters,* p. 90; William Howard Russell, *My Diary North and South* (New York: Harper, 1954), p. 77; "Agreement by Robert F. W. Allston to Purchase Hogs from the Slaves, 1859," in *The South Carolina Rice Plantation as Revealed in the Papers of Robert F. W. Allston,* ed. J. H. Easterby (Chicago: University of Chicago Press, 1945), p. 350; "Ben Graham," in *Slave Testimony,* p. 636.

36. Charles Ball, *Fifty Years in Chains; or, The Life of an American Slave* (Indianapolis: Asher, 18[37]), pp. 113-115; Clinkscales, *On the Old Plantation,* p. 21; John Michael Vlach, *Back of the Big House: The Architecture of Plantation Slavery* (Chapel Hill: University of North Carolina Press, 1993), p. 164.

37. "Sarah Fitzpatrick," *Slave Testimony,* p. 644; response of O. T. McCann, NQS; Elijah Tucker to "Sir," n.d., Southside Virginia Family Papers, UVAL; Perdue, Barden, and Phillips, eds., *Weevils in the Wheat,* p. 40; Mary Jones to Charles C. Jones, Jr., 18 Dec. 1855, in *The Children of Pride,* p. 178.

38. Rawick, ed., S1, Vol. 3, Pt. 3, p. 201 and Pt. 4, p. 243; Mary S. Mallard to Mary Jones, 20 Jan. 1861, Mary Jones to Ruth B. Jones, 22 Jan. 1861, and Mary S. Mallard to Mary Jones, 25 Jan. 1861, in *The Children of Pride,* p. 643, 644, 646.

39. Charles Manigault to Jesse T. Cooper, 10 Jan. 1848, in *Life and Labor on Argyle Island: Letters and Documents of a Savannah River Rice Plantation, 1833–1867,* ed. James M. Clifton (Savannah: Beehive, 1978), p. 62; Tattler, "Management of Negroes," *Southern Planter* 11 (Feb. 1851), p. 42.

40. Herbert G. Gutman terms such slave unions "prenuptial" in *The Black Family in Slavery and Freedom, 1750–1925* (New York: Vintage, 1976), pp. 61–67. See also n. 2 above.

41. Perdue, Barden, and Phillips, eds., *Weevils in the Wheat,* p. 40; Rawick, ed., S2, Vol. 16, Pt. 12, p. 35, and S1, Vol. 6, pp. 298, 313.

42. Rawick, ed., SS1, Vol. 10, Pt. 5, pp. 1946–1947; Boykin, "Management of Negroes," in *Advice among Masters,* pp. 244–245; "Discipline among Negroes," *Southern Cultivator* 14 (June 1856), p. 192.

43. Entry for Sept. 1863, *Mary Chesnut's Civil War,* ed. C. Vann Woodward (New Haven: Yale University Press, 1981), p. 465.

44. *The Old Pine Farm: or, The Southern Side. Comprising Loose Sketches from the Experience of a Southern Country Minister, S.C.* (Nashville, Tenn.: Southwestern Publishing House, 1959), pp. 186–187.

45. Rawick, ed., S1, Vol. 3, Pt. 4, p. 187. On the frequency of "abroad" marriages in Loudoun County, Va., see Brenda E. Stevenson, *Life in Black and White: Family and Community in the Slave South* (New York: Oxford University Press, 1996), p. 208.

46. Perdue, Barden, and Phillips, eds., *Weevils in the Wheat,* pp. 300–301. Also

Foby, "Management of Servants," *Southern Cultivator* 11 (Aug. 1853), and Francis Boykin, "Management of Negroes," both in *Advice among Masters*, pp. 308, 245. On the relationship between small and large slaveholders, see Eugene D. Genovese, "Yeoman Farmers in a Slaveholders' Democracy," *Agricultural History* 49 (Oct. 1975).

47. Lewis W. Paine, *Six Years in a Georgia Prison* (New York: n.p., 1851), p. 134; Benjamin Drew, *A North-Side View of Slavery. The Refugee, or the Narratives of Fugitive Slaves in Canada* (New York: Johnson Reprint, 1968), p. 54; "Henry Baker," in *Slave Testimony*, p. 655.

48. Pickard, *The Kidnapped and the Ransomed*, p. 118; Rawick, ed., SS2, Vol. 1, p. 6; entries for 28 July 1845, 29 Sept., 17 and 20-22 Nov. 1856, Sturdivant Collection (microfilm, SHC). On how slaves divided land and other property in the slave quarter (an issue that remains largely unexplored) see Larry E. Hudson, Jr., *To Have and to Hold: Slave Work and Family Life in Antebellum South Carolina* (Athens: University of Georgia Press, 1997), Chapter 2.

49. "Philip Coleman," in *Slave Testimony*, pp. 561-562; Rawick, ed., SS1, Vol. 11, p. 66.

50. Rawick, ed., S2, Vol. 13, Pt. 3, p. 233.

51. On the types of property that slaves accumulated and Virginia men who kept property at the homes of their wives, see Lynda J. Morgan, *Emancipation in Virginia's Tobacco Belt, 1850-1870* (Athens: University of Georgia Press, 1992), pp. 44-46. On the discrepancies in the age of marriage and first-time parenting for men and women, see Gutman, *The Black Family in Slavery and Freedom*, p. 50; Trussell and Steckel, "The Age of Slaves at Menarche and Their First Birth," pp. 489-492; Stephen Crawford, "The Slave Family: A View from the Slave Narratives," in *Strategic Factors in Nineteenth Century American Economic History*, ed. Claudia Goldin and Hugh Rockoff (Chicago: University of Chicago Press, 1992), p. 345; Richard H. Steckel, "Slave Height Profiles from Coastwise Manifests," *Explorations in Economic History* 16 (Oct. 1979), pp. 368-369. On efforts by slave men to feed their families through theft, see entry for 13 July 1857, John Edwin Fripp Diary, SHC; Perdue, Barden, and Phillips, eds., *Weevils in the Wheat*, p. 245; entry for 22 Oct. 1837, John G. Traylor Diary, ADAH; "Rosa Barnwell," in *Slave Testimony*, p. 698. On slave men securing fuel, see Rawick, ed., SS2, Vol. 4, Pt. 3, p. 1287; responses of P. F. Mitchell and O. T. McCann, NQS.

52. Blake Touchstone, "Planters and Slave Religion in the Deep South," *Masters and Slaves in the House of the Lord: Race and Religion in the American South, 1740-1870*, ed. John B. Boles (Lexington: University Press of Kentucky, 1988), pp. 99-100, 124; John W. Blassingame, *The Slave Community: Plantation Life in the Antebellum South*, rev. ed. (New York: Oxford University Press, 1979), pp. 168-170.

53. Eugene D. Genovese, *Roll, Jordan, Roll: The World the Slaves Made* (New York: Vintage, 1974), pp. 481, 475-476; "Some Recollections of Le Grand Tutwiler,

Former Slave of Dr. Henry Tutwiler of Greene Springs, Alabama," Henry Tutwiler Papers, UVAL; responses of P. F. Mitchell and the son of a Perry County planter, NQS; Diary of Rev. Francis Hanson, SHC, entries for 27 Dec. 1859; 29 Feb. 1860; 17 April and 20 Oct. 1863; 1 March 1865; Rawick, ed., S1, Vol. 5, Pt. 4, p. 142.

54. Holland Nimmons M'Tyeire, *Duties of Christian Masters* (Nashville, Tenn.: Southern Methodist Publishing House, 1859), pp. 98–100; *Journal,* P. E. Church of South Carolina, 1859 (Charleston, 1859), quoted in Blassingame, *The Slave Community,* p. 175. For statistics, see Blassingame, *The Slave Community,* pp. 169–170.

55. Emphasis in the original; quote from "Southern Presbyterian Review" 8 (1854), in Blassingame, *The Slave Community,* p. 175, see also pp. 168, 174; Frederick A. Bode, "The Formation of Evangelical Communities in Middle Georgia: Twiggs County, 1820–1860," *Journal of Southern History* 60 (Nov. 1994), p. 737.

56. Perdue, Barden, and Phillips, eds., *Weevils in the Wheat,* p. 158; "The law read to Joshua & Beck before their marriage," Slave Record Book, William Massie Papers, VSLA.

57. Response of James M. Davison, NQS; John Witherspoon DuBose, "Recollections of the Plantation," Part 2, *Alabama Historical Quarterly* 1 (Summer 1930), p. 115; entry for Feb. 1859, James M. Torbert Diary, ADAH; Richard H. Steckel, "Slave Marriage and the Family," *Journal of Family History* 5 (Winter 1980), pp. 406–421.

58. Perdue, Barden, and Phillips, eds., *Weevils in the Wheat,* pp. 231, 36. For an elaborate ceremony involving a black preacher, see Georgia Bryan Conrad, *Reminiscences of a Southern Woman* (Hampton, Va.: Hampton Institute Press, n.d.), p. 16. On clothing, see Mary Jones to Charles C. Jones, Jr., 31 Jan. 1856, in *The Children of Pride,* p. 186. On a less elaborate wedding, see Rawick, ed., S1, Vol. 2, Pt. 1, p. 124.

59. Rawick, ed., S2, Vol. 13, Pt. 3, p. 206; Perdue, Barden, and Phillips, eds., *Weevils in the Wheat,* p. 134.

60. Paine, *Six Years in a Georgia Prison,* p. 135; also response of D. M. McIntosh, NQS.

61. Perdue, Barden, and Phillips, eds., *Weevils in the Wheat,* p. 129, also p. 153; Rawick, ed., SS2, Vol. 8, Pt. 7, p. 3131, also Vol. 3, Pt. 2, p. 645. On broomstick weddings, see Blassingame, *The Slave Community,* pp. 166–167; Brenda E. Stevenson, *Life in Black and White,* pp. 228–229.

62. French, *Slavery in South Carolina and the Ex-Slaves,* p. 94; Perdue, Barden, and Phillips, eds., *Weevils in the Wheat,* p. 122. On the various responses following emancipation of former slaves who had married under slavery, see Ira Berlin and Leslie S. Rowland, eds., *Families and Freedom: A Documentary History of African-American Kinship in the Civil War Era* (New York: New Press, 1997), Chapter 6.

63. Rawick, ed., SS1, Vol. 11, p. 214; Perdue, Barden, and Phillips, eds., *Weevils in the Wheat,* p. 118; Thomas H. Jones, *The Experience of Thomas H. Jones Who*

Was a Slave for Forty-Three Years (New York: AMS Press, 1975), p. 30, emphasis in the original.

Epilogue

1. Elizabeth Keckley, *Behind the Scenes: or, Thirty Years a Slave, and Four Years in the White House* (New York: Oxford University Press, 1988).

2. Keckley, *Behind the Scenes,* pp. 18–20, 39.

3. Frederick Douglass, *My Bondage and My Freedom* (New York: Dover, 1969), p. 263; Keckley, *Behind the Scenes,* p. xii.

ACKNOWLEDGMENTS

Born in Bondage was conceived in a graduate seminar at the University of Maryland, College Park. There I encountered Philip Curtin's estimate that only 4.5 percent of the nearly ten million Africans enslaved in the Americas had been brought to the area that later became the United States. I knew that on the eve of the Civil War the United States had become the world's largest slaveholding nation, with more than four million men, women, and children in bondage. The slave population of the antebellum South had grown through human reproduction and included large numbers of children. Yet the picture presented in scholarly works and the popular press rarely included these children.

I had developed a scholarly interest in children and family in part as a result of my own parenting experiences. Knowing firsthand the challenges modern parents face in rearing children, I wanted to know how slaves had experienced parenthood and how children had learned to survive the oppression associated with chattel bondage. A search of the literature on slavery revealed that few scholars had considered the presence of children, let alone contemplated the nature of their experiences. I began this study in the belief that the existence of slave children mattered.

Many people helped to make this book possible. I am especially grateful to Ira Berlin, who not only directed the dissertation upon which this study is based but also offered comments on an early draft of the book manuscript, which has been considerably broadened in scope. Other colleagues, friends, and family supported this project in numerous ways. Wilma King, Paul Lachance, Ann Patton Malone, and Deborah Gray White provided thoughtful responses to various aspects of my research presented at professional conferences. Lester S. Brooks read the entire manuscript when it was nearly complete; Eve Sterne read an early draft; anonymous reviewers obtained by Harvard University Press read earlier and later versions. All offered helpful comments. Friends and colleagues read one or more drafts or papers from which chapters were developed: Ruth Wallis Herndon, the late Stuart Kaufman, Holly Kennedy, Joélle Rollo-Koster, and Steven F. Miller. Leslie S. Rowland, George Callcott, Barbara E. Finkelstein, Gay L. Gullickson, and Alfred A. Moss made helpful suggestions for turning my dissertation research into a book. Anne Apenys, E. Susan Barber, Mary Beth Corrigan, and Cynthia N. Kennedy lent their support throughout graduate school and beyond, often commenting on my ideas about slavery and children and sometimes responding to written passages. My editor at Harvard University Press, Joyce Seltzer, offered encouragement and concrete advice to improve the book. The detailed comments provided by David Lobenstine and copy editing by Mary Ellen Geer, also at Harvard University Press, proved very helpful as well. I also thank the University of Georgia Press, which in 1996 published a different version of the material on breastfeeding and weaning found in Chapter 1 (Marie Jenkins Schwartz, "'At Noon, Oh, How I Ran': Breastfeeding and Weaning among Slaves in the Antebellum South," in *Discovering the Women in Slavery*, ed. Patricia Morton (Athens: University of Georgia Press, 1996), and *Labor's Heritage*, the quarterly magazine of the George Meany Memorial Archives, which also in 1996 published a variant of my findings about slave children's labor in Alabama (Marie Jenkins Schwartz, "One Thing, Then Another: The Work of Slave Children in Alabama," *Labor's Heritage* 7 [Winter 1996], pp. 22–33, 56–61). This exposure generated conversations with other scholars that significantly improved this work.

I have received substantial institutional support for my work, for which I am grateful. Twice I have received funds from the National Endowment for the Humanities. An NEH Fellowship for College Teachers provided financial support to complete a draft of this manuscript. An earlier NEH Dissertation Year Fellowship furnished funding for concluding that stage of the project's development. The University of Rhode Island, Kingston, generously granted me a year's leave as well as financial assistance for completing the manuscript. Other organizations provided funds for travel to repositories for research: the American Historical Association; the Department of History at the University of Maryland, College Park; and the Virginia Historical Society. The Committee on Africa in the Americas at the University of Maryland, College Park, and the Department of History at the University of Rhode Island, Kingston, supported my attendance at professional conferences where I presented preliminary findings for peer review. The John Nicholas Brown Center for the Study of American Civilization, Brown University, provided funding for research and office space while I made revisions to the manuscript.

Staff members at a variety of archives and other repositories offered valuable assistance. I especially appreciate the help I received from the staff of the Alabama Department of History and Archives, Montgomery; McKelden Library, University of Maryland, College Park; Wilson Library, University of North Carolina, Chapel Hill; University of Rhode Island Library, Kingston; United States Agricultural Library, Beltsville, Maryland; University of Virginia Library, Charlottesville; the Virginia Historical Society, Richmond; and the Virginia State Library and Archives, Richmond.

My final acknowledgment is to my family. My husband, Ron, supported the project in numerous ways and read an early draft of the manuscript. I owe a special debt to our children, who made me aware that sons and daughters mold the lives of mothers and fathers as much as parents order the lives of children. I am glad that Dustin, Eric, and Brenda have helped to shape my life.

INDEX